DUMBARTON OAKS
MEDIEVAL LIBRARY

Daniel Donoghue, General Editor

THE ART OF MAKING VERSES

GERVASE OF MELKLEY

DOML 87

DUMBARTON OAKS MEDIEVAL LIBRARY

Daniel Donoghue, General Editor
Danuta Shanzer, Medieval Latin Editor

Jan M. Ziolkowski, Founding Editor

Medieval Latin Editorial Board
Julia Barrow
Thomas F. X. Noble
Daniel Nodes
Michael Roberts

Medieval Latin Advisory Board
Walter Berschin
Ralph Hexter
Mayke de Jong
José Martínez Gázquez
Kurt Smolak
Francesco Stella
Jean-Yves Tilliette

The Art of Making Verses

GERVASE OF MELKLEY

Edited and Translated by

TRAUGOTT LAWLER

DUMBARTON OAKS
MEDIEVAL LIBRARY

HARVARD UNIVERSITY PRESS
CAMBRIDGE, MASSACHUSETTS
LONDON, ENGLAND
2025

Copyright © 2025 by the President and Fellows of Harvard College
ALL RIGHTS RESERVED
Printed in the United States of America

First Printing

Library of Congress Cataloging-in-Publication Data

Names: Gervase, of Melkley, active 1200–1220, author. | Lawler, Traugott, editor, translator. | Gervase, of Melkley, active 1200–1220. Ars versificatoria. (Lawler) | Gervase, of Melkley, active 1200–1220. Ars versificatoria. English. (Lawler)

Title: The art of making verses / Gervase of Melkley ; edited and translated by Traugott Lawler.

Other titles: Dumbarton Oaks medieval library ; 87.

Description: Cambridge, Massachusetts : Harvard University Press, 2025. | Series: Dumbarton oaks medieval library ; DOML 87 | Includes bibliographical references and index. | Latin with English translation on facing pages; introduction and notes in English.

Identifiers: LCCN 2024038681 | ISBN 9780674290969 (cloth)

Subjects: LCSH: Poetry—Authorship—Early works to 1800. | Latin poetry—Early works to 1800.

Classification: LCC PA8310.G424 A88 2025 | DDC 871/.0109—dc23/eng/20241028

LC record available at https://lccn.loc.gov/2024038681

Contents

Introduction vii

The Art of Making Verses 2

Abbreviations 303
Note on the Text 307
Notes to the Text 313
Notes to the Translation 331
Bibliography 387
Index of Names 389
Index of Literary and Rhetorical Terms 393

Introduction

Gervase (known as Gervasius *de saltu lacteo,* "of the milky pasture," that is, of Melkley) was born at Melkley, alternatively Mentley, near the modern Hertfordshire town of Puckeridge, probably around 1175. He tells us that he studied under John of Hauville, the author of *Architrenius* (1184), who taught in Rouen. Though the date of *The Art of Making Verses (Ars versificatoria)* is uncertain, it can be guessed at from internal references. It cannot be before 1200, the year in which John Gray became bishop of Norwich, since it repeatedly quotes a poem celebrating that event, beginning "Magnus Alexander" and appearing along with it in Glasgow, Hunterian Museum (University of Glasgow), MS V.8.14, formerly MS 511 (manuscript H). It also mentions several other events from around the same time: the castration of the abbot of Hyde (1201), the death of Abbot Walter of Waltham Abbey (1201), and the death of William de Longchamp, bishop of Ely (1197). This confluence suggests that Gervase may have begun his work around 1200, but the version we have must have been completed considerably later, since it also gives an epitaph for Simon de Montfort, who died in 1218. Gervase was still alive in 1231, the earliest possible dating for a document he witnessed at Saint Paul's in London. I

date the completion of the work to 1220, though it was probably started about twenty years before that.

Clearly Gervase was a teacher, though we don't know where; he was also a poet, author at least of a poem on Mary that is also in manuscript H, but probably also of the poem *Homage to John Gray* and others in that manuscript, a number of epitaphs, and probably of the various verses in the text said to be by "someone." But he was also a valued administrator, probably working early with John Gray (bishop of Norwich, d. 1214), and certainly working later with Stephen Langton (archbishop of Canterbury, d. 1228).[1]

Gervase wrote at a time when, in both France and England, the writing of poetry and the teaching of poetry in the schools were at a high-water mark. Of the two poems he admired (and quotes) most, Bernard Silvester's *Cosmographia* appeared in 1150 and his teacher John of Hauville's *Architrenius* in 1184. Alan of Lille, whom he also cites and surely also admired, flourished in the second half of the twelfth century, and died in 1202. Though Gervase's own output was small, he clearly thinks of himself as belonging to this select company of modern poets. At 2.46, in a remarkably personal moment, he seems to express his desire to write poetry as good as Bernard Silvester's.

Criticism was flourishing too, along with poetry. Horace's *Ars poetica* was much in vogue, and Donatus's *Ars maior* still the standard school grammar. Matthew of Vendôme's *Ars versificatoria* had appeared in about 1165, and Geoffrey of Vinsauf, whose two prose treatises as well as the *Poetria nova* were well known to Gervase, was more or less his contemporary. He studied the poets but out of a kind of anxiety of influence seems to have thought hard about how to be dif-

ferent from the critics, and so produced a text that was at the same time animated by this literary world but also a new departure. He shows his determination to make his own mark by organizing his teaching of the art of verse in an entirely new way, dispensing with Matthew's and Geoffrey's categories such as "easy ornament" and "difficult ornament" to divide figurative language into the three categories of *identitas, similitudo,* and *contrarietas,* or sameness, likeness, and opposition.

Gervase's aim was to teach his students how to compose short sentences *(clausulae)* in an elegant, that is, "figured" way. In practice, this seems to mean verse couplets; see, for example, 1.46 and 1.47, where boys strive to manage two full verses. Indeed, nearly all Gervase's examples are couplets. He apparently gave considerable thought to classifying the figures in the best way for his elementary students to learn them.

What Gervase came up with was his idiosyncratic division into the three categories mentioned above. All the figures discussed under "sameness" maintain the literal sense of words and statements; most involve wordplay or patterns of repetition, but none involve symbolism or transfer of sense: the words refer literally to the thing or the action they name. "Rough sameness," his starting point, is plain thoughts in plain words: everyday speech. He hurries past that to get to "polished sameness": language that is still literal, but artfully shaped, which is his subject in part 1. Polished sameness involves either *conservantia* (which I have rendered "consistency") or mutation. Consistency is a little like rude sameness, something to get past—puns, mostly, and other sorts of repetition. Mutation seems like a contra-

diction of sameness: if there is change, how can it remain the same? But it turns out that all it means is changing from what you might have said to what you do say, so that, for instance, paralipsis (the figure of emphasizing something by mentioning its omission) counts as mutation: if you say, "I pass over his childish insults," you have changed from saying, "He insults people childishly." Anything you leave out is a change, any extra word or phrase you add, even just a modifier, is a change. The idea of calling all this mutation may seem disingenuous, but there it is. After subtraction and addition, the final mode of change is "diversion." This starts out with equality, which involves no more than using synonyms or synonymous phrases, saying something "equal" to what you would have said, or what you have just said. It actually celebrates what H. W. Fowler called "elegant variation,"[2] the mark nowadays of the debased style of sportswriters and many other journalists—but Gervase and his contemporaries loved it. A second mode of diversion is digression, which is "going away from the subject, or the sense." The first is benign: descriptions and the like. But how can "going away from the sense" be a mode of sameness? And when we learn that metonymy and synecdoche, always included by other writers among the tropes, are modes of digression, we feel at last that Gervase has gone too far with his "sameness" idea. "Decembers" are simply not the same as years, nor "gold" as a ring made of gold. Here Gervase's original categories simply don't hold up. Clearly he could not put these two tropes under "likeness," where he puts metaphor, since the issue in these tropes is not likeness, and he certainly could not have put them under opposition. He needed a fourth category: "relation," maybe,

INTRODUCTION

or "inclusiveness." He himself says, "We go away from the sense when we attribute to one thing what belongs to another, by reason of some inclusiveness" (1.69). But to be included in the same category as something else is hardly to be the same as it. The rest of the material treated under diversion does indeed belong to sameness—except for hyperbole, always treated as a trope by others, and by definition not "same."

A good example of the differences among the three modes —sameness, likeness, and opposition—occurs at 1.31, where Gervase gives an example of conjunction in all three modes: in the first Io gets a series of literal adjectives, in the second she is compared to other women ("a Marcia in judgment," and so on), and in the third Pyramus and Thisbe's situation is described in a series of oxymorons, nouns modified by contrary adjectives ("warlike peace," etc.).

The second and third modes (addressed in parts 2 and 3, respectively) are more straightforward than sameness. Likeness, as one would expect, is largely about metaphor, although Gervase begins by discussing coinages, that is, words made from like words. Granted this is likeness, but the discussion seems oddly trivial next to the discussion of metaphor. Opposition is the best section of all, distinguishing witty modes of irony and paradox, always clearly.

The poem on John Gray, quoted repeatedly throughout, shows Gervase putting his ideas into action. The major idea of the poem is that while John of Oxford, who has just died, was an excellent bishop, John Gray will be an even better one. The poem in its overall structure thus combines the two major modes the treatise advocates, similarity and opposition, and, like the treatise, it puts opposition in the cli-

INTRODUCTION

mactic position. Its final sentence, cited at 2.53 (under "likeness") as an example of comparison with accumulation, ends with a rush of metaphorical oppositions:

> For everything would be lamenting the death of your predecessor, John, and hard Gargara would not be refusing tears for that man; but your more abundant glory is silencing their groans, for a whale outweighs a trout, a camel beavers, a fountain a tumbler, the sun lamps, a line a point.

This is also synonymy, of course, the five metaphors all signifying the same thing, said at 1.35 to be good for concluding effectively. This brilliant sentence combines sameness, likeness, and opposition into a fit conclusion. The poem also constantly exhibits Gervase's key ideas of "advocation" *(advocatio),* literally one part of a sentence or paragraph "calling to" *(advocare)* another, and "accumulation" *(coadunatio),* or "everything coming together into one." Both make for what we call coherence. Along the way are instances of metaphorical paroemia (4.2), paradigm (2.51–52), disjunction (1.31), annomination (1.9–13), climax (1.17, 1.34), conversion (3.3), sentence-metaphor (2.44), reiteration (1.33), three instances of the use of *vel* to mean *etiam* ("or" for "even," 5.11), and paralipsis (1.29), and also many metaphors (throughout part 2), adjectives (1.36–44), and proper names (2.15–22). *Parmenides rupis,* the poem that in the Hunterian manuscript (H) comes right after *The Art of Making Verses* and right before *Homage to John Gray,* and which is thought to be Gervase's by everyone who has studied it, is likewise full of advocation, accumulation, and opposition: I see instances of coalescence

of phrases (1.31–32), conversion (3.3), unmodified antitheton (3.10), and reiteration (1.33), to name a few.

Edmond Faral spoke admiringly of the literary virtuosity of the work of Gervase, John of Hauville, and others of their age: "Above all we must realize that the poetry of this age has to be studied minutely in all its processes. Its practitioners were truly literate people, admirably schooled in the tradition; they didn't have our precious modern dictionaries, and yet they knew enough to say, for example, as Gervase does, that the word *velificatus* (sailed over) was a hapax legomenon of Juvenal's."[3] The author of *Tria sunt,* writing in Oxford around 1400, admired Gervase's treatise exceedingly, naming it the *Liber de eleganciis (Book of Refinements).* But the small number of manuscripts, three of them from the revival of rhetorical study in Oxford around 1400,[4] and the near absence of external references suggest that it never achieved the influence it deserved.

For the manuscripts, see the Note on the Text. There has been just one previous edition and one translation. The late Hans-Jürgen Gräbener edited the text from the Glasgow manuscript, with collations of the two Balliol College manuscripts, as his Münster dissertation in 1964, and published his edition in 1965.[5] It has thorough identification of Gervase's many citations, a detailed running commentary in the introduction, useful indices, and a breakdown of the entire text into its headings, subheadings, and sub-subheadings. Unfortunately, however, Gräbener's text is riddled with errors, some of them mere typos but many actual misreadings of the manuscripts. These shortcomings were amply laid bare in two reviews, by Rino Avesani and Franz Josef Worstbrock.[6] I have done away with Gräbener's elaborate system

of headings and subheadings, since it confuses rather than clarifies. Catherine Yodice Giles translated Gräbener's text as her Rutgers dissertation,[7] but she misunderstands several passages, and the value of her work is limited, since she failed to correct Gräbener's errors. Though I have striven to improve on both these works, I must acknowledge that both have often been helpful to me.

For the title, *Ars versificatoria (The Art of Making Verses)*, see Preface 1, the second sentence and the textual note. The H reading *versificaria,* which Gräbener prints, is erroneous; see Worstbrock's review.[8] Gräbener's title, *Ars poetica*, is merely a nod to Horace; it has no manuscript basis.

I had a lot of help with this book. I want to acknowledge above all the contributions of the late Alan Rosiene. He discussed Gervase with me by email in an enlightening way and would surely have continued to improve it if he had not died of COVID-19 early in the pandemic. I am grateful also to Martin Camargo for his many years of helpful advice on matters rhetorical. Nicole Eddy of the Dumbarton Oaks Medieval Library set me straight constantly, and Michael Roberts and Danuta Shanzer of the editorial board vetted my work with deep learning and eagle eyes. Finally, my wife Peggy was always there for me, as she has been for sixty-six years now.

Notes

1 The Gray connection was suggested by the late Alan M. Rosiene in a paper entitled "Space Shifting: The Diverse Life of Gervase of Melkley," delivered in 2017 at the meeting of the International Society for the His-

tory of Rhetoric in London. See the Note on the Text below. For the Langton connection, see Frederick M. Powicke, *Stephen Langton* (Oxford, 1928), 102–3.

2 H. W. Fowler, *Dictionary of Modern English Usage* (Oxford, 1926), 130–33.

3 My translation: "Surtout on comprendra que la poésie de cette époque doit être minutieusement étudiée en tous ses procédés. Ceux qui la pratiquaient étaient vraiment des gens de lettres, admirablement informés de la tradition; et, dépourvus de nos précieux lexiques modernes, ils savaient pourtant dire, par exemple, comme le fait Gervais, que la mot 'velificatus' etait un hapax legomenon de Juvénal"; Edmond Faral, "Le manuscrit 511 du 'Hunterian Museum' de Glasgow: Notes sur le mouvement poétique et l'histoire des etudes littéraires en France et en Angleterre entre les années 1150 et 1225," *Studi medievali* 9 (1936): 96. For Gervase's attribution of the word to Juvenal, see *The Art of Making Verses* 2.3.

4 Martin Camargo, "The Late Fourteenth-Century Renaissance of Anglo-Latin Rhetoric," *Philosophy and Rhetoric* 45 (2012): 107–33, especially 124 on the three Gervase manuscripts.

5 Hans-Jürgen Gräbener, ed., *Ars poetica: Kritische Ausgabe,* Forschungen zur romanische Philologie 17 (Münster, 1965).

6 Rino Avesani, review of Gräbener, *Ars poetica, Studi medievali* 7 (1966): 749–60; Franz Josef Worstbrock, review of Gräbener, *Ars poetica, Zeitschrift für deutsches Altertum und deutsche Literatur* 96 (1967): 99–107.

7 Catherine Yodice Giles, "Gervais of Melkley's Treatise on the Art of Versifying and the Method of Composing in Prose" (PhD diss., Rutgers University, 1973).

8 Worstbrock, review of Gräbener, *Ars poetica,* 99n.

THE ART OF
MAKING VERSES

Dilecto suo Iohanni Albo, non tam socio quam magistro, suus Gervasius de Saltu Lacteo hoc opusculum cum salute.

Armata est maiorum petitio et cognatissima iussioni. Hinc est quod, cum vestrae mihi petitionis auctoritas praecepisset ut versificatoriae vobis artis industriam explanarem, non praetemptata tanti operis difficultate, audax et improvidus vestrae parui iussioni. Hortantur fides et obedientia ne vel precis devotio vel iussionis maioritas contemnatur.

2 Scripserunt autem hanc artem Matthaeus Vindocinensis plene, Gaufroi Vinesauf plenius, plenissime vero Bernardus Silvestris (in prosaico psittacus, in metrico philomena). Timendum est igitur laborem praesumpsisse qui viros tam authenticos detinebat. Et mihi quidem discretius est silere quam tantum opus prosequi, vel promisisse. Malo tamen esse fidelis quam timidus, obediens quam discretus. Opus igitur promissionis aggredior, quod ne propter eorum scripta nugatorium videretur, brevis et valde compendiosus et facilis procedere destinavi.

3 Sed cum difficillimum sit sub dilucida brevitate procedere, mallem verbosus intelligi, quamvis authentica faciat volumina difficultas. Erit igitur in communibus ecliptica

PREFACE

To John White, beloved as his friend but more as his teacher, his own Gervase of Melkley offers this little work, and sends his greetings.

A request from one's superiors is armed and amounts to a command. That is why, when your authoritative request had bidden me to explain to you the workings of the art of making verses, without pausing to think about how hard it would be, I daringly, recklessly obeyed your command. My loyalty and obedience impel me not to undervalue either the love behind the request or the superior force of the command.

Others, of course, have written about this art: Matthew of Vendôme fully, Geoffrey of Vinsauf more fully, and Bernard Silvester (a parrot in prose and a nightingale in poetry), most fully. One ought to be afraid, then, to have taken up a job that has held the attention of men of such authority. I'd be smarter just to keep quiet than to go ahead with such a work, or even to have promised to do it. Still, I'd rather be true than afraid, obedient than prudent. So I'm setting out on the work I promised, and so that what they have written won't make it seem worthless, I have chosen to proceed, and to be brief, very succinct, and easy.

But since it is very hard to combine brevity and lucidity, I would rather be perceived as verbose and understood, even though it's difficulty that lends books authority. And so the teaching in this little work will be abbreviated in standard

opusculi huius traditio, in privatis vero perissologica, ut prosit rudibus garrulitas intellecta. Opusculum hoc rudium est! Dialecticos ad supradictos transmittimus. Consilium tamen est ne contemnant vel *Barbarismum* Donati vel *Poetriam* Horatii vel *Rhetoricas* Ciceronis.

4   Dupliciter enim ad rei notitiam pervenimus, directe et indirecte. Verbi gratia, naturam locutionis quattuor genera circumsistunt. Quaedam sunt prohibitionis, quaedam permissionis, quaedam praecepti, quaedam consilii. Prohibitiones consistunt in vitiis, permissiones in figuris—quae utraque Donatus exponit—praecepta in grammatica, consilia in rhetorica. Igitur circa grammaticae regulas intellecto quid vitium, quid figura, indirecte facilius quid sit consilium elucescet, item in debita quantum ad grammaticam et venusta quantum ad rhetoricam assignatione.

5   Directe nos instruunt Priscianus et Cicero, indirecte vero Donatus indecentias assignando. Oportet nos etiam in hac arte docenda tam vitia quam elegantias explanare. Sed satis de vitiis in Seneca *De controversiis* Ovidii Nasonis sententiam inspexistis. Rogatus enim Ovidius aliquando ab amicis ut tolleret tres versus, invicem petiit ut ipse tres excipere posset in quos eis nihil liceret. Conscripserant illi quos tolli vellent secrete, hic quos voluit privilegiare—in utrisque codicellis iidem versus erant, ex quibus primus fuit "Semibovemque virum, semivirumque bovem," ubi videtur esse perissologia, scilicet vitium superfluitatis. Patet ergo summi ingenii viro non iudicium defuisse ad compescendam licentiam carminum suorum, sed animum. Quaesitus ergo quare

matters, but redundant when I am presenting my own original ideas, so that my garrulousness may be understood by beginners, and profit them. This little book is for beginners! Those who have reached dialectic we leave to the writers named above. And yet my advice to them is not to despise the *Barbarismus* of Donatus or Horace's *Art of Poetry* or Cicero's *Rhetorics*.

We come to know something in two ways, directly and indirectly. For example, four categories make up the nature of speech: some speech is prohibition, some permission, some precept, some advice. Prohibitions apply to faults, permissions to figures—Donatus has explained both of these—precepts to grammar, advice to rhetoric. So once what is a fault and what is a figure are understood from the rules of grammar, what is advisable will shine forth, indirectly, more easily, with the attribution of what is correct to grammar and what is elegant to rhetoric.

Priscian and Cicero teach us directly, and Donatus indirectly by specifying what is not fitting. We too in teaching this art have to explain both faults and beauties. But you have clearly seen from Seneca's *Controversies* what Ovid thought of faults. Once his friends asked him to remove three lines, and he asked them in return if he might make an exception for three that they couldn't touch. They secretly wrote down the ones they wanted removed, and he the ones he wanted to protect—and the same three lines were on both sheets. The first was, "Both a half-bull man and a half-man bull," where there seems to be *perissologia*, that is, the fault of redundancy. And so it is clear that this man of the highest genius didn't lack the judgment to restrain the license of his poetry, but the will. When asked why he

illos non tolleret, ait decentiorem faciem esse in qua naevus aliquis appareret.

6   Ecce ex verbis ipsius Ovidii possumus fere colligere vitium esse vitio caruisse. Immo certe impossibile est aliquandiu sine vitio prosaica etiam oratione decurrere. Quicquid enim fuerit assignari facillimum, erit merito difficillimum evitari. Ostendam igitur vitia non ut a quibuslibet carminibus eliminentur omnia, sed partialiter singula secundum cuiuslibet facultatem. Oportet etiam et venustatem quandam rhetoricam et quasdam elegantias enodare, quae plenius quam doctrina usu possunt et exercitio comprehendi. Quippe infinita est venustatis elegantia, et nova cotidie surrepit inventio modernorum.

7   Magister Iohannes de Hauvilla, cuius ubera disciplinae rudem adhuc mihi lactaverunt infantiam, multas quidem elegantias adinvenit, plures auditoribus suis tradidit. In libello vero suo de peregrino philosopho quem Architrenium vocat, plurimas observavit. Cuius quidem libelli sola sufficit inspectio studiosa rudem animum informare. Idem de Claudiano, de Darete Phrygio, de Bernardo Silvestri. Idem de antiquioribus, scilicet Lucano, Statio, et Virgilio—maxima etiam de libellis Ovidii sentiatis. Sed *Anticlaudianus* indirecte nos instruit plenius quam directe.

8   In hac arte si assit exercitium, praecedet ingenium instructionem. Quippe practica rhetoricae, naturali industriae vicinissima, occurrit spontanea animo subtili, etiam theoricam ignoranti. Scio quendam qui, prius quam novisset an alia essent "attributa personae" vel "negotii," prius quam

wouldn't remove the lines, he said that a face is more beautiful if it has a blemish in it.

From these words of Ovid's we can almost gather that it's a fault not to have any faults. And surely it's impossible to proceed for very long even in prose without a fault. The easiest mistake to point out will of course be the hardest to avoid. Therefore, I am going to point out faults, not so that all of them can be eliminated from any and all poems, but so that particular ones can be partially eliminated according to the writer's ability. I need also to elucidate a certain rhetorical charm and its refinements, though they can be understood more fully by use and practice than by teaching. In fact the refinement of such charm is infinite, and another new discovery of the moderns creeps up every day.

Master John of Hauville, at the breast of whose learning my rude infancy was weaned, came up with many refinements and passed on several to his pupils. In his little book about the itinerant philosopher he calls Architrenius, he heeded many of them. A careful reading of that book alone is enough to educate a rude mind. The same goes for Claudian, Dares Phrygius, and Bernard Silvester. You should have the same experience with the older writers, namely Lucan, Statius, and Virgil—and especially with the books of Ovid. *Anticlaudianus,* though, teaches us by indirection rather than directly.

If you work at this art, native talent will be more important than instruction. For, to a subtle mind, even one ignorant of theory, the practice of rhetoric, since it is quite akin to natural industry, occurs spontaneously. I knew a boy who, before he knew whether there were such things as "attributes of persons" or "attributes of actions," and even before

etiam rhetoricam inspexisset, in fabula de Pasiphae, cum dandum erat Pasiphaen vaccam aeneam machinari et sese includere, quia res abominabilis fuit et auribus odiosa, tali usus est insinuatione:

> Dic, quid abhorret amans? Quid amans et femina?
> Tandem
> si sit amans mulier et generosa? Nihil.

Nec adhuc sumitur nomen "insinuationis," res tamen oculum ingenii non latebat. Ibi etiam, locorum adhuc ignorans nomina, triplici tamen usus est argumento: ab affectionibus, cum dixit "amans"; a natura, cum dixit "femina"; a fortuna, cum dixit "generosa." Generositatem enim, saltem dierum nostrorum, fortunae magis attribuo quam naturae. Nondum noverat quid esset a contrariis invenire sententiam, et tamen sic processit:

> Imperio scelus est sceleris nil scire, timentque
> hoc solum, regum sceptra timere nefas.

Cautum est igitur ut studiosis animis brevis sit huius artis theorica; in practica plenius elaborent, tam aliorum opera legendo medullitus quam propria componendo. Parum enim sufficit in legendis auctoribus soloecismos exponere, seu apparentia vitia, locos etiam rhetoricos et colores.

9 Notandum igitur quod quaedam regulae cuilibet sermonis generi sunt communes, quaedam tantum metricis, quaedam tantum prosaicis speciales. De hiis quae communia sunt prius censui proponendum.

PREFACE

he had studied rhetoric, in the story of Pasiphae, when he had to tell how Pasiphae had made a bronze cow and had enclosed herself inside it, because that was an abominable thing and hateful to hear, used this *insinuatio:*

> What does a lover abhor? What if the lover is also a woman? Finally, what if this woman lover is also noble? Nothing!

He had not yet learned the term "insinuation," but the thing itself was not hidden from the eye of his intelligence. There too, though he didn't know the names of the topics of invention either, he used a threefold argument: from affections, when he said "a lover"; from nature, when he said "a woman"; from fortune, when he said "noble." For I attribute nobility, at least that of our day, to fortune rather than nature. He hadn't learned yet what it is to invent a maxim from contraries, and still he went on:

> It is a crime for those in power to know nothing of crime, and they fear this alone: that it be a sin to fear the scepters of kings.

Care must be taken to keep the theory of this art short for eager minds; let them work more fully at practice, both in reading with close attention the works of others and in composing their own. In the reading of the authors, it is not enough just to point out solecisms, obvious faults, and the topics and colors of rhetoric.

It should be noted that some rules are common to every style of writing, some are special only to poems, some only to prose. I have decided to treat the common rules first.

I

Proposita quacumque materia, positae clausulae sub vulgari sermone sponte se offerunt recitanti. Est igitur clausula oratio sive perfecta sive imperfecta, dummodo vel per se vel per subintelligentiam perfectum constituat intellectum. Compositionis clausularum triplex est locus: alius ab eodem, alius a simili, alius a contrario. Identitas enim, similitudo, et contrarietas, si usui cognitionique tradantur, eloquentiae generant ubertatem.

2   Identitas est oratio sine omni transumptione vel contrarietate absolute prolata. Identitas alia rudis, alia polita. Rudis identitas ex simplici subiecto constat et simplici praedicato: quicquid adicitur vel deturpat clausulam vel decorat. Rudium identitatum alia rudis, alia rudior, alia rudissima. Rudis identitas in solis grammaticae praeceptis consistit et caret tam figura quam vitio quam colore. Rudior est in qua includitur aliqua improprietas quae non decorat sermonem, excusatur tamen necessitate aliqua, sive lege melica vel metrica vel rhythmica vel rhetorica—et sic introducitur "figura," cuius multae a Donato species assignantur. Rudissima est in qua includitur vitium inexcusabile, et talis introducit barbarismum vel soloecismum.

3   Vitiorum igitur, quaedam excusantur respectu speciali tantum, quaedam generali tantum, quaedam utroque, quae-

PART ONE

No matter what subject has been assigned, little phrases in ordinary language occur spontaneously to us as we speak. Such a phrase, therefore, is a form of speech, either complete or incomplete, as long as it constitutes a complete thought, whether by itself or by implication. There is a triple source for composing the parts of sentences: one is from sameness, one is from likeness, and one is from opposition. For sameness, likeness, and opposition, if they are accompanied with intelligence and practice, generate the richness of eloquence.

Sameness is discourse that moves forward nakedly, without any metaphor or opposition. It is either rough or polished. Rough sameness consists of a simple subject and a simple predicate: whatever is added either disfigures the phrasing or beautifies it. Rough sameness can be rough, rougher, or roughest. Rough sameness consists in the rules of grammar alone and has neither figure nor fault nor rhetorical color. Rougher sameness has some impropriety that does not beautify the discourse, but is excused by some necessity, some law of melody or meter or rhythm or rhetoric—in this way "figure" is introduced, many types of which are described by Donatus. The roughest sameness is the one that involves some inexcusable fault, and introduces a barbarism or solecism.

As for faults, some are excused in one particular respect alone, some in a general respect only, some in both, some in

dam neutro. Speciali tantum, ut si fieret liber quidam qui in quolibet versu contineret prosthesim vel epenthesim vel aliam figuram, quilibet versus suam posset figuram excusare, et tamen habito respectu ad totum inutilis esset liber ille— inde est quod liber Ennii condemnatur. Generali tantum, ut contingit in vitio quod non excusat aliqua necessitas— melica vel metrica vel huiusmodi—quid specialiter consideratur, sed in contextu totius ponitur ut totum ex eius naevo secundum Nasonis sententiam decoretur. Hinc forte est quod invenit Donatus exempla in Virgilio tam barbarismorum et soloecismorum quam figurarum. Hinc ait Rogerus Devoniensis in Virgilii *Aeneidis* omnia vitia et omnes figuras, omnes etiam colores rhetoricos, praeterea totam philosophiam et totam ethicam contineri. Utroque respectu excusantur figurae moderatae, neutro vitia immoderatissima.

4   Politur identitas duplici genere rhetoricae, coloribus scilicet et argumentis. Argumenta placent animis et colores auribus. Sensualitatem colores, rationem alliciunt argumenta. Vitia, figurae, et colores quadam similitudine vestiuntur; et sunt in multis ex aequo sibi respondentia, in multis excedentia pariter et excessa. Verbi gratia, Donatus dicit barbarismum fieri per immutationem litterae, ut "olli" pro "illi." Isdem in metaplasmi tractatu consequenter dicit, "Antithesis est litterae pro littera positio, ut 'olli' pro 'illi.'" Qui modus in coloribus mutatio vocatur, ut "praecones" pro "praedones." Potest igitur in huiusmodi vitium de facili latere sub umbra virtutis. Et ideo difficillimum est expressissimas inde differentias assignare. Quippe a peritis in melica

neither. In a particular respect only, in that if there happened to be a book that in some line had examples of prosthesis or epenthesis or some other figure, any one verse could justify its figure, but if that consideration were applied to a whole book that book would be unusable—that is why Ennius's book is condemned. In a general respect only, as happens with a fault that no necessity excuses, with no reason—whether of melody or meter or the like—why it should receive particular consideration, but that is situated in the context of the whole in such a way that the whole is actually beautified by its wart, according to Ovid's principle. That is perhaps why Donatus found examples in Virgil of barbarisms and solecisms as well as of figures. And that is also why Roger of Devon says that in Virgil's *Aeneid* are contained all the faults and all the figures, all the colors of rhetoric too, besides all of philosophy and all of ethics. In both respects moderate figures are excused, the most immoderate faults in neither respect.

Sameness is refined by two kinds of rhetoric, by colors and arguments. Arguments please minds and colors ears. Colors appeal to the senses, arguments to reason. Faults, figures, and colors wear very similar clothes; they are interchangeable in many ways, and in many ways exceed and are exceeded equally. For example, Donatus says that it makes a barbarism if you change a letter, as *olli* for *illi*. Then later, in treating metaplasm, he says, "Antithesis is putting one letter for another, as *olli* for *illi*." And among the colors this same device is called mutation, as *praecones* for *praedones*. Thus it is possible, even easy, with faults of this kind to conceal them under the shadow of a virtue. And that makes it very hard to specify their differences very precisely. Professional singers

facultate complexiones hominum distinguuntur. Alio cholericis, alio sanguineis, alio phlegmaticis, alio se credunt concentu melancholicis placituros. Quidam in mollibus, quidam in asperis delectantur. Qui mollibus gaudent, asperiores iudicant vitiosos. Non miremur igitur si in coloribus et figuris quosdam frequentiores, rariores alios invenimus. Certe cum in *Architrenio* durissimae translationes sint et frequentissimae, audivi tamen discretum virum dicentem vitiosum esse illum librum eo solo quod nullum versum contineat vitiosum. Ecce fere probabile videtur quod uni vitium est, hoc alii esse figuram, et alii colorem. Haec igitur exercentis industriae relinquimus distinguenda, cum nondum ars temperantiae sit inventa.

5 Item sunt quidam colores tantae propinquitatis quod non habent nomina sibi assignata propter affinitatem. Igitur cum opus fuerit, satis utile est indifferenter uti figurarum nominibus, vitiorum etiam et colorum. Item sciendum est quod quandoque mutatur quandoque permanet identitas colorata. Permanet quotiens nec similitudinarie nec contrarie coloratur. Mutatur quotiens subintrat locus "a simili" vel locus "a contrariis," et tunc non est identitas revera sed similitudo vel contrarietas. Identitas pura et permanens multipliciter coloratur. Colorum alius vocalis, alius realis. Sunt enim quidam colores qui adeo decorant ipsam vocem quod etiam non intelligentes alliciunt ad auditum, ut puta annominatio, leonitas, et huiusmodi; et isti vocales dicuntur. Sunt et alii qui plenius excitant intellectum et dicuntur reales.

differentiate people by their temperaments. They think that one harmony will please the choleric, another the sanguine, another the phlegmatic, yet another the melancholic. Some people delight in soft music, others in harsh music. Those who like soft music think harsher music is faulty. So let's not be surprised if we find some colors and figures often and others less often. Certainly although in *Architrenius* there are many very hard metaphors, I heard a man of discretion call that book faulty precisely because it doesn't have a single faulty line. It seems quite probable that one person's fault is another person's figure, and someone else's color. So I leave the distinguishing of these things to the industry of the practitioner, since the art of moderation has not yet been discovered.

Some colors are so like each other that they haven't been given special names because of their kinship. So should the need arise, it makes considerable sense to use the names of figures, faults, or colors without differentiation. Likewise you should know that colored sameness is sometimes changed and sometimes remains as it is. It remains as it is, as long as the color does not involve a similitude or opposition. It is changed whenever the topic "from likeness" or the topic "from contraries" comes in, and then it isn't really sameness anymore, but likeness or opposition. Pure permanent sameness is colored in a lot of ways. A color is either verbal or factual. Some colors so ornament speech by themselves that they entice even those who don't understand them to listen: for instance, puns, leonine rhyme, and the like; these are called verbal. Others appeal more fully to the understanding and are called factual.

6   Coloratur igitur identitas tum per conservantiam, tum per mutationem. Non miremini si novas hic inveniatis appellationes. Licet enim secundum Tullium causa doctrinae et causa evidentiae dictionum significationem vel restringere vel mutare.

7   Conservantia est identitas illa in qua nichil additur vel subtrahitur vel ab ordine divertitur ad sententiam decorandam (nisi hoc forte fuerit necessitate, metrica vel huiusmodi), sed quasi substantialiter habet in se quicquid decoris habet. Conservantia igitur consistit tum in simplici narratione, tum in loquendi vehementia, tum in quaestione et responsione.

8   Simplex narratio coloratur quandoque per tautoparonomion, quandoque per euphonomaton, quandoque per amphibolum. Tautoparonomion consistit in maturitate dicendi; et est quaedam species sententiae; et dicitur quasi "identitatis proverbium," scilicet omne proverbium quod a materia non recedit, qualia sunt haec: "Praevisa levius laedunt," "Levius communia tangunt," "Duplice post melior una loquela prior." De huiusmodi plenius dicetur inferius. Euphonomaton est consonantia orationis quae consistit in similitudine sive identitate replicata tum litterarum, tum syllabarum, tum etiam dictionum.

9   Tam litterarum quam syllabarum identitas vel est in principio vel in medio vel in fine dictionis. Si fuerit in principio vel in medio, annominationem facit. Litterarum, ut hic, "_Currere currentem vetuit violentia venti._" Syllabarum, ut hic: "Fronduit in plano platanus." In medio, ut hic: "Non convallibus sed Trivallis." Annominatio commode fit etiam si consonantia sit in principio unius dictionis et in medio alterius, sic: "Non gena sed ingenio fronduit Ulixes."

PART I

Sameness is colored sometimes by consistency, sometimes by change. Don't be surprised if you find new terminology here. Cicero says that it is allowable to restrict or change the meaning of words in order to teach or clarify.

Consistency is a sameness in which nothing is added or taken away or transposed to ornament a statement (unless perhaps this happens by necessity, metrical or otherwise), but, as it were, has in its own essence whatever it has of ornament. Therefore consistency takes the form sometimes of simple narration, sometimes of vehemence of speaking, sometimes of question and answer.

Simple narration is colored sometimes by *tautoparonomion*, sometimes by *euphonomaton*, sometimes by ambiguity. *Tautoparonomion* consists in maturity of expression; it is a kind of pointed observation and etymologically means "proverb of sameness," that is, any proverb that does not depart from the literal, such as: "Things foreseen hurt more lightly," "Shared troubles touch us more lightly," "One word beforehand is better than two afterward." There will be more about this later. *Euphonomaton* is harmony in speech that consists in likeness or sameness by repetition of letters, syllables, or even words.

Sameness of both letters and syllables occurs at the beginning, middle, or end of a word. If it occurs in the beginning or middle it creates annomination. Sameness of letters is like this: "The violences of the wind prevented the runner from running." Of syllables, like this: "The plane tree blossomed on the plain." In the middle, like this: "Not in valleys but in Trivalli." Annomination works even if the repeated sound is in the beginning of one word and the middle of the other, thus: "Ulysses blossomed not in the cheek but in

17

Bernardus Silvestris: "Fronduit in plano platanus, conv_alli_bus _al_nus." Et ideo venustior est annominatio quia est in illis syllabis in quibus principalis dominatur accentus.

10   Iuxta hunc colorem sumuntur duo schemata, paronomasia et paromoeon. Paronomasia vero hunc colorem excedit, comprehendit enim consonantiam finalem. Paromoeon vero consideratur per principia trium dictionum immediate positarum in quibus est eiusdem litterae vel syllabae repetitio, ut hic, "sole serena suo," et sic exceditur ab hoc colore. De hoc schemate dicit Isidorus quod si ternarius numerus excedatur, non erit schema sed schemati contrarium, id est vitium inexcusabile, ut in illo versu Ennii: "O Tite, tute, Tati, tibi tanta, tiranne, tulisti." Hoc bene observavit Bernardus in hiis versibus:

> Fronduit in plano platanus, convallibus alnus,
>   rupe rigens buxus, litore lenta salix.

Binario frequentius usus est, semel tamen trinario. Haec fuit Isidori sententia. Sed certe credo quod ipse aliquando cum discretione tamen excedere non negaret, ut in hiis versibus de quodam electo in episcopum:

> Hic est ergo vacans quem sedes exigit: huius
> spirat in amplexus, suspirat in oscula, votis
> aspirat, tantique viri connubia sperat.

PART I

supercheekiness." Bernard Sylvester: "The plane tree blossomed on the plain, the a̱lder in va̱lleys." This is a particularly elegant annomination because it is on the syllables that carry the main accent.

There are two figures that go along with this color, paronomasia (punning) and alliteration. Paronomasia goes beyond annomination because it includes end rhyme. Alliteration is seen when three words in a row start with the same letter or syllable, as, *sole serena suo* (serene in her own sun), and thus here too there is an advance beyond annomination. Of this figure Isidore says that if there are more than three words, it won't be a figure at all but the opposite of a figure, that is, an inexcusable fault, as in this line of Ennius's: "O Titus Tatius, you tyrant, you yourself have turned such troubles onto yourself." Bernard keeps to that rule well in these lines:

> The plane tree blossomed on the plain, the alder in valleys, the rough box tree on rocky cliffs, the willing willow on the shore.

He used two-word puns very often, but a three-word pun just once. This was Isidore's opinion. But I certainly think that Bernard did not refuse, sometimes, with discrimination, to go beyond the norm, as in these lines about a man elected to be a bishop:

> He is therefore the man the vacant see needs: it pants *(spirat)* for his embraces, it sighs *(suspirat)* for his kisses, it aspires *(aspirat)* for marriage, it hopes *(sperat)* to be wed to such a man.

Ad quaternarium transcendunt—et tamen a quibusdam pulcherrimi reputantur.

11 Item fit in quolibet tractatu annominationum frequens numerus, frequentissimus nequaquam, unde hii versus de Pyramo et Thisbe fere vitiosi sint:

> Imminet immeritis gravior quam carcer utrisque,
> semper in insidiis imperiosa parens.

In hiis dictionibus "gravior" et "carcer," *g* et *c* ex vicinitate soni annominationem faciunt; et praeterea nimium sonat in versibus illis haec littera *i*. Si ergo multi huiusmodi versus ad invicem vicini essent, certe vitium esset vitiosissimum. Eodem modo nimietas potest esse annominationum in duobus versibus, ut in versibus hiis de Myrrha:

> Dum furit in funus proprium prope femina fato
> quod nutrit nutrix insidiosa sedet.

Huiusmodi ergo cavenda sunt; vel, quia quaedam vitia decorant, nimietas talium caveatur.

12 Item est quaedam annominatio adeo ampla quod fere repetitionem parit. Retinetur enim tota dictio praeter modicam immutationem. Haec retentio tum fit in unica dictione, tum in pluribus unica tum extranea, tum cognata. Extranea, ut: "Stricta structura." Architrenius: "Fecundo fecunda mero facundia surgit." Cognata est ubi una inflectitur ex reliqua. Pulchrum igitur erit ut cuiuslibet tractatus duobus vel tribus versibus sit huiusmodi annominationum frequentia. Statius:

PART I

The pun climbs up to four words—and yet these lines are thought by some to be very beautiful.

Likewise in any piece of writing annominations are frequent, but not very frequent, for which reason these lines about Pyramus and Thisbe might almost be faulty:

> There hangs over them both, though they do not deserve it, a thing worse *(gravior)* than prison *(carcer)*, an imperious mother, always plotting against them.

In the words *gravior* and *carcer*, g and c create annomination from the nearness of their sound; furthermore, the letter *i* occurs very often in the lines. If many lines of this kind were near each other, surely the fault would be most faulty. Likewise there can be too much annomination in two lines, as in these about Myrrha:

> While the woman, near death, is furious for her own funeral, which her insidious nurse is nursing, she sits by.

Accordingly beware faults of this kind; or, since some faults adorn, beware of overdoing them.

Some annomination is so extensive that it almost turns into repetition, for the whole word is retained except for a tiny change. This retention occurs in one word or several; in one word, either with a cognate or noncognate word. Noncognate, as: "strict structure." Architrenius: "Abundant wit arises from abundant drinking." Cognate annomination is where one word is the inflected form of the other. It will be attractive to have a sequence of annominations of this kind in two or three verses of any piece of writing. Statius:

Iam clipeus clipeis, umbone repellitur umbo,
ense minax ensis, pede pes et cuspide cuspis.

Hic modus in figuris polyptoton appellatur. In pluribus fit haec retentio quasi per quandam derivationem, ut si dicatur, "Fortuna <u>fort</u>is <u>una</u>." Unde quidam egregius versificator ait de quodam Philippo, qui de honesto scholari factus est sodomita, sic, "Quicquid Philippus erat—phy!—lepus esse potest," ut sit haec syllaba "phy" interiectio contemnentis.

13 Fit etiam et alio modo annominatio, quando scilicet per eandem syllabam incipit sequens dictio per quam praecedens terminatur, ut hic: "Il<u>la</u> <u>la</u>tet." Quod autem recolitis Ciceronem huiusmodi condemnasse, intelligendum est de illis quae fiunt vel ex pondere syllabae vel ex nimio hiatu vitiosae, ut hic: "Diva, vale, ampla plais." Dicit tamen Bernardus, "Gardo brevis, longus barbulus, ampla plais." Commodius est exemplum: "Plus sitit auca cadum mortua, viva vadum." Commodissimum est illud Bernardi, "Ad Paridis raptus Ida datura rates."

14 Similitudo litterarum vel syllabarum in fine parit tum consonantiam, tum leonitatem. Consonantia dupliciter consideratur: quandoque ex eo quod diversae dictiones eandem habent ultimam vocalem, ut "in eis ait," quandoque ex eo quod ultima vocalis et quicquid sequitur idem est, ut "hinc inde," "venit, ait." Hic modus a Donato homoeoptoton appellatur. Isti modi quandoque tam in prosa quam in

PART I

> Now shield is repelled by shields, boss by boss, threatening sword by sword, foot by foot, and lance by lance.

This device among figures is called polyptoton. In several words this repetition occurs as if by derivation, for example if you say, *Fortuna fortis una* (Fortune and a brave man are one and the same thing). A certain exceptional maker of verses speaks thus of a certain Philip, a good student who became a sodomite, "Whatever Philip was, he can be—fie!—a hare," turning the syllable "phi" into an interjection of contempt.

Another form of annomination is when the next word starts with the same syllable the last one ended with, as in this case: *Illa latet* (She is hiding). You will remember that Cicero condemned this kind of thing, but you should realize that he meant those that are faulty, either from the weight of the syllable or involving too much of a hiatus, as in this case: *Diva, vale, ampla plais* (Goodbye, divine plump plaice). Bernard, however, says: *Gardo brevis, longus barbulus, ampla plais* (The short roach, long barbel, broad plaice). Here is a fitter example: *Plus sitit auca cadum mortua, viva vadum* (A dead goose thirsts more for an urn, a live one more for a pond). Most fitting is this one of Bernard's: *Ad Paridis raptus Ida datura rates* (Ida will provide ships' timber for Paris's rape).

Likeness of letters or syllables in the end brings about either consonance or leonine rhyme. Consonance is observed in two ways: either when two different words have the same final vowel, as *in eis sit,* or when both that vowel and what follows it are the same, as *hinc inde,* or *venit, ait.* Donatus calls this homoeoptoton. In both prose and verse these

metro magis quam leonitas comprobantur—minus apparens aliquando commendabilior invenitur.

15   Leonitas est consonantia in duabus ultimis syllabis. Haec parit duos colores qui dicuntur "similiter cadens" et "similiter desinens." Haec facit versus leoninos, quos vix contingit in aliquo opere authentico nisi casualiter invenire. Illi sunt cuilibet brevi materiae, utputa epitaphiis et proverbiis, specialiter deputati, dummodo in authentico volumine non ponantur. Nec enim Ovidius epitaphium Phyllidis voluit componere leoninum, dicens:

> Phyllida Demophon leto dedit hospes amantem.
>   Ille necis causam praebuit, illa manum.

Quaedam tamen leonitas satis commendabilis invenitur, quae consideratur in fine primi versus et in medio sequentis, mixta tamen cum alio colore. Architrenius:

>   Et Lucifer esse coactus
> Letifer est factus. Vanoque a numine venit
> quo Numa devenit.

Invenitur etiam alia brevior illa et ideo commendabilior. Sistit enim citra finem versus Architrenius: "Heu quam terribilis iudex immobilis." Similiter in descriptione Callistus inter socias Dianae, sic:

> Haec aliis melior, vita praestantior, arte
>   doctior, eloquio suavior, ore prior.

devices are more welcome sometimes than leonine rhyme—
and sometimes a less obtrusive instance comes off better.

Rhyme is a consonance in the last two syllables. It generates two colors, named *similiter cadens* and *similiter desinens*. This produces leonine verses, which one scarcely finds present in any work by our authors except inadvertently. They are just right for any sort of simple subject matter, such as epitaphs and proverbs, while they are not included in work by our authors. In fact Ovid did not want to compose his epitaph for Phyllis in rhyme, but wrote:

> Demophon (her guest) sent Phyllis (who loved him) to her death. He furnished the cause of her death, she the hand that performed it.

But rhyme can be found that is praiseworthy enough if it is mixed with another color—the one you see at the end of one verse and in the middle of the next. Architrenius:

> The one assigned to be Lightbringer was consigned to be Deathbringer. From an empty divinity he went to where Numa descended.

Another rhyme can be found too, shorter than this and for that reason more praiseworthy. Architrenius places it near the end of a line: *Heu quam terribilis iudex immobilis* (Oh, how terrible is an unmovable judge). Likewise in a description of Callisto among the friends of Diana:

> She is better than the others, superior in her life, more learned in art, more eloquent in speech, more excellent in beauty.

Hic modus a Donato dicitur homoeoteleuton, et comprehendit tantum casuales terminationes. Item de summo pontifice et rege:

> Hic sapit, ille capit; hic docet, ille nocet; acer
>   est hic, ille sacer; hic malus, ille salus.

Huiusmodi schema solet paronomasia appellari.

16   Identitas dictionum repetitionem parit, quae tum fit in principio clausularum et parit repetitionem antonomastice et stricte sumpto vocabulo, tum in fine et parit conversionem—quandoque utrimque et parit complexionem. Iuxta annominationem et repetitionem sumuntur duo colores, traductio et gradatio. Traducitur ergo vox quandoque ad diversos casus, et hoc fit per modicam immutationem et parit annominationem, ut hic: "Utraque mihi placet, utramque diligo, de utroque cogito." Quandoque traducitur vox ad diversos sensus, sed repetitur dictio tota, ut hic:

> Caelestes ora, da Christo pectus et ora.
> Omni sic hora caelestis quaeritur ora.

Et hic:

> Forti nexa fide tibi sunt bona, nec mala; fide,
>   vir, domino fide, vir bone plene fide.

PART I

Donatus calls this device homoeoteleuton, but restricts it to case endings. Here is one on the pope and a king:

> One knows, the other takes; one teaches, the other harms; one is fierce, one is holy; one is wicked, one saves.

The corresponding figure is usually called paronomasia.

Sameness of words brings about repetition, which occurs either at the beginning of clauses, where it creates repetition if the word is taken both literally and antonomastically, or at the end, where it creates conversion—or sometimes in both places, and then it creates complexion. Two colors take their place beside annomination and repetition: transplacement and climax. And so sometimes a word is moved to different cases, and since this involves only slight change it creates annomination, as in this case: "Both please me, I love both, I think about both." Sometimes the change is to different meanings but the word stays entirely the same, as here:

> Pray *(ora)* to the saints, dedicate to Christ your heart and mouth *(ora);* this is the way the celestial realm *(ora)* is sought at every moment *(hora)*.

And here:

> Things joined by strong faith *(fide)* are good for you and not bad; trust *(fide),* man, trust *(fide)* in the Lord, O good man full of faith *(fide)*.

Item:

> Mente manuque vires, virtus domat utraque vires,
> sed minor ad vires, Hector, Achille vir es.

Fiet autem hic modus commendabilius si leonitas caveatur, secundum quod dicuntur versus leonini, ut patet in conquestione Pyrami et Thisbes ad parietem, sic:

> Invide, dum teneris non cedis amantibus, ambos
> caedis, et illicito caedis amore furis!

Sub hac specie continentur illi versus iocosi:

> Non amor infelix, sed amo; non hamo, sed hamor;
> hamor, et hoc hamo pectus inescat amor.
> Non hamo, sed amo; qua non amor, hamor amoris
> hamo. Non hamans non amor; hamor amans.

17 Gradatio similiter, quae a Donato metalepsis dicitur, quandoque fit per inflectionem, quandoque per resumptionem. Inflectio tum fit casus in casum, ut hic:

> Ira movet litem, lis proelia, proelia mortem,
> mors lacrimas, lacrimae numina, numen opem.

Tum fit unius partis in aliam, ut hic:

> Sic solatur amor: urunt solatia, lenit
> ustio, lenimen angit, et angor alit.

Haec introducit annominationem. Per resumptionem fit, ut hic:

Again:

> You flourish *(vires)* in mind and hand, both virtues direct your strength *(vires)*, but, Hector, you are a man *(vir es)* lesser in strength *(vires)* than Achilles.

This style will be more praiseworthy if rhyme—what might give your verse the name of leonines—is avoided, as is clear in this complaint of Pyramus and Thisbe to the wall:

> O hateful one, while you don't give way *(cedis)* for tender lovers, you are killing *(caedis)* us both; you are crazed with illicit love for bloodshed *(caedis)*.

Into this category fall these humorous lines:

> Unhappy me, I am not loved but I love; I don't hook, I am hooked; I am hooked, and with this hook love ensnares my heart. I don't hook, but I love; because I am not loved, I am hooked by the hook of love. Not hooking, I am not loved; loving, I am hooked.

Climax, which Donatus calls metalepsis, is likewise created sometimes by inflection, sometimes by resumption. Inflection occurs both from case to case, as here:

> Wrath moves strife, strife battles, battles death, death tears, tears divinity, divinity help.

And from one part of speech to another, as here:

> Thus love consoles, consolations burn, burning relieves, relief pains, and pain sustains.

That example includes annomination. Climax is created by resumption, as in this case:

Venit et invenit, invenit et addidit arma;
   addidit et rabies tota Robertus erat.

Repetitionem prohibent quidam ternarium excedere, sed certe inveniam forte quaternarium, quem non audeam condemnare.

18   Amphibolum est oratio quae plures significat intellectus, ut: "Gallam subigo," "Crus fregi." Exeat illud a gravi materia, nisi fuerit in deorum responsis vel in quibuscumque divinationibus, ut hic: "Croesus perdet Halym transgressus plurima regna." In elegia amoris et in quibusdam frivolis invenitur. Statius in secundo:

> Nil transit amantes.
> Sentio, pervigiles acuunt suspiria questus.

Similiter de Nerone ait quidam ironice:

> Quis negat Aeneae magna de stirpe Neronem?
>   Sustulit hic matrem, sustulit ille patrem.

Equivoce usus est hac dictione "sustulit."

19   Extravaganter etiam contingit narrationem simplicem decorari. Sunt igitur quaedam dictiones quae sese contingunt vicinitate significationis, differunt tamen subtiliter intuenti, ut:

> Hii sapientiae nil gustant poculi,
> Argi pecuniae, sensus monoculi
> addiscunt animi; scrutantur oculi
> non locos logicos, sed loca loculi.

PART I

> He came, then he found me; he found me, then he brought weapons; he brought them, and Robert was all madness.

Some people prohibit repetition beyond the third instance, but I'm sure to find one that reaches four, and I wouldn't dare condemn it.

An ambiguity is a statement that can mean more than one thing, as, "I hammer away at my last," "I broke a leg." Keep this out of serious subjects, unless it be in the answers of the gods or in oracles, as here: "Once Croesus has crossed the Halys he will destroy many kingdoms." It is found in the love elegies and in some light verse. Statius in book two:

> Nothing escapes lovers. I feel it: sighs are sharpening your wakeful complaints.

Likewise someone writes ironically of Nero:

> Who denies that Nero is of the great line of Aeneas? Aeneas carried away *(sustulit)* his father, Nero made away with *(sustulit)* his mother.

He has used the word *sustulit* in two senses.

A simple story can also be ornamented another way. There are some words that are related by the nearness of their meaning, and yet differ for one who is paying close attention, as:

> These men taste nothing of the cup of wisdom; they are Arguses of money, but one-eyed men for learning things of the mind; their eyes study not the topoi of logic but the whereabouts of the money bag.

Et "ioci" et "ioca," "exemplum" et "exemplar." Item "haruspex," "augur," et "hariolus"; et "unguis" et "ungula." Huiusmodi ergo uti possumus ornatissime non exponendo differentiam expresse. Sed ita uti debemus ut ex positione dictionum lectori callido differentia praenotetur. Tale est hoc exemplum Ovidii secundum Isidorum, "Et non inventa reperta est." Nec enim haec sententia a contrariis est secundum Isidorum. Dicit quod invenimus quaesita, et reperimus inopinate occurrentia. Expressius est exemplum, de rege Ricardo dictum est: "Praeteriti exemplum fuit, exemplarque futuri." Gaufroi Vinesauf in conquestione Angliae de morte eiusdem regis ait,

> Quid ages? Volucrum rimaberis aure
> murmura? Vel motus oculo? Vel Apolline fata?
> Tolle mathematicos! Est augur surdus et auspex
> caecus et hariolus amens. Praesentia scire
> fas homini, solique Deo praescire futura.

20   Vehementia est quando quasi indignantes vel admirantes procedimus. Haec parit tres colores: correctionem, exclamationem, dubitationem. Correctionum alia adversativa, alia additiva. Adversativa dupliciter fit: tum negatione unius et positione alterius, ut hic, "Non in eo peperit pignus, sed tela, sed hostem." Tum fit positione utriusque, et hoc fit quando verbum unum vel una sententia videtur alii adversari et illam tollere—tunc apponitur dictio correctiva ostendens

PART I

Also *joci* and *joca, exemplum* and *exemplar*. Likewise *haruspex, augur,* and *hariolus;* and *unguis* and *ungula*. We can use pairs of this kind as ornament, not explaining the difference openly. But we should do it in such a way that the difference will already be clear to a smart reader from the position of the words. Such is this example from Ovid, according to Isidore, "And, unfound, you were (a lighter grief) than discovered." But according to what Isidore says, you can't switch the two words around: he says that we find things we are looking for, but we discover things that turn up unexpectedly. Here is a clearer example, said of King Richard: "He was an example from the past, and an exemplar for the future." Geoffrey of Vinsauf in his lament for England, on the death of that king says,

> What will you do? Will you search out birdsong with your ear? Or their movements with your eye? Or prophecies from Apollo? Away with astrologers! Augurs are deaf, observers of birds blind, and soothsayers brainless. It is right for man to know present things, for God alone to foreknow the future.

Vehemence is when we proceed as if angry or shocked. It engenders three colors: correction, exclamation, and indecision. Correction is either adversative or additive. Adversative correction occurs in two ways: one is to deny one thing and replace it with another, as in this case, "In him (Paris) she (Hecuba) didn't give birth to a child, but to weapons, to an enemy." The other is by including both; this is done when one word or one expression seems to be opposed to the other, and to cancel it—and then a corrective word is introduced that shows that both can simultaneously stand.

ea simul stare. Lucanus de Afranio veniam petente ait, "Gerit omnia victi / sed ducis." Quia haec dictio "victi" nimiam demissionem notare videretur, si ibi pedem sisteret oratio, ideo addidit "sed ducis," quasi diceret, "et non cuiuscumque victi." Simile de Pyramo et Thisbe:

> Invidia Famae patrum pervenit ad aures,
>   tempore consilium sed puerile brevi.

Quia haec dictio "consilium" sonare solet in sensum et in discretionem, ideo additur adversative "sed puerile." Fit etiam haec species correctionis per hanc dictionem "tamen," ut hic: "Pulchra, pudica tamen." Lucanus in primo: "Invita peragam / tamen omnia dextra." Invitus saepe facit, raro perficit; se tamen perfecturum dicit.

21 Additiva correctio est quando aliquid asseritur, sed additur aliquid novi. Haec fit competenter quando annominationi miscetur, ut hic: "Structa domus sed stricta fuit; satis alta sed arta." Fit autem competentius quando per gradationem fit processus, scilicet quando per gradus augetur vel minuitur sive bonum sive malum, ut in versibus de Troia:

> Non in eo peperit pignus, sed tela, sed ignem,
>   sed mala cuncta sibi, sed Priamo, sed suis.

PART I

Lucan says of Afranius asking for pardon, "He showed all the bearing of a beaten man—but a beaten general." Because the word *victi* (of a beaten man) might seem to denote too much dishonor, if the phrase stopped there, Lucan added *sed ducis* (but of a general), as if to say, "not just any beaten man." Similar is this of Pyramus and Thisbe:

> In a short time, by the envy of Rumor their plan reached the ears of both fathers—a plan, but a puerile one.

Because the word "plan" usually smacks of good sense and discretion, "but a puerile one" is added in opposition. This kind of correction is also made with the word "yet" or "still," as here: "Beautiful yet chaste." Lucan, in book one: "Though my hand will be unwilling, still I will do it all." An unwilling person often acts, but rarely completes his action; but he says he will complete it.

Correction by addition is when something is said and then something new is added. A good way to do it is to mix it with annomination, as here: "The house was constructed but constricted, tall but small." An even better way is to move forward by progression, when something either good or bad is enhanced or diminished in steps, as in these verses about Troy:

> In him she didn't give birth to a child but to weapons, but to fire, but to every evil for herself, for Priam, for her family.

Similiter de episcopo Norvicensi:

> Religio, pietas et clausae mente capaci
> virtutes latuisse velint; sed—praeco bonorum,
> sed tuba virtutum, sed honesti lucifer orbi—
> praedicat invitas largitio sola sorores.

Apparentior est tuba quam praeco, lucifer quam tuba. Architrenius de avaritia:

> O utinam sanctos haec citra viscera patres
> Ecclesiae pupugisset acus, ne vilior auro
> ara foret, sed libra libro, sed numine nummus.

Maius est numen quam liber.

22 Exclamatio est quando quasi dolore vel indignatione aliquid extollimus, ut hic,

> O dolor! O plus quam dolor! O mors! O truculenta
> mors! Esses utinam mors mortua!

Dubitatio est quando dubitando procedimus, ut patet in exemplo supradicto, "Quid ages?" etc. Et in illo noto, "Tu mihi te confers, homo, quo te nomine dicam?"

23 Color qui consistit in quaestione et responsione subdividitur in dialogum et subiectionem. Dialogus est sermo versatus inter duos, ut inter Didonem et Annam sororem suam, sic:

> "Anna, soror, morior." "Quare?" "Quia vivo." "Quid inde?"
>   "Talis enim vitae vespere vita foret."

PART I

Similarly, about the bishop of Norwich:

> Religion, piety, virtues enclosed in a capacious mind might try to stay hidden; but generosity—the herald of good deeds, the trumpet of virtues, the light-bearer of goodness for the world—advertises those unwilling sisters all by itself.

A trumpet is more striking than a herald, a light-bearer than a trumpet. Here is Architrenius on avarice:

> Oh, if only before this a needle had punctured the bellies of the holy fathers of the Church, so that the altar would not now be cheaper than gold, but pounds and shillings cheaper than books, coins than the will of God.

The will of God is greater than a book.

Exclamation is when we emphasize something as if in grief or anger, as in this case:

> O sorrow! O more than sorrow! O death! O cruel death! I wish you were dead, death!

Indecision is when we proceed hesitantly, as is clear in the example given above, "What will you do?" and so on. And in this well-known line, "You impose yourself on me, man; by what name shall I call you?"

The color that consists of a question and its answer is divided into dialogue and hypophora. Dialogue is a conversation between two people, as between Dido and her sister Anna, thus:

> "Anna, sister, I'm dying." "Why?" "Because I'm alive." "How so?" "Such would life be in the evening of life."

Et illud: "'Quid fers?' 'Poma fero.' 'Quot?' 'VII.' 'Da mihi!' 'Nolo.'" Huiusmodi contingit plenius invenire in Seneca tragoediarum. Huius species est ratiocinatio, quando scilicet de aliquo quaerimus quare ipsum sit, et postea confirmamus ratione quare ipsum sit. Et hoc sub dialogo, ut hic:

> Semper avarus eget. Quare? Quia cum petit usus,
> tangere parta timet. Cur? Ne minuatur acervus.

Melior est prima species et magis authentica.

Subiectio est quando quaestionem facimus, sed anticipamus nos ipsi respondentem, responsione quidem nostra aggravantes quaestionem, sic:

> O pater, O quid agis? Deus est quem spernis; et ipsum
>   qualiter effugies, terra cinisque, Deum?
> An fugies? Sed ubique latet. Fallesne? Sed idem
>   est cui semper idem quod fuit est et erit.
> An vinces? Sed cuncta potest. Illumne latebis?
>   Sed quodcumque latet vel patet ipse videt.
> Mors igitur vetiti te poena miserrima ligni
>   deprimet, in natis ius habitura tuis.

Hic color competenter fit quando ex praecedentibus sequitur conclusio. Per hunc modum competenter exclamatio decoratur.

Mutatio est identitas subtractione vel additione vel diversione aliqua colorata. Patet ergo quod tres sunt mutationis species: subtractio, additio, et diversio. Subtractio dividitur in praecisionem et prolepsim. Praecisio est quando

And this: "'What are you carrying?' 'I'm carrying apples.' 'How many?' 'Seven.' 'Give me one!' 'No.'" You can find many more of this kind in Seneca the tragedian. A type of this is reasoning by question and answer, when we ask someone why something is the case and then establish by reasoning why it is the case. This is achieved by dialogue, as here:

> A miser will always be needy. Why? Because when necessity requires it, he is afraid to touch what he has made. Why? So the pile may not get smaller.

The first type is better and more authentic.

Hypophora is when we ask a question, but ourselves anticipate the answerer, intensifying the question by our answer:

> O father, oh, what are you doing? It's God you are spurning, and how will you, dust and ashes, flee God himself? Or will you flee? But he is everywhere. Will you trick him? But he is the one to whom what was, is, and will be are always the same. Will you beat him? But he can do everything. Will you hide from him? But he sees everything, whether hidden or open. Death, then, the most terrible punishment of the forbidden tree, will overcome you, and will hold sway over your children.

This color is aptly used when the conclusion follows from what precedes. It makes a good ornament for exclamation.

Mutation is sameness colored by subtraction, addition, or diversion. So, evidently, there are three kinds of mutation: subtraction, addition, and diversion. Subtraction is divided into aposiopesis and prolepsis. Aposiopesis is when

praecidimus aliquid a dictione vel oratione. Haec fit dupliciter, vel per plenam subtractionem vel per interpolatam sumptionem quadam tamen simulatione non plene dicendi. Haec solet competenter incidere sub indignatione vel terrore, sub elegia etiam amoris vel cuiuslibet tristitiae. Iste modus raro vel nunquam fit competenter sub persona scribentis, sed per prosopopoeiam, id est per fictam personam, ut patet sub dialogo in hoc exemplo ad terrendum puerum:

> "Fles?" "Fleo." "Nonne taces?" "Non." "Vado vocare magistrum."
> "Vade!" "Magistrum visne vocem?" "Quae mea cura? Voca!"

Oratio etiam plena subtrahitur ex indignatione, ut in Lucano, ubi introducit Ciceronem exhortantem Pompeium ad civile bellum. Ut dilemma faciat Pompeio, dicit,

> Scire senatus avet, miles te, Magne, sequatur,
> an comes.

Et ex vehementia animi subticet efficaciam dilemmatis, scilicet hoc: "Si miles, duc, si comes, sequere."

Fit etiam praecisio per interpolatam sumptionem; secundum quod introducit Iohannes de Hauvilla Caunum interrogantem et Byblidem pavide respondentem cum invenisset eam Caunus dolentem, sic: "'Quis te laesit?' 'A. . .' 'Quis?' 'Am. . .' 'Quis?' 'Amo. . .' 'Quis?' 'Amor.'" Et iterum cum ipsa vexaret eum,

PART I

we cut off something from a word or a phrase. It is done in two ways, either by a full subtraction or by introducing a turn in the conversation in a kind of simulation of not completing a statement. This usually works well with anger or fear, or in an elegy for love or for any sort of sadness. This device is rarely or never used appropriately in the person of the writer himself, but by prosopopoeia, that is, by an imagined person, as in clear in the dialogue in this example for scaring a boy:

> "Are you crying?" "Yes, I'm crying." "Won't you stop?" "No." "I'm going to call the teacher." "Go ahead." "You want me to call the teacher?" "Why should I care? Call him!"

Also a complete statement is curtailed out of anger, as in Lucan, where he brings in Cicero exhorting Pompey to civil war. In order to create a dilemma for Pompey, he says,

> The senate would like to know, Magnus, whether it is following you as a fighter or as a companion.

In his passionate feelings, he suppresses the real point of the dilemma, which is this: "If we are fighters, lead us; if we are companions, follow us."

Aposiopesis is also made by introducing a turn in the conversation, just as John of Hauville brings in Caunus asking questions and Byblis answering fearfully when Caunus had found her weeping, with these words: "'Who hurt you?' 'L...' 'Who?' 'Lo...' 'Who?' 'Lov...' 'Who?' 'Love.'" And again when she was irking him:

"Quid tibi vis?" "Quod a...." "Quid?" "Quod ama...."
"Quid vis?" "Quod amare...."
"Quid?" "Quod amare ve...." "Quid vis?" "Quod amare velis."

Incidit autem color iste venustissime quando auctor praescindit aliquid sub persona introducta et ipsemet consequenter supplet sub propria. Bernardus in *Parricidali,* introducens patrem condonantem filio mortem suam, dicit,

"Condono mea, nate, tibi...." Cum dicere vellet
"funera," vox linguam nulla secuta suam.

Generaliter fit etiam praecisio per subtractionem verbi substantivi, ut hic: "Magna opera Domini" (subaudis "sunt"). Similiter: "Fidelia omnia mandata eius." Istud obtinet frequenter in omni genere sententiae, ut hic: "Duplice post melior una loquela prior." Alio modo venustissime fit praecisio quando facit dictionem semel positam teneri equivoce. Gregorius in *Dialogis:* "Fuit vir vitae venerabilis, gratia 'Benedictus' et nomine." Dialecticus bis diceret "Benedictus," sed nos contenti sumus semel positae, et praescindimus secundo positam. Simile: "Flores hic legit, ille libellos." Simile: "Aeneas patrem, Nero matrem sustulit." Fit etiam venustissime hic modus quando nomen aequivocum quasi cogitur per adiectivum aliquod distributivum ad significationem convenientem, ut hic: "Iacobus uterque nitet laurea." Est adhuc et alius modus venustior, quando attribuimus rei adiectivum vel adiectiva quae sunt illius vocis

PART I

"What do you want for yourself?" "That l. . . ." "What?" "That lo. . . ." "What do you want?" "That love. . . ." "What do you want?" "That love is what you w. . . ." "What do you want?" "That love is what you want."

This color is used most elegantly when the author cuts short a speech from a character he has introduced and appropriately completes it himself in his own person. Bernard in *The Astrologer,* when he brings in a father forgiving his son for killing him, says,

"I forgive you, my son, for my. . . ." When he tried to say "death," no sound obeyed his tongue.

Aposiopesis is regularly made by taking out the verb "to be," as in this case: "Great the works of the Lord" (understand "are"). Likewise: "Faithful all his commandments." This happens often in all sorts of maxims, as in this case: "One word beforehand better than two afterward." Another extremely elegant form of aposiopesis is when it causes a word introduced once to be taken in two ways. Gregory in the *Dialogues:* "There was a man of venerable life, 'Blessed' both by grace and by name." A dialectician would say "Blessed" twice, but we are content to just say it once and remove the second one. Like it: "One man picks flowers, one books." Or: "Aeneas carried off his father, Nero his mother." The most elegant form of this is when an ambiguous noun is forced, as it were, into the appropriate meaning by a distributive adjective, as here: "Each James shines because of his laurel." Another mode is still more elegant, when we attribute to a thing an adjective or adjectives that properly

43

proprie. Unde dictum est cuidam quae proprio nomine vocabatur Idonea, sic:

> Consona sit propriae communis, Idonea: gaude.
> Grata duplant nomen significata tuum.

"Idonea" communis, id est significata eo nomine prout est commune. "Idonea" propria, id est significata eo nomine prout est proprium. Simile de quodam Clemente: "Hic est ille Clemens uterque, tam communis quam proprius, nec dissonat proprius a communi."

27 Fit adhuc praecisio per plenam subtractionem alio modo, quando scilicet aliquis casus regitur a verbo, non ratione eiusdem verbi sed ratione alterius subintellecti et subtracti, ut si dicam, "Iste equus pascitur silvam," id est, pascendo vel dum pascitur, silvam corrodit. Ecce subtrahitur "corrodit." Fit autem venuste hic modus si tale verbum semel positum unum casum regat ratione sui, alium ratione verbi subintellecti, ut hic: "Pascitur Iohannis nemus et aperti gramine campi." "Pascitur nemus," haec impropria, id est pascendo corrodit. "Pascitur gramine," haec propria. Latentius et melius potest hic modus fieri in identitate casuum, ut hic: "Pater meus cum patrimonium suum diutissime tenuisset, tandem possessionem pariter et spiritum exhalavit." "Exhalavit spiritum," haec propria; "exhalavit possessionem," id est, exhalando amisit, haec impropria.

PART I

belong to its name. Accordingly the following words were addressed to a woman whose name was Idonea:

> Let the common word be in line with your proper name, Idonea: be happy. Such welcome meanings duplicate your name.

Idonea (suitable) is a common adjective; a woman is designated by it in so far as it conveys a common quality. And one properly named "Idonea" is designated by that name insofar as it conveys a feature proper to her. Likewise about somebody named Clement: "This is that double Clement, clement both in common and proper sense: no discord exists between the proper and common senses of his name."

A further aposiopesis involves full subtraction in another way, when a case is governed by a verb, but not by virtue of that verb but by virtue of another that is understood but unexpressed, as if I said, "This horse is grazing a forest," that is, by grazing or while he is grazing, he is eating the forest away. "Eating away" is simply left out. This mode is attractive if the verb that appears only once governs one case in its own right and another by reason of the understood verb, as here: "He is grazing John's grove and the grass of the open field." "He is grazing the grove" is an improper phrase, but means he is eating it away by grazing on it. "He is grazing the grass" is proper. This mode can be more subtle and better if the cases are the same, as here: "Though my father had kept his patrimony for a very long time, at last he breathed out both his property and his spirit." "He breathed out his spirit" is proper; "he breathed out his property," that is, lost it by expiring, is improper.

28 Prolepsis idem est quod anticipatio. Est ergo prolepsis quotiens clausula de novo apposita anticipat finem clausulae praeinceptae. Haec fit utiliter ex indignatione vel ira. Statius in sermone Tydei et Polynicis cum Eteocle:

> Haec pietas, haec magna fides! Nec crimina gentis
> mira equidem duco. Sic primi sanguinis auctor,
> incestique patrum thalami. . . .

Antequam plene dixisset, "Primi sanguinis auctor fuit incestus"—quasi modicum incepisset—praetermisit illam clausulam et incepit quiddam maius, dicens, "incestique patrum thalami." Hic modus frequenter contingit inter mutuo colloquentes, et maxime litigantes. Seneca tragoediarum sufficiat in exemplis.

29 Additionum alia occupatio, alia coadunatio, alia determinatio. Occupatio est additio quaedam dissimulationis in sententia proposita, quando scilicet simulamus nos nolle dicere quod dicimus. Haec tum fit ad iocum excitandum, ut hic,

> Quid referam quae forma tibi, quam sis speciosus,
>   quam sis par nano corpore, ventre bovi?

Tum fit ad taedium tollendum, unde dictum est de quodam qui, cum multas haberet virtutes, inter ceteras dives erat et pulcher, sic:

> Praetereo leviora loqui quae munera sumpsit
> vel formae vel opum; sed ei certamine dulci
> divitias Fortuna pluit, Natura decorem.

PART I

Prolepsis is the same as anticipation. It is prolepsis whenever a newly added phrase anticipates the end of a phrase that has already been begun. This is useful for expressing indignation or anger. Statius in the conversation between Tydeus (representing Polynices) and Eteocles writes:

> This is your piety, this your famous word of honor! The crimes of your family don't surprise me. Such was the founder of your line, such the incestuous beds of your ancestors....

Before he had finished saying, "The founder of the line was incestuous"—as if what he had begun was trivial—he skipped that remark and stated something bigger, saying, "the incestuous beds of your ancestors." This mode happens often between two people speaking with each other, and particularly in court cases. Seneca provides abundant examples in his tragedies.

Additions are either paralipsis, coalescence, or modification. Paralipsis is an addition of a kind of dissimulation into a statement, when we pretend we don't want to say what we are saying. It can be done either for comic effect, as in here:

> Why should I talk about your looks? Why should I say how handsome you are, how like a dwarf in your body, with a cow's belly?

Or for relieving boredom, like the lines about a man who among his many virtues was rich and handsome:

> I omit mentioning what slighter gifts he had of beauty or wealth, but in sweet rivalry Fortune rained riches on him, and Nature beauty.

30   Coadunatio est aggregatio dictionum vel orationum sub quadam similitudine et dissimilitudine. Coadunatio enim exigit vehementissime ut uniformitas pariter et diversitas observetur. Coadunatio tum fit in dictionibus, tum in orationibus. Coadunatio dictionum dividitur in polysyndeton et articulum—ut restringamus vocabulum figurae polysyndeton, quia large acceptum comprehendit etiam adiunctum. Polysyndeton ergo, prout hic accipitur, est coadunatio terminorum similium per coniunctionem vel coniunctiones, ut "et," "-que," "sed," "vel," "ut," et huiusmodi, ut "Acamasque Thoasque Neoptolemusque." Item:

> Non in eo peperit pignus, sed tela, sed hostes,
>   sed mala cuncta sibi.

Articulus est oratio consimiles continens dictiones, sed caesa verbis loco coniunctionis punctorum distinguitur intervallis, ut,

> Armis, classe, cibo dives mala castra petisti;
>   solus, inermis, inops, inglorius ecce redisti.

Hic modus inchoandis materiis aptissimus invenitur. Ablativis, ut hic:

> Divitiis, specie, fama, virtute, pudore,
>   ortu, consiliis Io serena fuit.

Adiectivis sic:

> Prompta, pudica, timens, humilis, facunda, fidelis,
>   docta, potens, locuplex, nobilis Io fuit.

PART I

Coalescence is the conglomeration of words or phrases by either likeness or unlikeness. It strongly forces the perception either of uniformity or of diversity. It is made both with words and phrases. Coalescence of words is divided into polysyndeton and *articulus*—though here we are restricting the meaning of the word for the figure polysyndeton, since taken more broadly, it also includes adjunction. Polysyndeton then, as understood here, is the coalescence of similar terms by means of a conjunction or conjunctions, as "and," "also," "but," "or," "as," and the like, as in "Acamas and Thoas and Neoptolemus." Again:

> She didn't give birth to a child but to weapons, but to enemies, but to everything bad for herself.

Articulus is a phrase containing similar expressions, but, split up into individual words, it is divided by intervening punctuation instead of conjunctions, as,

> Rich in arms, fleet, food you attacked the camp of wickedness; behold, you went home alone, unarmed, poor, without glory.

This mode is found to be particularly apt for beginning a subject. It occurs with ablatives, as here:

> In riches, beauty, reputation, virtue, modesty, birth, judgment Io was well favored.

With adjectives in this way:

> Active, modest, bashful, humble, well spoken, faithful, learned, able, wealthy, noble: that was Io.

Hic color alio nomine membrum orationis dicitur. Schesis onomaton figura consonat huic colori.

31   Orationum coadunatio alia aggregatio, alia reiteratio. Aggregatio est orationum coadunatio sine reiteratione. Haec coadunatio tum consideratur secundum verbum, tum secundum coniunctionem. Secundum verbum continet duas species, disiunctum et coniunctum. Disiunctum est quando singulis clausulis collectis singula verba attribuuntur, ut hic:

> Exhilarant frondes silvam, vacat imbribus aer,
>   murmure ludit aqua, flore superbit ager.

Huic colori schema consonat hypozeuxis, hic est utilis materiis inchoandis. Architrenius:

> Velificatur Athos, dubio mare ponte ligatur,
>   remus arat colles, etc.

Coniunctum est verbo semel posito diversa coniunctio clausularum. Hic similiter est utilis materiis inchoandis, sic:

> Insignis specie, vita preclara, faceta
>   eloquio, fulgens moribus Io fuit.

Non putetis istas species tantum circa identitatem consistere, sed frequentius. Contingunt enim quandoque etiam circa species similitudinis vel contrarietatis. Similitudinis, ut hic:

> Marcia consilio, gestu Lucretia, vita
>   Penelope, facie Tindaris Io fuit.

Contrarietatis, ut hic:

PART I

This color is also called comma. The figure *schesis onomaton* corresponds to this color.

Coalescence of phrases involves either accumulation or reiteration. Accumulation is the coalescence of phrases without repetition. Think of it as either by verb or by conjunction. By verb, it has two species, disjunction and conjunction. Disjunction is when a group of separate clauses each has its own verb, as here:

> Leaves gladden the woods, the air is free of rain, the stream babbles playfully, the meadow is proud with flowers.

The figure hypozeuxis corresponds to this color, which is useful for beginning a subject. Architrenius:

> Mount Athos is sailed over, the sea is spanned by a dubious bridge, oars plow the hills, etc.

Conjunction involves phrases separately joined to a single verb. It too is useful for beginning subjects, thus:

> Io was remarkable for beauty, distinguished in her life, gifted in her speech, brilliant in her character.

Beware of thinking that these devices rely only on sameness, though they do most frequently. Sometimes they occur also with types of likeness or opposition. Of likeness, as here:

> Io was a Marcia in judgment, a Lucretia in her conduct, a Penelope in her life, a Helen in beauty.

Of opposition, as here:

> Exhaurit miseros pax bellica, gloria tristis,
> dulcor amarus, egens copia, dirus amor.

Zeugma figura consonat huic colori, quam variant tripliciter: a superiori, ab inferiori, a medio.

32 Aggregatio orationum secundum coniunctionem considerata continet duas species, adiunctum et dissolutum. Adiunctum est aggregatio orationum per coniunctionem vel per coniunctiones copulatarum. Bernardus:

> Ossibus extrahitur elephas, dorsoque camelus
> surgit, et in bubalo cornua frontis honor.

Hucusque extenditur schema polysyndeton a Donato, quippe tamen ex descriptione ipsius schematis comprehendi non potest—praesumi tamen potest ex descriptione sui contrarii, dialyton. Dissolutum est aggregatio orationum nulla coniunctione mediante. Bernardus:

> Pisce natantur aquae, volucri discurritur aer,
> incedunt pecudes, vipera serpit humo.

Nec putetur hunc colorem disiunctum esse vel tantum cum disiuncto accidere. Provenit etenim et cum coniuncto et utilis est etiam materiis inchoandis. Bernardus in *Parricidali* ait,

> Miles erat Romae, probus armis, rebus abundans,
> urbe potens, felix coniuge, clarus avis.

PART I

The poor lovers were worn out by warlike peace,
mournful glory, bitter sweetness, needy abundance,
ill-omened love.

The figure zeugma corresponds to this color, which writers vary in three ways, placing the verb at the beginning, the end, or the middle.

Accumulation of phrases by conjunction has two types, conjoined and freed. Conjoined is the accumulation of phrases connected by a conjunction or conjunctions. Bernard:

> The elephant is lengthened by his tusks, and the camel is made taller by his back, and on the buffalo horns are the glory of his forehead.

The figure polysyndeton is extended by Donatus to include this, since, though from the description of the figure itself that can't be understood, still it can be assumed from the description of its opposite, dialyton or "freed," which is the accumulation of phrases without a mediating conjunction. Bernard:

> Waters are swum in by a fish, the air traversed by a bird, animals walk, the viper creeps on the ground.

And don't be thinking that this color is disjunction or occurs only with disjunction. For it also appears with conjunction, and it too is useful for beginning subjects. Bernard in *The Astrologer* says,

> There was in Rome a knight, proven in arms, abounding in possessions, powerful in the city, happy in his wife, distinguished in his ancestors.

Hic color schemati dialyton aequipollet adeo quod fidelissima interpretatione dialysis est "dissolutio," dialyton "dissolutum." Extra vagantia, fit etiam coadunatio secundum quamlibet sui speciem pulcherrime cum repetitione vocali. Bernardus:

> Quaerit ut expoliet venatibus, alite, pisce,
> gustus humum, gustus aera, gustus aquas.

Plusquam pulcherrime cum repetitione reali, ubi scilicet repetitur sensus dictionis et non vox. Haec fit per synonyma, ut de Pyramo et Thisbe dictum est:

> Vivendi modus est una gaudere, dolere
> coniunctim, pariter ire, sedere simul.

33 Reiterationem dividunt prius dicti repetitio, conduplicatio, interpretatio. Prius dicti repetitio est quando quod in fine est, ex ira vel indignatione reiteramus vel ex quacumque animi vehementia, ut hic: "Illud vobis supplicium contulit severitas, severitas quae non potuit verbis explanari. Explanari? Quis enim mentis illius venenum explicaret?" Et illud psalmistae: "O Domine, quia ego servus tuus, ego servus tuus et filius ancillae tuae." Conduplicatio est quando motu irae vel indignationis vel alicuius anxietatis principium iteramus, ut hic:

> Tune duos una, saevissima vipera, cena?
> Tune duos?

PART I

This color is equivalent to the figure dialyton to the extent that, by the most literal translation, dialysis means "separation," dialyton "separated." Getting back to the subject, coalescence in any of its types also combines very beautifully with verbal repetition. Bernard:

> Appetite seeks to despoil the earth of game, to despoil the air of birds, to despoil the waters of fish.

It is even more beautiful with repetition of the content, that is, when the sense is repeated but not the word. This is created by synonymy, as in this statement about Pyramus and Thisbe:

> Their way of living is to rejoice as one, to grieve together, to walk side by side, to be seated at the same time.

Reiteration is either repetition of the previous word, or duplication, or synonymy. Repetition of the previous word is when out of wrath or anger or any strongly held feeling we repeat what was at the end of the previous phrase, as here: "His severity inflicted that punishment on you, a severity that words could not explain. Explain? Who could explain the venom of that mind?" And this from the psalmist: "For I, O Lord, am thy servant, thy servant and the son of thy handmaid." Duplication is when, moved by wrath or anger or some anxiety, we repeat the beginning, as in this case:

> You poisoned two at one meal, you cruelest of vipers? You poisoned two?

Bernardus in *Parricidali:*

> Filius ille tuus, cuius rationis acumen,
> actus mirari, verba probare soles.
> Filius ille tuus, de quo quoque livor et hostis,
> de quo mentiri Fama vel ipsa timet.
> Filius ille tuus, quem praedicat orbis et omnis
> quae sub septeno climate terra iacet.

Interpretatio est sententiae prius dictae diversis verbis iteratio, ut hic:

> Supplicium delicta vocant, vindicta scelestos
> expectat, scelerum crimina poena manet.

Hic color in proverbiis faciendis satis utilis invenitur. Cum tamen perissologicus fere videatur et contra Ciceronis doctrinam, pluribus tamen modis non solum non vitium sed etiam competens est ornatus. Uno modo, si expositive teneatur. Bernardus: "Quicquid occurrit morbis, quicquid conciliat sanitatem." Expositive tenetur, sic enim occurritur morbis. Alio modo si elective, et erit competentior si uniformitas sententiae diversitate generum temperetur, ut in hiis versibus:

> Qui vel quae vel quod Polynici Tydea pridem
> nos hic iungat amor, pax ea, foedus idem.

Elective tenetur disiunctiva coniunctio.

Tertius modus est si quasi quadam gradatione in efficacia verborum exile notetur augmentum, ut hic, "Peto quatinus brevitas temporis quo coaluimus animas alliget, mentes as-

PART I

Bernard in *The Astrologer*:

> He is your son, whose sharpness of mind, whose actions you often wonder at, whose words you approve. He is your son, about whom envy, about whom enemies, about whom Rumor herself are afraid to lie. He is your son, whom the world crows over, and every land that lies beneath the seven zones.

Synonymy is repeating the previous statement in different words, as here:

> Crimes call for a penalty, vengeance awaits the wicked, punishment is in store for the commission of crimes.

This color is very useful in making up proverbs. Though it almost seems to be redundancy and contrary to what Cicero teaches, in fact in many modes it is not only not a fault but also a fitting form of ornament. One way is to use it to explain. Bernard: "Whatever combats diseases, whatever wins back health." This is explanatory, for that is how diseases are combatted. Another way is to offer choices, and it will work better if the uniformity of statement is tempered by diversity of genders, as in these verses:

> May this love, this peace, this selfsame pact that of old bound Tydeus to Polynices, bind us now.

The nouns, joined without conjunctions, are offered as choices.

A third way is if by a sort of climax a small increase is indicated in the force of the words, as here: "I beg that the shortness of the time in which we have grown together may bind our souls, tighten our minds, link together our hearts,

tringat, pectora concatenet, et sic duorum diversitas uniatur vel amore mutuo vel alterna pace vel foedere relativo." Plus enim quodam modo est constringere quam alligare, concatenare quam constringere.

35 Quartus modus est competentissimus, cum fit ratione competentius perorandi. Cum enim unicam habeamus tantum rationem ad aliquid persuadendum, rhetoricum est ita illam variare, et per dictiones synonymas ita frequenter resumere, ut appareat copia rationum. Verbi gratia, Pyramus et Thisbe, in persuasione sua ut paries ipsis caderet, dixerunt parieti,

> Iunge relativa quos nodat gratia, foedus
>   copulat alternum, mutuus unit amor.

36 Determinationum alia adiectiva, alia partitiva, alia appositiva, alia relativa. Sed partitivae et adiectivae excedentes sunt et excessae, et ideo de illis simul agamus. Adiectivorum igitur aliud notat causam, aliud differentiam, aliud signum, aliud effectum, aliud epitheton. Causam ut hic: "Hoc tempus humidum nocet segeti," id est, quia humidum ideo nocet. Venustissimum est sic positum adiectivum, Ovidius:

> Tres sumus imbelles numero: sine viribus uxor,
>   Laertesque senex, Telemachusque puer.

Istae determinationes—"senex," "puer," "sine viribus"—causative tenentur, quod manifestius esset si plena observaretur uniformitas, sic:

and in that way the difference between the two of us may be unified either by mutual love or by peace with each other or by a family-like pact." In a sense, tightening is more than binding, linking together more than tightening.

A fourth way, and most effective of all, is to use this device to conclude more effectively. For when we have only one argument for persuading someone of something, the rhetorical thing to do is to vary it so, and recapitulate it often in synonymous words in such a way, that there appears to be a heap of arguments. Pyramus and Thisbe, for example, when they were trying to persuade the wall to give way for them, said to it,

> Join us, whom reciprocal affection knots together, whom a shared pact conjoins, whom mutual love unites.

Modification is by adjectives, partitives, appositives, or relatives. But partitives and adjectives both add something extra to what they modify or fall short of it, and therefore let us deal with them together. Adjectives denote cause, or difference, or a sign, or effect, or an epithet. Cause, as this: "This wet weather is bad for the harvest." That is, it is bad for it because it is wet. It is most elegant to introduce an adjective in the following way, as in Ovid:

> We are three in number but unfit to fight: a wife without strength; Laertes, an old man; and Telemachus, a boy.

These modifiers—"old man," "boy," "without strength"—have causative force, which would be clearer if complete uniformity was observed, in this way:

Tres sumus imbelles numero tibi, debilis uxor,
　　Laertesque senex, etc.

Expone: uxor debilis, ideo imbellis; Laertes senex et ideo imbellis; Telemachus puer et ideo imbellis.

37　Adiectivum notat differentiam, ut hic: "Malus clericus legit in hac villa." Non exponitur "malus" quia malus; sed notat quod eius contrarium, scilicet bonitas, non insit ei. Talium aliud excludit suum contrarium, aliud suum simile. Contrarium, ut hic: "Albus homo currit," quasi diceretur ille non est niger. Simile excludit quando fit mentio de similibus et apponitur unum simile, ut si dicam, "Quidam amant viros eloquentes, quidam sapientes, sed fortes rex noster amat." Quasi diceret, non curat de eloquentia vel sapientia. Item simile excludit quamvis etiam de similibus nulla praecedat mentio. Sed hoc fit in derisoria prolatione, et tunc accentuandi modus et gestus pronunciantis adiuvant intellectum, ut si dicatur, "Fortis magister legit in hac villa," quasi diceret, non doctus vel sapiens.

38　Omne adiectivum differentiale mordet suum substantivum, et partitive tenetur, prout enim exponitur, "Ero morsus tuus, inferne." Qui mordet, partem accipit et partem relinquit. Eodem modo adiectivum differentiale partem accipit, partem relinquit. Omnis partitio ex divisione praecedente surgit. Cum igitur haec vera apud dialecticos, vel possit esse vera "Hominum alius albus, alius niger," haec congrua apud grammaticos, "Homo albus currit," apud rhetoricos vero adiectivum designans differentiam quandoque

PART I

> We are three in number but unfit to fight for you: a
> feeble wife, Laertes, an old man, etc.

To explain: the wife is feeble, and so unfit to fight; Laertes is old, and so unfit to fight; Telemachus is a boy, and so unfit to fight.

An adjective denotes difference, as here: "A bad cleric is teaching in this town." "Bad" here doesn't mean that he is wicked; but it does indicate that he doesn't possess its opposite, goodness. In such cases some adjectives exclude their opposite, some their likeness. Opposite, as here: "A white man is running," as if it said he isn't black. It excludes likeness when mention is made of like things and then a further like thing is added, as if I should say, "Some people love eloquent men, some wise men, but our king loves brave men." As if to say, he doesn't care about eloquence or wisdom. Sometimes likeness acts to exclude even if there was no prior mention of like things. This happens in derisory discourse, and then the way the speaker places the emphasis and his gestures assist understanding, as is the case if someone said, "A brave teacher is teaching in this town," meaning not a learned or a wise one.

Every adjective that implies difference takes a bite out of its substantive, and has partitive force, for as the text goes, "Hell, I will be thy bite." The person who bites takes part and leaves part. In the same way an adjective that implies difference takes part and leaves part. Every partition arises from a preceding division. Though this partition, "One man is white, another black," is true, or can be true, for dialecticians, and "A white man is running," is proper for grammarians, among rhetoricians an adjective designating difference

satis competenter determinat nomen proprium ratione aequivocationis, ut "Aiax Locrius, Scipio Africanus." Cum enim haec vera apud rhetoricos, "Duorum Aiacum alius Locrius, alius Telamonis filius," haec competens et ornata: "Aiax Telamonius."

39 Partitionum alia uniformis, alia inuniformis. Uniformis est quae fit in identitate casuum, quae tum fit per signum partitivum, ut "aliquis homo," tum per dictionem adiectivam, ut "homo albus." Inuniformis est quae non fit in identitate casuum. Inuniformium alia directa, alia indirecta. Directa, quando praecedit terminus partiens et sequitur partitus, ut "aliquis hominum." Indirecta, quando e converso, ut "creatura salis," quia creaturarum alia sal, alia non sal. Directa tum fit ornatissime quando terminus non casualis cogitur partiri in termino casuali, ut "tunc temporis," "inde loci," "ubicumque locorum." Bernardus:

Inde loci Venus est, quae seminis et geniturae
vires humecti plena caloris habet.

Indirecta similiter partitio, quam nominant dialectici "intransitivam constructionem genitivi," venustissimus est ornatus. Bernardus in descriptione divinae mentis: "Erat fons luminis, seminarium vitae, bonum bonitatis divinae, plenitudo scientiae, quae mens Altissimi nominatur."

40 Adiectivum designat signum in hoc exemplo usitato: "Haec urina est sana," id est, signum sanitatis. Simile in *Architrenio,* ubi dicit auctor,

sometimes quite appropriately modifies a proper name, because the name can mean more than one person, as, "Locrian Ajax, Scipio Africanus." Since this differentiation is true for rhetoricians, that "There are two Ajaxes, one Locrian, one the son of Telamon," this partition is appropriate and an adornment: "Telamonian Ajax."

Some partition is uniform, some nonuniform. Uniform partition is when words are in the same case. Sometimes it involves a partitive signifier, as "some man," sometimes an adjective, as "a white man." Nonuniform partition is when there is more than one case. It is either direct or indirect. Direct, when the differentiating term comes first and the differentiated second, as "someone of men." Indirect is the opposite, as "creature of salt," for some creatures are salt and some aren't. A particularly attractive form of direct nonuniform partition is when an indeclinable word is made to act like a declinable word, as "in that then *(tunc)* of time," "in that thence of *(inde)* of place," "in wherever *(ubicumque)* of places." Bernard:

> In that thence of place is Venus who, filled with moist
> heat, has the powers of sowing and generation.

Similarly, indirect partition, which dialecticians call "the intransitive construction of the genitive," is a very elegant adornment. Bernard in his description of the divine mind: "It was the fountain of light, the seedbed of life, a good from the divine goodness, the fullness of knowledge: it is called the mind of the Most High."

The adjective designates a sign in this familiar example: "This urine is healthy," that is, it is a sign of health. Likewise in *Architrenius,* where the author says,

> Non sum cui serviat auri
> turba vel argenti . . . vel cui facunda smaragdus
> disputet in digitis.

"Facunda" dicit quia smaragdus in oratoris digito signum est facundiae. Effectum designat adiectivum, ut hic: "Haec medicina est sana." Bernardus: "Plana soporatum terra papaver habet." Ab effectu, quia efficit soporatum. Ovidius: "Tristia per vacuos horrent absinthia campos." Tristia, quia efficiunt tristes vel colentes vel gustantes.

Epitheton apud Graecos idem est quod "adiectivum" apud nos. *Epi* enim idem est quod "in" vel "ad" vel "super," *epitheton* "interpositum" vel "appositum" vel "superpositum." In hoc loco tamen restringitur ut dicatur tantum "superpositum," ut haec dictio "super" notet abundantiam superfluitatis saltem apparenter, ut "albus olor," "dira Celaeno." Epitheton aliud designat laudem, aliud vituperium, aliud praerogativam quamcumque, aliud solam veritatem. Laudem, ut hic, "Hector fortis"; vituperium, ut hic, "Byrrhia lentus"; praerogativam, ut "Helena pulcherrima," "fortis Achilles," "facundus Ulixes," "magnus Alexander," quia illis nemo par diebus suis sive locis suis. Nec ponitur "fortis" ad differentiam alterius Achillis non fortis, sed fortis praerogative—non dico antonomasice, quia antonomasia in substantivo consistit.

Epitheton praerogativum ostensivum est. Unde Donatus dicit quod etiam per Antonomasiam et per epitheton "vel vituperamus aliquem vel ostendimus vel ornamus." Ostentio igitur huiusmodi vel est absoluta vel respectiva. Absoluta inutilis est omnibus facete loquentibus, immo quandoque et

PART I

> I am not one with a pile of gold or silver at his command . . . or one whose spokesman would be the eloquent emerald on his fingers.

He says "eloquent" because an emerald on the finger of a speaker is a sign of his eloquence. An adjective designates effect, as in this case: "This medicine is healthy." Bernard: "The plain possesses the sleepy poppy." That's from effect, since it makes one sleepy. Ovid: "Sad wormwood bristles throughout the empty fields." Sad, because it makes people sad, both those who grow it and those who taste it.

Epitheton in Greek is the same as "adjective" for us. *Epi* means "in" or "to" or "above," *epitheton* "put between" or "put by" or "put above." Here, though, it is restricted only to mean "put above" insofar as the word "above" may denote an abundance of excess, at least apparently, as "a white swan," "dread Celaeno." Epithet can denote praise, abuse, preeminence in anything, or just what is true. Praise, as, "Hector the brave"; abuse, as "lazy Byrrhia"; preeminence, as, "Helen the most beautiful," "Achilles the brave," "Ulysses the eloquent," "Alexander the great," because nobody was their equal in their time and place. "Brave" isn't used to distinguish Achilles from some other Achilles who isn't brave, rather he is preeminently brave. I am not speaking of antonomasia, which is always a noun.

An epithet of preeminence is demonstrative of something. Donatus says that both by antonomasia and by epithet "we abuse or adorn someone, or put them on show." A demonstration of this kind is either absolute or specific. Absolute demonstration is useless for anyone speaking humorously, and sometimes even for those speaking as a

grammatice loquentibus, ut si dicam, "Ego video hominem mortalem." Respectus vero quandoque determinatur facto ipso, quandoque voce. Quando facto determinatur, notat maiorem certitudinem vel aliquid huismodi, ut si videret Polynices duas filias Adrasti et nesciret utra quo nomine vocaretur, et diceret Adrastus, "Argivam maiorem dabo tibi." Haec dictio "maiorem" ibi non discernit aequivocationem, sed apponitur ut quam per proprium nomen nesciret discernere per adiectivum discernat. Et determinatur respectus huius praerogationis ex re ipsa, ex eo scilicet quod Polynices reliquam videt. Sed secundum hoc potest dici quod non tenetur puṛe adiective sed fixe et includit in se articulum, ut sit sensus, *Argiva la plus graunde,* Gallice. Sed hoc grammaticis relinquatur.

43 Voce determinatur respectus quando vicine appositum est vel suum contrarium vel suum simile, ut si dicam, "Deorum sunt factura niger corvus et albus olor." Cum fit mentio de rerum diversitatibus, ibi apponitur commodissime proprie proprium. Ut si enumerans opera divina dicam,

> Rerum summa tenent vagus aer, fervidus aether;
> sunt infra tellus fixa, Thetisque fluens.

Et ut authenticum habeamus exemplum, Bernardus:

> Surgit Athos, consurgit Eryx, sic alta Cithaera,
> sic ardens Liparis, sic terebinthus olens.

PART I

grammarian, as is the case if I should say, "I see a mortal man." The specific is sometimes determined by the circumstances themselves, sometimes by language. When it is determined by the circumstances, it denotes a greater certitude or something of the kind, as is the case if Polynices were to see the two daughters of Adrastus and didn't know either's name, and Adrastus said, "I shall give you the older of these Argive girls." The word "older" here doesn't clear up the ambiguity but is added so that he can distinguish by the adjective the one he could not distinguish by her name. And the specificity of this preeminence is determined by the situation itself, that is, because Polynices can see the other sister. And accordingly it can be said that its force is not purely adjectival, but a permanent fixture and includes the article, so that the sense is in French, *Argiva la plus grande,* the older Greek girl. But let this matter be left to the grammarians.

The specific is modified by another word when either its opposite or something similar to it is introduced near it, as if I should say, "The black raven and the white swan are both the handiwork of the gods." Since there is mention of a diversity of things it makes sense to specify separately what is proper to each. As if enumerating the works of God, I should say, 43

> The wandering air and the glowing ether occupy the loftiest places of creation; below are the fixed earth and the fluid sea.

And, to take an example from our authors, Bernard:

> Athos rises, Eryx rises also, so too high Cithaeron, and burning Lipari, so too the scented terebinth.

Sed quid hoc dictu, "Socrates ambulat super terram fixam," ex quo nullus ibi habetur respectus? Certe fere dico hunc versum Ovidii vitiosum: "Ad vada Maeandri concinit albus olor." Hunc versum computandum censeo inter illos qui suo vitio libri faciem decorabant. Sola veritas notatur huiusmodi epitheto sic posito.

44   Adiectivum solam veritatem notans est ab omni carmine repellendum per immediatam constructionem appositam. Cum adhuc in dubio sit an congruitas admittat talem determinationem, Parvipontani olim, quicquid nunc dicamus, hanc censuerunt incongruam, "Socrates, qui est albus, currit," similiter et hanc, "Socrates albus currit." Dixerunt enim quod officium huius relativi "qui" sit semper discretive teneri, similiter et talis dictionis adiective sic positae immediate. Unde, cum non posset discretionem facere in termino discreto, incongruam censuerunt. Moderni vero nostri dicunt quod haec dictio "qui" quandoque amittit officium discretionis et retinet tantum officium referendi. Similiter adiectivum est quandoque nota veritatis tantum; sed sive sit congrua sive incongrua, hic est naevus qui totam libri faciem appositus deturparet.

    Quae appositio est immediata coniunctio unius substantivi cum alio substantivo, ut "Mons Ossa." "Immediata," dico, non semper voce tenus, sed quoad sensum, ita scilicet ut terminus appositus intelligatur ex eadem parte ex qua est principale substantivum, ut "Maria, virgo virginum, portavit Christum."

But what about this statement, "Socrates is walking on the firm earth," in which nothing is specified? I would certainly almost call this line of Ovid's faulty: "By the shallows of the Meander sings the white swan." I think this line has to be counted among those that beautify the face of a book by their very faultiness. Only a truism is indicated by an epithet used in this way.

An adjective that just expresses a truism has to be banished from every poem by putting an appositive construction right after it. Since it is still in doubt whether correct usage admits such a modifier, the Parvipontani, whatever we may say now, used to consider the sentence "Socrates, who is white, is running" incorrect, and the sentence "White Socrates is running" as well. For they said that the role of the relative "who" should always be thought of as making a distinction, just like the role of such a word placed directly next to the noun as an adjective modifier. And since you can't make a distinction with just one term, they thought it incorrect. But our moderns say that the word "who" sometimes loses the role of making a distinction and keeps only the role of referring. Likewise, an adjective is sometimes only the mark of a recognized truth. But whether it is correct or incorrect, it's a blemish that, if placed in apposition, would disfigure the whole face of the book.

Apposition is putting a noun right next to another noun, such as "Mount Ossa." When I say "right next to," I don't always mean the wording, but the sense, in such a way that the appositional term is understood from the same perspective as the principal noun, as in "Mary, the virgin of virgins, bore Christ."

45   Relativa determinatio fit per dictionem relativam, ut "Maria, quae est virgo virginum, portavit Christum." Tam appositionum quam relativarum determinationum quaedam fit ratione communitatis specificandae, ut "Mons Ossa," "Homo qui est albus currit." Secundum hoc haec incongrua: "Socrates, qui est crispus, currit." Et fit in hiis exemplis partitio uniformis sed indirecta. Quandoque fit utraque ratione aequivocationis determinandae. Secundum hoc termino etiam discreto potest terminus communis apponi, ut "Leo homo pugnabit cum Hectore," vel "Leo, qui est homo ...," "Canis, marina belua, amarus est."

46   Hic modus appositionis usitatissimus est in vulgari sermone, ut "Iohannes, filius Anselmi, studet in iuris peritia." "Filius Anselmi" appositio est. Quandoque fit utraque ratione commendationis vel vituperationis, vel cuiuscumque excellentiae vel qualiscumque infamiae. Ovidius: "Credidimus blandis, quorum tibi copia, verbis." Si ratione solius veritatis fiat, inutilis est, ut, "Homo albus currit." Haec grammatico incompetens, nobis incompetentior. Tam appositionis quam relationis determinatio utilis est dicentibus exquisite. Verbi gratia, "Terminet has lacrimas tandem mors, meta malorum," vel sic, "Mors, ultima linea rerum, / finiet has lacrimas." Isti modi valent ad brevem materiam prolixius proferendam, ut si vellet quis in duobus versibus dicere, "In morte redditur cuique secundum merita sua," et diceret,

> Mors meritum vitae cunctis metuenda ministrat—
> hora nimis properata malis sed tarda beatis.

Ecce ultimus versus totus est appositio.

Relative modification is made through a relative pronoun, as with "Mary, who is the virgin of virgins, bore Christ." Both appositions and relative modifications are made in order to specify a commonality, as "Mount Ossa," "A man who is white is running." According to this principle, this is incorrect: "Socrates, who is curly, is running." In these examples we have uniform but indirect partition. Sometimes both of these serve to disentangle an ambiguity. In accordance with this a common term can be set against a term that applies to only one, as "Leo, a man, will fight with Hector," or, "Leo, who is a man . . . ," "The dog, a beast of the sea, is fierce."

This style of apposition appears most in everyday conversation, as "John, Anselm's son, is in law school." "Anselm's son" is in apposition. Both forms are sometimes used either for commendation of some excellence or abuse of some sort of shame. Ovid: "I believed your flattering words, which you had a lot of." If it serves only to express a truism, such as "The white man is running," it is of no value. This is lame, according to grammarians, and even lamer for us. Both apposition and relative modification are useful for those who want to speak with refinement: for example, "May death, the end of evils, finally stop these tears," or thus, "Death, the finishing line of existence, will put an end to these tears." These modes are valuable for stretching brief subject matter, as if somebody wanted to say in two lines, "In death each is repaid according to his merits," and said,

> Fearsome death gives everybody what their life has deserved—an hour that comes too soon for the wicked but too slowly for the blessed.

The whole second line is an apposition.

47 Tum sumitur haec appositio extra materiam, tum in materia. "Extra," ut hic patebit: Quidam, cum dixisset Pyramum et Thisben planxisse de die, hanc materiam, "Nox non caruit suo planctu," sufficere fecit duobus versibus hoc modo:

> Hora gravis miseris, sed amantibus apta beatis,
> non caruit planctu nox inimica suo.

In eo sumitur extra quod in principali materia nulla fit mentio de beatis amantibus. Unde haec dictio "sed" ibi inutiliter adversatur. Melius dixisset e converso, "Hora apta beatis, sed gravis miseris." Modus iste inutilior et minus commendabilis.

48 In materia sumitur, ut hic patebit. Cum quidam haberet hanc materiam, "Tantum victorem devicit senectus," volens eam sufficere duobus versibus usus primo appositione, postea relativa determinatione, dicens,

> Tantum victorem lentae spes ultima mortis
> devicit tandem quae vincit cuncta senectus.

Utraque determinatio ad rem est. Ecce, "spes ultima lentae mortis" appositio est et utilis. Cum enim mors multis infirmitatibus temptaverit hominem, nec posset eum vincere, immo forte nec etiam vexare, in sola senectute videtur esse

PART I

This apposition can be taken either from outside the subject matter or from within it. Here is what I mean by "outside": When a certain boy had said that Pyramus and Thisbe had complained about day, he took the subject "Night didn't lack its complaint either," and made it last for two lines in this way:

> The hour that is burdensome for wretches but just right for happy lovers, nasty night was not without its complaint.

Here the apposition is from outside because in the main subject there is no mention of happy lovers. And so the word "but" is useless: there is nothing to be adverse to. He'd have spoken better if he'd said instead, "The hour just right for the happy, but burdensome for wretches." His way is no good, not to be recommended.

Apposition is also taken from inside the subject matter, as this example will show. When a boy was given the subject "Old age conquered so great a conqueror," and wanted enough for two lines, first he used apposition, and then relative modification, saying,

> At last old age, that last hope of a death slow in coming, old age that conquers everything, conquered so great a conqueror.

Both modifiers belong to the subject. See how "that last hope of a death slow in coming" is an apposition, and effective. For since death tested the man with many infirmities, but could not conquer him, indeed perhaps could not even trouble him, his hope is seen to lie in old age alone. For it is

spes eius. Necesse est enim quod senectute moriatur. Relativa determinatio perficit versus, scilicet haec, "quae vincit cuncta."

49 Tam adiectivorum quam appositionum quaedam sunt vacua, quaedam onerata. Vacua, ut hic, "Prompta, modesta, timens Io fuit." Non dicitur, "prompta in hoc et in hoc." Similiter, "Mons Ossa est altus." Onerata sunt quae secum deferunt quasdam determinationes, ut hic:

> Insignis specie, vita praeclara, faceta
> eloquio, fulgens moribus Io fuit.

Similiter hic: "Senectus, spes ultima lentae mortis, hunc vicit." Haec dictio "spes" est principalis appositio sed defert secum caudam suam. Vacua per multiplicem coadunationem faciunt polysyndeton et articulum. Onerata vero per multiplicem coadunationem faciunt adiunctum et dissolutum.

50 Notabilis est adhuc extravaganter quaedam elegantia quae communis est tam adiectivae determinationi quam appositivae quam etiam relativae. Quaelibet istarum quandoque notat determinationem causae vel temporis vel consequentiae. Et secundum hoc non construitur immediate cum substantivo subiecti sed potius mediate mediante, scilicet quolibet verbo praeter substantivum, id est copulativum et vocativum. Si enim dicatur, "Mons est Ossa" vel "Mons vocatur Ossa" vel "Homo est albus" vel "Plato erit facundus," rudis est identitas. Unde notandum quod multipliciter resolvitur verbum. Quandoque in rem verbi et consignificationem, unde dicitur quod haec duplex, "Anima Antichristi necessario erit," cum hoc verbum "erit" habeat in se rem,

necessary that from old age comes death. A relative modification, "that conquers everything," finishes off the couplet.

Of adjectives and appositions, some are empty, some are packed. Empty, as "Io was active, modest, bashful." She is not said to be active in this or in that. Likewise, "Mount Ossa is high." The packed ones are those that bring some modifications with them:

> Io was remarkable for beauty, distinguished in her life,
> gifted in her speech, brilliant in her character.

Likewise, "Old age, the last hope of a death slow in coming, conquered him." The word "hope" is the primary appositive, but it drags its tail along with it. Empty ones by multiple coalescence produce polysyndeton and *articulus*. Packed ones, though, by multiple coalescence produce adjunction and asyndeton.

To digress, there is further a noteworthy refinement that is common to modification by adjective, apposition, or relative clause. Any one of these sometimes denotes modification of cause or time or effect. The refinement is not to construe it immediately with the noun of the subject, but with something in between, some verb besides the substantive verb, that is, copulative and naming verbs. If we say, "The mountain is Ossa," or "The mountain is called Ossa," or "The man is white," or "Plato will be eloquent," all that is rough sameness. Accordingly it should be noted that there are many ways to break down a verb into parts. Sometimes it is broken down into both the root meaning of the verb and its accompanying signifier. Thus the sentence "The soul of Antichrist will necessarily be" is said to be double, since the verb "will be" has its own root meaning (namely, the

THE ART OF MAKING VERSES

scilicet hoc accidens "esse," et consignificationem futuri, quae potest intelligi per hoc verbum "conveniet." Sed hoc magis logicorum est quam nostrum.

51 Quandoque resolvitur in rem verbi sui et verbum substantivum. Secundum quod dicitur a Prisciano auctore quod omne verbum includit in se verbum substantivum et potest quodlibet verbum exponi per verbum substantivum et suum participium, ut "Socrates amat," id est, "est amans." Unde dicitur quod hoc verbum "est" radix est omnium verborum, et secundum hoc intelligitur semper verbum substantivum ante rem verbi in constructione. Non est sensus, "Socrates amat," id est, "Socrates amans est," sed sic: "Socrates est amans." Hic modus ad grammaticos spectat.

52 Tertio modo—sed magis improprie—resolvitur quodlibet verbum, excepto substantivo et vocativo, in suum participium et verbum substantivum—non dico radicem, sed vel tertium adiacens vel purum substantivum. Omne enim verbum includit in se tertium adiacens saltem consecutive, sicut "Homo animal," quia "Si est homo, est animal." Eodem modo: "Si amat, est aliquid." Hoc patere potest in hoc exemplo: "Filius meus a Bononia redibit facundus." Non est sensus, "Filius facundus ad differentiam non facundi redibit," sed is: "Filius rediens erit facundus," id est, "Cum redibit, erit facundus." (Notandum igitur quod in talium resolutione consignificatio non intelligitur circa rem verbi principalis, sed circa tertium adiacens.) Idem in appositione: "Veni ad me, quia venies Hercules vel Aeneas," id est, tam dilectus hospes ut fuit Hercules vel Aeneas. Iuvenalis: "Venies Tyrinthius aut minor illo / hospes." Non est sensus, "Tu existens

accident "to be") and an accompanying signifier of the future, which can be understood to mean, "It will be fitting." But these are matters more for the logicians than for us.

Sometimes it is resolved into the content of the verb and a substantive verb. This is in accordance with what the authority Priscian says, that every verb includes in itself the verb "to be," and any verb can analyzed as its participle plus the verb "to be," as "Socrates loves," that is, "is loving." And so it is said that the verb "is" is the root of all verbs, and therefore a substantive verb is always understood to precede the content of the verb in its makeup. The sense isn't "Socrates loves," that is, "Socrates, loving, is," but this: "Socrates is loving." This mode is a subject for grammarians.

A third way—a more improper way—to break down any verb except the verb "to be" and verbs of calling or naming, is into its participle and the verb "to be"—I won't say the root, but either a third predicate element or pure substantive. Every verb includes in itself this third predicate element at least as a consequence, as "Man an animal," that is, "If he is a man, he is an animal." In the same way: "If he loves, he is something." This can be clarified in the following example: "My son will return from Bologna eloquent." The sense isn't "My eloquent son will return," as opposed to someone who is not eloquent, but this: "My son, returning, will be eloquent," that is, "When he returns, he will be eloquent." (Note that in analyses like these the cosignifier is not the content of the principal verb but the third predicate element.) It is the same with apposition: "Come to me, for you will come as Hercules or Aeneas," that is, as welcome a guest as Hercules or Aeneas was. Juvenal: "You will come as Hercules or the guest lesser than him." The sense isn't "You,

Tyrinthius aut Eneas venies," sed, "Cum venias vel si venias, eris mihi Tyrinthius aut Aeneas." In hiis exemplis "appositionem" dico esse, quia in eis non exprimitur principale regimen substantivi sequentis ex parte appositi. Regitur tamen re vera ex verbo apposito ratione verbi substantivi subintellecti. Simile etiam in relativa determinatione: "Achilles veniet, qui Hectorem superabit," id est, veniens erit qui superabit.

53 Hec tertia verbi expositio, in suam rem et "tertium adiacens," magis impropria est, et ideo nobis utilior. Improprietates enim excusabiles sermonum elegantiis sunt facundae; et illis additur literatura, et per illas oportet frequenter in minutas partiunculas resolvere dictionem. Unde dictum est, "Frange dictiones et intelliges scripturas."

54 Est adhuc elegans positio terminorum quam dicimus "absolutam," ubi scilicet ponuntur termini casuales—tam nominativus quam et genitivus quam alii—absque verbo, tamen ob hoc ut habeat locum sequens relatio vel sequens partitio. Sequens relatio, ut hic: "Iupiter, eius genitivus est Iovis." Bernardus Silvestris:

> Obriguit Boreas, maduit Notus; Auster et Eurus
>   hic tempestates, ille serena facit.

Obliquus hic: "Lapidem quem reprobaverunt aedificantes, hic factus est, etc." Sequens partitio, ut hic, Bernardus:

being Hercules or Aeneas, will come," but "When or if you come, you will be Hercules or Aeneas to me." In these examples, I say there is "apposition" because in them it is apparently not the function of the apposed verb to govern a subsequent noun. But it is in fact governed by the apposed verb by virtue of the understood substantive verb. The case is similar with modification by a relative clause: "Achilles will come, who will overcome Hector," that is, he will be coming who will overcome.

This third analysis of a verb, into its meaning and a "third predicate element," is more irregular but thereby more valuable for us. For excusable improprieties, because of their linguistic refinement, convey eloquence; literature is enhanced by these means, and because of them it is often necessary to analyze a word into very small components. Thus the dictum, "Break down the words and you will understand texts."

There is further an attractive organization of terms that we call "absolute," that is, where the terms are introduced in declined form—nominative, genitive, and the other cases—without a verb, but so that they can be replaced by a subsequent pronoun or partitioning. A subsequent pronoun, as here: "Jupiter: the genitive of it is Jovis." Bernard Silvester:

> The North Wind was chill, the South Wind wet; of the West and East the latter brings storms, that former fair weather.

An oblique example: "The stone that the builders rejected, that has become, etc." A subsequent partitioning, as here, Bernard:

> Cur gelidus Boreas mollisque Favonius, alter
> floribus expoliet, vestiat alter humum?

Haec dictio "alter" bis posita partitive respicit illos duos terminos absolute positos, "Boreas," "Favonius."

Item est quaedam elegantia quam "simplicitatem" possumus appellare. Haec communis est tam adiectivae determinationi quam relationi quam etiam appositioni. Adiectivum igitur quandoque simpliciter determinat, quandoque simpliciter determinatur, quandoque simpliciter respicit. Simpliciter determinat, quando nomen aequivocum vel quasi, positum in una significatione, determinatur adiectivo pertinente ad aliam significationem. "Vel quasi" dico, quia quam si non videatur nobis quod esse nomen aequivocum, videbitur tamen quod esse nomen quasi aequivocum ex eo quod potest teneri materialiter vel significative. Materialis positio est quando agitur de voce ipsa; significativa positio est quando agitur de vocis appellato. Contingit ergo, quod nomen positum significative determinatur adiectivo pertinente ad ipsum nomen prout materialiter tenetur, ut hic: "Consona sit propriae communis, Idonea." Hoc nomen Idonea significative tenetur et etiam duplici significatione, ut dictum est supra. Et tamen adiectiva pertinent ad tertiam positionem, scilicet ad materialem. Idonea enim nomen ipsum est commune vel proprium, non res nominis. Secundum hunc modum potest de facili peccari, si dicam "Aiax Locrius" pro "Aiax Thelamonius." Caute igitur fiant huiusmodi.

PART I

The cold North Wind and the gentle West Wind, why would the one strip the earth of flowers and the other clothe it?

The word *alter,* introduced twice to make a distinction, refers back to those two terms that are introduced absolutely "North Wind" and "West Wind."

Here is another refinement, which we can call "simplicity." It applies equally to modification by adjectives, to relatives, or to apposition. An adjective sometimes modifies simply, sometimes is modified simply, sometimes refers back simply. It modifies simply when an ambiguous or quasi-ambiguous noun, used in one of its meanings, is modified by an adjective that pertains to another meaning. The reason I say "or quasi-ambiguous" is that, even if it doesn't seem an ambiguous noun to us, it will still be seen to be a quasi-ambiguous noun because it can be used materially or meaningfully. Material use is when the focus is on the word itself; meaningful use is when the focus is on what the word names. Thus it happens that a noun used meaningfully is modified by an adjective that pertains to the noun itself as it is thought of materially, as in this case: "Let the common word be in line with your proper name, Idonea." The name Idonea is understood meaningfully and also in a double meaning, as was said above. And yet the adjectives pertain to the third use, the material. What is common or proper is the noun Idonea, not the subject named. In this form of expression it is easy to make an error, if I should say "Locrian Ajax" for "Telamonian Ajax." So let things of this kind be practiced with caution.

56 Simpliciter determinatur adiectivum aequivocum quando sumitur in una significatione, sed respicitur a sua determinatione tamquam poneretur in alia. Verbi gratia, "intumescere" in una significatione idem est quod "ingrossari," in alia "indignari" vel "irasci." Dictum est de quodam macilento qui effectus est pinguis, "Pellis demissa iam dudum ossibus maritata novae carnis separatur coniugio de interpositione non notae paelicis intumescens." Haec dictio "intumescere" ibi re vera ponitur pro "ingrossari," sed ubi dicit "paelicis" respicit aliam significationem, et bene exsequitur translationem inceptam.

57 Adiectivum quandoque respective tenetur, ut dictum est supra, in huiusmodi exemplis: "Deorum sunt factura niger corvus et albus olor." Huiusmodi igitur adiectivum quandoque simpliciter respicit. Bernardus:

> Aesculus alta solo, caelo directa cacumen
> pinus, et exiguae Phillidis esca nuces.

Quia nuces, quas gerit pinus, grossae sunt, ad hoc respiciens ad differentiam dicit, "et exiguae Phillidis, etc."

58 Simplex relatio est quando dictio substantiva tenetur in una significatione et sequitur relativum respiciens aliam significationem, ut si dicerem, "Iupiter est nominativi casus et ipse est deus." Unde dictum est de quodam, cum multa essent de eo vitia enumerata, sic:

PART I

An adjective with two meanings is modified simply when it is used in one meaning but by its modification is perceived as if it were used in the other meaning. For example, "swell up" in one meaning is a synonym for "get fat," in another for "get angry" or "get mad." It was said of a certain thin man who had gotten fat, "His flabby skin, long since married to bones, is separated therefrom by an alliance with new flesh, swelling up through the intervention of some unknown mistress." The word "swell" is certainly used here for "get fat." But when he says "mistress," he looks to another meaning, and successfully follows through with the metaphor already begun.

56

An adjective is sometimes used with an additional reference, as I said above, in examples of this kind: "The black raven and the white swan are both the handiwork of the gods." Thus an adjective of this kind sometimes makes a simple reference. Bernard:

57

> The tall oak bending toward earth, the tip of the pine reaching to heaven, and its nuts, the food of little Phyllis.

The nuts which the pine produces are fat; with reference to this his wording points to a difference: "the food of poor Phyllis."

Simple relation is when a noun carries one meaning and is followed by a pronoun referring to another of its meanings, as if I said, "Jupiter is the nominative case and he himself is a god." In accordance with this the following was said of someone, when many of his vices had been enumerated:

58

83

> Ulteriore malo premitur, quod nomen abhorrent
> saecula: Iudaica seditione nocet.

Hoc nomen "seditione" significative tenetur, relativum respicit ipsam vocem.

Appositio simplex est quae respicit aliud quam illud pro quo tenetur terminus cui apponitur, Verbi gratia, "Intumescere" aequivocum est, ut dictum est. Item, Iupiter "deus," Iupiter "aer superior." Statius igitur volens dicere Inachum fluvium ingrossari ex inundatione aquarum descendentium ex aere superiori, ait, "Inachus intumuit genero Iove." "Genero" appositio est et respicit fabulam de Iove et Io. Bernardus elegantissime, cum ageret de novem ordinibus angelorum, ubi perventum est ad Virtutes, ait,

> Virtutes sacer ordo facit, miracula rerum,
> cum propriae causas utilitatis habent.

Exponitur: "Sacer ordo facit Virtutes," id est, in ordinis serie post superiores angelos succedunt Virtutes, scilicet ordo angelorum sic vocatus. Sequitur appositio: "miracula rerum, etc." Non dicit hoc propter illas Virtutes, sed propter istas inferiores quattuor quas dicimus cardinales, quae sunt plus quam mirabilia quotiens propter se appetuntur, secundum philosophos.

Fit etiam ex simplici respectu vocis simplex appositio, quando scilicet vox tenetur significative et apponitur ei terminus respiciens materialem suppositionem. Statius de Eteocle parante insidias Tydeo, sic:

> He is oppressed by a further vice, whose name the ages despise: he does harm with his pernicious treachery like Judas's.

The noun "treachery" is used in its regular meaning, while the pronoun *(quod)* refers to the word itself.

A simple apposition is one that refers to something other than the meaning of the term to which it is apposed. For example, "swell up" is ambiguous, as has been said, and Jupiter means both "the god" and "the upper air." Thus Statius, wanting to say that the river Inachus is swollen by an inundation of water coming from the upper air, says, "Inachus is swollen by Jupiter, his son-in-law." "Son-in-law" is in apposition, and refers to the myth of Jove and Io. Bernard says most elegantly, treating the nine orders of angels, when he gets to the Virtues,

> The sacred plan produces the Virtues, miracles of creation, for they have the causes of their own usefulness.

It is explained "The sacred plan produces the Virtues," that is, in the sequence of the plan, after the superior angels come the Virtues, meaning the order of angels so called. Then an apposition follows: "miracles of creation, etc." He doesn't say that because of those Virtues, but because of the inferior four ones that we call the cardinal virtues, which are more than wondrous whenever they are sought for their own sake, according to philosophers.

Simple apposition also occurs from the simple reference of the word: namely, when a word is used meaningfully and a term is apposed to it referring to the word as word (material use). Statius on Eteocles preparing an ambush for Tydeus, thus:

Sollicitat—sanctum populis per saecula nomen—
legatum insidiis tacitoque invadere ferro.

In hoc loco cautum censeo praemuniri ne unum inconsulte attribuamus uni aequivocorum quod est alterius, ut Ovidius:

Filia purpureos Nisi furata capillos
pube premit rapidos inguinibusque canes.

Et alibi, "Praeterita cautus Niseide navita gaudet"; id est, praeterita filia forti, quia illa mutata est in monstrum marinum, ut patet in undecimo *Methamorphoseon*. Oportet nos carminum nostrorum licentiam compescere; sua illi auctoritas relinquatur. Item non praetereat memoria simplicem demonstrationem—Statius: "Tales in bella venimus."

61 Diversio est quotiens causa ornatus ab ordinis planitie digredimur. Diversionum alia aequalitas, alia egressio, alia transversio, alia transcensus. Ad hanc distinctionem elementares pueri transferantur. Aequalitas est quotiens sumendo aequipollens pro aequipollenti clausulam decoramus. Haec fit tum necessitate concidentiae, tum ratione latentis argumenti, tum ratione uniformis variationis. Fit autem necessitate concidentiae tum metrice, tum prosaice. Metrice, ut in Lucano: "Caesar in arma furens." Non potuit dicere, "Julius in arma furens," ratione metri. Prosaice concidentiae necessitate fit, ut patet scientibus prosas artificiose componere. Bernardus: "De confuso, de turbido prius egreditur vis

> He urges them to make an attack on the ambassador—a title sacred to peoples through the ages—in ambush with unheard swords.

In this place I think a caution should be offered to guard against thoughtlessly assigning one person an ambiguous term when it should be another, as Ovid does:

> Nisus's daughter, having stolen his purple hair, inflicts ferocious dogs on her genitals and groin.

And elsewhere, "The cautious sailor is happy once he has passed Nisus's daughter"; that is, having passed a fearsome daughter, because she was changed into a sea monster, as we see in *Metamorphoses* 11. We, though, have to hold in check the freedom of our poems: leave his established usage to him. Likewise do not fail to remember simple description — Statius: "That is how we are coming to war."

It is digression whenever, for the sake of ornament, we depart from the level course of any sequence. Its kinds are synonymy, egression, transversion, and transcendence. Let elementary students be directed to this section of the book. It is synonymy whenever we adorn a phrase by substituting one equivalent form of language for another. This happens sometimes from the requirements of rhythm, sometimes by reason of a hidden argument, sometimes by reason of uniform variation. It occurs for requirements of rhythm both in verse and in prose. In quantitative verse, as in Lucan: "Caesar, raging for arms." He couldn't say, "Julius, raging for arms," because of the meter. Synonymy from requirements of rhythm occurs also in prose, as is clear to those who know how to compose artistic prose. Bernard: "From confusion

ignita." Propter musicam prosae suae non potuit dicere "vis ignea," ut patebit in tractatu dictandi. Huiusmodi mutatio, si fieret in prosa non artificiosa, non esset aequalitas sed potius rudis identitas.

62 Ratione latentis argumenti fit quandoque aequalitas, ut, si diceret quis sub rudi identitate, "Telemachus necessario erit callidus," sub aequalitate potius diceret, "Filius Ulixis necessario erit callidus"—et hoc ratione latentis argumenti, scilicet quia filius Ulixis, cum pater adeo callidus esset. In hac vero, "Filius Penelope callidus erit," non subiacet argumentum. Propter huiusmodi cautum censeo *Rhetoricas* inspicere et sollicitiori studio consulere Ciceronem quae sunt attributa personae, quae negotii, ut argumentandi ratio plenius elucescat. Ovidius pro hac, "A Theseo credatur reddita virgo?" quanto venustius et efficacius ait, "A iuvene et cupido credatur reddita virgo?" Iam patet in parte aequalitatis mutatio, scilicet circa terminos casuales. Verbum etiam aequalitate mutari potest multipliciter. Verbum enim aut est substantivum, aut tertium adiacens, aut aliquid verbum adiectivum. Substantivum aut purum aut determinatum. Si purum, in nullum convertitur, nisi in hoc verbum "existit." Potest tamen et illud aequalitate mutari, quamvis non in simplex verbum—puta quaeratur aliquod verbum saltem oneratum, quod cum eo convertatur. Verbi gratia, si "Est in rerum numero," "Comprehenditur," vel "Auget rerum numerum." Item verbum substantivum aliter poterit

and turbulence the fiery power first emerges." On account of the rhythm of his prose, he could not say "the power of fire," as will be clear in the section on dictamen. A change of this kind, if it occurred in unartistic prose, wouldn't be synonymy but rough sameness.

Synonymy sometimes occurs by reason of a hidden argument, as, if someone said with rough sameness, "Telemachus is bound to be clever," with synonymy he would say instead, "The son of Ulysses is bound to be clever"—and this is by way of a hidden argument: namely, he was clever because he was the son of Ulysses, since the father was so clever. But in this, "Penelope's son will be clever," there is no underlying argument. But here I think a caution is in order, to look at the *Rhetorics* and pay especially close attention to what Cicero says are the attributes of persons, what of actions, so that the rationale of the argument will be entirely clear. Ovid, instead of "Is it to be supposed she was sent back a virgin by Theseus?" wrote, so much more pleasingly and effectively, "Is it to be supposed she was sent back a virgin by a young man, one full of desire?" Now it is obvious that synonymy can involve change, at least in words with case endings. And in synonymy a verb too can be changed multiple times. For a verb is either the verb "to be," or the copula, or some added verb. The verb "to be" is either pure or modified. If pure, it is only converted into the verb "to exist." Still, even it can be changed by synonymy, although not into a simple verb—just find a verb, loaded however slightly, that can be exchanged for it. For example, for "It is in the number of things," "It is comprehended in the number of things," or "It augments the number of things." Again, the verb "to be" can be changed by synonymy in another way—

aequalitate mutari secundum scilicet rei naturam cui assignatur. Verbi gratia, rudis est identitas haec, "Socrates est." Cum igitur Socrates sit contentum huius generis "animal," competens est aequalitas simplex, "Socrates vivit," est aequalitas onerata locutio, "Socrates vitales auras trahit." Bene dico, "secundum subiecti naturam," quia haec aequalitas non posset competenter arbori assignari. Sed arbori sic: "Arbor viget," "Arbor entelechia vegetatur." Si vero sit verbum substantivum determinatum, verbi gratia, "Arbor est in hoc solo," erit aequalitas talis, "Arbor ducit radices in hoc solo," vel sic, "Arbor ramos extendit in hoc solo," vel sic, "Coartat in hoc solo." Sed quaeratur semper haec mutatio et in subiecti natura et in intentione dicentis.

63 Si vero determinatur modali determinatione, consulite dialecticos. In modalium aequipollentiis erit aequalitatem invenire. Verbi gratia, "Anima Caesaris necessario est," "Anima Caesaris non potest non esse." Idem obtinet quocumque verbo modaliter determinato. Bernardus pro hac, "Hyle necessario turbabatur," ait, "Non turbari non potuit id quod ab omni natura tam multiformiter pulsaretur."

64 Si verbum sit tertium adiacens, vel determinatur adiectivo vel substantivo. Si adiectivo, ex verbo et determinatione potest inveniri simplex aequalitas, ut, "Plato est albus," "Plato albet." Et talia verba eisdem possunt casibus onerari, quibus et nomina adiectiva, ut "Cicero est callidus ingenio," "Cicero callet ingenio." Bernardus: "Et te, Natura, quia calles ingenio, sociam operis non dedignor." Haec igitur

namely, according to the nature of the subject to which it is assigned. For example, "Socrates is" is rough sameness. Since Socrates is contained in the genus "animal," the simple synonymy is appropriate, "Socrates lives." A loaded synonymy is the locution "Socrates draws in the breath of life." I am right to say, "according to the nature of the subject," because this synonymy could not appropriately be assigned to a tree. But for a tree: "The tree is healthy," "The tree has reached its perfection." If it is the verb "to be" that is modified—for example, "The tree is in this ground"—synonymy will take this form: "The tree has spread its roots in this ground." Or this: "The tree is extending its branches on this ground," or "is confining its branches on this ground." You always want to make a change that suits both the nature of the subject and what you want to say.

63 If it (the verb "to be") is modified modally, have recourse to the dialecticians. The synonymy will be found in equivalences of modal expressions. For example, "Caesar's soul necessarily is," "Caesar's soul cannot not be." The same thing obtains for any verb modified modally. Bernard, instead of "Matter was necessarily being thrown into confusion," said, "What was being pounded in so many ways by all of nature could not not be thrown into confusion."

64 If the verb is the copula, it is modified either by an adjective or a noun. If by an adjective, from the verb and the modifier a simple synonymy can be found, as "Plato is white," "Plato is whitened." And such verbs can be loaded by the same cases as adjectives, as "Cicero is knowing by natural genius," "Cicero knows by natural genius." Bernard: "And since you, Nature, know by natural genius, I will not scorn to have you as ally in my work." And so this brief sentence,

clausula, "Telemachus necessario erit callidus," poterit tota per aequalitatem mutari. Pro "Telemachus" ponatur "filius Ulixis"; pro hac dictione "necessario" ponatur "non contingit non" vel "non poterit non"; pro hac "esse callidus" ponatur "callere" et oneretur suo ablativo, et habebimus hanc, "Filius Ulixis non poterit ingenio non callere."

65 Si determinetur nomine substantivo, ex natura rei substantivi eiusdem debet elici aequalitas, et potest copula cum eodem substantivo pariter commutari, ut "Socrates est homo," "Socrates humana facie decoratur." Appone determinationem praepositionalem sic, "Socrates inter tot animalium genera humanae naturae gaudet privilegio." Hic modus etiam quandoque immutat casum subiecti, ut "Plato est homo," "Platonem informat humanitas." Verba vero alterius modi, ut "videt," "diligit," aequalitate possunt commutari vel per convertibilitatem vel per consequentiam, ut "Socrates videt Platonem," "Socrates visuales radios dirigit in Platonem," "Thisbe diligit Pyramum," "Thisbe suspirat in amplexus Pyrami." Fit etiam multis aliis modis haec mutatio quae dictatoribus sponte se offerunt—tractandi tamen compendium dedignantur.

66 Ratione uniformis variationis fit aequalitas duplex: Uno modo quando aliqua dictio substantiva est diversorum generum et suscipit diversa adiectiva, quorum unum sit unius generis, reliquum alterius. Verbi gratia, "specus" est idem quod "fossa," et tam est masculini generis quam feminini. Ovidius:

"Telemachus will necessarily be clever," can be completely changed by synonymy. For "Telemachus," put "the son of Ulysses"; for the word "necessarily," put "does not not happen" or "will be unable not"; for the phrase "be knowing," put "know," and let it be loaded up with its ablative, and then we will have, "The son of Ulysses will be unable not to know by natural genius."

If the modification is by a noun, a synonymy should be derived from the nature of the thing named, and the copula can be changed along with the same noun, as "Socrates is a man," "Socrates is adorned with a human face." Add a prepositional modifier in this way: "Socrates, among so many kinds of animals, enjoys the privilege of a human nature." This mode sometimes also changes the case of the subject, as "Plato is a man," "Humanity informs Plato." Other kinds of verbs besides "to be," such as "see" or "love," can be changed by synonymy by employing either convertibility or consequence, as "Socrates sees Plato," "Socrates aims the rays of his eyes toward Plato," "Thisbe loves Pyramus," "Thisbe sighs for the embraces of Pyramus." This change is made in many other ways that offer themselves spontaneously to writers—but they don't lend themselves to being treated concisely.

Synonymy is created by means of uniform variation in two ways: One, when a noun is of different genders and takes different adjectives, one of one gender and the other of another. For example, the word *specus* (cavern), a synonym for *fossa* (ditch), is both masculine and feminine. Ovid:

Est specus exesi structura pumicis asper;
  non homini facilis, non adeunda ferae.

Est et alius modus multo decentior et est contrarius cuidam modo supra dicto ubi est frequentia annominationum cognatarum, ut in hiis versibus, "Iam clipeus clipeis, umbone etc." Ibi enim retinetur rerum identitas et etiam nominum praeter exilem vocis immutationem. Hic vero sub identitate rerum plena nominum diversitas observatur. Verbi gratia, sunt quaedam nomina synonyma, ut "Marcus," "Tullius," ut "lorica," "thorax"; quaedam fere synonyma, ut "mucro," "ensis," ut "prora," "puppis," "carina," et huiusmodi. Talia igitur fere synonyma sub hoc modo pro synonymis accipiantur. Fiat igitur frequens collectio talium synonymorum hoc modo:

Iam scuto clipeus, mucrone repellitur ensis,
  lorica thorax, lituo tuba, missile telo.

Magister Iohannes de Hauvilla hunc modum plenius approbavit, et ideo poterit huiusmodi exemplum in *Architrenio* plenissime inveniri. Processio igitur huiusmodi "ratione uniformitatis" vel sit penitus similium, ut in hoc exemplo, "Iam clipeus clipeo, etc.," vel sit penitus dissimilium, ut in illo exemplo, "Iam scuto clipeus, etc." Non est tutum mixtim procedere, unde hos versus Bernardi censeo vitiosos,

PART I

> There is a cavern, rough (*asper,* m.) because of its structure of corroded pumice, not easily approached (*adeunda,* f.) by man or beast.

There is another way, much more fitting and the opposite of a certain mode mentioned above where there is an accumulation of plays on cognate words, as in the lines, "Now shield (is repelled) by shields, boss (by boss), etc." For there we had both sameness of things and sameness of names except for the slight difference in case endings. But in the present case for the same things we see a complete diversity of names. For example, there are synonymous nouns, such as "Marcus" and "Tullius," or "corselet" and "breastplate"; nearly synonymous nouns, such as "sword point" and "sword," or "prow," "stern," and "keel," and similar groups. In this mode such near-synonyms are treated as synonyms. And so an accumulative combination of such synonyms should be made in this way:

> Now shield is repelled by buckler, sword by sword point, corselet by breastplate, trumpet by horn, missile by spear.

Master John of Hauville used to praise this mode quite highly, and so examples of the sort will be found in *Architrenius* with the greatest ease. And so a sequence of this kind, "by means of uniformity," should be either of words utterly the same, as in the example of "Now shield by shield, etc.," or of words utterly different, as in "Now shield by buckler, etc." It isn't safe for the sequence to be mixed, and so I consider these verses of Bernard's to be faulty:

> Est igitur proba iuncta probo, formosa decoro,
> callida sensato, religiosa pio.

In hiis enim dictionibus "proba . . . probo" fallit uniformitas dissimilitudinis. Item et hii vitiosi sunt:

> Laetatur Tereo sua Progne, coniuge coniux,
> dux duce, regina rege, puella viro.

In hiis dictionibus "puella viro" fallit uniformitas similitudinis. Melius diceretur "virago viro."

67 Digressio est exitus a materia vel a sententia, ex vicinitate vel comprehensione rerum acceptus. Nec enim hanc vicinitatem appello similitudinem, ut Donatus. Eximus igitur a materia per colorem quem appellamus digressionem. Digressio est quando eximus ad aliquid materiae conveniens. Haec tum fit poetico figmento, ut Statius fingit Iovem coadunare deos et deponere bellum Thebanum, ubi introducit Iovem dicentem,

> Dire senex! Meruere tuae, meruere tenebrae
> ultorem sperare Iovem. Nova sontibus arma
> iniciam regnis.

Tum fit per comparationem, tum per descriptionem. De comparatione alibi dicemus. Descriptio est demonstratio proprietatis alicuius rei, puta vel hominis, vel loci, vel temporis vel huiusmodi. Descriptio autem in nulla materia fieri

> Thus a worthy woman was united with a worthy man, a beautiful woman with a handsome man, a clever woman with a smart man, a religious woman with a pious man.

In the words "worthy . . . worthy" the uniformity of difference is contravened. These lines too are faulty:

> His Procne rejoices in Tereus, spouse in spouse, leader in leader, queen in king, girl in her man.

In the words "girl in her man" uniformity of sameness is contravened. It would have been better to write "woman in her man."

Digression is a departure from the subject or from the sense, undertaken on the grounds of proximity to the subject or of inclusiveness. This proximity I don't call similitude, as Donatus does. We depart from a subject by means of a color that we call digression. It is digression when we go away to something that touches on our subject. Sometimes this is done by a poetic fiction, as Statius imagines Jove gathering the gods and sending down war on Thebes, when he brings in Jove saying,

> Terrible old man! Your darkness has deserved, truly deserved, to hope for Jove as your avenger. I will send new strife on the guilty kingdoms.

Sometimes it is achieved by comparison, sometimes by description. We will speak of comparison elsewhere. Description is showing the properties of anything—say, of a man or a place or a time, or the like. In any subject, however, the only description that should be made is the kind from which

debet, nisi talis ut auctor ex ipsa eliciat aliquod argumentum. Verbi gratia, in fabula de Pyramo et Thisbe describitur bustum Nini, ut audita opportunitate loci probabile sit amantes illuc libentius convenire. Descriptio vero nihil ad rem faciens vel nulla sit vel brevissima. Haec descriptio Babylonis superflua est in illa fabula:

> Orbis honor, Babylon, orbis laus imminet, orbis
> effigies, orbis balsamus, orbis apex.

Quid enim ad rem de statu Babylonis? Nihil de materia probabilius efficitur per hanc descriptionem. Describitur autem res tum intrinsecus, tum extrinsecus. Intrinsecus scilicet ex circumstantia ipsius corporis vel loci. Hic modus generalis est. Extrinsecus scilicet ex aliquo famoso actu vel huiusmodi. Secundum hoc usus est Statius digressione in consecratione Archemori interfecti, ut ex magnis actibus haberentur septem reges Argivi magis auctentici. Similiter describit Lucanus locum ubi victus erat Curio—describit, inquam, a famosis actibus, scilicet a lucta Herculis et Antaei et a victoria Scipionis, ut per hoc innuat Curionem ibi audatius dimicasse, ubi consuetudinaria fuit victoria Romanorum. Unde adiecit,

> Curio laetatus tamquam fortuna locorum
> bella gerat.

68 Hic periphrasis consideranda, quae "circumlocutio" interpretatur. Est enim circumlocutio quasi quaedam rei descriptio. Est enim aequipollentia quaedam nominis alicuius

the author can extract some argument. For example, in the story of Pyramus and Thisbe there is a description of the tomb of Ninus, so that once the opportunity that place presents is described, it is probable that the lovers will choose to meet there. But a description that contributes nothing to the subject should be made very briefly or not at all. This description of Babylon is superfluous in that story:

> Babylon, the glory of the world, the praise of the world attends you, you the very image of the world, the balm of the world, the apex of the world.

How is the prestige of Babylon to the point? Nothing in the subject is made more probable by this description. Further, a thing is described either intrinsically or extrinsically. Intrinsically from the circumstances of its body or place. This is the usual mode. Extrinsically, from some famous deed or the like. Thus Statius uses digression in the consecration of the slain Archemorus, so that from their great feats the seven Argive kings will be considered more prestigious. Likewise, Lucan describes the place where Curio was conquered—he describes it, I mean, from famous actions, the wrestling of Hercules with Antaeus and the victory of Scipio, thus suggesting that Curio had fought unusually daringly, in a place where Roman victory was the norm. And so he adds,

> Curio was happy, as if the luck of the place were waging the battle.

Here we should consider periphrasis, translated into Latin as "circumlocution." Circumlocution is a kind of description of a thing. It is using some equivalent of the name

rei pro ipso nomine posita, ut in hac propositione: "Animal ad imaginem domini factum salvabitur." Subiectus terminus periphrasis est "hominis." Statius: "Tandem sua monstra profundo / reddit habere Iovi." Haec vox "profundo Iovi" periphrasis "Plutonis." Similiter in *Architrenio* haec vox, "hora nimis properata malis, sed tarda beatis," periphrasis est "mortis." Huiusmodi circumlocutiones quandoque appositive ponuntur, quando scilicet apponuntur nominibus quorum sunt periphrases. Hic modus etiam usque ad verba extenditur, ut dicatur periphrasis huiusmodi "verborum mutatio"—quando scilicet pro hac, "Iste decessit," dicitur "Iste debitum naturae persolvit," et cetera huiusmodi. Hic modus etiam utilis est materiae prolongandae. Verbi gratia, haec materia, "fabula est sititiva," brevis est ad unius versus compositionem; potest autem sufficere, si pro hac dictione "fabula" per periphrasim ponatur huiusmodi vox, "oratio longa" vel "protractio fandi." Pro hoc vero praedicato "est sititiva," ponatur haec, "reddit potandi cupidum." Et sic fit hic versus: "Reddit potandi cupidum protractio fandi."

69 A sententia eximus quando uni attribuimus quod est alterius ratione alicuius comprehensionis. Hoc fit per antonomasiam, per metonymiam, per circuitionem, per synecdochen. *Antonomasia* Graece idem est quod "pronominatio" Latine, scilicet nominis unius pro alio positio, hoc est generalioris pro minus generali. Haec positio semper quandam praerogativam notare debet, ut hic, "Apostolus dicit," id est Paulus. "Poeta," id est Virgilius. Sic teneri est excellenter et praerogative. Unde fidelissima est expositio: "Poeta," id est "excellens inter poetas" vel "optimus inter poetas." Propter

of a thing instead of the actual name, as in this proposition: "An animal made in the image of the Lord will be saved." The term suppressed in the periphrasis is "man." Statius: "At last he gave Underworld Jove's monsters back to him." The term "Underworld Jove" is a periphrasis for "Pluto." Also this statement in *Architrenius,* "the hour that comes too soon for the wicked, too slow for the blessed," is a periphrasis for "death." Sometimes circumlocutions of this kind are introduced as appositives—namely, when they are placed next to the nouns they are periphrases of. This mode is also extended to verbs, so that periphrases of this kind are called "verb mutation"—namely, when for "He died," we write "He paid the debt of nature," and so on. This mode is also useful for prolonging a subject. For example, the subject "A story makes me thirsty" is too short to make a complete line; but it is long enough if we replace the word "story" by a periphrasis with a phrase such as "long talking" or "protracted speaking." And for the predicate, "makes me thirsty," we can say, "makes me want to drink." And so we have a line: "Protracted speaking makes me want to drink."

We go away from the sense when we attribute to one thing what belongs to another, by reason of some inclusiveness. This is done by antonomasia, metonymy, circuition, and synecdoche. *Antonomasia* in Greek is the same as "pronomination" in Latin: namely, replacing one name for another, that is, a more general name for one less general. This replacement should always mark some special status, as in "the Apostle says," for Paul, or "the Poet" for Virgil. To be referred to in that way is a mark of excellence and special status. Hence this interpretation is most faithful: "the Poet," that is, "outstanding among poets" or "the best of

hanc affinitatem quam habet cum superlativo, tenetur quandoque superlative et determinatur genitivo, ut "poeta poetarum"; "virgo virginum," id est, dignissima virginum vel castissima; "rex regum," id est potentissimus.

70 "Metonymia" idem est quod "transnominatio." *Meta* enim "trans," *onoma* "nomen." Huius a Donato tres species assignantur, ut ponatur inventum pro inventore vel e converso, possessio pro possessore vel e converso, continens pro contento vel e converso: "Lascivo murmure garrit ager." Donatus dicit se haec tria exempla diligentibus proposuisse. Docebit ergo diligentia ad imitationem istorum metonymice:

- Materiam ponere pro materiato, ut videtur. Ut: "Auro superbit manus," id est, anulo cuius materia est aurum.
- Causam pro causato, ut "Amor me peremit," id est, stultitia quam feci per amorem.
- Signans pro signato, ut per Thetidem signatur aqua, per Lyaeum vel Bacchum vinum, quia ipse est deus vini: "In cratere meo Thetis coniuncta Lyaeo."
- Antecedens pro consequente, ut "Camena" pro "carmine"; prius enim utimur Camena quam carmen habeamus.
- Consequens pro antecedente, ut "pallet" pro "timet." Et item, pro hac, "Non emo tanti stuprum," dixit Demosthenes, "Non emo tanti poenitere," ut testatur A. Gellius *Noctium Atticarum*.
- Concomitans pro concomitante, ut "plectrum" pro "cithara."

poets." Because of the affinity this has with the superlative, it is sometimes treated as a superlative and modified by a genitive, as "poet of poets"; "virgin of virgins," that is, the most worthy or most chaste of virgins; "king of kings," that is, the most powerful.

"Metonymy" means the same thing as "transnomination." *Meta* corresponds to *trans* (across) and *onoma* to *nomen* (name). Donatus lists three kinds of this trope: the invention may be put for the inventor, or vice versa, the possession for the possessor, or vice versa, the container for the thing contained, or vice versa: "The field is chattering with a playful murmur." Donatus says he has given these three examples for the diligent. The same diligence will instruct then, in imitation of these, on the subject of metonymies:

- The material for what is made with the material, when apparent. Thus: "His hand vaunts itself with gold," that is, with a ring made out of gold.
- Cause for effect, as "Love has destroyed me," that is, the stupid things I did out of love.
- Sign for thing signified, as when Thetis stands for water, or Lyaeus or Bacchus for wine, because he is the god of wine: "In my bowl is Thetis joined with Bacchus."
- Antecedent for consequent, as "the Muse" for "poetry," since we call on the Muse before we have a poem.
- Consequent for antecedent, as "he is pale" for "he is fearful." Again, instead of saying, "I won't pay that much to disgrace myself," Demosthenes said, "I won't pay that much to feel regret," as we know from Aulus Gellius's *Attic Nights*.
- One concomitant for another, as "plectrum" for "lyre"

- Partem pro toto, ut "testudo" pro "cithara." Horatius: "Me quater undenos sciat implevisse Decembres," id est annos. Pars autem large intelligatur tam pars exigitiva quam constitutiva; et secundum hoc punctum est pars lineae, superficies corporis.
- Item proprietatem pro subiecto, ut "Clementia regis nobis profuit," id est, rex clemens.

Sed hic modus circuitionem facit sive emphasim. Immo ubicumque est hic modus, est emphasis. Est et una species metonymiae secundum quosdam cum attribuitur insensatae rei sensus. Lucanus:

> Vis illic ingens pelagi semperque laborant
> aequora ne rupti repetant confinia montes.

Laborare animalium est. Hic autem modus causa doctrinae efficacius potest ad similitudinem retorqueri.

71 "Emphasis" Graece, "permutatio" Latine. Emphasis est quotiens attribuimus accidenti quod est subiecti, ut in praedicto exemplo. Unde plerique Latini, magis rem intuentes quam vocem, emphasim dicunt expressionem sonare quia secundum eius digniorem positionem aliquam exprimit vehementiam circa subiectum, scilicet vel intensionem sui accidentis, ut hic, "Davus est ipsum scelus," id est, in eo est accidens hoc "sceleratum" valde intense, vel intensionem alicuius intellecti circa suum accidens, ut hic, "Maria est virginitas," id est, in ea est castitas valde intensa. Non dico hoc accidens "virgo," quia virginitas non potest intendi vel remitti.

PART I

- Part for whole, as "sounding board" for "lyre." Horace: "Let him know that I have completed forty-four Decembers," that is, years. For a part may be understood largely as both exigitive and constitutive, so that a point is part of a line and a surface part of a whole body.
- Property for the subject, as, "The leniency of the king was good for us," that is, the lenient king.

This mode entails either circumlocution or emphasis. In fact, wherever this mode appears there is emphasis. Some people consider it a type of metonymy to attribute senses to an insensate thing. Lucan:

> Mighty there is the power of the sea, and its waters labor to prevent the severed mountains from renewing their contact.

To labor is a quality of animals. For teaching purposes this mode can more effectively postponed for treatment under likeness.

"Emphasis" in Greek is "permutation" in Latin. It is emphasis whenever we attribute to an accident what belongs to the subject, as in the previous example. Many Latin speakers, focusing on the thing rather than the word, say that emphasis lends force to an expression because its prominent position in the sentence communicates vehemence about a subject, that is to say, either an intensification of an accident, as here: "Davus is crime itself," that is, the accident "criminal" is exceedingly pronounced in him, or an intensification of something understood about its accident, as here: "Mary is virginity itself," that is, chastity is exceedingly pronounced in her. I don't say the accident "virgin," since virginity cannot be increased or diminished.

72 Emphasis optima est pueris instruendis. Verbi gratia, sumatur rudis identitas, haec scilicet, "Tempus nocet segeti." Quaeratur utrique substantive adiectivum causale, sic: "Tempus humidum nocet segeti nutriendae." Omne adiectivum copulans habet substantivum praeiacens a quo denominative sumitur. Mutetur ergo utrumque adiectivum in substantivum, et fiet emphasis utrimque. Oportet ergo mutari utrumque priorum substantivorum in genitivum, quod potest etiam fieri cum verbi mutatione, sic: "Temporis humiditas subtrahit segetis nutrimentum." Tandem cuilibet substantivae conferre potes suum adiectivum si placet, hoc modo: "Ventosi temporis infelix humiditas crescenti segeti solare subtrahit nutrimentum." Quid vero, si esset verbum absolutum, ut "curro," "vado," "iaceo," "dormio," et huiusmodi? Talia vel pure ponuntur vel determinantur. Si pure ponuntur, mutari possunt, ut supra dictum est in tractatu aequalitatis. Si determinantur, utputa praepositionali determinatione, mutari possunt in verbum transitivum, cuius transitionem determinet res quam importat praepositionalis determinatio. Ut pro hac, "Sol lucet super parietem," habeatur haec, "Sol illuminat parietem." Addantur adiectiva sic: "Sol serenus illuminat planum parietem." Loquamur emphatice et addamus adiectiva, sic: "Amoeni solis iocunda serenitas totam illuminat parietis planitiem incandentis." Possumus etiam satis apte clausulam circa subiectum tantum emphasi decorare, circa praedicatum adiective tantum et ablativo instrumentali, sic: "Amoeni solis iocunda serenitas suae claritatis immensitate totum parietem illuminat." Fit etiam emphasis e converso quando scilicet attribuitur subiecto quod est proprietatis, ut hic:

PART I

Emphasis is the perfect thing to teach boys. For example, take unsubtle predictability such as, "The weather is bad for wheat." Find a causal adjective for each noun, thus: "Wet weather is bad for nutrient-needy wheat." Every adjective that can be joined to a noun has an underlying noun from which it is derived. If we change each adjective into its noun, we will have emphasis in both. Both previous nouns have to be changed to the genitive case, and this can be accompanied by a change of the verb, thus: "The wetness of the weather has taken away the nutrition of the wheat." Finally to any noun you can add its adjective as you please, in this way: "The unfortunate wetness of the windy weather has removed solar nutrition from the growing wheat." But what if it's an intransitive verb such as "run," "walk," "lie," "sleep," and so on? Such words are either modified or unmodified. If they are unmodified, they can be changed, as was described above in treating synonymy. If they are modified, as with a prepositional phrase, they can be changed into a transitive verb, and the object of the preposition should become the object of the transitive verb. Thus, instead of "The sun shines on the wall," have "The sun illuminates the wall." And adjectives are added thus: "The clear sun illuminates the flat wall." Then let us speak emphatically and also add adjectives, thus: "The jocund clarity of the beautiful sun illuminates the whole flat surface of the glowing wall." We can also adorn the sentence appropriately by using emphasis for the subject alone, and just an adjective, along with an ablative of means, for the predicate, in this way: "The jocund serenity of the beautiful sun illuminates the whole wall by the immensity of its brightness." Conversely, emphasis also occurs when something that belongs to a property is attributed to the subject, as here:

Qui cito dat, bis dat, meritum dilata minorant
munera; plus laudis hinc fluit, inde minus.

"Munera dilata," id est "dilatio munerum."

73 Notandum autem quod idem est circuitio in coloribus quod emphasis in figuris, sane intelligantur huiusmodi. Notandum autem quod tunc fit emphasis venustissime quando unica dictio respicit duo verba unum proprie, reliquum emphatice. Unde Hegesippus, in oratione Herodis hortantis filios ad pacificam unitatem, ait, "Manete fratres, nolite exuere quod generati estis." Haec dictio "quod" pro fraternitate supponit et respicit verbum "exuendi" sine emphasi, verbum vero "generandi" cum emphasi. Ab hac elegantia non recedit, si pari modo ponantur duo nomina, scilicet relativum et antecedens, alterum emphatice, reliquum vero sine emphasi, ut si dicerem, "Nolite fraternitatem exuere, qua tanto tempore permansistis." Huic consonat illud regis Bramanorum scribentis regi Alexandro de statu patriae sue et dicentis, "Mulieres nostrae nesciunt in augenda pulchritudine plus affectare quam natae sunt."

74 Synecdoche est quando aliquid vel aliqua toti attribuimus genera partis vel e converso parti genera totius, ut hic: "Inspice mulierem, sed oculis castigatis," propter totum castigatum. Toti genera partis, ut hic: "Caesar est crispus," propter caput crispum. Virgilius: "iam formosissimus annus," propter illam partem anni. Hic dubitari potest an ubicumque est synecdoche sit metonymia, an metonymia

PART I

He who gives quickly gives twice, delayed gifts diminish merit; more praise flows from the one, less from the other.

"Delayed gifts," that is, "delay of gifts."

You should note that circumlocution in colors is the same as emphasis in figures—at least they should be so understood. You should also note that emphasis is most elegant when a single word refers to two verbs, one in its proper sense, the other by emphasis. Thus Hegesippus, in a speech of Herod's exhorting his sons to make peace in unity, says, "Stay brothers, don't throw away what you were born to." The word "what" stands for brotherhood and relates to the verb "throw away" without emphasis, but to the verb "born to" with emphasis. And the elegance remains even if two nouns are paired, namely a relative and its antecedent, one with emphasis, one without, as if I were to say, "Don't throw away brotherhood, in which you have remained for so long a time." This conforms to what the king of the Brahmins wrote to King Alexander about the state of his country, saying, "Our women cannot aspire by beautifying themselves to exceed what they were born with."

Synecdoche is when we attribute some property or properties of a part to the whole, or properties of the whole to a part, as here: "Look at the woman, but with restrained eyes," instead of restrained in every way. Properties of a part for the whole, as here: "Caesar is curly," because of his curly hair. Virgil: "now the year most beautiful," for that part of the year. Here there arises a doubt whether every synecdoche is a metonymy; or whether metonymy is observed

attendatur tantum in suppositione, synecdoche in attributione, an non adeo generaliter intelligenda sit metonymia, ut supra dictum est. Nec enim generalitatem illam expresse accepimus a Donato.

75   Synecdoche alia simplex, alia determinata. Simplex, ut "Caesar est crispus." De tali dicit Donatus, "Meminisse debemus ubi totum a parte ostendimus, ab insigniore parte hoc esse faciendum." Determinata synecdoche est quam sequitur accusativus, ut "Caesar est albus caput." Huiusmodi fit de parte minus insigni, ut "nuda pedes." Ovidius: "Laudabat nudos media plus parte lacertos." "Nudos plus," id est, maiorem partem media parte. Color iste satis communis, satis proprietati vicinus, secundum quod determinatur adiectivum synecdocha determinatione, ut hic: "Socrates est albus pedem." Fit autem pulchrius si quasi aequivoce cum determinatione duplici procedamus, ut in hoc exemplo: "Albus uterque fuit, totus hic, ille manus." Fit adhuc color iste magis improprie, sed multo venustius, cum determinatur synecdoche substantivum, ut hic, "Erat Benedictus mentem monachus et cucullam," id est, habuit et mentem et cucullam monachalem. Statius in decimo: "Sed consanguinei quamvis atque omnia fratres, / tu prior." "Omnia fratres," id est, habentes omnia fraterna.

76   Transversio est exitus a verbo identitatis per vocalem aliquam commutationem. Haec dividitur in inversionem et transmutationem. Inversio est vocalium ordinis perversio per similitudinem proximantem sententiam efficiens dissimilem. Hac utimur frequentius ad contemptum. Haec tum fit per adiectionem, ut, "Isti sunt iuris perditi qui leges legunt" pro "periti"; tum fit per abiectionem, ut "carnales

only in substitution, synecdoche in attribution; or whether metonymy should not be understood in a general sense, as was described above. However, we have not received that general sense in so many words from Donatus.

Synecdoche is either simple or modified. Simple, as "Caesar is curly." On this Donatus says, "We should remember that when we show a whole from a part it should be done from some significant part." Modified synecdoche is when there follows an accusative, as "Caesar is white on the head." A similar effect is possible with a lesser part, as "naked of foot." Ovid: "He praised the arms, naked more than halfway." "Naked more," that is, a part greater than half. The color is pretty common, and very like property, according to which an adjective is modified by a synecdochal modifier, as here: "Socrates is white of foot." It is more beautiful, though, if we proceed, as it were, equivocally with a double modifier, as in this example: "Both were white, one all white, the other just his hands." This color is more irregular, but much more elegant, when a noun is modified synecdochally, as here, "Benedict was a monk in both mind and cowl," that is, he had both the mind and the cowl of a monk. Statius in the tenth book: "But though you two are of one blood, and brothers in all respects, you take precedence." "Brothers in all respects," that is, having all things brothers do.

Transversion is avoidance of repeating a word by changing letters. It is divided into either inversion or transmutation. Inversion is changing the spelling of a word, thereby producing a dissimilar meaning from a basic similarity. Often we use it to express contempt. Inversion is achieved by addition, as in the case, "Those people who read laws are law's reprobates *(perditi)*" for "experts" *(periti);* by

pontifices" pro "cardinales pontifices"; tum fit per mutationem, ut "praedones" pro "praecones," "archidiabolus" pro "archidiaconus"; tum fit per mutationem factam sive in unica dictione sive in diversis, ut "latro" pro "lator," "displicina" pro "disciplina," "Cullius turrit" pro "Tullius currit." Juxta hunc locum inveniuntur methaplasmi illi: anathesis, ut "olli" pro "illi," et metathesis, ut "Evandre" pro "Evander."

77 Transmutatio est transversio vocis non efficiens sententiam dissimilem. Haec fit multipliciter. Quandoque mutatur adiectivum in genitivum demonstrativum essentiae, ut pro hac "vir fortis" dicatur "vir fortitudinis," et ponitur huiusmodi genitivus excellenter. Unde Gaufroi Vinesauf primo posuit adiectivum, postea quasi augmentantem genitivum, dicens,

   Quid, miles perfide, miles
perfidiae, miles pudor orbis et unica sordes
militiae. . . .

Quandoque ponitur gradus pro gradu, positivus pro comparativo, ut hic: "Bonum est sperare in domino quam, etc."; comparativum pro positive, Bernardus: "Abundantior enim malignitas quibus insedit sedibus, funditus non recedit." Et hic modus excellentiam notat, et exponitur "abundantior," id est, "valde abundans." Quandoque ponitur finitum pro infinito, ut "nunc" pro "aliquando." Boethius: "Nam nunc quidem ad communem hominum mensuram se cohibebat. Nunc vero pulsare caelum verticis cacumine videbatur." Quandoque fit commutatio praedicamenti. Bernardus:

subtraction, as "carnal prelates" for "cardinal prelates"; by alteration, as "robbers" *(praedones)* for "heralds" *(praecones)*, "archdevil" *(archidiabolus)* for "archdeacon" *(archidiaconus)*; and the mutation can be in a single element or in several, as "thief" *(latro)* for "bearer" *(lator)*, "displeasure" *(displicina)* for "learning" *(disciplina)*, "Rullius is tunning" for "Tullius is running." Here are located these metaplasms: anathesis, as *olli* for *illi*, and metathesis, as *Evandre* for "Evander."

Transmutation is the adaptation of a word without changing the meaning. This takes numerous forms. Sometimes an adjective is changed to a genitive that expresses its content, so that "a man of bravery" is said instead of "a brave man"; such a genitive usage is commendable. Thus Geoffrey of Vinsauf put the adjective first, then the genitive as if to strengthen it, saying,

> Why, perfidious soldier, soldier of perfidy, soldier shame of the world and unparalleled defilement of the army. . . .

Sometimes one degree of comparison is put for another, here the positive for the comparative: "It is good (that is, better) to hope in the Lord than, etc."; the comparative for the positive, Bernard: "A more abundant (that is, abundant) malignity does not withdraw completely from the locations where it has settled." This mode also denotes excess, and "more abundant" is taken to mean "very abundant." Sometimes a definite word is used for an indefinite, such as "now" for "sometimes." Boethius: "For now she confined herself to normal human size, now she seemed to strike the sky with the top of her head." Sometimes an alteration is made in

"Terra, vides, quomodo ex elementorum fecunditate concepta nunc fluviis, nunc graminibus, nunc silvis comantibus hilarescit." "Nunc" pro "hic" ponitur, et est ibi metalepsis figura, ex eo quod "dictio gradatim pergit ad id quod ostendit": "nunc" pro "hic" intelligitur, et "hic" pro "alicubi." Quandoque mutatur modus pro modo, ut "audire" pro "audiebant." Statius: "Tunc horrere comae, sanguisque in corde gelari." Quandoque ponitur praeteritum imperfectum ex sui variabilitate pro coniunctivo, ut "amabant" pro "amarent" vel "possent amare." Bernardus de intricatione circulorum Veneris et Mercurii ait, "Et nisi commissuras nodosque intersectionum Urania intentior deprehendisset, viarum ambagibus ad solem, unde venerant ferebantur." Id est, "possent ferri" vel "ferrentur."

78   Quandoque per interpretationem transvertitur vox. Verbi gratia, usus est Latinorum ut quibusdam nominibus, tam Graecis quam barbaris, utantur sub modica immutatione et notha faciant. Dicunt enim Graeci "tragoedía," "comoedía," nos "tragédia," "comédia," unde propter litterae immutationem mutamus accentum Graecorum. Similiter dicunt Anglici "Yxewirde," Latini "Yxewirdia." Item Anglici "Melclege," Latini "Melcleia," et Latinos accentus observant. In huiusmodi igitur quandoque causa ornatus transvertimus nomen ipsum per interpretationem. Verbi gratia, "Melclege" componitur ex duobus integris Anglice et interpretatur fideli expositione "lactis saltus." Causa igitur ornatus ubi dicendum erat "Melclege" potest dici "lactis saltus" vel "saltus lacteus."

categories. Bernard: "You see how the earth, conceived from the fertility of the elements, rejoices now with rivers, now with grasses, now with leafy forests." "Now" is used for "here," and we have here the figure metalepsis insofar as "the language moves by stages toward what it is displaying": "now" is for "here," and "here" for "somewhere." Sometimes one form of the verb is changed for another, as "to hear" for "they heard." Statius: "Then his hair was standing on end, and his blood freezing in his heart." Sometimes the imperfect indicative, because of its flexibility, is used for the subjunctive, as *amabant* (they loved) for *amarent* (they would love) or *possent amare* (they could love). Bernard, on the intermingling of the orbits of Venus and Mercury, says, "And if Urania had not paid special attention to the knots and conjunctions of their intersections, they were borne by circuitous paths back to the sun, where they came from." That is, "they could be borne" or "would be borne."

Sometimes a word is adapted by translation. For example, the practice of Latin speakers is to utter some nouns, both from Greek and other languages, with a small change and make them hybrids. For the Greeks say *tragoedía, comoedía,* and we say *tragédia, comédia;* because there is change of a letter, we change the accent of the Greeks. In the same way the English say "Yxewirde," the Latins *Yxewirdia*. Again, the English say "Melkley," the Latins *Melcleia,* and they keep Latin accent. In names of this kind, then, for the sake of ornament we adapt the name by translation. For example, "Melkley" is composed of two separate words in English and literally means "pasture of milk." For the sake of ornament, then, instead of saying "Melkley" it can be called "the pasture of milk" or "the milky pasture."

79   Sunt et alia transmutationis genera, ut hypallage, in hac: "In nova fert animus." Et Lucanus: "Ut primum maestum tenuere silentia coetum." Item hendiadys, ut in hac: "Arma virumque cano." Et si plura huiusmodi inveniantur, non invideo.

    Transcensus est excessus in verbo vel sententia. Hic dividitur in tres species: hyperbaton, litoten, et hyperbolen. Hyperbaton est transcensio quaedam verborum ordinem turbans. Huius species sunt hysteron proteron, anastrophe, tmesis. Qui has intelligere voluerit, Donatum consulat. Sunt et aliae duae nobis utiliores, interpositio et synchysis. Pulchre tamen fit tmesis quandoque, ut hic: "Quo me cumque rapit tempestas, etc." Similiter et hic secundum quosdam, "Inque vicem...." Quod apud nos interpositio, hoc in figuris parenthesis nuncupatur. Est igitur interpositio quotiens unam orationem interserimus antequam alia finiatur. Haec, licet indistincte, plerumque fiat; quibusdam modis utilius fit quam aliis. Fit enim peroptime quando aliquid horrendum vel abominabile dicendum est. Interpositio enim illa temperat terrorem et abominationem. Virgilius: "Frigidus—o pueri, fugite hinc!—latet anguis in herba." Ecce antequam plene illud horrendum dixisset, temperavit terrorem promittendo salutem per fugam. Bernardus Silvestris in *Parricidali* maluit separare haec tria verba "occidet patrem suum" quam coniungere, dicens,

PART I

There are also other kinds of transmutation, such as hypallage, in this: *In nova fert animus (mutatas dicere formas corpora)*. (My mind impels me toward speaking of forms changed into new bodies.) And Lucan: "As soon as silence held the sorrowing crowd." Also hendiadys, as in this phrase: "I sing of arms and a man." And I have no objection to finding more examples of this kind.

Transcendence is excess of word or thought. It has three kinds: hyperbaton, litotes, and hyperbole. Hyperbaton is an excess that disturbs the order of words. Its kinds are hysteron proteron, anastrophe, and tmesis. Anyone who wants to learn them should consult Donatus. There are two other kinds more useful to us, interposition and synchysis. Sometimes tmesis is elegantly fashioned, as here: "Where the storm ever takes me, etc." Some people like this one too: "And in turn. . . ." What I am calling interposition is called parenthesis among the figures. Anyway, it is interposition whenever we insert one phrase before another is finished. Let this be used often, though not too ostentatiously; some forms of it are more useful than others. The best time to use it is when you have to say something dreadful or disgusting. Such an interposition moderates the horror and disgust. Virgil: "A cold snake—oh, boys, get out of here!—is hiding in the grass." You see, before Virgil finished mentioning the scary thing, he moderated the fear by urging them to escape by flight. Bernard Silvester in *The Astrologer* preferred to separate the three words "will kill his father" rather than keep them together, saying,

79

> Patrem—sed taceo nisi quod premis, arguis, instas—
> occidet, fato sic agitante, suum.

Ecce una parenthesis est inter "patrem" et "occidet," alia inter "occidet" et "suum." Et alibi, loquens de sideribus hoc promittentibus, ait,

> Spondebant—sed flere magis quam dicere fas est,
> proh dolor!—auctorem funeris esse tui.

Et alius quidam haec verba, "contra cognatum steti," quia abominabilia sunt, sic divisit:

> Contra cognatum—fateor, ubi vincla, quod absit,
> sanguinis abrumpat gratia laesa—steti.

Duplex est hic interpositio. Una inter duo prima verba et ultimum—quicquid ibi ponitur est interpositio; praeterea est et alia minor, scilicet haec, "quod absit." Modus iste pulchrior est per ironiam. Fit etiam frequenter. Statius in sermone Eteoclis ubi respondet fratri suo mediante Tydeo:

> Te penes Inachiae dotalis regia dono
> coniugis, et Danaae—quid enim maioribus actis
> invideam?—cumulentur opes.

Fit etiam interpositio satis optime quandoque admirative, ut in fabula de Pyramo et Thisbe:

PART I

His father—but I would remain silent if you weren't pressing me, urging me, insisting—he will kill, since his fate is driving him to it.

You see the interposition between "father" and "will kill," and another between "will kill" and "his." And later, speaking of stars predicting this, he says,

They affirmed—but it is right rather to weep than to speak it, alas!—him to be the author of your death.

Another poet has divided up the words "I stood against my kinsman," because they are shocking, in this way:

Against my kinsman—I confess, whenever ruptured goodwill should break the bonds of blood (perish the thought)—I stood.

The interposition here is double. One is between the two first words and the last—everything between them is an interposition; there is also a second, lesser one: namely, "perish the thought." This mode is more beautiful if there is irony, and it's also common. Statius in the speech of Eteocles, where he answers his brother through the intermediary Tydeus:

You have been endowed with a kingdom by the gift of your Argive wife; let your Greek riches—for why should I envy your greater deeds?—pile up high.

Sometimes an interposition serves well to express wonder, as in the story of Pyramus and Thisbe:

> Ecce patet pueris—quid enim celatur amantes?—
> parva nec artifici cognita rima suo.

81   Synchysis est hyperbaton ex omni parte confusum, ut patet in fabula de Pyramo et Thisbe in hiis versibus:

> Invidia famae patrum pervenit ad aures
> tempore consilium sed puerile brevi.

Male separatur necessitate metri hoc substantivum "tempore" ab hoc adiectivo "brevi." Et neque secundum hoc exemplum, neque secundum exemplum quod ponit Donatus, est synchysis color sed tantum figura, quia vitium est, sed excusabile. Talem versum composuit Vindocinensis, dicens,

> Christe, tibi sit honor, sit laus qui cum patre regnas,
> rex cum rege, deus cum sine fine deo.

Iuxta hoc schema tamen sumitur quidam color, quem "singula singulis" nuncupamus. Singula singulis est ad invicem sese respicientium multiplex terminorum divisio sed collectiva. Respectus ille tum fit in re et constructione, tum in re tantum. In re et constructione, ut hic: "Cicero, Caesar, Actaeon scribit, militat, venatur." Secundum hunc modum fiunt hii versus:

> But see, there is visible to the young people—for what is hidden from lovers?—a small crack not even known to the builder.

Synchysis is hyperbaton that is disordered in every respect, as is clear in the story of Pyramus and Thisbe in these verses:

> But their teenage plan reached the ears of their fathers in a short, by the envy of rumor, time.

Because of the demands of meter, the noun "time" is clumsily separated from its adjective "short." And neither in this example nor in the example Donatus gives is synchysis a color but only a figure, because it is a fault, though an excusable one. Matthew of Vendôme composed such a verse, saying,

> Christ, to you be honor, to you be praise, who reign with the father, king with king, God with without-end God.

Alongside this figure, though, we do place a certain color, the one we call "each to each." Each to each is a multiple distinction of terms that relate mutually to each other but as a collective. This relation sometimes applies both to the content and the construction, sometimes just to the content. To the content and the construction, as in this case: "Cicero, Caesar, Actaeon writes, fights, hunts." The following verses adopt this mode:

Iuno, Tisiphone, Pallas, Bellona, Dione
aptat, maestificat, manifestat, tradit, amicat
primitias, Erebum, subtilia, vulnus, ephebum
naturae, sceleri, Musis, hosti, mulieri
conceptu, poena, speculo, mucrone, catena
vitae, terroris, animi, Mavortis, amoris.

Hic modus synchysim facit, nec colorem certe dixerim sed figuram quam, salva pace Donati, certe vel figuram audeam vix nominare. Deturpat enim adeo quod excusabilis non videtur; ab operibus authenticis huiusmodi dixerim eliminanda, maxime ubi verborum separanda diversitas invenitur. Et tamen Anticlaudianus ait,

> Frons lilia, balsama naris,
> dens ebur, osque rosam parit, offert, reddit, adequate.

In re tantum fit respectus ut hic: "Achilles et Aiax interfecerunt Hectorem et Paridem." Plana est constructio. Et tamen est ibi respectus realis divisus ex eo quod Achilles Hectorem et Aiax Paridem interfecit. Hic modus non excusat sed decorat, ut in illa epistula Byblidis ad Caunum:

> Pagina maeroris et littera caeca lituris
> scripta dolente venit femineaque manu.

Haec dictio "dolente" causative respicit hanc dictionem "maeroris," scilicet quia ex dolente manu ideo est pagina maeroris. Haec dictio "feminea" respicit hunc terminum

PART I

> Juno readies the first fruits for Nature by the conception of life. Tisiphone saddens Erebus for crime with the pain of terror. Pallas manifests subtleties for the Muses with the mirror of the mind. Bellona gives a wound to her enemy with the sword of Mars. Dione ingratiates a young man to a woman by the chain of love.

This mode creates synchysis, and I certainly would not call it a color but a figure—indeed, *pace* Donatus, I would scarcely dare even to call it a figure. For it disfigures to such a degree that it does not seem excusable. I would say that such things should be removed from the works of standard authors, especially where we find a variety of words that have to be separated off. Nevertheless, Anticlaudianus says,

> The forehead lilies, the nose balsam, the tooth ivory, and the mouth rose engenders, offers, mirrors, in likeness.

The relation is only in content, as here: "Achilles and Ajax killed Hector and Paris." This construction is straightforward. And yet there is here a distinction in the content of the relationship, because Achilles killed Hector and Ajax Paris. This mode doesn't exculpate but ornaments, as in the letter of Byblis to Caunus:

> This page of grief, this letter illegible with smearing, comes written by a sorrowing and feminine hand.

The word "sorrowing" bears a causal relationship to the word "grief," since, because it is from the sorrowing hand, it is a page of grief. The word "feminine" bears a causal rela-

"caeca lituris" causative. Cum enim haec vox "caeca lituris" abundantiam fletus notet et marium quamvis dolentium non sit flere, bene dicit "feminea." Architrenius:

> Combussit Phrygium pastorem, Pergama, Graecos
> a Veneris surgens faculis amor, ignis et ira.

Hic, salva aequivocatione et singulari numero huius dictionis "combussit," nihil derogatur constructioni, quia amor, ignis, et ira combusserunt Paridem, Pergama et Graecos. Item in descriptione busti Nini:

> Lascivit radio, dulcedine, murmure, fructu,
> flos ibi, gramen ibi, fons ibi, morus ibi.

Nihil derogaretur constructioni si tantum verbum pluraliter poneretur. Sed verbi singularitas notat verbum multotiens resumendum. Illud tamen singularitatis vitium exilissimum est et fere nullum. Fit etiam modus hic quandoque venustissime sub diversitate verborum, non tamen in constructione necessario separandorum, ut in hiis versibus:

> Impedior studio, gemitus pluo, scripta lituro
> corpore, corde, manu morbida, maesta, tremens.

Excepta synchysi secundi versus nihil derogatur constructioni, cum haec constructio plana sit: "Iste homo morbidus, esuriens, dolens languet, comedit, et suspirat." Quippe

tionship to the phrase "illegible with smearing." Since that phrase "illegible with smearing" denotes a lot of crying, and though males may grieve they don't weep, "feminine" is well said. Architrenius:

> Love arising from the torches of Venus, fire, and wrath consumed the Phrygian shepherd, Troy, and the Greeks.

Here, aside from the ambiguity and the singular number in the word *combussit* (consumed), there is nothing to object to in the construction, seeing that love, fire, and wrath consumed Paris, Troy, and the Greeks. Likewise in the description of Ninus's tomb:

> There exults in brilliance, in sweetness, in murmuring, in fruit, here the flower, here the grass, here the fountain, here the mulberry tree.

Nothing would be wrong with the construction if only the verb were plural. But the singular form of a verb denotes that it is to be repeated again and again. And so the fault of using the singular is very slight, almost nothing. This device is used very elegantly sometimes with several different verbs that need not be separated in construction, as in these lines:

> I am prevented from study, I rain groans, I erase what I have written, in body, heart, and hand sick, sad, trembling.

Except for the synchysis in the second line there is nothing wrong with the construction, since the construction is straightforward: "This man—sick, hungry, sorrowing—languishes, eats, and sighs." Wouldn't it be a valid sentence to

nonne haec vox, "Morbidus comedit," est bona constructio? In mutuo tamen respectu singula singulis invenitur.

Litotes fit ubi minus dicitur et magis intelligitur, ut si dicam, "Aliquid est diligere eo animo quo dilexerunt se Pylades et Orestes." Aliquid, id est magnum. Bernardus:

> Debetur nonnullus honos et gratia Silvae,
> quae genitiva tenet.

Nonnullus, id est, magnus. "Hyperbole est dictio fidem excedens augendi minuendive causa," secundum Donatum, "augendi, ut 'candidior nive,' minuendi, ut 'tardior testudine.'" Et est hyperbole superlatio vel excessio in sententia, et color nomine "exsuperatio" nuncupatur. Haec utilis est in descriptionibus faciendis. Haec tamen fiet bene quando sub aliqua aggregationis specie gradatim procedimus, semper scilicet hyperbolen augmentando, ut hic:

> Virginis ad vultum marcet rosa, lilia pallent,
> languet luna, latent sidera, Phoebus ebet.

Hic incidunt simul hyperbole, disiunctum, et gradatio.

Circa diversionem extravaganter notetur quod, cum aliqua concomitantia simul sunt assignanda, optime fiet si a nominibus identitatis causa maturius dicendi divertimur ad effectus vel ad causas vel ad aliquid huiusmodi circumiacens, breviter tamen et succinte. Verbi gratia, pro hac, "Cato fuit temperatus et iustus et prudens et fortis," ait Lucanus,

say, "The sick man eats"? Still, in the mutual relationship we have the color "each to each."

Litotes is when less is said and more is meant. As if I should say, "It's something to love as heartily as Pylades and Orestes loved each other." Something: that is, a great thing. Bernard:

> No small honor and thanks are owed to Silva, who possesses what gives life.

No small, that is, great. "Hyperbole," according to Donatus, "is a word that goes beyond the truth in order to amplify or diminish: to amplify, as 'whiter than snow,' to diminish, as 'slower than a turtle.'" Hyperbole is exaggeration or excess in meaning, and as a color it is called "exsuperation." It is useful in composing descriptions. It will work well when we proceed step by step with the appearance of aggregation, always increasing the hyperbole, as here:

> Before the face of the girl, the rose fades, lilies pale, the moon dims, the stars hide, Phoebus fades.

Here we have hyperbole, disjunction, and climax all at once.

On the subject of diversion, it may be noted in addition that, when attendant details are to be presented altogether, the best way to do it, in order to write more maturely, is if we turn from the synonymous nouns to effects or causes or some such relevant consideration—briefly and succinctly, though. For example, Lucan, instead of saying, "Cato was temperate and just and prudent and brave," says,

> Haec duri immota Catonis
> secta fuit: servare modum finemque tenere,
> naturamque sequi, patriaeque impendere vitam.

Per primum notat temperantiam ubi dicit, "servare modum," et sic per ordinem prudentiam, iustitiam, fortitudinem.

84 Est et hic alius modus elegantissimus praenotandus qui quidem utilis est productis materiis breviandis. Verbi gratia, sumatur haec materia: "Melius sub bona spe pati quam properare et decipi." Hic notantur quattuor: duo coniunctim, spes et patientia, item alia duo coniunctim, festinantia et deceptio. Possumus ergo sic dicere, "Utiliora sunt spes et patientia quam festinantia et deceptione." Sed hic stare non placet. Possumus adhuc utrimque alterum concomitantium in adiectivum mutare, sic: "Utilior est sperans patientia quam festina deceptio." Secundum hoc fit hic versus, "Durior est properans deceptio quam mora sperans," vel sic, "Quam lapsus properans praestat patientia sperans." Secundum hoc scilicet artificium fit hic versus de hac materia, "Melius est mentiri pro habendo gaudio quam pro veritate dicenda perdere," "Falsa lucrativa malim quam vera nociva."

PART I

> This was the inflexible rule of severe Cato: to keep moderation and hold on to a limit, to follow nature, to give his life for his country.

In the first phrase he alludes to temperance when he says, "keep moderation," and in the same way in order to prudence, justice, fortitude.

There is also this other very elegant device worth noting, which is indeed useful for shortening lengthy subject matter. Take this subject, for example: "It is better to suffer with good hope than to hasten and be deceived." Here four things are referred to: one pair, hope and patience, and another, haste and deception. We can therefore say the following: "Hope and patience are more beneficial than haste and deception." But to stop at that is not satisfying. We can still change one member of both pairs into adjectives, thus: "Hopeful patience is more beneficial than hasty deception." And then turn it into verse: "Hasty deception is more harmful than hopeful delay," or "How hopeful patience beats a hasty slip." With the same device, from the following subject, "It's better to lie and enjoy happiness than to lose it for telling the truth," is produced this verse: "I would prefer profitable lies to damaging truths."

84

2

Similitudo est prolatio vocis aliqua similitudinariam aequipollentiam assignantis, sive expresse sive inexpresse. Similitudinum alia assumptio, alia transumptio, alia homoeosis. Assumptio est accomodatio vocis ad significationem vel consignificationem quam ex institutione non habet per similitudinem extra sumptam. Similitudo extra sumpta est quae contrahi non potest ex aliqua significatione dictionis habita ex principali institutione, ut haec vox "achillior" assumitur ad significandum idem quod haec vox "fortior"; et non contrahitur similitudo ex sui principali institutione quae nulla est, sed sumitur extra in alia dictione, scilicet in hac dictione "Achilles," quia haec vox "Achilles" fortem hominem significat.

2 Assumptionum quaedam vocis non significativae, quaedam est vocis significativae. Vox non significativa accomodatur ad significandum multipliciter. Quandoque contingit quod habemus nomen barbarum quod apud nos per casus non inflectitur, ut "Adam," "Abraham." Loco igitur obliquorum secundum quosdam assumimus voces non significativas et accomodamus ad significandum. Dicunt enim quod isti obliqui "Adae," "Abrahae" sunt voces non significativae accomodatae ad significandum. Secundum enim analogiam deberemus dicere "Adamus," "Adami," "Abrahamus," "Abrahami"; sed dicimus "Adae," "Abrahae" ratione exilis similitudinis. Rectus enim nulli declinationi adeo similis ut primae, saltem accusativo primae similis est in terminatione.

PART TWO

Likeness is an utterance of a word that signifies an equivalence based on likeness, explicitly or implicitly. Likenesses are either assumption, metaphor, or homoeosis. Assumption is accommodating a word to a meaning or implication that it does not have originally by means of an external likeness. An external likeness is one that cannot be drawn from any meaning that the word has originally; for instance, the word "achillier" is taken by assumption to mean the same thing as the word "braver," and the likeness is not drawn from the original meaning, which is of no significance, but is taken externally, from another word, namely the word "Achilles," because the word "Achilles" means "a brave man."

One kind of assumption is of a word without a meaning, another of a word with a meaning. A meaningless word is adapted to produce meaning in many ways. Sometimes we happen to have a foreign word that is indeclinable in Latin, such as *Adam* or *Abraham*. According to some, to supply the oblique cases we take by assumption words that have no meaning and adapt them to convey meaning. For they say that oblique forms such as *Adae* or *Abrahae* are meaningless words adapted to convey meaning. By analogy we ought to have said *Adamus, Adami, Abrahamus, Abrahami*, but we say *Adae, Abrahae* by reason of a slight likeness. For the nominative is like no declension more than the first, or at least its ending is like the accusative of the first declension.

3   Quandoque contingit quod habemus penuriam dictionum compositarum. Possumus tum per expressum simile satis aptam dictionem invenire, semper forsitan inauditam. Verbi gratia, habemus hanc in usu: "mellifluus." A simili possumus dicere "murrifluus," "balsamifluus," "venenifluus." Item invenimus "semibos," "semivir." A simili possumus dicere "semicamelus," "semi[porc]us," si opus fuerit. Magister Iohannes dixit "vernifluus" ad similitudinem veris, scilicet hilaris vel pulcher. Numquam forte invenitur hoc participium "velificatus" nisi in Iuvenali. Forsitan ipse invenit cum dixit, "velificatus Athos."

4   Nova enim verba contingit quandoque per similitudinem invenire, ut "tantalizat," "pregnat," "detunicat," "primitiat." Et haec omnia confirmavit Iohannes de Hauvilla fieri licere auctoritate Horatiis dicentis,

>   Licuit, semperque licebit
> signatum praesente nota producere nomen.

Exposuit enim sic: "nomen" (id est quamcumque dictionem) "signatum nota" (id est, expressa ratione inventionis) "praesente." Unde non licet mihi invenire hoc vocem "buba" ad significandum Platonem.

5   Notarum alia exprimitur intrinsecus et extrinsecus, alia intrinsecus tantum. Intrinsecus et extrinsecus: quando per principium ipsius dictionis patet ratio suae inventionis, nihilominus tamen determinatur alia dictione significativa

PART 2

Sometimes we happen to have a paucity of compound 3
words. But we can from a distinct likeness invent a suitable
word, though perhaps an entirely unprecedented one. For
example, we have the usage "mellifluous" (flowing with
honey). By likeness we can say "myrrhifluous" (flowing with
myrrh), "balsamifluous" (flowing with balm), "venenifluous"
(flowing with poison). Also we have *semibos* (half cow), *semivir* (half man). By likeness we can say "semicamel" or "semi-
pig," if we need to. Master John of Hauville said "vernifluous" (spring-flowing), to represent what spring is like — that
is, gay or lovely. The past participle *velificatus* is perhaps
never found except in Juvenal — who may have made it up
when he wrote, "sailed-over Athos."

Sometimes new verbs happen to be invented by likeness, 4
verbs like *tantalizat* (he teases), *praegnat* (she is pregnant), *detunicat* (he undresses), *primitiat* (he initiates). And John of
Hauville confirmed that all these were permissible by the
authority of Horace, who said,

> It was allowed, and always will be allowed,
> to bring out a noun stamped with a current mintmark.

His reasoning is as follows: "a noun" (that is, any word)
"stamped with a mintmark" (that is, with a clear reason for
inventing it) "that is current." So it is not allowed for me to
invent the word "buba" to mean Plato.

Some coinages are produced both intrinsically and ex- 5
trinsically, others only intrinsically. Both intrinsically and
extrinsically: when the reason for an invention is made obvious at the beginning of the word, but it is nevertheless still
modified by another, meaningful word that expresses the

exprimente rationem inventionis, ut hic: "Ista mulier praeliliat lilia, id est praecellit lilia in candore." Unde quidam ait,

> Lilia vernifluo Thisbe praeliliat ore,
> praeradiat radios, praerosulatque rosas.

Haec autem nimium incompetens esset: "Ista praeliliat nivem," et adeo vitiosa quod nullo modo tolerabilis.

6 Intrinsecus tantum exprimitur nota, ut hic, "Facies tua dumescit pilis." Haec dictio "dumescit" exprimit in se rationem suae inventionis. Patet enim per principium quod a "dumo" trahitur, et est sensus, "Faciei tuae pili similes sunt dumo vel dumis."

Quandoque autem exprimitur nota intrinsecus tantum, sed extrinsecus exprimitur significatio verbi inventi—non dico ratio inventionis—ut hic, "Crystallantur aquae glacie temporali." "Crystallus" nota est huius verbi "crystallantur," sed haec determinatio "glacie temporali" ostendit significationem. Est enim sensus, "crystallantur," id est "imitantur crystallum." Si vero dicam, "Crystallantur aquae apud Thylem glacie perpetua," haec alia determinatio alium potest sensum exprimere, hunc scilicet, "Crystallantur, id est fiunt crystallus." Talis est enim rei veritas, ut dicunt physici.

7 Quandoque longe extra exprimitur significatio, ut hic:

rationale of the invention, as here: "That woman outlilies the lily, that is, exceeds the lily in whiteness." Accordingly someone said,

> With her vernifluous complexion Thisbe outlilies the lilies,
> Outrays the sun's rays, outroses the roses.

But "She outlilies the snow" would be too inept, and so utterly faulty as to be intolerable in every way.

A coinage is produced only intrinsically, as here: "Your face is becoming a thicket of hair." The word *dumescit* contains in itself the reason for its invention. For it is clear right away that it is drawn from *dumus* (thicket), and the sense is, "Your hairy appearance is like a thicket or thickets."

Sometimes, however, a coinage is produced only intrinsically, but the meaning of the invented word—I don't say the reason for its invention—is expressed extrinsically, as here: "The waters are crystallized by seasonal ice." "Are crystallized" is a coinage from the word "crystal," but the modifying phrase "by seasonal ice" shows its meaning. For the sense is, "they are crystallized," that is, "they imitate crystal." But if I were to say, "The waters at Thule are crystallized by perpetual ice," this new modification can express a different sense, namely, "They are crystallized, that is, they become crystal." For that is the truth of the matter, as the physicists say.

Sometimes the meaning is expressed externally at some length:

Ut sol lucens in beryllo
transit illum, nec in illo
repugnat integritas,
sed vis crescit et augetur
qua decrescit et deletur
frigoris vicinitas,
sic est caro lucis orta
de puellae clausa porta,
sic beryllat virginem
incarnatus rex caelestis:
vitiorum tota pestis
per hunc perit hominem.

Significatio huius dictionis "beryllat" exprimitur per illud principium: "Ut sol lucens in beryllo." Notat enim non quod virgo fiat beryllus, sed quod in hoc sit similis beryllo.

8   Satis apte etiam, si inveniatur participium aliquod ficticium in auctoribus, ex eo potest et verbum fingi. Iuvenalis: "velificatus Athos"; Iohannes Hauvillensis: "velificatur Athos." Ex Graeco etiam dictiones licenter possumus extorquere, ut Bernardus extorsit haec nomina "cosmographia," "microcosmus," "megacosmus," Iohannes Hauvillensis hoc nomen "Architrenius." Similiter adiectiva, si placet, callide. Graeci dicunt "pantomorphon." Bernardus: "Oyarses igitur circuli, quem 'Pantomorphen' Graecia, Latinitas nominat 'Omniformem,' formas rebus omnes omnibus et associat et ascribit." Ego audacter dicerem, pro hac clausula, "Sumpsisti tibi mulierem meretricem," "Duxisti tibi Thaidem pantomorpham," id est, omniformem sive variabilem.

9   Inveniuntur etiam frequenter et ornatissime quaedam participia, quae appellantur "participia sine verbi origine."

PART 2

> Just as when the sun shines on beryl it passes through it and does not lose its integrity therein but its force, by which any nearby cold is diminished and eliminated, is increased and augmented, so the flesh of light, born from the closed portal of a girl, so the incarnate king of heaven beryls a virgin: the whole scourge of sins perishes through this man.

The meaning of the word "beryls" is expressed at the beginning: "Just as when the sun shines on beryl." It means not that the virgin becomes beryl, but that she is like beryl in this respect.

This also works: if a made-up participle should be found in the authors, a verb can be made out of it. Juvenal: "Athos the sailed over"; John of Hauville: "Athos is sailed over." Again, we can freely twist out words from Greek, as Bernard twisted out the nouns "cosmography," "microcosm," and "megacosm," and John of Hauville the name "Architrenius." Adjectives too, if you want, and are clever enough. The Greeks say "pantomorph" (shape-shifter). Bernard: "And so the Usiarch of that sphere which is called in Greek *Pantomorphos*, and in Latin *Omniformis*, conveys and assigns all forms to all things." I might audaciously have said, for the phrase, "You have taken a whore to wife," "You have married Thais the shape-shifter," that is, the omniform or variable.

Also, there are often found certain very attractive participles, called "participles without an original verb." They

Quae tantum absoluta sunt, ut "comans," "viridans." Transitiva non recolo me vidisse. Theodolus:

> Ore columba suo ramum viridantibus ultro
> contulerat foliis.

Bernardus: "Terra ex elementorum fecunditate concepta, nunc silvis, nunc graminibus, nunc fluviis comantibus hilarescit." Possunt decenter et licite verba consimilia inveniri, ut de "herba" "herbidare." Bernardus: "Quarta prior e circulo more viridantis Aegypti in diversa florum gramina novamentis vernalibus herbidabat."

Ornatissime etiam contingit comparativas quasdam dictiones invenire, quae multipliciter transformantur, quandoque a substantivo in quo scilicet excellit res comparativi, pro quo ponitur, verbi gratia, "Qui sedet hac sede ganymedior est Ganymede." Sed huiusmodi ludicra sunt et ab operibus auctenticis eliminantur. In huiusmodi doctrinae exemplum Iohannes de Hauvilla hunc versum composuit: "Petrior est petra, tigre tigrior, hydrior Hydra." Visa tamen doctrina, abradi iussit et hunc apponi, "Hydra, tigris, petra plus Hydra, tigre, petra." Sunt tamen quaedam nomina appellativa et substantiva quae ratione accidentis subintellecti elegans abusio comparavit, ut "tyro," novus miles: "Erat Hector in armis tyronior quam Achilles," id est novior. "Melodia," suavis cantus; "melodior," suavior: "Tympanizat psittacus, et psittaco melodior philomena." "Tyrannus," crudelis dominus: "Iste miles tyrannior est Herode."

only stand by themselves—*comans* (luxuriant), for instance, or *viridans* (verdant). I don't recall seeing other forms. Theodulus:

> In her mouth the dove spontaneously brought a branch with verdant leaves.

Bernard: "The earth, brought to conception by the fecundity of the elements, rejoices now in rivers, now in grasses, now in luxuriant forests." Verbs like these can be invented, properly and permissibly, such as *herbidare* (become green) from *herba* (grass). Bernard: "The first quarter of the circle, like verdant Egypt, greened up into various flowering plants with the renewings of spring."

Another way to beautify is to invent certain comparative words, which can be transformed in various ways. Sometimes from a noun in which the idea of the comparative arises the comparative is put for it, for example, "He who sits in this seat is ganymedier than Ganymede." Such usages are playful, and are kept out of authentic works. To exemplify this teaching, John of Hauville composed this line: "He is rockier than a rock, tigrier than a tiger, hydrier than Hydra." But once we saw this lesson, he had us erase it and put this instead, "He is more a Hydra than Hydra, more a tiger than a tiger, more a rock than a rock." All the same, there are some nouns, both appellatives and substantives, that because of their underlying connotation tasteful distortion has given a comparative form to, nouns such as "tyro," a novice soldier: "In weaponry, Hector was tyronier than Achilles," that is, more of a novice. "Melody," tunefulness; "melodier," more tuneful: "The parrot has a call, but the nightingale is melodier than the parrot." "Tyrant," a cruel lord: "This soldier is tyranter than Herod."

11 Sunt etiam quaedam adiectiva positiva quae tamen accepta per se perfectionem notant. Qualia sunt haec: "plenus," "perfectus," et eorum adverbia, quia pleno nihil plenius—et tamen in solemni usu habentur eorum comparativa, ratione abundantiae notandae. Sunt et alia minus usitata, ut "tersus," "elimatus," "purgatus," "praesens," "inclinatus," "defectus," "defaecatus," "inquisitus," "exactus," "pressus," et huiusmodi, et talium adverbia. Hiis omnibus assumimus comparativa, utentes etiam illis quandoque pro positivis. Bernardus Silvestris: "Erat igitur videre velut in speculo tersiore," id est valde puro. Et alibi: "Cumque quam fert Silva grossitiem elimatius expurgasset," id est elimate et perfecte. Inveniri etiam possunt "purgatius," "inclinatius," "inquisitius," "exactius," "pressius." Item "praesentius," id est citius; "defectius," id est debiliter et imperfecte; "defecatius," id est valde munde. Possumus etiam eleganter activae terminationis participia comparare, ut "amantior," "florentior," et talia maxime de quibus super egimus, scilicet "comantior," "viridantior."

12 Superlativa pari vice aliquotiens assumuntur. Verbi gratia, medio nihil magis medium, et tamen "medioximum" invenitur. Bernardus: "Eorum singulo occupato domicilio ad quod consensu materiae inclinatius ferebatur, sedit tellus, ignis emicuit, aer, aqua medioximi substiterunt." Item quadam quasi abusiva comparatione ipsa comparativa, immo etiam et superlativa, aliquotiens similitudinarie comparamus per adiectionem huius vocis "plusquam," ut si dicat

PART 2

Furthermore, there are certain positive adjectives that when taken alone imply in themselves perfection, such as "full," "perfect," and their adverbs, since nothing is fuller than the full—and yet their comparatives appear in formal writing in order to emphasize abundance. There are other examples too, though less common ones: "clean," "refined," "purged," "present," "bent down," "worn out," "purified," "unexamined," "exact," "depressed," and the like, and their adverbs. For all these we adopt comparatives, even using them sometimes as positives. Bernard Silvester: "It was possible then to see as if in a cleaner mirror," that is, exceedingly clear. And elsewhere: "And when she had purified the coarseness that Silva produces in a more refined way," that is, refinedly and perfectly. You can also find "in a more purged way," "in a more downward bent way," "in a more unexamined way," "more exactly," "in a more depressed way." Also "more presently," that is, "more quickly"; "in a more worn-out way," that is, weakly and imperfectly; "more purifiedly," that is, exceedingly cleanly. We can also tastefully make comparative participles with an active ending, such as "more loving," "more flourishing," and especially the ones we treated above, namely, "more luxuriant," "more verdant."

Sometimes superlatives are employed in a similar move. For example, nothing is more middling than the middle, and yet we find the word "middlemost." Bernard: "When each of these bodies had occupied the abode to which it was most disposed to be carried by the consent of matter, the earth sank down, fire sprang upward, and air and water settled middlemost." Also by a kind of abuse of comparison, we sometimes in similar fashion compare the comparative itself, and even the superlative too, by adding the phrase "more than," as if the parrot should say to the nightingale,

psittacus philomenae, "Veni, plusquam dilecta, plusquam dilectior, plusquam dilectissima, ut uterque sub fago patula audienti Tityro tympanizet." Verba sunt Iohannis Hauvillensis. Quid similiter si dicerem circa verbum hoc modo: "Diligo te certe, sed plusquam diligo?"

13 Propria etiam nomina quandoque sibi pluralia assumunt, quod fit dupliciter. Quandoque per similitudinem quam habet singulare cum appellativo, ex eo scilicet quod sicut appellativum plura comprehendit eodem modo et proprium, quamvis hoc univoce, illud equivoce, ut "Duorum Aiacum alter Locrius, alter Telamonis filius," id est vocatorum hoc nomine Aiax. Bernardus:

> Secana prosiliit, ubi grandia germina regum
>   Pipinos, Karolos bellica terra tulit.

Martialis Coquus:

> Marone felix Mantua est,
> . . . .
> Nasone Paeligni sonant,
> duosque Senecas unicumque Lucanum
> facunda loquitur Corduba.

Id est, "vocatos hoc nomine Seneca."

Quandoque per similitudinem quam habet cum appellativo, ex eo quod aliquod appellativum designat aliquod accidens expresse, et proprium dat intelligere illud idem, quamvis inexpresse, ut "fortis" significat hoc accidens "forte"; "Achilles" vel "Hercules" dat idem cointelligere. Secundum hoc dici potest, "Veniunt plusquam CC milites, omnes Hectores vel Aiaces." Martialis:

PART 2

"O more than dear, more than dearer, more than dearest, come let us both make our music beneath the spreading beech with Tityrus as audience." John of Hauville wrote that. What if I talked similarly with a verb, thus: "I love you surely, I more than love you?"

Sometimes proper nouns employ plurals, in two ways. Sometimes this happens because of the likeness that the singular has to a common noun, for just as any common noun has a plural, so can a proper noun, in the same way (though simply, where the common noun does so equivocally), as: "Of the two Ajaxes," that is, the two men called by the name Ajax, "one is Locrian, the other the son of Telamon." Bernard:

> The Seine rises up where a warlike land bore the great ancestors of kings, the Pippins and Charleses.

Martial the Cook:

> Mantua is happy in Maro . . . the Paeligni resound with Naso, eloquent Cordoba speaks of the two Senecas and the single Lucan.

That is, "those called by the name Seneca."

And sometimes because of the likeness it has to the common noun, in that a common noun designates an accident directly, and a proper noun gives one to understand the same thing, but indirectly, as "a brave man" signifies the accident "bravery"; "Achilles" or "Hercules" gives one to understand the same thing, so that one can say, "Here come more than two hundred soldiers, all of them Hectors or Ajaxes." Martial:

> Insanis! Omnis gelidis quicumque lacernis
> sunt ibi, Nasones, Virgiliosque vides.

Sunt quidam qui dicunt huiusmodi dictiones de quibus supra egimus inveniri non licere, sicut nec illa comparativa "petrior," "ganimedior," et exponunt illum versum Horatii, "Licuit semperque licebit, etc."

De transumptione metaphorica dicentes licuit semper producere, id est extendere ad aliam significationem per metaphoram "nomen signatum" (intellige "praesente nota") id est, manifesta ratione transumptionis, ut hic: "Ulmosque maritat vitibus," id est coniungit individua coniunctione iuxta descriptionem matrimonii. Sed quid dicerent de hiis versibus?

> Candida morus erat niveique puerpera fructus,
>   sed roseat byssum, purpura poma cruor.

Condemnabuntne hoc verbum "roseat"? Quid de hoc verbo "enucleat" pro "manifestat"? Videtur enim inventicium et ficticium esse. Quid de verbis tranformatis ab omnibus fere comparativis, ut "altiorat," "peiorat," "maiorat"? Sed dicunt forte huiusmodi verba esse inventa ab antiquis, sed ipsi defectum dictionum suppleverunt; modo sufficiunt dictiones et quicquid apponeremus ex superfluo esset. Magister vero Iohannes sententiam suam confirmavit per alium versum Horatii, "Multa renascentur quae iam cecidere," dicens

PART 2

> Crazy! Everybody you see there, freezing in their raincoats; they're all Ovids or Virgils.

There are those who say that inventing words of the sort I have been treating above is not allowed, just as they say comparatives such as "cliffier" and "ganymedier" aren't, and they have their own interpretation of Horace's line, "It was allowed, and always will be allowed, etc."

Speakers have always been permitted, by means of metaphorical transference, to draw out—that is, to extend to another meaning—by metaphor a "coined noun" (understand "with an immediately evident significance"), that is, with a clear rationale for the transference, as in this case: "And he marries elms to vines," that is, joins them in an indivisible joining, just like the description of matrimony. But what would they have said about these verses?

> White was the mulberry and pregnant with snowy fruit, but blood rosies the linen veil and the purple fruit.

Will they condemn the verb "rosy"? What about the verb "unshell" for "make plain"? It seems made up, factitious. What about the verbs derived from almost any comparative, verbs such as "highers," "worsens," "largers"? They may say, of course, that yes, verbs of this kind were invented by the ancients, but the ancients compensated for a deficiency of words; we have enough words now, anything we might add would be superfluous. Master John, though, backed up his opinion with another line of Horace's, "Many things that have now fallen away will be reborn," implying, perhaps,

forte huiusmodi verba non nunc primo inventa sed ab antiquo usu lapsa iterum renasci. Et per illum:

> Et nova fictaque nuper habebunt verba fidem si
> Graeco fonte cadant, parce distorta.

Item per illum:

> Dixeris egregie notum si callida verbum
> reddiderit iunctura novum.

Sed nulla ratio adeo fortis quae confutari non possit vel vere vel imaginarie. Consulat igitur unusquisque discretionem suam, et vel nullam novam inveniat dictionem, vel quod melius est inveniat.

Inventam tamen excuset subtilitas inventionis—etiam raritas et dicendi puritas veniam mereatur. Quidam adeo rigidi—nescio dicam an pavidi sunt—quod neque frequentativa, neque meditativa, neque inchoativa, neque possessiva, neque patronymica, neque diminutiva audeant invenire. Non simus uter adeo demissi ut suscipiamus huiusmodi "petrior," "ganimedior," "praeliliat," "praerosulat," neque tam rigidi ut ille qui condempnavit hanc dictionem "Iovina" quia in bibliotheca theologica non invenitur. Quis audeat Bernardo derogare qui tamen usus est hiis dictionibus "praegnat," "primitiat," dicens,

> Illic temperies, illic clementia caeli
> floribus et vario germine praegnat humum.

that words of this kind are not newly invented but have fallen from the use of antiquity and are born again. He would also cite:

> New and recently made-up words will be trusted if they spring from a Greek font, minimally adapted.

And this:

> You will have spoken well if a clever juxtaposition has made a word new.

But no reasoning is so powerful that it cannot be countered, whether in truth or in appearance. In short, everyone should consult his own discrimination, and either invent no new word, or invent something better.

All the same, an invented word may be excused by the subtlety of the invention—and rarity and purity of speech may also earn indulgence. There are some people who are so rigid—I don't know whether I should say so fearful—that they don't dare invent anything, whether frequentative or meditative, or inchoative verbs, possessives, patronymics, or diminutives. We should not be either so permissive as to accept words such as "rockier," "ganymedier," "she outlilies," "she outroses," nor as rigid as the person who condemned the word "Jovine" because it is not found in the theological corpus. Who would dare to question Bernard, who used the words "pregnate" and "primitiate," writing,

> There the mildness of the climate, there the kindness of heaven pregnates the earth with flowers and various fruits.

14

Item:

> In caelo divina manus caelique ministris
> omne creaturae primitiavit opus.

Videtur certe mihi in huiusmodi euphoniam cum ratione plenius operari. Scio magistrum Rogerum Devoniensem non consentire quibusdam supradictis, qui versum illum Horatii, "Licuit semperque licebit, etc.," speciali suo modo exposuit de memoria comparanda. Sed auctori credendum est potius quam lectori: illi scripserunt, ipse legit. Expositores inveniunt litteram meretricem; scriptores vero auctorum molestias, auctorum necessitates et indigentias sunt experti. Inventicium videtur hoc nomen "infantaria"— propter sui saltem raritatem. Et tamen Martialis Coquus ait,

> Infantes secum semper tua Bassa, Fabulla,
> collocat et lusus deliciasque vocat,
> et, quo mireris magis, infantaria non est.
> Ergo quid in causa est? Pedere Bassa solet.

Item Servius: "Demosthenes, rogatus ut pro re publica os suum aperiret, ait, 'Non possum synanchen patior.' Responsum est ei, 'Non synanchen, sed argyranchen.' Acceperat enim, ut putabatur, argentum tacendi causa."

15 Per onomatopoeiam etiam invenerunt antiqui quaedam nomina, sicut puteus inferni a sono suo dicitur "Tartara"; similiter "obba" monachorum. Item clangor tubarum et tinnitus aeris. Hic modus inveniendi apud modernos nullus vel rarus est.

PART 2

Again:

> From heaven and the ministers of heaven the divine hand primitiated every work of creation.

He certainly seems to me, for euphony of this kind, to be acting perfectly reasonably. I know that Master Roger of Devon does not agree with some of the things I have been saying. He used to explain Horace's line, "It was allowed, and always will be allowed," in his own special way, as about acquiring memory. But the author must be trusted, rather than a reader: they wrote, he just reads. Critics find a text corrupt, but writers have experienced authorial vexations, compulsions, and needs. The noun "infantary" ("baby-minder") seems like a coinage—at the very least because of its rarity. And yet Martial the Cook says,

> Your friend Bassa, Fabulla, always gathers babies around her and calls them her toys and her sweethearts, and what will surprise you all the more, she is not an infantary. But what's the reason? Bassa is always farting.

Likewise Servius: "Demosthenes, asked to open his mouth on behalf of the state, said, 'I can't, I have laryngitis.' They said back, 'Not laryngitis, but silveritis.' For they thought he had been paid to be silent."

The ancients also invented some nouns by onomatopoeia: the pit of hell is called "Tartarus" from its sound, and the monks' *obba* (fat-bottomed bowl) is similarly named. Also the clangor of tubas and the tinkle of brass. This mode of invention comes up rarely or never nowadays.

16 Vox significativa assumitur per similitudinem extra sumptam, et hoc quando dictio quae uno modo est significativa assumitur alio modo secundum quod non est significativa, quod fit multipliciter. Contingit enim quandoque quod dictio que est tantum singularis numeri assumitur pluraliter, ut si pro hac, "tres boni milites," dicam "tres Achilles." Quandoque contingit quod illa quae brevis est per naturam subtilitate quadam producitur, vel e converso, ut patet in hoc versu, "In nobis amor, in reliquis sit amor," hac scilicet exili similitudine ut, sicut prima huius dictionis "amor" hic longa fit, eodem modo longum significet amorem vel, si vultis ut dicam, consignificet longitudinem. Similiter, "Qui spernunt decus, dedecus assit eis."

Quandoque contingit quod vox aliqua assumitur ad aliud significandum, quia illa vox quae assumitur et res ad quam assumitur uno et eodem modo repraesentantur, verbi gratia: data magistro Iohanni de Hauvilla materia de quodam cratere aureo quem vulgariter "cuppam" appellamus, ut per prosopopoeiam faceret illam dicere se totam valere quinque marcas auri, dixit, "De tali censu sum, marcas tota valens v." Ecce assumitur haec vox "v" vocalis ad significandum "quinque," quia figura ipsius repraesentat ipsam vocem et etiam illum numerum; et bene dicitur fieri per similitudinem extra sumptam, quia, quamvis haec vox "v" sit significativa et aequivoce appellet duo, scilicet se ipsam et figuram incausti illam, tamen neutra illarum significationum operatur ad assumptionem. Possit enim "v" vox ipsa non esse nomen sui ipsius vel nomen figurae, et tamen repraesentari per figuram et eadem ratione assumi. Hii duo modi ultimi subtiles sunt

PART 2

A signifying term is used because of an external likeness, 16 when a word that signifies in one way is used in another way with a significance it does not properly bear. This is done in several different ways. Thus, it happens sometimes that a word that occurs only in the singular is used plurally, as if for "three good soldiers" I say, "three Achilleses." Sometimes it happens that what is short by nature is subtly lengthened, or vice versa, as is evident in this line of verse, "There is long love in us, let there be short love in the others," with this slight analogy that just as the first syllable of the word *amor* (love) is here made long, in the same way it signifies a long love, or, if you prefer this wording, it carries the additional meaning of length. Likewise, "Let those who spurn honor have dishonor."

Sometimes it happens that a word is appropriated to mean something else, because the word that is appropriated and the subject for which it is appropriated are represented in one and the same way. For example, Master John of Hauville was given the subject of a golden bowl that we call in English a cup, and in order to make it declare by personification that in total it was worth five marks of gold, said, "I'm so wealthy: in total I am worth five marks." The word "v," as a word, is appropriated to mean "five (marks)," because its shape represents that word and also that number, and it is rightly said to function by external likeness because, even though the word "v" is meaningful and ambiguously summons up two things, that is, itself and the shape of the ink, still neither of those meanings causes the appropriation. For the word "v" itself could also be not its own name or the name of the shape, and yet be represented by the shape and employed in the same way. These last two modes

et apti iocantibus, non sunt tamen operibus auctenticis imponendi.

17 Non procul hinc catachresim censeo, quae interpretatur "abusio," et est usurpatio nominis alieni, ut parricidam dicimus eum qui occidit fratrem, et piscinam quae pisces non habet. Haec enim nisi extrinsecus sumerent vocabula sua non haberent. Videri enim potest catachresim citra transumptionem propter imperfectam rationem transumendi. Huius species videri potest quidam modus ornatissimus, scilicet quando quodam modo coartamus dictionem aliquam ad quandam novam significationem vel consignificationem ratione necessitatis, non propter aliquam similitudinem. Secundum hoc Cicero quandoque distinguit inter "laetari" et "gaudere." Hegesippus etiam distinctione utitur hiis verbis "assumere" et "accipere," per verbum asssumendi connotans violentiam, per verbum accipiendi libertatem sive iustitiam, dicens, "Longe dicebant Archelaum Herode intolerabiliorem futurum, cum iste assumpserit regnum, ille acceperit." Herodes enim electione Caesaris sive dono accepit, Archelaus violenter usurpavit quasi heres Herodis.

18 Transumptio est translatio vocis a propria significatione ad alienam per similitudinem intransumptam. Intransumpta est similitudo quae sumitur a vocis significatione quam habet ex principali institutione. Transumptionum alia dictionis, alia orationis. Dictionis, ut "Pratum ridet"; orationis, ut "Litus aratur." Transumptio dictionis metaphora dicitur a Donato, et ab ipso per "animale" et per "inanimale" quadrupliciter dividitur—quam divisionem nos omittimus. Metaphorarum alia absoluta, alia respectiva. Absoluta est

are subtle: good for witty play, but not to be introduced into serious writing.

17 I consider catachresis not far from this. It means "misuse," the usurping of the name of something else, as we call someone who kills his brother a parricide, and speak of a *piscina* (fishpond) which has no fish. There would be no word for these things unless they received them from outside. It can seem right for catachresis to come before metaphor because of its incomplete justification for transference. There is a certain very pretty mode that can be thought of as a kind of catachresis, I mean when to some degree we force a word into a new meaning or additional meaning out of necessity, and not because of any likeness. Thus Cicero sometimes distinguishes between *laetari* (to feel pleasure) and *gaudere* (to feel joy). Hegesippus too makes a distinction between the words *assumere* (to take) and *accipere* (to receive), introducing the connotation of violence with *assumere* and of freedom or justice with *accipere,* saying, "They said that Archelaus would be far more intolerable than Herod, since he took the kingdom, Herod received it." For Herod received the kingdom by Caesar's selection of him, or by his gift; Archelaus violently usurped it as Herod's heir.

18 Metaphor is the transference of a word from its proper meaning to a different one by means of an untransferred likeness, that is, a likeness inherent in the meaning the word had originally. Metaphors are either of a word or a sentence. Of a word, as "The meadow is laughing"; of a sentence, as "The beach is being plowed." Transference of a word is called metaphor by Donatus and divided by him into four kinds under both "animate" and "inanimate"—a division we are leaving out. Metaphors are either absolute or respective.

metaphora ubi dictio transumpta non respicit aliam dictionem appositam coadiuvantem eius transumptionem, ut hic: "Pratum ridet," id est floret. Haec fit multipliciter secundum diversas partes orationis.

19 Nomen igitur proprium quandoque transumitur ad tenendum appellative et hoc tum substantive, tum adiective. Substantive, et secundum hoc distributionem admittit sicut appellativum, ut si pro hac, "nullus bonus miles," dicam, "nullus Hector" vel "nullus Achilles." Pro "amica" similiter ponitur "Phyllis," "Corinna," "Amaryllis," "Galathea": "Nullam puto Phyllida nosti," id est, nullam amicam. "Tuus Pamphilus," id est, tuus amicus. Similiter pro hac, "Amicus amico salutem," solet dici, "Pirithoo suo suus Theseus salutem," et consimiles. Pro hac dictione "tyrannus" poni possunt haec et huiusmodi: "Herodes," "Nero," "Phalaris," "Busiris." Verbi gratia, in epitaphio dictum est,

Hic iacet Herodes Herode tyrannior: huius
spiritus infernum polluit, ossa solum.

Quandoque transumitur ad tenendum pro forma aliqua emphatice, ut hic:

Dantur item fato casuque cadunt iterato
Simone sublato Mars, Paris atque Cato.

Mars, id est militia; Paris, id est pulchritudo; Cato, id est sapientia.

20 Notandum ergo quod ex intentione transumentis transumptae dictionis significatio variatur. In huiusmodi enim transumptione, quandoque respicitur status ipsius cuius nomen transumitur, quandoque tantum vicina convertibilitas

PART 2

In an absolute metaphor, the transferred word does not look to another nearby word to aid the metaphor, as here: "The meadow is laughing," that is, blooming. This is done in many ways according to the different parts of speech.

Sometimes a proper noun is transferred to act in a common role, either as a noun or as an adjective. When it acts as a noun, it admits the same usage as a common noun, as if instead of "no good soldier," I should say "no Hector" or "no Achilles." Likewise for "girlfriend," put "Phyllis" or "Corinna" or "Amaryllis" or "Galatea": "You have no Phyllis, I think," that is, no girlfriend. "Your Pamphilus," that is, your boyfriend. Again, instead of "A friend greets a friend," it's often said, "His Theseus greets his Pirithous," and like names. Instead of "tyrant" we can say "Herod," "Nero," "Phalaris," "Busiris," and so on. For example, there was an epitaph with the words,

> Here lies a Herod more tyrannical than Herod; his soul is polluting hell, his bones this soil.

Sometimes a proper noun is transferred to serve as an emphatic form of some word, as here:

> Simon is dead, and Mars, Paris, and Cato succumb again to fate; they fall in a second fall.

Mars, that is, military might; Paris, that is, beauty; Cato, that is, wisdom.

It is important to note that the meaning of the metaphoric term varies with the intention of the maker of the metaphor. For in a metaphor of this kind, sometimes the point is the condition of the person whose name is transferred, sometimes only the close interchangeability of

terminorum, illius scilicet qui transumitur et illius pro quo transumitur. Status respicitur ut si dicam: "Iste est alter Tantalus." Quia fuit Tantalus in divitiis quibus uti non potuit, ideo transumo hanc dictionem "Tantalus" ad significandum idem quod haec vox "indigens in copia" vel "egenus in abundantia": "Parisius dego, Tantalus alter ego." Respicitur vicina convertibilitas terminorum, ut si dicam, "Pirothous est alter Theseus." In hac non respicio statum Thesei, sed transumo hanc dictionem "Theseus" ad significandum idem quod haec vox significat, "volens omnia quae Theseus," quia illi duo termini fere convertuntur. Patet ergo quod secundum diversam transumentis intentionem haec dupliciter potest intelligi, "Iste est alter Pyramus." Si respicitur status, exponi potest "Pyramus, id est, amicus exclusus a voluntate." Unde illud, "Vivit adhuc Pyramus, Thisbe dilectissimus." Si convertibilitas, exponi potest "Pyramus, id est, omnia volens quae Pyramus." Unde illud,

> Nodus amoris eos constrinxit et altera Thisbe
> Pyramus, et Thisbe Pyramus alter erat.

21 Quandoque transumitur nomen proprium ad significandum adiective. Sed tunc quandoque propter obscuritatem locutionis exigit determinari ablativo sub electione exprimente pro quo adiectivo ponitur. Verbi gratia, si velim dicere Agenor pulcher erat et dicam "Agenor erat Paris," obscurus est sermo. Nescitur enim an intendam dicere eum esse lascivum an pulchrum an debilem. Apponitur ergo ablativus hoc modo, "Agenor erat Paris ore." Haec dictio "ore"

terms—namely, the one that is transferred and the one in place of which the transference is effected. Condition is referred to if I should say, "This man is a second Tantalus." Since Tantalus was placed among wealth that he could not use, I transfer the word Tantalus to mean the same as "needy in the midst of wealth," or "poor in the midst of abundance": "I live in Paris, I'm a second Tantalus." Close interchangeability of the terms is in question if I say, "Pirithous is a second Theseus." In this example, I ignore the condition of Theseus but transfer the name "Theseus" to carry the sense of the phrase "wanting all that Theseus wants," because the two terms are almost interchangeable. It is clear, then, that depending on the intention of the transferer, the phrase "This man is a second Pyramus" can be understood in two ways. If his condition is referred to, "Pyramus" can be understood to mean "a lover shut out from his desire," thus, "Pyramus is alive today, most dear to his Thisbe." If interchangeability, "Pyramus" means "wanting all that Pyramus wants," and so,

> The knot of love bound them together: Pyramus was a second Thisbe and Thisbe a second Pyramus.

Sometimes a proper noun is taken over to carry an adjectival sense. But then sometimes the expression is so obscure that it has to be modified by an ablative chosen to make clear what adjective it is being used for. For example, if I want to say that Agenor was handsome, and I say "Agenor was a Paris," the sentence is obscure because it is not clear whether I want to say he was lustful or handsome or weak. And so an ablative is added in the following way, "Agenor was a Paris in looks." The word *ore* (face) offers two meanings

21

duo praetendit sub electione, pulchritudinem et turpitudinem. Haec dictio "Paris" formam eligit. Sub hoc modo loquendi per aggregationem ornatissime possumus quempiam vel commendare vel vituperare. Commendare marem hoc modo:

> Ore Paris, fama Pelides, viribus Hector,
>   censu Croesus, avis Caesar: Agenor erat.

Feminam hoc modo:

> Marcia consilio, gestu Lucretia, vita
>   Penelope, facie Tyndaris: Io fuit.

Vituperare sic:

> Actibus Herodes, animo Nero, Byrrhia verbis,
>   fraude Sinon, Proteus pectore: Davus erat.

22   Quandoque transumitur nomen patris mediante auxilio adiectivi ad significandum hoc accidens filius, et sumitur similitudo ab illo generali, "Saepe solet similis filius esse patri." Virgilius, in conquestione Didonis de discessu Aeneae, ait, "Utinam mihi parvulus aula luderet Aeneas," id est, filius Aeneae repraesentans ipsum tamquam filius patrem.

Alio etiam modo transumitur nomen proprium quando scilicet aliquis auctenticus vir assumpsit nomen illud vicini a proprietate, alius vero imitando eum quodammodo a longe sumpsit illud remotius a proprietate. Videns Iuvenalis Virgilium sumpsisse hoc nomen Aeneas pro hoc appellativo filius, similiter assumpsit, non tamen pro filio Aeneae sicut Virgilius. Dicit enim Iuvenalis,

to choose from, good looks or brazenness, but the word "Paris" selects "good looks." If we amass phrases of this kind, we can praise or blame somebody very eloquently. We can praise a man in this way:

> In looks a Paris, in fame an Achilles, in strength a Hector, in wealth a Croesus, in ancestry a Caesar: that was Agenor.

We can praise a woman in this way,

> A Marcia in her thoughtfulness, a Lucretia in her bearing, a Penelope in her life, a Helen in her beauty: that was Io.

We can blame thus:

> A Herod in his actions, a Nero in spirit, a Byrrhia in his talk, a Sinon in his lies, a Proteus at heart: that was Davus.

Sometimes a father's name is transferred with the help of an adjective to mean the accident, his son, the likeness depending on the proverb, "Like father, like son." Virgil, in Dido's complaint about Aeneas's departure, says, "If only a little Aeneas of mine were playing in the palace," that is, a son of Aeneas's, standing for him as the son the father.

A proper noun is transferred in another fashion, namely, when some actual person has taken up that name of a relation appropriately, but another, imitating him after a fashion, has taken it up from afar and further afield from what is appropriate. Juvenal, seeing that Virgil had taken the name Aeneas for the common noun "son," likewise had recourse to it, but not as Virgil did for a son of Aeneas's. For Juvenal says,

> Dominus tamen et domini rex
> si vis tu fieri, nullus tibi parvulus aula
> luserit Aeneas.

Id est filius. Uterque transumpsit, sed Iuvenalis magis: similitudo enim Iuvenalis non potest bene dici intransumpta. Simile alibi: Ucalegon proprium nomen erat cuiusdam personae in Virgilio qui in combustione Troiae res suas transtulit anxius. Virgilius eo nomine proprie usus est, dicens, "Iam proximus ardet Ucalegon," scilicet vicinus Aeneae. Iuvenalis transumpsit illud idem nomen ad quemcumque vicinum in tali necessitate detentum, dicens, "Iam poscit aquas, iam frivola transfert Ucalegon." Eodem modo alibi loquitur Iuvenalis de Romanis qui adulantur divitibus cum sint in mari, et sacrificant diis ut possint divites evadere tempestates, dicens,

> Pueris et frontibus ancillarum
> imponet vittas et si qua est nubilis illi
> Iphigenia domi. . . .

Iphigenia, id est, filia quam possit sacrificare. Et hoc ideo dicit, quia a Virgilio habuit Iphigeniam filiam Agamemnonis adiudicatam sacrificio in Aulide insula. Eadem ratione, si vellem admovere aliquem ut rediret domum, quia ipse habet domi uxorem et patrem et filium, dicerem ornatissime,

> Ut redeas tua Penelope ferventius instat:
> sunt tibi Laertes Telemachusque domi,

ad imitationem Ovidii dicentis, "Tres sumus imbelles numero, etc." Ipse proprie usus est propriis nominibus, ego transumptive.

PART 2

But if you want to be lord and a king among lords, no little Aeneas should be playing in your palace.

That is, no son. Both have practiced a transference, but Juvenal more distantly: the likeness he draws can hardly be spoken without a metaphor. Here is a similar instance: Ucalegon was the proper name for a character in Virgil who when Troy was in flames carried off his things in a panic. Virgil used his name in its proper sense, saying, "Now next to him Ucalegon is burning," that is, near Aeneas. Juvenal made a metaphor of the same name, using it for any neighbor caught in such a crisis, saying, "Ucalegon is already shouting 'Water, water!,' already moving out his odds and ends." In the same way in another place Juvenal speaks of Romans who flatter the rich when they are at sea, offering sacrifices to the gods to enable the rich to escape storms:

> He will put sacrificial bands on his slave boys and on the foreheads of his slave girls, and if there is a marriageable Iphigenia in the house. . . .

Iphigenia, that is, a daughter he could sacrifice. He says it because he knew from Virgil that Iphigenia, Agamemnon's daughter, was sentenced to be sacrificed on the island of Aulis. In the same way, if I wanted to urge someone to go back home because he had a wife and a father and a son at home, I might say, very prettily,

> Your Penelope is pressing you very eagerly to come home: you have a Laertes and a Telemachus there,

in imitation of Ovid's saying, "Three in number, we are unfit for war, etc." He used those proper names properly, I am using them metaphorically.

23 Nominum appellativorum aliud substantivum, aliud adiectivum. Substantivum transumitur multipliciter: quandoque ad tenendum pro adiectivo, quandoque pro substantivo. Pro adiectivo multipliciter: Quandoque absque determinatione, ut si pro hac, "Hostes nostri non venient desides, sed feroces," dicam, "Non venient asini, sed leones." Hic modus tum fit per appositionem, ut hic: "Nascitur et puero vagit nova pagina versu." Puero, id est novo. Quandoque cum determinatione, et hoc tum praepositionis, tum ablativi, tum etiam genitivi. Praepositionis, ut hic, "In prosaico psittacus, in metrico philomena." Ablativi, ad similitudinem propriorum nominum, ut hic, "Iste fuit nanus corpore, mente gigas." Genitivi, ut hic, "Succedet asinus nequitiae."

24 Substantivum transumitur pro substantivo, ut si pro hac dictione "candor" ponam "lilia" vel "ebur," pro "rubore" "rosam," pro hac voce "suavis odor," "balsama," "lacrimas" pro "petitione lacrimabili," quae scilicet fit cum lacrimis. Bernardus: "Has lacrimas tener orbis habet." Item, pro "serie" ponitur "textus," quia sicut textus successivus est, et in texendo quiddam expressa successione prius, quiddam posterius fit, eodem modo in serie quacumque, et maxime temporis. Bernardus: "Illic exarata supremi digito dispositoris textus temporis, fatalis series, dispositio saeculorum." Et hic fit illa realis repetitio supradicta, quia "textus," "series," "dispositio" hic pro synonymis habentur. (Sed notandum quod non fit competens transumptio si pro hac, "Albedo est color disgregativus visus," dicam, "Ebur est color disgregativus visus" vel "Lilia sunt color, etc.")

Oportet ergo quod huiusmodi transumptio determinetur vel remote vel proxime. Remote, scilicet ex alia parte

PART 2

Common nouns are either substantives or adjectives. The substantive is transferred in many ways: sometimes to be used for an adjective, sometimes for a noun. For an adjective, in many ways: Sometimes without a modifier, as if, instead of, "Our enemies won't come idle but fierce," I should say that they "won't come asses but lions." This mode also occurs through apposition, as here: "A new page is born and wails in infant verse." Infant, that is, new. Sometimes with modification by a prepositional phrase, an ablative, or even a genitive. By a prepositional phrase, as "A parrot in prose and a nightingale in poetry." By an ablative, just as with proper nouns, as "He was a dwarf in body, a giant in mind." By a genitive, as "An ass of wickedness will follow."

A noun is transferred for a noun, as if for the word "whiteness" I should put "lilies" or "ivory," for "redness" "rose," for the phrase "sweet smell," "balms," "tears" for "a tearful request" (that is, one made with tears). Bernard: "These tears the tender world has." Also "text" is put for "series," since—just as a text involves a succession, and in composing a text in an obvious succession one thing is earlier, another later—the same process applies in any series, especially one of time. Bernard: "There, inscribed by the finger of the supreme arbiter, was the text of time, the series of fate, the arrangement of the ages." And here we have that repetition of content that I spoke of earlier, because "text," "series," and "arrangement" are synonyms here. (Note, though, that it is not a true metaphor if for "Whiteness is a color that dazzles the vision" I should say, "Ivory is a color that dazzles the vision," or "Lilies are a color, etc.")

A metaphor of this kind has to be modified, either remotely or proximately. It is modified remotely from another

constructionis, ut "Lilia mixta rosis faciem pinxere puelle." Haec dictio "faciem" ex parte praedicati determinat transumptionem quae fit ex parte subiecti, quia per hanc dictionem "faciem" patet manifeste quod haec dictio "lilia" ponitur pro candore. Proxime, ut hic:

> Consona sunt aliis oris rosa, balsama naris,
>   nix auris, menti lilia, dentis ebur.

25   Item nota quod frequentissime contingit poni in transumptione antecedens pro consequente, ut si lucem alienam appellem "diem" per transumptionem, ut hic: "Stellarum contenta die lunaeque sereno / ivit. . . ." Sed huiusmodi sunt exempla mutationis de qua supra egimus. Nec miremur si ad unum et idem diversis modis pervenimus. Notandum tamen quod in hoc differe videntur mutatio et transumptio, quod secundum quosdam in mutatione frequenter dicimus substantivum pro verbo, in transumptione vero dicimus id ad quod transumitur vox.

26   Commune est nomini proprio et appellativo quod utrumque transumitur quandoque ad supponendum collective. Secundum hoc haec dictio "rex" supponit quandoque ipsum hominem cum statu, ut appelletur status ipse habitus—omnia scilicet vestimenta sua et omnia arma. Unde secundum hoc conceditur quod rex est plura. Unde dicitur, "Iste percussit regem in galea qui galeam percussit; tetigit puellam qui tunicam eius tetigit; calcavit super eam qui super vestes eius calcavit." Ratio huius transumptionis est quod ea quae ad ornatum rei sunt quasi de esse eius sunt. Sunt enim partes exigitivae et adiacentes.

part of the same sentence, as "Lilies mixed with roses painted the girl's face." The word "face," part of the predicate, modifies the metaphor that is part of the subject, because it is the word "face" that makes it clear that "lilies" stands for whiteness. Proximately, as here:

> Harmonious with each other are the rose of her mouth, the balms of her nose, the snow of her ear, the lilies of her chin, the ivory of her tooth.

Again, note that very often the antecedent is put by metaphor for the consequent, as is the case if I call moonlight "day" by metaphor, as in this case: "Content with the day of stars and the cloudless moon, she went. . . ." Effects of this kind are examples of mutation, which we have treated above. Nor should we be surprised if we arrive at one and the same thing in different ways. All the same, you should note that mutation and metaphor seem to differ in this regard, that (according to some) in mutation we often use a noun for a verb, but in metaphor we specify what a word is transferred to.

A proper noun and a common noun share this property, that either sometimes suggests by transference a collective sense. Thus the word "king" sometimes suggests the man with his regal status, so that his very regalia—his clothing and all his weapons—is his status. So we just have to grant that "king" has multiple senses. And so it is said, "He who has struck the king's helmet has struck the king by striking the helmet; he who has touched a girl's dress has touched her; he who has stepped on her clothing has stepped on her." The rationale of this metaphor is that the things that serve to adorn something are of its essence. For parts are not just adjacent but exigitive.

27   Nomen adiectivum transumitur ad tenendum pro alio adiectivo, ut si dicam "fenestratum" pro "apertum," ut hic, "rete fenestratum." "Tunicatus," id est, "opertus" vel "clausus"; Bernardus: "Dividit in species tunicata legumina tellus." "Defaecatus," id est, "purgatus." Cum enim proprie loquor, "Nihil defaecari potest nisi quod faecem habet," Bernardus tamen transumptive ait, "Ex aetheris serenitate et liquore aeris defaecatam opifex puritatem excepit." Item "agninus," "roseus," et huiusmodi transumuntur. Cum enim proprie agninum sit quod de agno est, ut caro et vellus, per transumptionem tamen dicitur agninum quod mite est ut agnus, et huiusmodi. Verbi gratia, "Agninus dominus facit ut sit verna caprinus."

28   Ut secundum Donati ordinem procedatur, pronomen quoque quandoque transumitur, et hoc tum ratione vicinae convertibilitatis terminorum. Sed nota: quandoque affectus tuus nomen operi tuo imponit. Et circumscripta voluntate omnis actus indifferens, et nihil hominem approbat vel condempnat plenius quam voluntas. Ideo tam proprium nomen quam pronomen potius transumitur ad supponendum voluntatem ipsius qui supponitur proprie per illum terminum. Ut si dicam, "Thisbe est Pyramus," id est, "voluntas Pyrami," ut emphatica sit locutio. Quae emphasis dupliciter potest intelligi, scilicet "quae nihil vult vel desiderat nisi Piramum," vel "quam vult Pyramus." Secundum hunc modum transumitur pronomen, et quoad significationem et quoad constructionem, ut si dicam, "Ego moritur," id est, "voluntas mea"; emphatice, id est, "amica mea" vel "quae omnia vult quae ego," vel "quam ego volo," vel "cuius velle ego volo." Magister Iohannes de Hauvilla ait, "Dii faciant sine me ne moriatur 'ego,'" et alius,

PART 2

An adjective is transferred to serve for another adjective, as if I should say "windowed" for "open," as here, "a windowed net." "Jacketed" for "covered" or "enclosed"; Bernard: "Earth divides the jacketed legumes into species." "Freed of feces," that is, "purged." For when I speak literally, nothing can be freed of feces except if it has feces, but Bernard says, metaphorically, "From the clarity of the ether and the liquid of the air, the Maker extracted feces-free purity." Again, "lamblike," "rosy," and the like are metaphors. Though literally "lamblike" refers to what is taken from a lamb, such as meat and sheepskin, still by metaphor what is soft as a lamb is said to be lamblike, and so on. For example, "A lamblike master causes a servant of his household to become goatlike."

To proceed in Donatus's order, a pronoun is also transferred sometimes by reason of close convertibility of terms. But note: sometimes an emotion of yours imposes a noun on your work. If the will is set aside, every action is indifferent; but nothing justifies or condemns a man more than his will. Therefore either a proper name or a pronoun is rather transferred to represent the will of the person who is properly represented by that term. As if, in order to speak emphatically, I should say, "Thisbe is Pyramus," that is, "Pyramus's desire." The emphasis can be taken in two ways, either "one who wants or desires nothing but Pyramus," or "whom Pyramus wants." A pronoun too is transferred in the same way, both in meaning and in grammatical function, as if I should say, "My I is dead," that is, "my desire"; emphatically, that is, "my lover," or "who wants everything I want," "whom I desire," or "whose wishes I wish for." Master John of Hauville said, "May the gods grant that my 'I' not die without me," and another said,

> Dum Cirrhae latices libavimus alter uterque
> vixit, eras ego tu tuque secundus ego.

Pronomen etiam quandoque transumitur ad supponendum, scilicet collective, ipsam rem et rei ornatum. Ovidius: "Pars minima est ipsa puella sui." Haec dictio "sui" consupponit puellam et vestes eius omnes, collective. Sed in hoc ampliatur improprietas, quia antecedens non transumitur et relativum transumitur. Haec dictio enim "puella" ibi supponit tantum unum, haec dictio "sui" plura, et est "simplex relatio." Respicit enim haec dictio "sui" suum antecedens non pro significatione quam hic habet, sed pro alia significatione, scilicet transumpta, secundum quod concedimus per transumptionem quod puella est plura, ut supra dictum est.

Verborum et participiorum transumptio exemplorum suppositione luce clarius elucescet. Fere enim quodlibet verbum de facili transumi potest. Verbi gratia, "amare": "Ulmos vitis amat," id est, crescit plenius in ulmis. "Docere": "Liber docet quid agendum." "Legere":

> Aethera scribuntur stellis, caelique libello
> astrologus ventura legit.

Id est, inquirit tamquam legens. "Audire": "Imperavit dominus ventis et mari, audierunt venti et siluerunt," id est, imitabantur audientem. "Vagire": "Hebe vagit infantia"; vagit, id est, tenera est. Architrenius: "Nascitur et puero vagit

PART 2

> While we drank the waters of Cirrha, both lived as the other—you were I and I a second you.

A pronoun is also sometimes transferred to suggest, simultaneously, both a thing itself and its adornment. Ovid: "The girl herself is the smallest part of herself." The phrase "of herself" connotes simultaneously both the girl and all her clothing. But impropriety is amplified in the process, because the antecedent is not subject to transference and what relates back to it is. For here the word "girl" suggests only one thing, the phrase "of herself" several, and bears a "simple relation." For "of herself" looks back to its antecedent not with regard to the meaning the antecedent has there but with regard to another meaning, a metaphorical one, according to which we grant by metaphor that the girl is several things, as was said above.

Metaphors of verbs and participles will shine more clearly than daylight by the introduction of examples. Almost any verb can easily be subject to transference. "To love," for example: "A vine loves elms," that is, it grows more fully on elms. "To teach": "A book teaches us what is to be done." "To read":

> The text of the heavens is inscribed by the stars, and in the book of the sky the astrologer reads things to come.

That is, he inquires into them as if he is reading. "To hear": "The Lord gave a command to the winds and the sea; the winds heard and became silent," that is, they imitated a person hearing. "To cry": "A baby cries because it can't talk yet," that is, "is of tender age." Architrenius: "A new page is born

nova pagina versu." "Texo, texis"; Bernardus: "Quae de optatis texebatur oratio, delicias fecerat audiendi." "Vireo, vires"; Statius: "Sed prole virebat feminea." Eodem modo, "loquitur," "fatetur": "Monachi loquuntur digitis," "Fateatur opus quis fecerit auctor." Eodem modo, "inebrio," "devoro": "Inebriabo sagittas meas sanguine, scilicet et gladius meus devorabit carnes." "Sapit": "Hic homo curam sapit." Per haec exempla patet manifeste et de participio, verbi gratia, "Dumescente pilis facie," et alibi, "Me noctescente, diescat hic liber."

30 Adverbia quoque consimili ratione transumuntur, ut "funditus" vel "medullitus" pro "penitus." Verbi gratia: "Veri dialectici sunt qui rerum naturas medullitus investigant." Bernardus: "Abundans malignitas quibus insedit sedibus funditus non recedit." Similiter "pressius," quod si propriam haberet significationem significaret "magis presse," et ponitur pro "firmius" vel pro "funditus."

Coniunctiones, praepositiones, interiectiones vel penitus non transumuntur, vel earum transumptiones assignare potius erit subtilitatis dialecticae quam utilitatis vel venustatis rethoricae. Non curamus igitur de solutionibus illorum qui moderno tempore exponunt has, "Socrates est tantus quod potest attingere trabes," "Socrates videt Platonem," et e converso.

31 Respectiva transumptio est quotiens aliquae duae dictiones sese mutuo respiciunt ad hoc quod utraque transumatur. Verbi gratia, "Iste quandoque est calidus, quandoque est frigidus," id est, iste est inconstans. Expone verbo ad

and is crying in childish verse." "I weave, you weave"; Bernard: "The speech that was woven from favorite things had caused delight in its hearing." "I flourish, you flourish"; Statius: "But he flourished with female progeny." Likewise, "he speaks," "he declares": "Monks speak with their fingers," "Let the work declare what author wrote it." Likewise, "I make drunk," "I devour": "I will make my arrows drunk with blood, and my sword shall devour flesh." "He smacks of": "This man smacks of worry." From these examples the usage is entirely clear with participles too, for example, "His face, becoming bushy with hair," and here, "With my all-nighting, let this book see the light of day."

Adverbs are capable of transference too, in much the same way, as "from the ground up" or "intimately," for "thoroughly." For example: "True dialecticians are those who investigate the nature of things intimately." Bernard: "Abundant malignity does not quit locations in which it has taken up residence from the ground up." Likewise, *pressius*, which if it had its proper meaning would mean "more closely," is also put for "more firmly" or "utterly."

Conjunctions, prepositions, and interjections are either just not subject to transference, or their transference will be assignable to dialectical subtlety rather than to rhetorical utility or elegance. And so we don't spend time on the solutions that people come up with these days to explicate "Socrates is so tall he can touch the ceiling beams," "Socrates sees Plato," and the reverse.

Referential metaphor happens whenever two words refer mutually to each other to produce a double transference. For example, "This man is sometimes hot, sometimes cold," that is, he is inconstant. To explain word by word: "He is

verbum: "Est calidus," id est, vult unum; "Est frigidus," id est, vult eius oppositum. Ratio transumptionis est ex eo quod inconstantia versatur circa opposita. Pro hac igitur, "Iste est constans," nihil valet dicere, "Iste est calidus," quia non exprimitur respectus huius dictionis "calidus." Hoc autem utilis: "Iste vel semper est calidus vel semper est frigidus."

32   Huius modi exempla in diversis partibus orationis diverse inveniuntur. In propriis nominibus, sic: "Iste homo nunc Thebas Eteocli, nunc Thebas adiudicat Polynici." Thebas, id est quodcumque bonum vel gratiam suam; Eteocli, id est uni parti; Polynici, id est oppositae. Et tamen nulla similitudo est inter Thebas et gratiam vel inter Polynicem et partem simpliciter, sed habito respectu ad controversiam Polynicis et Eteoclis propter Thebas. Similiter, "Animus huius nunc Romam nunc Parisius evagatur."

In appellativis substantivis, sic: "Nunc equum exigit, nunc asellum." In adiectivis: "Utinam calidus esses, aut frigidus, sed quia tepidus es, evomam te." "Calidus," id est, amicus per fidem; "frigidus," id est, hostis apertus. "Sed quia tepidus," id est, inter utrumque, "evomam," id est susceptum relinquam.

In pronominibus secundum hunc modum ponitur finitum pro infinito, ut si de quodam qui me nunquam vidit, dicam, "Nunc meus, nunc tuus est." Vel sic, "Huius et illius voluntatis est," id est, variabilis. Huius, id est alicuius, et illius, id est alterius modi. "Continue" post hoc intellige. Bernardus: "Illud igitur inconsistens, et convertibile huius et illius conditionis qualitatis et formae . . . , elabitur incognitum, vultus vicarios alternando."

hot," that is, he wants some thing; "He is cold," that is, he wants its opposite. The rationale of the metaphor is that inconstancy involves opposites. If you want to say, "He is constant," it does no good to say, "He is hot," because there is no mention of what "hot" refers to. This, however, does work: "He is either always hot or always cold."

Various examples of this idea are found with various parts of speech. With proper nouns in this way: "This man awards Thebes now to Eteocles, now to Polynices." Thebes, that is, every good he has and every favor; Eteocles, that is, to one party; Polynices, that is, to the opposite party. Yet there is no literal likeness between Thebes and favor, or between Polynices and a party, but only with reference to the disagreement between Polynices and Eteocles over Thebes. Similarly, "This man's mind wanders now to Rome, now to Paris." 32

In common nouns in this way: "At one moment he demands a horse, at another an ass." In adjectives: "I wish you were hot or cold, but because you are lukewarm, I will vomit you out." "Hot," that is, my friend, because of your faithfulness; "cold," that is, my open enemy. "But because you are lukewarm," that is, between the two, "I will vomit you out," that is, though I took you in, I will drop you.

With pronouns in this usage, a definite pronoun is put for an indefinite pronoun, as if I should say about a man who never saw me, "Now he is mine, now he is yours." Or, "He is of this mind—or of that," that is, variable. Of this, that is, of one way; and of that, that is, of another way. Understand "continually" after these words. Bernard: "It (matter), inconsistent and changeable from one condition of quality or form to another . . . , slips along unrecognized, exchanging successive appearances."

In verbis quoque si pro hac, "Socrates Aeschinem diligit," dicas, "Socrates Aeschinem bibit," inutilis fere est transumptio. Haec tamen utilis: "Cicero Pompeium nunc bibit, nunc evomit," id est, quandoque diligit, quandoque odit. In huiusmodi contingit frequenter totam orationem transumi, et tamen computatur in transumptionibus dictionum, quia habetur respectus ad partes.

Antequam ad alia procedamus, circa dictionum transumptionem quaedam sunt regulae praenotandae. In primis tamen utile est nosse quid sit advocatio.

33 Advocatio est qualitas respectiva que inest alicui dictioni ex eo quod, mediante proprietatis significatione quam habet, consona est alii dictioni vel aliis dictionibus in eadem oratione contentis. Secundum hoc, verbum advocandi exigit accusativum casum designantem rem respectu cuius inest illa proprietas. In hac igitur clausula, "Hebe vagit infantia et flos cunis egrediens amantum amplexibus relativis arridet"—in hac, inquam, clausula, haec vox "vagit" advocat hanc dictionem "infantia" et e converso, quia infantis proprium est vagire. Haec vox "cunis egrediens" advocat hanc vocem "arridet," quia surgens a cunis, matri libenter arridet.

34 Huiusmodi advocationum quaedam intrinseca, quaedam extrinseca. Intrinseca in re ipsa consideratur, extrinseca in rei respectu. Verbi gratia, cum dico, "Veris lascivia pubescentis decrepitam hiemis eliminat senectutem," haec dictio "lascivia" advocat hanc dictionem "pubescentis" intrinseca advocatione. Puberes enim frequentius sunt lascivi. Item haec dictio "pubescentis" advocat hanc dictionem "senectutem," non quia pubertas sit senectus vel puberes senes, sed

PART 2

In verbs too, if instead of "Socrates loves Aeschines" you should say "Socrates drinks in Aeschines," the metaphor is almost unusable. But this is viable: "Cicero now drinks Pompey in, now vomits him out," that is, loves him sometimes, hates him sometimes. In examples like this it happens often that the entire sentence becomes a metaphor, but it still counts as transference of words because the focus is on parts of speech.

Before we go on to other matters, some rules about transference of words must be stipulated. But the very first thing is to know what advocation is.

33 Advocation or evoking is the referential quality that a word has because through the medium of its proper meaning it accords with another word or words contained in the same sentence. A verb that evokes needs an accusative designating the topic to which its proper sense refers. So in this little sentence, "Hebe cries in her infancy, but when her flower comes out of the cradle, she smiles at the reciprocal embraces of those who love her"—in this sentence, I say, "cries" evokes the word "infancy," and vice versa, because crying is proper to an infant. "Comes out of the cradle" evokes "smiles," because when the baby is taken out of the cradle it readily smiles at its mother.

34 Some advocations of this kind are intrinsic, some extrinsic. Intrinsic are observed in the subject itself, extrinsic in reference to a subject. For example, when I say, "The wantonness of pubescent spring dispels the decrepit old age of winter," "wantonness" evokes "pubescent" by an intrinsic advocation, because those going through puberty very often display wantonness. Also, the word "pubescent" evokes "old age," not because puberty is old age or boys old men, but by

extrinseca advocatione: respicit enim senectutem ut suum contrarium, et in quam iuventus saepe violentiam exercet. Item, "Cura aufert candorem" dici potest hoc modo: "Candoris nivem curarum flamma remittit." Haec dictio "flamma" advocat hanc dictionem "nivem" extrinseco respectu. Non enim flamma est nix, sed in nivem agit. Hoc verbum "remittit" advocat utramque, quia flamma remittit, nix remittitur.

35 Tunc pulcherrima erit transumptio, cum similitudo intransumpta Janus erit et utramque partem respiciet. Quandoque enim respicit tantum alteram, quandoque utramque, quandoque neutram. Tantum alteram, ut in hoc exemplo: "Maciei flamma remittit quam dederat natura nivem." Haec dictio "flamma" transumptive tenetur pro violentia maciei, si transitiva sit constructio, vel pro ipsa macie, si intransitiva—sed sumitur similitudo tantum ex parte praedicati, quia sicut flamma nivem consumit, eodem modo macies candorem. Sed macies ipsa re vera non urit, neque in colore similis est flammae. Unde dempta hac dictione "nivem," haec est inexcusabilis: "Maciei flamma decorem expulit." Macies enim potius est similis cineri quam flammae!

Utramque partem respicit similitudo ut in his exemplis: "Curarum flamma decorem exurit." Haec dictio "flamma" respicit praedicatum competenti similitudine, quia sicut flamma quamcumque rem consumit, ita curae decorem. Unde bene advocat hanc dictionem "exurit." Item respicit hanc dictionem "curarum" competenter, quia idem est effectus curae et flammae: utraque enim accendit et exaestuat. Exaestuant enim ignis, amor, ira, cura.

Simile hic: "Rufum caput est rogus fidei." Haec dictio "rogus" competenter transumitur ratione utriusque partis.

an extrinsic advocation: youth refers to old age as its opposite, and as a state on which it often works violence. Also, "Care takes away beauty" can be expressed this way: "The flame of cares melts away the snow of beauty." The word "flame" evokes the word "snow" by an extrinsic relation. Flame isn't snow, but it has an effect on snow. The phrase "melts away" evokes both: flame melts, snow is melted.

Then a metaphor will be very beautiful, since the untransferred likeness will be Januslike and look both ways. For sometimes it refers only to one, sometimes to both, sometimes to neither. Only to one, as in this example: "The snow that nature had given, the flame of emaciation melts." "Flame" serves as a metaphor for the violence of emaciation, if the construction is transitive, or for emaciation itself, if it is intransitive—but the likeness depends only on the role of the predicate, because just as flame consumes snow, so emaciation consumes beauty. But emaciation itself in reality does not burn, nor is it colored like flame. Consequently if you take out "snow," the expression "The flame drives out beauty" is indefensible. Emaciation is more like ashes than flame!

A likeness refers to both ways as in these examples: "The flame of cares burns up beauty." "Flame" refers to the predicate with an apt likeness, because just as flame consumes everything, so cares consume beauty. Thus it evokes appropriately the word "burns." It also refers aptly to "cares," because flame and cares have the same effect: each sets on fire and seethes up. Fire, love, anger, care: they all seethe.

This example is similar: "Red hair is the funeral pyre of faithfulness." "Pyre" is an apt metaphor on the basis of

35

Ratione subiecti, quia rufum caput simile est rogo in colore. Ratione praedicati, quia sicut rogus mortuum designat, ita rufum caput fidem quasi mortuam. Non igitur dicerem adeo competenter, "Rufum caput est sepulchrum fidei." Hic enim dependens est similitudo tantum ex altera parte.

Incommendabilior vero est transumptio ubi neutram partem respicit advocatio, ut hic: "Humiliaverunt colla cordium suorum sub praeceptis Domini." Neque haec dictio "cordium" neque haec dictio "praeceptis" advocat hanc dictionem "colla." Gregorius in libro *Dialogorum* melius ait, dicens, "Humiliaverunt colla cordium suorum sub suave iugum nostri redemptoris." Haec dictio "iugum" advocat hanc dictionem "colla," et e converso. Cassiodorus: "Indecens est Christianum, vas caelesti gratiae mancipatum, saeculares haurire delicias." Haec dictio "vas" advocat hanc dictionem "haurire" et etiam hanc dictionem "Christianum," quia homo simpliciter quoddammodo similis est vasi. Unde legitur in *Dialogis* Gregorii vox diaboli de Iudaeo qui se signaverat signo crucis, sic: "Hic iacet vas vacuum sed signatum." Item aliud exemplum: de homine pessimo dici potest, "Iste est dolium scelerum." Si vero homo ille grossitiei magnae fuerit, tunc competentius erit dictum eum esse dolium scelerum.

Secundum dicta patet quod in Tobia haec commendabilis est, "Baculum senectutis nostrae tulistis." Haec autem, "Basim senectutis nostrae tulistis," non esset adeo commendabilis.

36 Item secundum praedicta patet quod advocatur metaphora quandoque per aliam metaphoram, quandoque per

its relation to both parts of the sentence. By reason of the subject, because red hair is like a pyre in color. By reason of the predicate, because just as a pyre indicates a dead person, so red hair, as it were, indicates a faithfulness that is, as it were, dead. I would not have said, "Red hair is the grave of faithfulness" so appropriately, because in this case the likeness depends only on one side.

Even less praiseworthy is a metaphor where neither side is evoked, as here: "They bowed down the necks of their hearts beneath the precepts of the Lord." Neither the word "hearts" nor the word "precepts" evokes the word "necks." Gregory speaks better in the *Dialogues,* saying, "They bowed down the necks of their hearts beneath the gentle yoke of our redeemer." Here the word "yoke" evokes the word "necks," and vice versa. Cassiodorus: "It is not fitting for a Christian, a vessel subject to heavenly grace, to drink in the sweets of the world." The word "vessel" evokes the word "drink" and also the word "Christian," because a man, taken in his essence, is in a way like a vessel. Thus we read in Gregory's *Dialogues* the cry of a devil about a Jew who had made the sign of the cross over himself: "Here lies an empty but marked vessel." Another example: of a very wicked man you might say, "He is a tub full of crimes." And if the man himself is of great girth, calling him a tub full of crimes is even more apt.

According to what has been said, it is clear that we should admire this verse in the book of Tobias: "You have taken the staff of our old age." This wording, "You have taken the foundation of our old age," would not be so admirable.

What has been said also makes clear that a metaphor sometimes is evoked by another metaphor, sometimes by a

36

proprietatem. Per metaphoram, ut hic: "Curarum flamma remittit quam dederat natura nivem." Tam haec dictio "flamma" quam haec dictio "nivem" transumitur, et utraque advocat reliquam. Per proprietatem, ut hic: in conquestione magistri Gaufredi *De rege Ricardo,* ubi voluit dicere, "Qui maxime delectabat oculos et aures et mentem," ait,

> Ipse fuit sol in oculis, et dulcor in aure,
> et stupor in mente.

Ecce quia nihil oculis pulchrius sole videtur, bene haec dictio "sol" advocatur per hanc dictionem "oculis." Et tamen haec dictio "oculis" proprie tenetur, haec dictio "sol" transumptive. Similiter de hac dictione "dulcor" et hac dictione "aure," quamvis "dulcor" generaliter pertineat tam ad gustum et nares quam ad aures, et magis proprie, unde satis optime—et specialius et melius—ut mihi videtur, dixisset, "concentus in aure," ibi enim specialior esset advocatio. Quod sequitur, "et stupor in mente," optime dictum est. Nihil enim pressius tangit animum quam stupor.

In adiectivis transumptis solet advocatio frequentius deesse (ut hic: "Facies nivea placet intuenti," "nivea" pro "alba")—licet possit dici huiusmodi non esse transumptas sed tantum proprias, et quod haec dictio "niveus" et haec dictio "lacteus" adeo propriae notae sunt similitudinis sicut et materiae. Et sicut haec est propria, "Caseus lacteus est," id est, de materia lactis, eodem modo "Facies est lactea," id est, lacti similis.

37   Item in qualibet oratione secundum partem transumptam duo sunt attendenda, proprietas et transumptio. Alia dictio erit proprietatis, et alia transumptionis, ut si dicam,

PART 2

word used literally. By a metaphor, as here: "The snow that nature had given, the flame of cares is melting." Both words, "flame" and "snow," are metaphors, and each evokes the other. By a word used literally, as in this case: in Master Geoffrey's *Complaint of King Richard,* when he wanted to say, "Who most delighted our eyes and ears and minds," he wrote,

> He was the sun in our eyes and sweetness in our ears
> and amazement in our minds.

Since nothing is more beautiful to our eyes than the sun, the word "sun" is evoked well by the word "eyes." And yet "eyes" is used literally, "sun" metaphorically. It is the same with the words "sweetness" and "ear," though "sweetness" usually pertains to taste and smell rather than to ears, and he might more properly, and so ideally—more precisely and better— have said, "harmony in the ear," and the evocation in that case would have been more precise. What comes next, "and amazement in our minds," is very well said, for nothing hits the mind more powerfully than amazement.

Advocation is customarily quite rare in the case of metaphorical adjectives (as in this case: "A snowy face is pleasing to the beholder," "snowy" for "white")—although expressions of this kind can be said to not be metaphorical at all but only literal, and the words "snowy" and "milky" are just as literal markers of appearance as of substance. And just as "Cheese is milky," that is, "made from milk," is literal, in the same way "Her face is milky," that is, "is like milk," is literal.

Further, in any sentence two aspects of its metaphorical part must be observed, the literal and the metaphorical. One word will be literal and another metaphorical, as, if I

37

"Lilia candoris propter doloris imminentiam recesserunt," haec dictio "lilia" transumptionis est, haec dictio candoris proprietatis. Regula igitur est in quacumque oratione, habitis in principio duabus dictionibus, altera proprietatis, reliqua transumptionis, non subsequatur aliqua dictio quam non advocet vel propria vel transumpta. Verbi gratia, haec utilis: "Delectantur aures cordium nostrorum in cithara praeceptorum Domini," quia haec dictio "aures" advocat hanc dictionem "cithara." Item haec utilis: "Humiliamus colla cordium nostrorum in suave iugum nostri redemptoris." Haec autem inutilis: "Delectantur aures cordium nostrorum in suavi iugo domini." Hanc igitur philosophi clausulam non commendo: "Oris nardus ad examen narium delicatas odoris epulas efferebat." Haec dictio "nardus" non advocat hanc dictionem "epulas," cum utraque transumptionis sit; item nec haec dictio "delicatas" advocatur ab alio, eius enim transumptio a cibo trahitur, cuius nulla praecessit mentio.

Item propter principium transumptionis notandum est quod haec advocatio maxime locum habet, ubi per genitivum vel ablativum exprimitur significatio transumpta, ut hic, "veris lascivia," id est, iocunditas. Nesciretur enim pro quo teneretur haec dictio "lascivia" nisi per hunc genitivum "veris." Item, "philosophus facie," id est, macer facie.

38   In hiis igitur maxime notandum quod similitudo intransumpta tum sumitur a persona, tum a negotio. Persona duplex: illa ad cuius significationem transumitur dictio, et alia a cuius significatione transumitur. Inter has igitur quandoque est similitudo essentialis, scilicet non habito respectu

should say, "The lilies of whiteness have faded because sorrow is looming," the word "lilies" is a metaphor, the word "whiteness" literal. The rule then is in any sentence that starts with two words, one literal, the other metaphorical, no word should follow that is not evoked by the preceding words, either the literal or the metaphorical. For example, this is successful: "The ears of our hearts delight in the lyre of the precepts of the lord," because the words "ears" and "lyre" evoke each other. This too is successful: "Let us bow the necks of our hearts under the sweet yoke of our redeemer." But this is not successful: "The ears of our hearts delight in the sweet yoke of the lord." Nor do I approve of this sentence of a philosopher: "The nard of her mouth gave off a sumptuous banquet of odors for the nose to sample." The word "nard" does not evoke the word "banquet," though each is a metaphor, nor is the word "sumptuous" evoked by another word, since its metaphorical usage is drawn from food, which hasn't been previously mentioned.

Again, on the matter of beginning a metaphor it should be noted that an evocation is especially appropriate when the transferred meaning is brought out by a genitive or ablative, as in "the wantonness of spring," that is, joyfulness. The point of the word "wantonness" wouldn't be clear without the genitive "of spring." Again, "a philosopher in the face," that is, emaciated looking.

A major thing to note about metaphor is that an untransferred likeness is derived either from a person or an action. From a person, doubly: the word to whose meaning the transfer is made and the word from whose meaning the transfer is made. And of these, sometimes the likeness is essential, that is, without regard to any exterior action, as

38

ad aliquem actum exteriorem, ut inter hoc significatum "bos" et hoc significatum "segnis." In huiusmodi transumptionibus dictio transumpta quandoque sine determinatione ponitur, ut "Iste est bos" (id est, segnis), quandoque cum determinatione, sed ablativi tantum, ut "Iste est bos animo," "Iste est philosophus facie" (id est, macer).

Quandoque est inter illas similitudo habito respectu ad aliquem actum specialem exteriorem. Sed secundum hoc determinari vult transumptio vel genitivo vel praepositionali determinatione, et ibi sumitur a negotio. Secundum hoc, qui nec miles nec militi similis miles dici potest cum determinatione genitivi. Ut, si dolosus sit aliquis, dicatur "miles doli," si luxuriosus, "miles veneris," id est, amator vel exercitator veneris. Sicut enim miles laboriosus est in militia et sollicitus, sic iste in venere. Similiter quia psittacus optime avium loquitur continua oratione et prosa consistit in continua oratione, potest dici quod iste est "psittacus in prosa," id est, optime loquens prosaice. Similiter, "Iste est in metrico philomena," quia philomena optime avium cantat, et metrum consisitit in cantu.

39 Sciatur ergo quod tunc venustissime procedet transumptio cum prima dictio transumptionis respiciet pariter personam et negotium—personam sive ratione similitudinis sive ratione professionis vel essentiae vel huiusmodi, negotium vero ratione transumptionis tantum, ut in praedicto exemplo, "Rufum caput est rogus fidei." Vel, ut dixit quidam de quodam discipulo scholari qui in corporis deformitate maxime similis erat cultori agri, ut latens esset ironia, inquit, "Hic est grammaticae cultor studiique colonus." Et alius de quodam qui professus est philosophiam sed maxime luxuriosus erat, inquit, "Hic est philosophus veneris."

between "ox" and "slow." In metaphors of this kind the transferred word is sometimes used without a modifier, as "He is an ox" (that is, slow), sometimes with a modifier, but in the ablative only, as "He is an ox in the brain," "He is a philosopher in the face" (that is, emaciated).

Sometimes the likeness in these cases is with regard to some exterior activity. But in such a case the transference needs to be modified by a genitive or a prepositional phrase, and in that instance the transference is derived from an activity. Thus a man who is neither a soldier nor like a soldier can still be called a soldier with a modifying genitive. As if someone is deceitful, he may be called "a soldier of guile," if licentious, "a soldier of sex," that is, a lover, or practitioner of sex. For just as a soldier is energetic and devoted in soldiery, so is he in sex. Likewise, because a parrot talks in a constant flow of words better than any other bird, and prose consists of a constant flow of words, you can say that somebody is "a parrot in prose," that is, best at speaking in prose. Similarly, "He is a nightingale in verse," because the nightingale sings better than any other bird, and verse consists of song.

Be assured, then, that a metaphor will proceed in the most elegant way when its first term refers both to a person and activity—to the person either by reason of likeness or occupation, or essence, or the like, but to an activity by way of metaphor only, as in the previously cited example, "Red hair is the funeral pyre of faithfulness." Or as someone said about a teaching assistant in school who in his misshapen body was very like a tiller of the soil, to hide the irony, "He is a cultivator of grammar and a tiller of learning." And somebody else said of a man who taught philosophy but was licentious in the extreme, "He is a philosopher of sex."

Item sive hoc sive alio modo fiat transumptionis inceptio, ut pulcherrime procedatur, per successionem clausularum plurium incepta transumptio fideliter observetur, adeo ut frequens sit intermixtio dictionum quarum altera per transumptam, altera per propriam advocetur. Tanto tamen erit ornatior si incepta sit ut proximo praemonstravi. Verbi gratia, de clerico luxurioso:

> Hic est
> Philosophus veneris, quem mollis pagina lecti
> non libri reficit, [cui], dum magis approbat album
> incaustum tripusque nigrum, nocturna placere
> non lucis scriptura solet, rubeoque libello
> inspuitur calamo delectans littera caeca.

Ecce quomodo istae duae dictiones, "philosophus" et "veneris," successive advocant dictiones sequentes. Et vide in fine: haec dictio "veneris" advocat hanc dictionem "rubeo," haec dictio "philosophus" hanc dictionem "libello," haec dictio "veneris" hanc dictionem "inspuitur," et sic per ordinem.

De magistro simili colono, hoc modo: "Hic homo, grammaticae cultor et colonus studii, instimulat pueros ad discendum, et prata lenioris litterae facili transitu orationis percurrit. Sed acuto rationis vomere confringit saxa sententiae durioris."

Istius modi repertor et auctor extitit Claudianus. Hic notandum est quasdam duras transumptiones in huiusmodi casibus competenter admitti propter latens argumentum et uniformitatem procedendi. Turpiter enim transumerem dicens, "Vomer rationis tuae," nisi sic latenter innuerem: te similem esse colono. In *Anticlaudiano* tamen magister Alanus auctoritate sua contentus ait,

PART 2

Again, whether a metaphor begins in this or another way, so that it may proceed in the most beautiful way, let the initial metaphor be maintained faithfully by a series of numerous clauses to the extent that there is a regular intermixing of words of which some are evoked by a metaphorical and some by a proper sense. This will be all the more elegant if it is started the way I have just been showing. For example, on the licentious cleric:

> He is a philosopher of sex, whom the soft sheet of a bed, not of a book, refreshes, who, while he commends white ink and black stool, customarily prefers night writing to daylight, and a delightful but invisible letter is spattered on a pink book from his pen.

See how the words "philosopher" and "sex" evoke in turn the words that follow them. And at the end too: the word "sex" evokes the word "pink" and "philosopher" "book," "sex" "is spattered," and so on in succession.

On the teacher likened to a farmer, it is achieved in this way: "This man, a cultivator of grammar and a tiller of learning, inspires students to learn and runs through the meadows of easier texts with a ready course of speech. But with the sharp plowshare of reason he breaks up the rocks of a harder passage."

The original founder of this way of writing was Claudian. Here it should be noted that some harsh metaphors are rightly admitted in cases of this kind because of a hidden argument and consistency of proceeding. I would be making a wrong use of metaphor with the words "the plow of your reason" if I weren't insinuating that you are like a farmer. Master Alan, though, confident in his own authority, wrote in *Anticlaudianus,*

> Optimus excultor morum, mentisque colonus,
> more suo Seneca mores ratione monetat.

Eum qui facetissimus et fere doctissimus hominum fuit, colonum vocat, quod si in alio non peccasset, certe coloni non est monetare.

40 Est igitur nisi in casibus praedictis et consimilibus omnis dura transumptio fugienda. Unde haec approbanda non est: "Nondum veneranda senectae / albet olore coma." Cum enim multiplex sit constructio dictionis transumptae cum suo genitivo, duae sunt magis commendabiles: transitiva, ut hic, "lilia faciei" (id est, candor faciei), et intransitiva, ut hic, "Lilia candoris" (id est, lilia, quae sunt candor). Est et alia constructio transitiva sed minus probabilis, ut hic: "Lilia senectutis depingunt caput tuum," id est, candor quem facit senectus. Haec autem adhuc minus commendabilis: "olor senectutis," id est, candor quem facit senectus. Cum enim candor penes superficiem attendatur, magis sunt consona superficiei nix vel lilia quam olores. In illis igitur, "Nondum veneranda senectae / albet olore coma," remota est constructio et ratio remotior transumendi.

41 Est et alius modus commendabilis, quando scilicet sumimus aliquod dictum authenticum, vel dimidium vel quamcumque partem dicti, et eo ordine quo auctor proprie usus est nos utimur transumptive. Verbi gratia, Bernardus Silvestris de proprietate herbarum ait,

PART 2

> In his customary way Seneca, the best cultivator of morals and husbandman of the mind, coins morals with the die of reason.

He takes a man who was the most eloquent and almost the most learned of men and calls him a farmer, but even if he had made no other mistake, it is certainly not a farmer's role to mint coins.

And so except in the foregoing cases and others like them, every hard metaphor is to be avoided. So this is not to be commended: "My hair is not yet white and venerable with the swan of old age." Though there are many ways to construct a metaphorical word with a dependent genitive, two are especially to be recommended: the transitive relation, as in "lilies of face" (that is, whiteness of face), and the intransitive, as "lilies of whiteness" (that is, lilies that are whiteness). There is also another transitive construction that is less approvable, as here: "The lilies of old age are painting your head," that is, the whiteness that old age causes. But the following is even less commendable: "the swan of old age," that is, the whiteness that old age causes. Since the whiteness is only observed on the surface, snow or lilies suit this surface more than swans. In short, in the words "My hair is not yet white and venerable with the swan of old age," the construction is farfetched and the rationale of the metaphor still more so.

There is another praiseworthy mode, namely, when we take a phrase from an author, or half a phrase or some part of a phrase, and use the same sequence metaphorically that the author used literally. For example, Bernard Silvester says of the properties of plants,

> Narcissos fontana tenent, saepesque ligustra;
> horti forma rosae, lilia vallis honor.

Proprie usus est hiis dictionibus "lilia," "rosae." Alius in descriptione virginis sic ait,

> Depinxere genas oculo sub utroque tumentes,
> collis forma rosae, lilia vallis honor.

42   Contingit item ornatissime unicam dictionem poni simul et semel proprie et transumptive; verbi gratia, "Sedent virgines in virgulto, tenentes flores in manibus, et relucent ibi lilia facierum pariter et hortorum." Et sic haec dictio "lilia" tenetur equivoce. Quippe equivocationem sic desiderat rethorica, sicut logica dedignatur. Unde sicut sine transumptione aequivocatio commendatur, eodem etiam modo, sed et plenius, cum transumptione. Architrenius: "Canduit Alcides Veneris Nessique veneno." Haec dictio "veneno" ponitur aequivoce. "Veneno Nessi" proprie dictum est, veneno "Veneris" transumptive. Similiter alibi,

> Alciden pudeat quod eodem pollice pensum
> Anteique necem, nunc vir, nunc femina nevit.

Haec dictio "nevit" aequivoce tenetur. Videtur tamen magis commode dixisse, "filum Anteique necem, etc." Quam praeclare Hegesippus, libro tertio, de Ascalone loquens cui insurrexerunt cives Hierosolymitani, hunc typum observans,

PART 2

> Springs have narcissuses, hedgerows the cowslip; the roses are the beauty of a garden, the lilies the glory of a valley.

He uses the words "lilies" and "roses" literally. Someone else, describing a young girl, says,

> Roses, the beauty of a hillside, and lilies, the honor of a valley, below each eye painted her full cheeks.

It also is a very elegant turn of phrase to use a single word literally and metaphorically at one and the same time; for example, "The girls are sitting in an arbor holding flowers in their hands, and there the lilies of their faces and of those gardens give light in tandem." The word "lilies" is used in two senses. The fact is that rhetoric welcomes double meaning as eagerly as logic disdains it. Accordingly, just as double meaning wins approval without metaphor, in the same way it does still more with metaphor. Architrenius: "Hercules was aflame with Nessus's poison and Venus's." The word "poison" is used with a double meaning here. "Nessus's poison" is literal, "Venus's" metaphorical. Likewise in another place,

> Hercules should be ashamed that with the same hand he spun his quota of wool and the death of Antaeus, at one time as a man, at another as a woman.

The word "spun" is used with a double meaning. It seems, though, that he might better have written, "thread and the death of Antaeus, etc." How excellently Hegesippus in observance of this mode, speaking in his third book about Ascalon, against which the citizens of Jerusalem had risen up,

42

ait, "Haec septingentis ac viginti stadiis ab Hierosolymitana urbe discernebatur et odiis ingentibus." "Discernere," prout proprie tenetur, locale est.

43 Regulariter item notandum quod quodlibet adiectivum quanto magis a purissima proprietate recedit, tanto nolentius admittit aliam dictionem loco sui positam transumptive. "Purissimam proprietatem" adiectivi intelligo quotiens adiectivum ponitur secundum quod institutum est primaria institutione. Scilicet, si sit denominative sumptum a qualitate, in purissima proprietate tenetur si notet qualitatem a qua sumitur ita inesse essentialiter ut sufficiat ad denominandum. Item si sit denominative sumptum a substantia, in purissima proprietate tenetur si notet materiam, ut "Iste caseus est lacteus," id est, de lacte materia. Similiter "globus niveus," id est, de nive materia. Si igitur dicam, "Nivem cano in te: / candida iam floret canis properantibus aetas," hoc adiectivum "candida" a purissima proprietate recedit. Candor enim non est forma aetatis sed substantiae. Sed dicitur aetas candida quia efficit candidum. Loco huius dictionis "'candida" minus idonee diceretur "lactea" per transumptionem. Simile in fabula de Pyramo et Thisbe: pro hac clausula, "Mora revera erant nigra sed fabula ea fingit alba," dictum est, "Candida cerussant nigrum, mendacia verum." Mendacia dicuntur candida non quia in mendatio sit color aliquis, sed quia mendacia fuerunt de colore candoris. Similiter verum dicitur nigrum quia veritas fuit de nigredine. Cum igitur haec adiectiva tantum recedant a proprietate, loco sui non admittunt alia transumpta. Unde versus iste

says, "This town was separated from the city of Jerusalem by 720 stades and by massive hatreds." "Separate" in its literal meaning refers to location.

As a general rule it should be noted that the more any adjective departs from purest literalness, the more unwillingly it admits being replaced by another word used metaphorically. By "purest literalness" of an adjective I mean whenever an adjective is used in accordance with what was established as its original, primary meaning. That is, if it is derived from a quality, it is used in purest literalness if it denotes that the quality it refers to so constitutes its essence as to suffice for the derivation. Again, if it is derived from a substance, it is used in purest literalness if it denotes the substance, as "This cheese is milky," that is, from the substance milk. Likewise, "a snowy ball," that is, from the substance snow. And so if I say, "I sing of the snow on you: as the white hairs come in a hurry, your white age is already flowering," the adjective "white" departs from purest literalness. For whiteness is not a feature of age but of a substance. But age is said to be white because it makes a person white. It would have been less fitting if instead of the word "white" the metaphor "milky" were used. There is a similar example in the story of Pyramus and Thisbe: in place of the expression "The mulberries were in fact black, but the story pretends they were white," the wording was substituted, "The white masks the black, lies the truth." Lies are said to be white not because in a lie there is any color, but because the lies were about the color white. Likewise the truth is called black because the truth concerned blackness. Therefore, since these adjectives depart so far from literalness, other metaphors cannot be used

non esset adeo commendabilis, "Lactea cerussant piceum, mendacia verum." Ioseph in Darete suo, hunc modum loquendi observans in descriptione Helenae, inquit, "Totosque per artus / candida materni spirant mendacia cigni." Non dixit "lactea."

44 Transumptio orationis est translatio vocis complexae a propria significatione ad alienam secundum se totam, hoc est, non habito respectu ad partes, ut si dicam, "Iste lavat laterem," id est, inutile opus exercet. Haec vox enim "lavat" non transumitur ad alienam significationem, sed totalis oratio.

Oratio sic transumpta dividitur in asteismon et aenigma. Asteismos, qui "floritio" sive "florentia" interpretatur, generali significatione quamlibet rethoricam comprehendit. Namque asteismos secundum Donatum putatur esse illud dictum quod caret rustica simplicitate et faceta satis urbanitate est expolitum. Restricta tamen significatione species est orationalis transumptionis, ut hic,

Qui Bavium non odit, amet tua carmina, Mevi,
atque idem iungat vulpes et mulgeat hircos.

Id est, in nugis consumat tempus suum.

Asteismos autem secundum hoc multiplex est numerosaeque virtutis. Et ideo multipliciter assignatur: tum per apparentiam, tum per aequipollentiam, tum per alterius rei similitudinem. Per apparentiam, eo quod aliquis unum faciendo videretur callido inspectori aliud facere, quamvis impossibile, ut, si quis anxie alium sequitur in cursu potest

instead of them. And so this verse would not be so admirable, "The milky masks in white the pitch-black, lies what is true." Joseph of Exeter, in his version of Dares, observed this mode of speaking in describing Helen, saying, "The white beguilements of the maternal swan breathe through all her limbs." He didn't say "milky."

Sentence metaphor is the transference of a collective expression from its literal meaning to another complete in itself, that is, without reference to its parts, as if I should say, "He is washing a brick," that is, doing something pointless. The word "wash" isn't transferred to another meaning, the whole sentence is.

Sentence metaphors are classified as either asteismos or enigma. Asteismos, which means "blossoming" or "blooming," includes broadly anything rhetorical. According to Donatus, any wording that lacks rustic simplicity but has some polish of urbanity and wit is considered *asteismos*. But in a more restricted meaning it is just a species of sentence metaphor, as in this case:

> If he doesn't hate Bavius, then let him like your songs too, Maevius, and let him yoke foxes and milk billy goats!

That is, let him waste his time on trivialities.

In this definition, then, asteismos is many-sided and has numerous capabilities. And therefore it is indicated in various ways: by appearance, by equivalence, by likeness to something else. By appearance, in that someone who is doing one thing may seem to a keen observer to be doing something else, even something impossible, as is the case when, if a man follows another urgently at pace, he can seem to be

videri eius colligere vestigia. Lucanus: "Generoque legit vestigia Caesar," id est, anxie sequitur generum.

45 Talium apparentiarum alia sensualitatis, alia rationis. Sensualitatis est quod sensui apparet, ut puta solem oriri a mari. Unde pro hac, "Sol oritur," potest dici, "Exit ab undis Phoebus." Unde quidam ait, "Qualis exit Cynthia Thetidis ab unda." Hoc nomen etiam "Cynthia" a sensualitate est. Dicta est enim luna Cynthia quia videbatur quibusdam existentibus iuxta Cynthum montem lunam exire de monte illo. Per sensualitatem etiam adinventa sunt multa nomina deorum et dearum, et etiam multae fabulae gentilium — sed de daemonibus nihil ad praesens. Secundum sensualitatem etiam dictum est illud praedictum exemplum, "Generoque legit vestigia Caesar."

46 Rationis apparentia est quae non oculis, verum solo descernitur intellectu. Haec detraxit multipliciter animos in errorem; haec deorum numerum et nomina sua constituit fantasia. Non enim ex sensualitate dicta est stella aliqua — Mercurius (id est, mercator), Kyrios (id est, dominus) — sed rationabili quadam et fantastica disciplina. Secundum hanc apparentiam, quamlibet rem quodammodo fingimus animatam, et loquimur de quibuscumque tamquam haberent humanum corpus, humanam animam, et humanas penitus actiones. Secundum hanc etiam, rem inanimatam deum vel deam fingimus. Orationes igitur huiusmodi fictum intellectum proprie significantes, frequentius transumuntur ad designandum rem mediante qua intellectus proprius fingebatur. Hic est modus dicendi qui maxime decorat sententias

tracking his footprints. Lucan: "Caesar tracks the footprints of his son-in-law." That is, he urgently follows his son-in-law.

Some of these appearances involve the senses, some reason. A sensory appearance is what appears to one of the senses, as the sun rising out of the ocean, so that instead of saying, "The sun is rising," you can say, "Phoebus is emerging from the waves." Or, as someone wrote, "As Cynthia comes from the waves of Thetis." The name "Cynthia" is also derived from sensory perception. The moon was called Cynthia because to some people who lived near Mount Cynthus the moon appeared to come from that mountain. A lot of other names of gods and goddesses and also many of their myths of pagans were derived from sense impression—but no more about demons for the present. The example I just gave, "Caesar tracks the footprints of his son-in-law," also depends on sensory perception.

A rational appearance is one that is discerned not with the eyes but solely with the mind. This has drawn minds into error in many ways; it has created with its fantasy the number of the gods and their names. For it is not from sensory impression that a star gets its name—Mercury (that is, merchant), Kyrios (that is, lord)—but from a kind of reasoned but fantastical learning. According to this appearance, somehow we pretend that a thing is animated, and we speak about things as if they have a human body and human life, and do whatever humans do. In the same way too we imagine that an inanimate thing is a god or a goddess. Therefore, expressions of this kind that signify literally such a false understanding are more commonly transferred to designate the thing by means of which the literal idea was imagined. This is a way of speaking that more than any other

per quem auctores plenius commendantur. O, quanto desiderio versus quosdam Bernardi audivi commendari, qui pro hac, "Mentula impedit ne genus humanum moriatur," inquit,

> Militat adversus Lachesim sollersque renodat
> mentula Parcarum fila resecta manu.

Scio quod possetis dicere huiusmodi sententias falsas esse, et dici falsum pro vero, et hos versus pertinere ad idemptitatem. Sed non curo qualiter solvatur, dummodo pateat artificium sic dicendi. Rationabiliter censeo eas transumptas cum manifesta sit ratio similitudinis apparentia: sicut enim hostes adversantur ad invicem, sic mors et mentula.

Alibi, pro hac, vel quadam consimili, "Cygnus potest esse exemplum vitae contemnendae, qui moritur canendo," inquit,

> Et solus qui sentit olor discrimine quanto
> vivitur, et spreto funere cantor obit.

Alibi, pro hac, "Pavo est opus deliciosae pulchritudinis," inquit, "Naturae ludentis opus, Iunonius ales."

Item Martialis Coquus pro hac, "Vir bonus famosus est etiam post mortem," inquit,

> Duplicat aetatis spatium sic vir bonus, hoc est,
> vivere bene, vita posse priore frui.

beautifies sentences for which authors are lavishly praised. Oh, with what desire have I listened to some of Bernard's verses being praised! Bernard, instead of saying, "It is the penis that keeps the human race from dying out," said,

> The penis makes war on Lachesis and skillfully reattaches the threads severed by the hand of the Fates.

I know you could say that sentiments of this kind are false, and the false is being said for the true, and that these verses belong under sameness, not likeness. But I don't care how these objections are answered, as long as the artfulness of this way of speaking is made clear. I think that these metaphors accord with reason, because the reason is clear in the appearance of likeness: just as enemies are opposed to each other, so are death and the penis.

In another place, in place of, "The swan, which sings as it dies, can be an example of despising life," or something like it, he says,

> And the swan, the only creature that realizes how great is the risk in living, and dies a singer, defying death.

In another place, for "The peacock is a creation of entrancing beauty," he says, "Juno's bird, the creation of Nature made in sport."

Similarly, Martial the Cook, for "A good man is spoken of even after he dies," says,

> In this way a good man doubles the length of his life, that is, in living well and being able to derive satisfaction from his earlier life.

Qui enim bene vixit, apparet rationabili intellectui ipsum in aliis exemplariter vivere etiam post mortem. Hic modus plus commendat veteres quam modernos. Ait tamen unus modernorum de viro quodam qui magnae aetatis existens seram mortem sustinuit, propter aetatem sic,

> Inde Sibyllinos cum iam fastidiat annos
> morbidus et Parcae digitis languentibus aevi
> fila trahant, contenta situ sine forcipis usu
> putrida longaevae labuntur stamina vitae.

Apparet enim rationabili intellectui, secundum fabulas praeinventas, quod Parcae ex lassitudine torquendi digitos haberent languentes, cum revera neque Parcae sint neque fila. Videri etiam potest quod fila illa propter nimiam aetatem per se rumperentur.

Secundum hunc modum dictum est de Willelmo de Nunchamp epitaphium hoc modo:

> Mors huic invidit aut signa senilia vidit,
> virtutum numerum male credens esse dierum.

47 Aequipollentia consideratur in fine generali. Est enim finis generalis vel ineptum vel turpe, vel utile vel honestum. Cum igitur duarum praedicationum idem sit finis generalis, praedicatio illa quae expressius finem illum designat ponitur frequenter pro illa quae inexpressius. Verbi gratia, pro hac, "Iste est durae cervicis ad quamlibet doctrinam," ponitur

PART 2

For if someone has lived well, he appears to rational understanding to live again in others because of his example even after death. The metaphor, though, redounds to the credit of those living in past times more than those living now. Still, one of the moderns, of a man who lived to be very old and died at a great age, says with regard to his age,

> And so when a man has gotten sick and tired of being as old as the Sibyl, and the Fates are drawing the threads of his lifespan with feeble fingers, the rotten strands of the long life, only kept together by mold, give way without the use of scissors.

It appears to a reasoning mind, according to previously invented fables, that the Fates have feeble fingers because they are exhausted from winding, when in fact there aren't any Fates and there aren't any threads. It can also be seen that the threads break by themselves because they are so old.

An epitaph was made in this mode for William of Nunchamp:

> Death envied him or saw signs of age, believing mistakenly that the number of his virtues equaled that of his days.

A double meaning is something to consider in cases of general conclusions. For a general conclusion is either awkward or clumsy, or effective or fetching. Therefore when two predicates produce the same general conclusion, the one that communicates the conclusion more forcefully is often used in preference to the less forceful one. For example, instead of "He is stiff-necked toward any teaching," is

haec, "Iste est asinus ad lyram." Similiter in actionibus contingit, "Qui cito dat, placentius agit quam qui simpliciter dat." Item, "bis dat" similiter. Ideo pro hac, "Qui cito dat valde placenter agit," ponitur haec, "Qui cito dat, bis dat." Item si viderem aliquam castissimam mulierem aliquem procari, vel aliquod huiusmodi opus inutile facere, per aequipollentiam dicerem, "Iste arat litus," vel "Iste lavat laterem." Similiter pro hac, "Iste devincet hostes," ait Merlinus, "Colla eorum sub pedibus suis conculcabit." Similiter pro hac, "Iste erit magnae probitatis," dicitur, "Iste vindicabit Hectorem," id est similis erit, ac si posset Hectorem vindicare. Sed huiusmodi transfert frequentius ironia, et hoc etiam tum per hyperbolen, tum per litoten. Quandoque enim pro hac, "Iste erit valde probus," dicitur, "Iste adhuc trahet fabas ex olla."

48 Similitudo aliena in rebus extraneis consideratur. Verbi gratia, cum flos infans non sit nec cunas habeat, dicitur per transumptionem ad similitudinem puerorum, pro hac, "flos tener," "flos cunis egrediens." Statius pro hac, "Nunc praeparo me ad principale propositum," ait, "Nunc tendo chelyn," sumpto simili a citharoedo qui cum tendit praeparat se ad canendum.

49 In orationis transumptione notanda est quaedam dicendi elegantia, praeviso quod in oratione transumpta quaelibet dictio quasi syllabice tenetur. Dicemus igitur eleganter si una dictio semel posita uno respectu pars sit orationis

substituted, "He is an ass to the lyre." Similarly, there is a saying in the courts that "he who pays promptly wins more goodwill than he who just pays." "Pays twice" is a similar phrase. So we don't say, "He who pays promptly acts in a very acceptable fashion," but "He who pays promptly pays twice." Likewise, if I saw somebody accosting a most chaste woman, or doing something similarly futile, I would say, with a double meaning, "He is plowing a beach," or "He is washing a brick." Similarly, instead of "He will conquer the enemy," Merlin says, "He will trample their necks beneath his feet," and for "He will be of great moral standing," you say, "He will be a match for Hector," that is, be like him, as if he could match Hector. But metaphors of this kind are often made ironically, and also sometimes by hyperbole, sometimes by understatement. For sometimes instead of "He will be a very honorable man," we say, "He will yet draw beans from a pot."

A distant comparison is observed between things that are very different from each other. For example, although a flower is not a baby and does not have a cradle, yet for "a tender flower," using a metaphor based on a similarity to children, it is called "a flower just emerging from its cradle." Statius, for "Now I am preparing myself for my main theme," says, "Now I am tuning my lyre," the simile being taken from a lyre player, who when he is tuning is getting ready to play.

There is an elegant way of speaking in a metaphorical expression that needs to be mentioned, though first it has to be understood that in a metaphorical expression each word is as it were syllabic. And so we will speak elegantly if a single word in one regard is part of an expression that is wholly

secundum se totam transumptae, alio respectu proprie teneatur, et sic proprie et improprie, syllabice et dictionaliter teneatur. Verbi gratia, mulieri turpissimae quae faciem lavat nec tamen decoratur, dici potest, "Tu faciem lateremque lavas," id est, faciem lavas et inutile opus exerces. Simile Ovidius: "Demophoon, ventis et verba et vela dedisti." Haec enim, "Tu dedisti vela ventis," propria est, cum "dare" in una significatione idem sit quod "tradere." Haec autem, "Dedisti verba ventis," transumpta est secundum se totam ad significandum idem quod haec, "Infideliter locutus es." Et haec est transumptio secundum rationis apparentiam.

Supradicta orationis transumptio a Donato appellatur "allegoria," qui hoc exemplum ponit, "'Est iam tempus equum fumantia solvere colla,' id est, carmen finiri." Sed quod ipse dicit per allegoriam, "aliud significari quam dici," solvat theoricus; nos in practica detinemur. Allegoria cum similitudine et contrarietate excedens est et excessa.

Praeter igitur supradictas, eminent allegoriae species sex. Una quae ad similitudinem pertinet est aenigma. Aenigma est quaelibet obscura sententia probans ingenium divinandi, ut hic:

Quis dedit huic operi lucem? Vis nomen haberi?
Adde caput *gaure* cum transposita *suis aure.*

Item et illud:

Filia sum solis et sum cum sole creata,
sum decies quinque, sum quinque decemque vocata.

metaphorical, but in another regard is taken literally, and thus it is used both literally and figuratively, as a word and as part of a word. For example, to a very ugly woman who is washing her face without looking any better, you could say, "You are washing your face and a brick," that is, you are washing your face and wasting your time. Ovid's line is similar: "Demophoon, you have given your words and your sails to the winds." "You have given your sail to the winds" is literal, since one meaning of "give" is "hand over." But "You have given your words to the winds" is wholly metaphorical, meaning the same as "You spoke dishonestly." Also, this is a metaphor based on a rational appearance.

Donatus calls this form of metaphorical expression that I have been discussing "allegory," and gives this example: "'And now it is time to loosen the smoking necks of my horses,' that is, for the poem to be over." But as to his saying that through allegory "something else is meant than is said," let a theorist explain his meaning; we stick to practice. If allegory involves both likeness and opposition at once, it's both too much and too little.

Besides those already described, there are six kinds of allegory that present themselves. One kind that relates to likeness is enigma. Enigma is a dark statement that tests skill in detecting meaning, as in this example:

> Who gave light to this work? Do you want to find his name? Add the head of *gaure* to *suis aure* reversed.

Also this:

> I am the daughter of the sun and was created with the sun. I am ten times five (L), I am called five (V) and ten (X).

Dicitur tamen prout ad allegoriam pertinet aenigma specialius a Donato obscura sententia per rerum similitudinem occultata, ut, "Mater me genuit, eadem mox gignitur ex me," quod significat aquam in glaciem converti et glaciem in aquam resolvi. Huiusmodi raro inveniuntur in operibus authenticis, quamvis propter obscuritatem suam transumptive dicantur opera Aristotolis aenigmata.

Homoeosis est "minus notae rei per similitudinem eius quae magis nota est demonstratio." Haec habet tres species: icon, paradigma, comparatio. Icon secundum Donatum est collatio personarum ad invicem vel eorum quae personis accidunt, ut in hoc exemplo: "Os humerosque deo similis."

Paradigma est positio exempli dum tamen deterreat vel hortetur: deterreat, ut si dehortans aliquem ne dominum suum relinquat, dicas, "Iudas dominum suum tradidit et laqueo se suspendit"; hortetur, ut si movens aliquem ad conversionem, dicas, "Petrus flevit et dimissum est ei peccatum." Per coadunationem autem decoratur paradigma et est utilis materiis inchoandis. Unde quidam, volens hortari episcopum ut suspenderet parumper summas utilitates et audiret minores, inquit,

> Magnus Alexander bellorum saepe procellas
> immixtis fregit studiis, Socratesque studendi
> continuum solitus interrupisse laborem
> Threicias tremulo numeravit pollice chordas;
> cessit Athlas oneri, etc.

Et secundum hunc modum Iohannes Hauvillenis *Architrenium* inchoavit.

Paradigma etiam alio modo subdividitur. Quod enim Donatus "paradigma" nuncupat, hoc vocat usus modernus vel

PART 2

But with regard to its relation to allegory, enigma is specifically called by Donatus a statement darkened by the likeness of things, as, "My mother bore me and soon she herself is born from me," which means that water is turned into ice and ice is turned back to water. Enigmas are rarely found in the works of standard authors, although on account of their obscurity Aristotle's books may metaphorically be said to be enigmas.

Homoeosis is "indicating some unfamiliar thing by comparing it to something better known." It has three kinds: icon, paradigm, and comparison. Icon, according to Donatus, is comparing people or their attributes to each other, as in this example: "Like a god in his face and shoulders."

Paradigm is using an example to deter or encourage: to deter, as if, in encouraging someone not to leave his master, you should say, "Judas betrayed his master and hanged himself with a halter"; to encourage, as if, in urging someone to change his life, you should say, "Peter wept, and his sin was forgiven him." Paradigm is embellished by accumulation and is effective for beginning a subject. Thus one writer who wanted to encourage a bishop to suspend important activities for a while and attend to lesser ones, began,

> Great Alexander often interrupted the storms of war with intervals of study, and Socrates used to interrupt his constant work of studying to pluck the Orphean strings with agile thumb; Atlas rested from his burden, etc.

Also, John of Hauville began *Architrenius* with this device.

Paradigm is also subdivided in another way. For what Donatus calls "paradigm," the custom today is to call "fable" or

"apologum" vel "parabolam." Apologus vel parabola est cum, adducta rerum similitudine, quod de uno dicitur de alio intelligitur; sed apologus circa irrationabilia consistit, qualis est illa responsio Aristotelis: Cives quidam inituri erant foedus cum aliis, eo pacto ut removerent ab urbe sua quosdam civium suorum quos adversarii tumultuosos vocabant, eisque nominatim expressis consuluerunt super hoc Aristotelem, qui rescripsit per apologum, dicens, "Lupi quondam inierunt foedus cum ovibus eo pacto ut canes abigerentur a caulis."

Parabola circa animata consistit, quale est illud evangelii, "Homo quidam descendebat ab Ierusalem in Iericho," etc. Unde alibi, "Iam non in parabolis loquar vobiscum."

53 Comparatio est rerum dissimilium collatio, sicut icon similium. Haec a Donato parabole nuncupatur. Haec tum fit expresse, tum inexpresse. Expresse per dictionem exprimentem similitudinem, quales sunt haec: "sic," "sicut," "sicuti," "veluti," "quantus," "qualis," et huiusmodi. Consilium est talibus parcius uti. Fama enim nobilissimae *Thebaidos* ob comparationum frequentiam vix permansit illaesa. Inter omnes tamen, sive comparationes sive icon, nobilissima est quae fit per coadunationem dum tamen quaelibet pars brevibus verbis claudatur. Ut in versibus de quodam episcopo dictum est quod diu fuerat inutilis, "veluti sine pollice Tiphys, / aut Hector mucrone carens, aut Tullius ore." Haec icon est, quoniam rationabilium est collatio. Claudianus: "veluti sine remige puppis, / vel lyra quae reticet, vel qui non tenditur arcus." Haec comparatio est, quia non rationabilium est collatio; et notat uniformitatem. Haec enim comparatio esset inutilis, "veluti sine pollice

"parable." It is fable or parable when, employing the similarity between subjects, what is said of one is understood of the other; fables, though, deal with unrealistic events, as with this answer of Aristotle's: Some citizens were to enter into a pact with others, on the condition that they remove from their city certain of their citizens whom their adversaries called troublemakers. Giving their names, they consulted Aristotle on the matter, and he wrote back with a fable, saying, "Wolves once entered into an agreement with sheep on condition that dogs be kept away from the sheepfolds."

A parable is about living beings, as in the gospel story, "A certain man went down from Jerusalem to Jericho," etc. And elsewhere, "I will no more speak to you in parables."

Comparison brings together dissimilar things, as icon does similar things. Comparison is what Donatus calls parable. It is sometimes explicit, and sometimes implicit. Explicitly, by using a term of likeness, such as "so," "as," "even as," "as great as," "such as," and so on. The advice is, use such words sparingly. For the fame of the most noble *Thebaid* has hardly gone without injury because of its abundance of comparisons. But among all comparisons or icons, the noblest is that which is made by accumulation, provided each part is confined to a short phrase. As in verses about a bishop it was said that he was for a long time ineffective, "like Tiphys without his thumb, or Hector without his sword, or Cicero without his mouth." This is icon because it compares rational beings. Claudian: "like a ship without an oarsman, or a lyre that remains silent, or a bow that isn't drawn." This is comparison, because it is between nonrational objects, and it displays equivalence. For this comparison would not be legitimate, "like Tiphys without his thumb, or a lyre that

Typhis / vel lyra quae reticet, vel qui non tenditur arcus," propter inuniformitatem.

Inexpressa est comparatio sive icon ubi subtrahitur dictio exprimens similitudinem, et si per coadunationem fiat, venustior resultabit, ut hic:

> Praedecessoris lugerent cuncta, Iohannes,
> fata tui, lacrimasque viro nec dura negarent
> Gargara, sed patriae gemitus fecundior aufert
> gloria; pensat enim tructam balena, camelus
> castora, fons cyathum, sol lampada, linea punctum.

Similitudinarie posita sunt haec exempla. At ubi dici debuit "veluti pensat," dixit simpliciter "pensat."

Homoeosis igitur quaecumque, et si sit sine transumptione vel contrarietate, tamen absolute non profertur, sed semper habito respectu ad aliud.

remains silent, or a bow that isn't drawn," because it lacks equivalence.

A comparison or icon is implicit when the term of likeness is removed, and if it is done by accumulation, it will be all the more elegant, as in this case:

> For everything would be lamenting the death of your predecessor, John, and hard Gargara would not be refusing tears for that man; but your more abundant glory is silencing their groans, for a whale outweighs a trout, a camel beavers, a fountain a tumbler, the sun lamps, a line a point.

These examples are used as comparisons. And where he might have said "just as" these things outweigh, he just said they outweigh.

Therefore, every assimilation, even one without metaphor or opposition, is offered not absolutely but always with respect to something else.

3

Contrarietas est a rebus vel dictionibus contrariis ornata sententia, cuius species sunt allegoria et enthymema. Allegoriae species ad contrarietatem pertinentes sunt quinque: ironia, antiphrasis, charientismos, sarcasmos, paroemia. Nota vero quod istae species contrarietatem in voce non continent, sed tantum in intellectu.

Ironia est tropus per contrarium quod dicit ostendens, et hanc nisi gravitas pronuntiantis adiuverit, confiteri videbitur quod negare intendit. Martialis:

> Nullus in urbe fuit tota qui tangere vellet
>   uxorem gratis, Maeciliane, tuam
> dum licuit, sed iam positis custodibus ingens
>   turba fututorum est: ingeniosus homo es.

Haec tamen fit competenter par exclamationem, ut hic: "O magnum aurigam qui nomina nescit equorum!"

Antiphrasis est unius verbi ironia. Charientismos est tropus quo dura dictu gratius proferuntur, ut, interroganti, "Quaesivit me aliquis?" respondetur, "Bona fortuna," ut sic intelligatur, "Neminem me quaesisse." Sarcasmos est plena odio atque hostilis irrisio. Statius:

>   Me opponite regi
> cuius adhuc pacem egregiam et bona foedera gesto.

PART THREE

Opposition is an expression embellished by opposing things or words. Its kinds are allegory and enthymeme. Five kinds of allegory pertain to opposition: irony, antiphrasis, euphemism, sarcasm, and proverb. Note, though, that the opposition in these kinds does not consist in the words but only in how we understand them.

Irony is a trope communicating the opposite of what it says, and it will seem to assert what it intends to deny unless the emphasis of the speaker assists it. Martial:

> There wasn't a man in all Rome who wanted to touch your wife for free, Maecilianus, when it was allowed; but now that guards have been posted, there is a huge crowd of fuckers. You are one smart guy.

An effective way to be ironic is by exclamation, as in this case: "What a great charioteer! He doesn't know the names of his horses."

Antiphrasis is one-word irony. Euphemism is a trope in which hard things are worded in a kinder way, like the answer to the man who asked, "Did anyone miss me?": "Good luck," which he should take to mean, "Nobody missed me." Sarcasm is a hostile sneer, packed with contempt. Statius:

> Put me in front of the king. I'm still bearing the marks of his exceptional peace and his honest covenant.

Martialis:

> Quid mihi reddat ager quaeris, Line, Nomentanus?
> Hoc mihi reddit ager; te, Line, non video.

De paroemia infra dicetur.

2   Enthymema tam vocis quam sensus contrarietatem comprehendit. Quid sit enthymema habemus in *Topicis* Marci Tullii ad Trebatium dicentis, "Rhetorum 'ex contrariis conclusa' enthymemata appellantur, non quod non omnis sententia proprio nomine enthymema dicatur, sed, ut Homerus per excellentiam commune 'poetarum' nomen efficit apud Graecos suum, sic, cum omnis sententia enthymema dicatur, quia videtur ea quae ex contrariis conficitur acutissima, sola proprie nomen commune possedit. Eius generis sunt haec: 'Hoc metuere, alterum in metu non ponere.' 'Eam quam nihil accusas, dampnas; bene quam meritam esse aestimas, dicis male mereri?' 'Id quod scis prodest nihil; id quod nescis obest?' Hoc disserendi genus attingit omnino vestras quoque in respondendo disputationes, sed philosophorum magis, quibus est cum oratoribus ills ex repugnantibus sententiis communis conclusio, quae a dialecticis 'tertius modus,' a rhetoribus 'enthymema' dicitur." Hactenus Cicero.

3   Enthymematum species sunt contrarium, conversio, adversitas, metathesis, contentio, antitheton. Contrarium est quando, duobus repugnantibus positis, alterum probatur vel improbatur per reliquum, ut hic: "Qui sibi non parcit, mihi vel tibi quomodo parcet?" "Qui sua divulgat probra, credis

PART 3

Martial:

> You ask me, Linus, what profit my property near Nomentum gives me? Here's the profit it gives me, Linus: it keeps me from seeing you.

The proverb will be treated below.

Enthymeme includes opposition both of words and sense. We have a definition of enthymeme in Cicero's *Topics* to Trebatius, which says, "The rhetoricians' 'conclusion by contraries' is called enthymeme, not that it isn't a proper term for any expression, but, just as Homer has made the common noun 'poet' his own because of his excellence, so, though any expression may be called an enthymeme, because the one that is made by contraries seems most pointed, it has come to own the common noun alone as its proper name. Here are examples: 'Fear this, don't fear that.' 'You condemn a woman whom you accuse of nothing; are you saying that one you think deserving deserves to be punished?' 'What you know doesn't help you; is what you don't know hurting you?' This way of arguing is certainly relevant for your litigation, particularly in answering objections, but is even more relevant to philosophers, who share with orators the conclusion by contrary statements that the logicians call the 'third way,' the rhetoricians 'enthymeme.'" Thus far Cicero.

The types of enthymeme are contrary, conversion, adversity, metathesis, contention, and antithesis. Reasoning by contraries is when two opposites are set forth and one is proven or disproven by the other, as here: "How will a person who doesn't spare himself spare me or you?" "Do you believe a person who makes his own disgrace public will

quod mea celet?" "An metues aegrum quem sanum despiciebas?" "An soli cedes quem cum socio superabas?"

Conversio est quando ordo prius observatus convertitur, ut hic: "Iste vorator non comedit ut vivat, sed vivit ut comedat." Secundum hoc dictum est cuidam abutenti proprio filio, "Alii futuunt ut generent; tu generas ut futues." Seneca contra servum nolentem dare venenum domino petenti ait, "Non morieris domini arbitrio, morietur tuo?" Et alibi, "Alam eum qui propter debilitatem alitur, non alam eum qui propter alimenta debilitatur." Secundum hunc modum papa noster Innocentius tertius in postcommunione quadam ait, "Quod a te, Domine, descendit ad nos, ad te, quaesumus, a nobis ascendat, ut purificet quos redemit."

4 Adversitas multiplex est. Quandoque loquimur de duobus, quorum unum est ad aliud tamquam essent adversa. Lucanus: "Pugnare ducem quam vincere malunt." Loquitur tamquam haec duo, "pugnare" et "vincere," simul stare non possent, cum tantum propter victoriam pugnetur. Scio quosdam sic supplere, "quam vincere," "scilicet sanguine." Sed haec expositio grammatici simplicis est, non rhetorici, legentis, non docentis. Lucanus certe nullo modo determinationem illam in versu vellet apposuisse. Simile de quodam paupere proco dicente lenoni, "Adiuva me decipere filiam illius divitis ut eam habeam." Qui respondit, "Adiuvabo libenter, si non malis eam decipere quam habere." Ecce per prioris verba, deceptio illa fuit ad hoc ut haberet, responsum vero est tamquam decipere et habere essent adversa.

hide mine?" "Will you fear someone when he's sick whom you despise when he is healthy?" "Will you give way to one alone whom you overcame when he had a partner?"

Conversion is when an initial order is reversed, as in this case: "This glutton doesn't eat to live, but lives to eat." According to this, a man who was abusing his own son was told, "Others fuck to have children; you have children to fuck." Seneca said to a slave who, when his master asked him for poison, refused to give it to him, "You won't die by the will of your master, but he will die by yours?" And again, "I will feed a man who is fed because he is frail, I will not feed a man who is frail because of his eating." Pope Innocent III used this mode when he said in a post-Communion prayer, "We beg, Lord, that what has come down to us from you may go up from us to you in order to purify those whom it has redeemed."

4   Opposition is multiple. Sometimes we speak of two things, of which one is in relation to the other as if they were opposites. Lucan: "They would rather their general fight than win." He writes as if the two verbs, "fight" and "win," couldn't stand together, although fighting is only for winning. I know that some add, after "than win," "that is, with bloodshed." But that is the explanation of a simple grammarian, not a rhetorician, of a reader, not a teacher. In no way, surely, would Lucan want to add that qualifier to his line. It is a similar case with a poor suitor who said to a pimp, "Help me trick the daughter of that rich guy so that I can have her." He answered, "I'll be glad to help you as long as you wouldn't rather trick her than have her." In the first speech the point of tricking her was to have her, but the pimp answers as if tricking and having were opposites.

Quandoque ironice loquimur de duobus quae quasi concomitantia sunt tamquam simul esse non possint. Seneca: "Sacerdos vestra adhuc in lupanari viveret nisi hominem occidisset." Loquitur ironice, tamquam hominem occidere purgasset reliquum, cum utrumque malum sit. Quandoque de eodem tamquam essent adversa loquimur ratione diversorum statuum. Unde pro quodam homicida in se contra negantem ei sepulcrum, Seneca: "Irascere interfectori, sed miserere interfecti." Quandoque de adversis loquimur tamquam essent unum vel tamquam unum essent ad aliud. Seneca: "Movet me respectus omnium virginum, si in civitate nulla inveniri possit, neque meretrice castior neque homicida purior." Loquitur tamquam esse meretricem faceret in parte castitatem. Quandoque loquimur de eo quod commodum est tamquam esset incommodum. Lucanus: "Hoc hostibus unum, quod vincas, ignosce tuis." Victoria sua commodum suum fuit, et ideo sic dixit ut per hoc innueret se in nullo deliquisse, et ideo de facili veniam dandam. Exponat aliter qui voluerit.

5   Metathesis est rerum transpositio. Verbi gratia, cuiusdam filius propter meretricem abdicatus ex ea sustulit filium, qui moriens illum patri commendavit; adoptavit pater nepotem. Contradicitur sic, "Adoptavit eius filium propter quam eiecerat suum." Ecce transpositio rerum, potius enim videretur debuisse proprium filium non abdicasse propter meretricem quam eiusdem meretricis filium adoptasse. Secundum hoc dictum est, "Quam magnum est non laudari et esse laudabilem." Ordo rerum debitus est ut laudabilis laudetur.

PART 3

Sometimes we speak ironically of two things that are, as it were, coexistent as if they could not both be true at once. Seneca: "Your priestess would still be living in a whorehouse if she hadn't killed a man." He speaks ironically, as if to have killed a man would have wiped out the other, though both are bad. Sometimes by means of different conditions we speak of the same thing as if there were opposites. And so, speaking for a suicide against one who would deny him burial, Seneca: "Be angry with the killer, but pity the victim." Sometimes we speak about opposites as if they were a single thing, or as if they were a single thing with respect to something else. Seneca: "I am moved by respect for all virgins, if no one can be found in the city more chaste than a whore or purer than a murderer." He speaks as if being a whore made one a little bit chaste. Sometimes we speak of something advantageous as if it were hurtful. Lucan: "Forgive your enemies their one sin, that you are the winner." Caesar's victory was to Afranius's advantage, and so the latter spoke in such a way as to indicate that he had done nothing wrong, and so forgiveness should be granted him easily. Let anyone explain this differently if he wants to.

Metathesis is transposition. For example, a certain man had disinherited his son over a whore. The son then brought up a son by her, and as he lay dying commended him to his father, and the father adopted his grandson. This is spoken against, as follows: "He adopted the son of the very woman who had caused him to throw his own son out." Look how things are changed around: he'd have seemed to have done better not to disown his son because of a whore than to adopt the whore's son. In the same way it is said, "How great it is to deserve praise and not be praised." The natural thing

Hic modus competenter fit per coadunationem transumptionum, ut, si inveniatur indignior in aliquo praeponi digniori, hoc modo dici potest,

> Hic Nero praecedis, sequeris Cato; Byrrhia faris,
> Marce taces; Dave surgis, Homere iaces.

6   Contentio est sententia continens contrarias dictiones, veritatis tamen vel possibilitatis apparentiam non excedens. Removetur enim impossibilitatis apparentia per determinationem loci vel temporis vel rei. Loci, ut hic:

> Pompeius in Ponto fuit felix, in Graecia miser.

Temporis, ut hic,

> Res homo vana. Placet, sordebit; abundat, egebit;
> floret, marcebit; stat, cadet; est, nec erit.

Per determinationem rei removetur ut si dicam, "Diligit vetulas et puellas." "Vetula" et "puella" contraria sunt, sed talis res assignatur quae cum utroque stare potest, scilicet "diligere," quia unus homo potest utrasque diligere. Secus esset, si dicerem, "Tu diligis veterem puellam," istud enim non posset stare ad apparentiam litterae. Secundum hunc modum ait Martialis, "Arrigis ad vetulas, fastidis, Bassa, puellas." Habito respectu ad vetulas et puellas, fortior enim videtur contrarietas inter verbum et accusativum. Repugnat enim accidens vetulae quodammodo ei quod est arrigere.

is to praise the praiseworthy. This mode works well with the accumulation of several metaphors, as, if someone less worthy in some respect is preferred to a more worthy, it can be expressed in this way:

> Here Nero, you go first, Cato, you follow; Byrrhia, you talk, Cicero, you be silent; Davus, you rise up, Homer, you sink down.

Contention is a sentence that contains antithetical words, though without exceeding the appearance of truth or possibility. The appearance of impossibility is avoided by a modifier of place or time or subject. Of place, as here:

> Pompey was happy in Pontus, wretched in Greece.

Of time, as here:

> Man is an idle thing. He is pleasing, he will become repulsive; he is wealthy, he will be needy; he flourishes, he will fade; he stands, he will fall; he is, he will not be.

It is avoided by modification by a thing, as if I should say, "He loves old women and girls." "Old woman" and "girl" are opposites, but a thing is attributed to them that can hold true with either one, namely "love," since one man can love both. It would be otherwise if I were saying, "You love an old girl," since in its literal appearance it could not hold true. In this mode Martial says, "You are turned on by old women and turned off by girls, Bassa." Since reference is made to both old women and girls, the opposition between verb and accusative seems stronger, since the attribute of an old woman as object somewhat contradicts the notion of being turned on.

7 Huiusmodi contrarietatum alia localis, alia temporalis, alia realis. Localis temperatur per determinationem temporalem, ut hic, "Heri fui Parisius, hodie Rotomagi." Temporalis similiter per localem, ut in eodem exemplo. Iuxta temporalem contrarietatem Marcialis ait,

> Cras vives? Hodie iam vivere, Postume, serum est.
> Iste sapit quisquis, Postume, vixit heri.

Realem intellige per remotionem loci vel temporis, ut in hiis exemplis Senecae: "Si invitus pares, servus es; si volens, minister." Item, "Secrete ammone amicos, palam lauda." "Secrete" et "palam" contraria sunt. Huiusmodi est illud exemplum Ciceronis, "Hoc metuere: alterum in metu non ponere." Item Lucanus: "Dux sit in hiis castris senior dum miles in illis." (Miles, id est tiro.) Martialis:

> Mentiris iuvenem tinctis, Laetine, capillis,
> tam subito corvus, qui modo cignus eras.

Et illud Lucani: "Hoc petimus, victos ne tecum vincere cogas," et illud, "Sufficit huic tumulus cui non suffecerat orbis." Et illud de beata Virgine,

> Salve clavis prophetiae,
> de qua puer Isaiae,
> David gigas, nascitur.

PART 3

Some oppositions of this kind are local, some temporal, some pertain to a subject. A local opposition is qualified by a temporal modifier, as in this case: "Yesterday I was in Paris, today I am in Rouen." And a temporal opposition is balanced by a local modifier, as in the same example. As for a temporal opposition, Martial says,

> You will live tomorrow? Today is already late to be living, Postumus. The wise man, Postumus, is the one who lived yesterday.

You can recognize an opposition relating to a subject by the absence of reference to time or place, as in these examples from Seneca: "If you obey unwillingly, you are a slave; if willingly, you are an accomplice"; "Admonish your friends in secret, praise them openly." "In secret" and "openly" are contraries. Cicero's example is of the same type, "Fear this; don't fear the other." And Lucan: "Let the general on our side be older, provided that the soldiers on their side are older." ("Soldier" here means new recruit.) Martial:

> Laetinus, you are faking youth with your dyed hair, so suddenly a crow, you who were just now a swan.

Also this from Lucan: "This we ask, that you don't force us you've conquered to become conquerors with you." And, "A little mound is enough for one for whom the whole world hadn't been enough." And this on the blessed Virgin:

> Hail, key of Isaiah's prophecy, from whom the son, David's giant, is born.

7

Contingere autem potest in huiusmodi tam determinantia quam determinata contraria esse, ut si sic dicerem, "Si invitus pares, servus es, si volens, liber." Hic modus per coadunationem contrarietatum pulcherrime fit, ut hic:

> Mutuo distingue scola curia, bractea ferrum,
> stella lutum, verum fabula, gemma vitrum.

Et item,

> Fetidus est ille, redolens ego; sordidus ille,
> mundus ego; nugax ille, severus ego.

Fit etiam hic modus quandoque satis venuste per colorem quem "Singula singulis" appellamus. Martialis:

> Cum facias versus nulla non luce ducentos,
> Vare, nihil recitas. Non sapis, atque sapis.

Singula singulis hic reddenda sunt. Fiet autem modus hic venustissime si assit color quem "singula singulis" nuncupamus, et etiam coadunatio contrarietatum. Ut hic:

> Carmina qui quondam studio florente peregi;
> Flebilis heu maestos cogor inire modos.

Item de quodam qui in iuventute sua fuit ob vitae honestatem populis dilectissimus, in senectute ob vitae turpitudinem factus omnibus odiosus, sic,

PART 3

It can happen, though, in verse of this kind that both the modifiers and the words modified are opposites, as is the case if I were to say, "If you obey unwillingly, you are a slave, if willingly, you are free." This mode is achieved very pleasingly by accumulation of opposites, as here:

> Distinguish from each other school from court, gold leaf from iron, star from mud, truth from fable, gem from glass.

Likewise,

> He is smelly, I am fragrant; he is dirty, I am clean; he is frivolous, I am strict.

This mode is sometimes made quite elegant by means of the color we call "each to each." Martial:

> Though no day goes by, Varus, when you don't turn out two hundred lines, you recite nothing. You're a fool, and no fool.

Here the phrases mutually respond to each other. But the most elegant way of achieving this mode will be if you combine the color which we call "each to each" and accumulation of opposites too, as in this case:

> I who once wrote poems with youthful zeal, alas, am forced to turn in tears to sad refrains.

Again, here is a poem about a man who when he was young was most beloved by the people because of the uprightness of his life, but when he was old because of the wickedness of his life was hated by all:

> Gloria felicis olim viridisque iuventae
> vincitur, heu—misero commaculata sene.

Contra hanc dictionem "gloria" ponitur "heu," contra hanc dictionem "felicis," "misero," contra "olim" hoc verbum praesentis temporis "vincitur," contra "viridis," "commaculata," contra "iuvente," "sene."

8 Antithetum est sententia continens contrarias dictiones superfluitatis, sed et quandoque impossibilitatis apparentiam praetendentes—in intellectu tamen subtilis investigatoris solutio delitescit, ut hic, "Nimia humilitas superbia est"; "Nihil mihi donat qui omnia mihi donat." Sensus: nimia humilitas in apparentia, superbia est in existentia. Similiter, nihil mihi donat effectu qui omnia mihi donat promisso. Et hoc ideo dicitur, quia "Largissime promittere parum est facere."

Antithetum aliud inexpressum, aliud expressum. Antithetum inexpressum debile est, tum quia determinatione solvitur, tum quia a remotis sumitur. Determinatione solvitur ut in hiis versibus factis de abbate de la Yde quem ementulaverunt monachi proprii, sic:

> Abscidit patri genitalia filius, ut sic
> viveret in carne non caro mente pater.

Haec dictio "mente" debilitat antithetum. Melius esset subintellecta quam dicta.

A remotis sumitur multipliciter. Quandoque coassignantur aliqua duo quae non solent concomitari. Verbi gratia, non contingere solet quemquam luscum esse et bene videre. Martialis:

PART 3

> The glory of my once happy and flourishing youth is vanquished, alas—disgraced by a wretched old man.

"Alas" is opposed to the word "glory," "wretched" to the word "happy," "once" to the present tense verb "is defeated," "disgraced" to "flourishing," "old man" to "youth."

Antitheton is an expression containing terms opposite to excess, and even sometimes presenting the appearance of impossibility—though in the understanding of a subtle interpreter the solution may lie hidden. "Too much humility is pride"; "He who gives me everything gives me nothing." The sense is that the appearance of too much humility is pride in reality. Likewise, someone who promises me everything is in fact giving me nothing. And so there is a saying, "To promise lavishly is to do little."

8

Antitheton is either implicit or explicit. An implicit antitheton is weak, either because it is diluted by a modifier or because it is farfetched. It is diluted by a modifier, as in these lines about the abbot of Hyde who was emasculated by his own monks:

> The son cut off his father's genitals so that in this way he might live in the flesh not as flesh, but as a father in spirit.

"In mind" weakens the antitheton. It would be better understood than stated.

An antitheton is farfetched in many different ways. Sometimes two things are jointly attributed that don't usually go together. For example, it isn't usual for someone one-eyed to see well. Martial:

> Iliaco similem puerum, Faustine, ministro
> lusca Lycoris amat. Quam bene lusca videt!

Quandoque assignantur duo aliqua quorum unum est occulta privatio alterius, vel quasi. Verbi gratia, scelus et ignorare scelus, haec duo non concomitantur; unum est occulta privatio alterius. Dictum tamen est, "Imperio scelus est scelus ignorare." Quasi privatio, in Virgilio, "Una salus victis, nullam sperare salutem." Quandoque ex collatione duorum bonorum occulte colligitur quoddam malum. Verbi gratia, "Timere proprie est bonum, malum enim timore fugitur." Item, "Timere nefas est bonum." Ex hoc tamen et illo malum colligitur ex eo quod unum aliud determinat, ut hic:

> Imperio scelus est scelus ignorare, timentque
> hoc solum: regum sceptra timere nefas.

Quandoque sumitur antithetum a remotis per consequentiam. Verbi gratia, sumamus antithetum expressum, et videbimus inexpressum. Expressum est hoc: "Senes locupletes diligere odire est." Qui odit, per consequens posset dicere, "Morere." Martialis:

> Munera qui tibi dat locupleti, Gaure, senique,
> si sapis et sentis, hoc tibi ait, "Morere!"

Item cum nihil sit in rebus humanis perfectum, nihil est quod in aliquo saltem accusari non possit. Sit ergo

PART 3

> Faustinus, Lycoris with her one eye loves a boy like the page from Troy. How well the one-eyed woman sees!

Sometimes two attributions are made, one of which is the implicit negation of the other, or seems to be. For example, crime and being ignorant of crime are two attributes that don't coexist: one is the implicit negation of the other. Yet it has been said, "It is a crime for those in power to know nothing of crime." A seeming negation, as in Virgil: "The only hope of safety for the defeated is not to hope for safety." Sometimes by the comparison of two good things something bad is implicitly inferred. For example, "To fear in its proper sense is good, for evil is fled out of fear." Again, "It is good to fear wickedness." But from the two evil is inferred because one modifies the other, as in this case:

> It is a crime for those in power to know nothing of crime, and they fear this alone: that it be a sin to fear the scepters of kings.

Sometimes a farfetched antitheton depends on logical consequence. For example, let us take an explicit antitheton, and we will also see an unstated one. The explicit one is this: "To love rich old men is to hate them." Whoever hates them, could in consequence say, "Die." Martial:

> Gaurus, you are rich and old. Whoever gives you gifts — if you have any sense and wits about you — he is telling you, "Die!"

Again, since nothing in human affairs is perfect, there is nothing that can't be accused at least of something. Let

exemplum in virginibus. Pulcherrimas inspicimus, at in aliquibus accusamus secundum praedictam Ovidii sententiam. Turpes, vero, cum in omnibus accusabiles sint, ex more nostro praeterimus sub silentio et in nullo accusamus, quasi ex indignatione. Ex hoc fit antithetum expressum, sic: "Quam in nullo accusas, in omnibus accusas." Inexpressum vero per consequentiam fit. Quicquid enim in omnibus accusas, iudicio tuo dampnabile est; unde ait Cicero, "Eam quam nihil accusas, dampnas."

9 Antithetum expressum est in quo ponuntur verba expressam contrarietatem significantia. Talium antithetorum illud determinatum, aliud indeterminatum. Determinatio est appositio aliciuus verbi ex quo colligi potest solutio contrarietatis expressae. Verbi gratia, haec incompetens: "Servire regnare est." Si vero dicam, "Deo servire regnare est," haec dictio "Deo" hic appellatur determinatio, quia per illam presumitur solutio contrarietatis.

Notandum enim quod omne fere huiusmodi antithetum in intellectu habet latentem determinationem vel latentes determinationes quae subintelligendae quidem sunt, apponendae tamen non sunt, ut, cum dicitur, "Deo servire regnare est," sensus potest esse, "Qui Deo servit, imperat mundo." Talium determinationum quaedam perimens, quaedam augmentans, quaedam mediocris. Perimens est quae aufert suo contermino significationem vel suppositionem naturalem, ut, si dicam, "Falsus denarius non est denarius," "Sophisticum aurum non aurum," "Nihil mihi donat qui turpiter donat," et talia, videntur potius facere apparens antithetum quam verum.

young women serve as an example. We look at the most beautiful of them, and yet we find something to accuse them of, according to the previously mentioned opinion of Ovid. The ugly ones, though, since they are accusable in everything, we customarily pass over in silence and accuse them of nothing, as if in disdain. From this an explicit antitheton is created, in this way: "The woman you accuse of nothing you accuse of everything." But an implicit one depends on logical consequence. Anything that you accuse in everything is worthy of condemnation in your judgment; so Cicero says, "If you accuse a woman of nothing, you condemn her."

An explicit antitheton is one that contains words that signify an explicit opposition. These are either modified or unmodified. Modification is the introduction of a word that makes it easy to unpack an explicit antitheton. For example, it's pointless to say, "To serve is to reign." But if I should say, "To serve God is to reign," this word "God" here is called a modifier, because by it the unpacking of the opposition is understood.

It should be noted that nearly every antitheton of this kind has an understood, latent modifier or modifiers that are to be supplied but not stated, as to say, "To serve God is to reign" can mean, "Anyone who serves God rules the world." Some of these modifiers are elliptical, some supplementary, and some neutral. An elliptical one takes the meaning, or the word you'd naturally supply, away from its complementary term, so that, if I should say, "A false penny isn't a penny," "Philosophers' gold isn't gold," "He who gives grudgingly gives me nothing"—these statements seem to create an apparent antitheton rather than a real one.

Augmentans est quae vocis apparentia aggravat antithetum. Verbi gratia, magis est aperte esse malum quam esse malum. Seneca: "Aperte mala mulier quando est, tunc demum est bona." Colligitur igitur expositio ab hac dictione "aperte." Est enim is sensus, "Aperte mala quando est mulier, tunc minus est nocens."

Item, semper bene olere magis est quam simpliciter bene olere. Martialis Coquus:

> Hoc mihi suspectum est, quod oles bene, Postume,
> semper.
> Postume, non bene olet qui bene semper olet.

Id est, non bene olet per naturam qui bene olet semper, quia hoc non potest esse nisi per artificium.

Mediocris est quae nec perimit nec aggravat, et tales specificant sententias qualis appositio dativi vel accusativi. Lucanus: "Arma tenenti omnia dat qui iusta negat." Item Gaufroi Vinesauf de rege Henrico:

> Sufficit huic tumulus cui non suffecerat orbis:
> res brevis est ampla cui fuit ampla brevis.

Item: "Senes locupletes diligere odire est." Per accusativos istos scimus hunc sensum: diligere in apparentia odire est in veritate. Huius speciei est illud Ieronimi in libro quem fecit contra Iovinianum; ait enim contra tactum muliebrem, "Cum tactus depingat sibi etiam praeteritas voluptates,

PART 3

A supplementary modifier is one that intensifies an antitheton by the appearance of a single word. For example, to be openly bad is something more than to be bad. Seneca: "When a woman is openly bad, then finally she is good." The interpretation is understood from the word "openly." For the sense is, "When a woman is openly bad, then she is less harmful."

Again, to always smell good is something more than just to smell good. Martial the Cook:

> It is suspicious to me that you always smell good, Postumus. Postumus, a man who always smells good does not smell good.

That is, a man who always smells good does not smell good naturally, because that can only be by artifice.

A neutral modifier is one that is neither elliptical nor intensifying, and such things make sentences specific just as adding a dative or accusative does. Lucan: "He who denies what is right grants everything to one bearing arms." Similarly, Geoffrey of Vinsauf on King Henry:

> A little mound is enough for one for whom the whole world hadn't been enough: a small compass is large for one to whom a broad one was little.

Again: "To love rich old men is to hate them." From these accusatives we know that the sense is, to love in appearance is to hate in truth. An example of this type is what Jerome wrote in the book he composed against Jovinian; he says, to warn against touching women, "When the sense of touch depicts to itself even past pleasures, by remembering its sins

recordatione vitiorum cogit animam compati, et quodammodo exercere quod non agit." Haec dictio "quodammodo" determinatio est.

Indeterminatum dicitur antithetum per privationem determinationis. Talium aliud fit per positionem, aliud per remotionem. Positum antithetum est quod nihil abnegando contraria continet. Talium aliud regulare, aliud anomalum. Regulare quod secundum regulam aliorum falsum est ad litteram, et indiget expositoria quadam subtilitate, ut si dicam, "Byrrhia, totus in mendacio deditus, in sola falsitate fidelis est, stabilis in instabilitate." Hic ponuntur "fidelis" et "stabilis" abusive, habent enim ex institutione in bonum sonare.

Antithetum regulare, cum in multis sit utile materiis, plenius tamen invenitur circa fortunae materiam et amoris. Huiusmodi antitheti positio tum fit per adiacentiam, ut hic, "Amor est molle malum"; tum per appositionem, ut hic, "Mobilitas, statio fortunae, cuncta gubernat"; tum fit per verbum copulativum, ut hic, "Amicitia Neronis odium est"; tum fit per aliud verbum adiectivum, ut hic:

> Ad Venerem veniens Martem Mars exuit: horror
> blanditur, feritas supplicat, ira rogat.

Isti modi in multas et pulcherrimas extenduntur sententias. *Anticlaudianus* in descriptione domus Fortunae:

> Hic est Fortunae sua mansio, si tamen usquam
> res manet instabilis, residet vaga, mobilis haeret,
> cuius tota quies lapsus, constantia motus,
> volvere stare, situs decurrere, scandere casus.

it forces the soul to share the feeling, and in certain way to perform what it is not actually doing." The wording "in a certain way" is the modifier.

An unmodified antitheton is expressed by removing all modification. One way is by insertion, another by removal. An inserted antitheton is one that retains the opposites without denying either one. It is either regular or anomalous. The regular is what is literally false according to the standards of others, and it needs a certain subtlety to interpret, as if I should say, "Byrrhia, wholly given to lying, is faithful in falsity only, stable in instability." Here "faithful" and "stable" are misused, for in standard use they have to have a good sense.

Regular antitheton, although it is useful in many subjects, nevertheless is employed more frequently on the subjects of fortune and love. Its positioning is sometimes in juxtaposition, as, "Love is a soft evil"; sometimes in apposition, as, "Fickleness, the constant state of fortune, governs everything"; sometimes with a copulative verb, as here, "Nero's friendship is hatred"; and sometimes it employs a different, supplementary verb, as in this case:

> Coming to Venus, Mars lays aside Mars: terror wheedles, fierceness begs, anger pleads.

These modes are extended to many very beautiful sentiments. *Anticlaudianus,* describing Fortune's house, says,

> Here is Fortune's mansion, if something unstable can stand still, if a wanderer settles down, if a restless one stays in place. All of her rest is falling, her constancy movement; she stands when she is spinning, her stable state is to run onward, her climbing is tumbling.

Bernardus de revolutione firmamenti et aliis Noys operibus ait,

> Figit utrosque polos circumque volubile caelum
> flectit et aeternum volvere stare fuit.

Item, de damno ex quo postea sequitur commodum dici potest hoc modo, "O iactura placens, laetus dolor, utile damnum." Patet per praedicta exempla quod per coadunationem decorari potest iste modus. Notandum igitur quod in huiusmodi coadunationibus possunt pulcherrime substantiva sonare in bonum et adiectiva in malum, ut in conquestione Pyrami et Thisbes,

> Exhaurit miseros pax bellica, gloria tristis,
> dulcor amarus, egens copia, dirus amor.

E converso—substantiva possunt sonare in malum, adiectiva in bonum, ut hic:

> Scylla placens, blandae Sirenes, laeta Charybdis,
> fel sapidum, virus mulcebre, suavis amor.

Potest enim haec dictio "amor" indifferenter sonare in bonum et in malum propter contrarios sui effectus—efficit enim nunc gaudere, nunc dolere. Tertio modo sonabit pulcherrime unum substantivum in bonum, reliquum in malum. Similiter de adiectivis, si tamen ita ordinetur oratio ut prima dictio notet unum oppositorum, secunda reliquum, et sic per ordinem, ut hic,

PART 3

Bernard, speaking of the revolution of the firmament and other works of Noys, says,

> She fixes both poles and bends round the circumambient firmament; its eternal revolution was the cause of stability.

Again, a loss from which something good afterward comes can be expressed in this way: "Oh pleasing loss, happy sorrow, useful injury." It is clear from earlier examples that this mode can be embellished by accumulation. It should be noted that in accumulations of this kind, for the nouns to have a good sense and the adjectives a bad sense can have a special appeal, as in the complaint of Pyramus and Thisbe,

> We poor lovers are exhausted by warring peace, sad glory, bitter sweetness, needy abundance, cruel love.

Or the reverse—nouns can communicate a good sense, adjectives a bad, as in this case:

> Pleasing Scylla, flattering Sirens, happy Charybdis, delicious venom, soothing poison, sweet love.

For the simple word "love" can communicate either a good or a bad sense on account of the opposite effects it can have—for it can make you rejoice today and grieve tomorrow. In a third, very attractive, way one noun communicates a good sense and the rest a bad sense. It is similar with adjectives, as long as the sentence is so arranged that the first word denotes one of the opposite ideas, the next another, and so on sequentially, as in this case,

Falsa fides, odium mansuetum, dira voluptas,
 ira benigna, nocens gratia, poena placens.

11 Verborum adiectivorum positio per pulchras sententias extenditur. Martialis:

Extra Fortunam est quicquid donatur amicis:
 Quas dederis solas semper habebis opes.

Bene dicitur antithetum, quia dare et semper habere simul stare non possunt. Hic modus tum praetendit minus apparentem falsitatem, tum vero plenissimam impossibilitatem, falsitatem tantum, ut in illo versu sigilli in quo sculpta est imago virginis, habente sic, "Virgo patens celat quod littera clausa revelat." Contraria sunt "patens," "clausa"; contraria sunt "celare" et "revelare"; contraria sunt haec, "patens" et "celat," sicut haec, "clausa" et "revelat." Nec enim veri simile est "patentem celare," neque "clausam revelare."

Impossibilitatem quandoque praetendit haec positio. Verbi gratia, Iuvenalis, *Satira* sexta, ubi loquitur de Nerone Caligula, avunculo magni Neronis, cui Caesonia uxor sua dedit philtrum et fecit eum furere, dixit, "Tremulumque caput descendere iussit in celum." Ne imperatoribus detrahere videretur, qui post mortem deificari censerentur, "caelum" pro "inferno" posuit. Per hoc quod dicit "in caelum," honorat imperatores, per hoc quod dicit "descendere," tangit rei veritatem. Simile dixit quidam paginae suae quam misit viro magno, "Ad sacros ascende pedes." Lucanus similiter demonstrato Hercule inquit, "Huc, Antaee, cades." Hic modus per coadunationem pulcherrime procedit, similiter et per gradationem, ut in hoc exemplo:

PART 3

False faith, gentle hatred, cruel pleasure, benign wrath, hurtful thanks, pleasing pain.

The introduction of supplementary verbs is continued in beautiful sentiments. Martial:

> Whatever is given to friends is beyond the reach of Fortune: the only wealth you will always have is what you give away.

It is right to call this antitheton, since to give away and to always have cannot coexist. This mode sometimes offers falsity that is not immediately apparent, but sometimes utter impossibility: falsity plain and simple, as in the line on a seal on which is embossed an image of a young girl with the words, "This visible girl is hiding what the enclosed letter reveals." "Visible" and "enclosed" are opposites, as are "hide" and "reveal"; but "visible" and "hide" are opposites too, and "enclosed" and "reveal" as well. Neither phrase—"conceal what is visible" nor "reveal what is enclosed"—is plausible.

Sometimes the wording presents an impossibility. For example, Juvenal in the sixth *Satire*, where he speaks of Nero Caligula, uncle of the great Nero, whose wife Caesonia gave him a potion and made him go crazy, said, "And she ordered the trembling head to go down into heaven." Lest he seem to detract from emperors, who were thought to become gods after they died, he put "heaven" for "hell." In the phrase "into heaven" he honors emperors, in the phrase "go down" he glances at the truth of the matter. A poet said something similar in a page he sent to a great man, "Go up to the blessed feet." Lucan likewise said (as Hercules), "You will fall this way, Antaeus." This mode goes very nicely with accumulation, and likewise with climax, as in this example:

> Sic solatur amor: urunt solacia, lenit
> ustio, lenimen angit et angor alit.

12 Anomalum est antithetum quoddam quod solutione praedicta non indiget, quia, cum impossibile vel videatur, vel sit, falsum tamen non est. Ipsa enim quandoque impossibilitas veritas est. Hoc theologicum est et gloriosissimum antithetum. Secundum hoc dicitur:

> Sempiternum temporalem,
> moriturum immortalem
> virgo parit filium.

Et alibi:

> Fit aeternus temporalis
> et immensus fit localis.

Et item: "Fecunda virginitas." Et versus ille calicis: "Incircumscriptus hic circumscribitur auro." Omnia haec vera ad litteram. Gregorius etiam in libro *Dialogorum,* "Mortalitas nostra virtutem immortalitatis assumpsit, ex quo firmitas salvatoris nostram induit infirmitatem."

13 Per remotionem fit antithetum per negationem expressam, ut in hoc exemplo Ovidii, "Et non inventa reperta est." Secundum magistrum Rogerum, qui sic exponit: "'Et non inventa est' in propria forma, 'inventa sive reperta est' in aliena forma." Removetur autem tum concomitans, tum identitas. Concomitans ut in illo exemplo de igne illo qui ubique terrarum apparuit, et videbatur cuilibet civitas ei proxima accendi, cum tamen nusquam revera esset aliquis talis ignis. Unde ait Willelmus Lundoniensis, "Nusquam fuit

PART 3

Here is how love brings comfort: the solace burns, the burning soothes, the soothing hurts, and the pain nourishes.

An anomaly is an antitheton that doesn't need the explanation previously mentioned because, though it seems or is impossible, it is nonetheless not false. For sometimes impossibility itself is truth. This antitheton is theological and most wonderful. Here is an example:

> A virgin bears a son eternal and temporal, about to die and immortal.

And elsewhere:

> The eternal one becomes time-bound, and the immeasurable becomes local.

Again: "Fertile virginity." And the hexameter on a chalice: "Here the uncircumscribed one is circumscribed in gold." All of these are literally true. Also Gregory in the *Dialogues* writes, "Our mortality has taken on the power of immortality, because the strength of the savior has clothed our weakness."

Antitheton by removal employs explicit negation, as in this example from Ovid: "And although unfound she was discovered." This is according to Master Roger, who explains it thus: "She was both 'not found' in her proper form, and 'was found or discovered' in an alien form." Removal employs either coincident or identical words. Coincidence, as in the example of the fire that appeared everywhere on earth—and to everyone, the city next to him seemed to be burning, when in fact there was no such fire anywhere. And so William of London said, "What shone everywhere was

quod ubique refulsit." "Refulgere" et "esse" concomitantia sunt ignis. Simile Martialis:

> Qua factus sit requiris ratione,
> qui nunquam futuit pater Philenus?
> Gaditanus, Avite, dicat istud,
> qui scribit nihil et tamen poeta est.

"Scribere" et "poetam esse" concomitantia sunt.

Removetur identitas, id est, illud idem quod ponitur, ut in hoc exemplo: "Nihil mihi donat qui omnia mihi donat." Haec ergo remotio tum fit per nomen abnegativum, ut si dicam pro Caesare et Pompeio, "Qui utrumque diligit, neutrum diligit." Sensus est, "Qui utrumque diligit apparenter, neutrum diligit vere." Item: "Quam in nullo accusas, in omnibus accusas." Sensus est, "Quam in nullo accusas ore, in omnibus accusas mente." Ovidius: "Etsi pulvis nullus erit, tamen excute nullum." Sensus est, "Pone ibi pulverem esse et excute pulverem positive, nullum tamen veritate."

Quandoque fit haec remotio per verbum abnegativum. Unde ait quidam dominus et dilectus meus de monacho de Hyda, qui ementulavit abbatem suum, sic,

> Filius abscidit patris genitalia patri;
>   posset ut esse pater, abstulit esse patrem.

Sensus est, "Posset ut esse pater spiritualis, abstulit esse patrem carnalem." Item, propter quosdam praesumptuosos dici solet, "Non est parum scire se nihil scire"—iuxta illud sapientis, "Magnum est intelligere se nihil intelligere," et iuxta illud alterius sapientis, "Hoc solum scio, me nihil scire."

nowhere." "Shine" and "be" are concomitants of fire. Likewise Martial:

> You ask how it happened that Philenus, who never has fucked, is a father? Gaditanus can tell you, Avitus, since he writes nothing and yet is a poet.

"Write" and "be a poet" are concomitants.

Removal employs identity, that is, repetition of the same expression, as in the following example: "Who gives me everything gives me nothing." This removal is sometimes made by means of a negative noun, as if I should say about Caesar and Pompey, "Who loves both loves neither." The sense is, "He who apparently loves both loves neither truly." Again: "The woman you accuse of nothing you accuse of everything." The sense is, "The woman you do not accuse out loud, you accuse of everything in your heart." Ovid: "Even if there is no dust there, flick away that nothing." The sense is, "Pretend there is dust there and flick off the imagined dust, but flick off nothing in reality."

Sometimes this removal employs a verb of abnegation. Accordingly a certain master and a dear friend of mine says of the monk of Hyde who emasculated his abbot,

> The son cut off his father's genitals; so that he could be father, he removed the possibility of fatherhood.

The sense is, "So that he could be a spiritual father, he took away the possibility of fatherhood." Again, it is often said about certain presumptuous people, "It is no small thing to know that one knows nothing"—according to the saying of a wise man, "It is great to understand that one understands nothing," and also the saying of another wise man, "The only thing I know is that I know nothing."

Quandoque fit haec remotio per adverbium abnegativum. Martialis:

> Vult, non vult dare Galla mihi, nec credere possum
> quod vult quod non vult, quid sibi Galla velit.

Item Martialis:

> Matrem quae cupit esse se sororem
> nec matrem iuvat esse nec sororem.

Idem:

> Hostem cum fugeret se Fannius ipse peremit.
> Hoc plus quam furor est, ne moriare mori.

Hanc sententiam amplexans, Hegesippus in oratione Iosephi ait, "Timidus est et qui mori non vult quando oportet, et qui vult quando non oportet. Quis enim ignorat femineae libertatis esse et muliebris fortitudinis 'ne moriare mori' velle?" Secundum hunc modum dictum quoddam a Ieronimo in libro quem edidit contra Iovinianum in principio memoria dignum censeo. Condemnans enim difficultatem litterae suae, ait, "Iovinianus in libris suis totus tumet, totus iacet: attollit se per singula, et quasi debilitatus coluber in ipso conatu frangitur." Et post pauca, "Quotiescumque eum legero, ubi me defecerit spiritus, ibi distinctio est. Totum incipit, totum pendet ex altero, nescias quid cui cohaereat; et exceptis testimoniis scripturarum, quae ille venustissimae eloquentiae suae flore mutare non ausus est, reliquus sermo omni materiae convenit, quia nulli convenit."

PART 3

Sometimes this removal employs a negative adverb. Martial:

> Galla both wants yet doesn't want to open up to me, nor can I believe, since she wants what she doesn't want, what Galla intends.

Martial again:

> A mother who would rather be sister isn't happy being mother or sister.

And again:

> While fleeing the enemy Fannius killed himself. This is more than madness, to die lest you die.

Embracing this idea, Hegesippus in the speech of Josephus says, "Both the man who doesn't want to die when he should and the man who wants to when he shouldn't are cowards. For who doesn't know that it is characteristic of female freedom and womanly courage to want 'to die lest you die'?" In relation to antitheton, I think that the words of Jerome in the beginning of the book he wrote against Jovinian are worth mentioning. Condemning the opacity of Jovinian's style, he says, "In his books Jovinian is all swollen, and all flat. He raises himself here and there, but like a wounded snake is defeated in the very attempt." And after a bit, "Every time I read him, where my breath gives out comes punctuation. Everything is a beginning, everything depends on something else; you can't tell what goes with what, and except for the citations from scripture, which he has not dared to change because of the flower of their so very elegant eloquence, the rest of what he writes fits any subject because it fits none."

4

Praesentem adusque terminum distulimus paroemiam, ut de ea coniunctim ageremus. Nascitur enim tum ex identitate. tum ex similitudine, tum ex contrarietate. Paroemia igitur idem est quod "proverbium." Proverbiorum aliud est epiphonema, aliud translaticia, aliud enthymema. Epiphonema idem est quod identitatis proverbium, quod alio nomine "tautoparonomion" appellatur; et dicitur epiphonema ab *epi,* quod est "in" et *phonos,* quod est "sonus," quasi "in ipsa materia sonans," qualis est haec sententia: "Duplice post melior una loquela prior." Item: "Melius est sub bona spe pati quam properando decipi." Huiusmodi circa materiam suam coartantur, ut si dicerem, "Disseramus de venturis, quia 'Duplice post melior una loquela prior.'" Simile:

> Crescentisque frequens incendia foederis auget
> mentio; mortifero cura nociva malo est.

Huiusmodi est hoc exemplum: "Magis nocent insidiae quae latent." Et hoc: "Sera est erroris deprehensio cum pudeat confiteri."

[2] Translaticia est sententia ab una materia in aliam per similitudinem translata, ut si dicam, "Scribere non audeo: recens scriptor detractores timeo; ad suspicionem vulneris tiro pallescit." Ovidius:

> Adde quod et partus faciunt breviora iuventae
> tempora; continua messe senescit ager.

PART FOUR

We have put off paroemia until this end of the book so as to treat it all in one place. It arises from sameness and likeness and opposition. The word has the same meaning as "proverb." Proverbs are either epiphonemes, metaphorical, or enthymemes. An epiphoneme is the same as a proverb of sameness, also called *tautoparonomion,* and comes from *epi,* which is "on" and *phonos,* which is "sound," as if "sounding (only) on the actual subject matter," as in this sentence: "One word beforehand is better than two afterward." Also: "It is better to suffer with good expectations than to hurry and be deceived." Things of this kind are closely tied to their subject, as if I said, "Let's talk about what's to come, because 'One word before better than two after.'" Similarly:

> Harping on it fans the flames of the growing pact;
> harmful anxiety leads to deadly evil.

Here is another example: "Hidden snares do more damage." And this: "The detection of an error comes too late should one be ashamed to confess it."

The metaphorical paroemia involves a transference from one subject to another because of a likeness, as if I should say, "I don't dare write: as a young writer I'm scared of back-biters; a novice soldier goes white at the mere suspicion of a wound." Ovid:

> Besides, births shorten the period of youth; a field
> ages with constant harvesting.

Et nota quod eadem sententia quae translaticia est potest esse epiphonema propter mutationem materiae, ut si dicam, "Noli agrum hunc quolibet anno serere, quia continua messe senescit ager."

3 Enthymematis proverbium fit rationibus supradictis, et illud ad contrarietatem pertinet. Verbi gratia, "Innocentes occidit qui nocentes liberat." Item: "Amoris vulnus idem qui sanat facit." Item: "Miserum te iudico quod nunquam fuisti miser."

De hiis tribus modis mentionem faciens, Seneca *De controversiis* de amico suo locutus est, dicens, "Solebat Latro meus hoc genere exercitationis uti, ut nihil praeter epiphonemata aliquo die scriberet, aliquo die nihil praeter enthymemata, aliquo vero die nihil praeter has 'translaticias,' quas proprie 'sententias' dicimus, quae nihil habent cum ipsa controversia implicitum, sed satis apte et alio transferuntur, tamquam quando de fortuna, de crudelitate, de saeculo, de divitiis dicuntur; hoc genus sententiarum 'suppelectilem' vocabat." Paroemia venustissime intereretur materiis, venustissime materias inchoabit, venustissime terminabit.

PART 4

And notice that the same proverb that is metaphorical can be an epiphoneme if the subject changes, as if I should say, "Don't plant this field every year, because a field ages with constant harvesting."

An enthymemic proverb is made according to the principles given above, but pertains to opposition. For example, "He who lets criminals go free kills the innocent." Or: "The one who heals a love wound is the one who causes it." Or: "I think you are unhappy because you have never been unhappy."

Seneca mentions these three modes when speaking of his friend in the *Controversies:* "My friend Latro used to practice a kind of exercise in which on one day he would write nothing but epiphonemes, another day nothing but enthymemes, another day nothing but those 'metaphorical' expressions that we properly call 'adages,' that have no necessary connection with the *controversia* but can be transferred aptly enough to another context, as when the subject is fortune or cruelty or the age or riches; he called adages of this kind 'stock.'" A paroemia will go neatly in the middle of a subject, it will start it neatly, and it will end it neatly.

5

Quia superius mentionem fecimus de uniformitate, notandum quod circa tractandi genera in omnibus est, et super omnia munditia est conservanda. Haec consistit in uniformitate et diversitate et debita positione dictionum. Notandum ergo quod uniformitas et diversitas aequis passibus ambulant. Debent enim in uniformitate diversitas et in diversitate uniformitas observari, adeo ut quaelibet oratio polita dici possit vel uniformitas diversa vel diversitas uniformis.

Uniformitas consideratur in conservantia aequali rerum vel vocum; diversitas in earundem variatione. Quod patebit manifestius in exemplis. Statius: "Iam clipeus clipeis, umbone repellitur umbo, etc." Uniformitas consideratur in principiis istarum dictionum "clipeus, clipeis," diversitas in fine. Item diversitas consideratur in eo quod prius loquitur de clipeis, postea de umbonibus, postea de ensibus, et sic per ordinem. Uniformitas vero in eo quod sicut prius fit sermo de clipeis per nominativum et ablativum, ita postea de umbonibus, ita tertio de ensibus, et sic per ordinem. Si ergo diceretur, "Iam clipeus clipeis, clipeoque repellitur umbo," laederetur primo loco diversitas, secundario uniformitas diversitatis. Item isti versus sunt fere maxime commendati in Statio, et tamen laeditur uniformitas ubi dicitur, "iam clipeus clipeis." Fit enim in hiis versibus sermo de umbonibus in identitate numeri, similiter de ensibus et de pedibus at de cuspidibus. Non sic de clipeis, cum una dictio sit

PART FIVE

Since we mentioned uniformity above, it should be noted that it applies to every kind of writing, and above all purity of style has to be maintained. This consists in uniformity and diversity, and the fitting placement of words. Note, then, that uniformity and diversity march in step with each other. In uniformity diversity has to be preserved, and in diversity uniformity, so that any polished writing can be called either diverse uniformity or uniform diversity.

Uniformity is seen in the equal preservation of subjects and language, diversity in varying them. This will be made clearer by examples. Statius: "Now shield is repelled by shields, boss by boss, etc." The uniformity is seen in the beginnings of the words *clipeus* (shield) and *clipeis* (by shields), the diversity in the endings. Uniformity is also seen in the fact that he first talks about shields then bosses, then swords, and so on in order. It is uniformity, though, in the fact that just as he speaks first of shields in the nominative and ablative, he goes on to speak thus of bosses, then thirdly of swords, and so on in order. For had he said, "Now shield is repelled by shields, and boss by shield," diversity would have been marred in the first place, and also the uniformity of diversity. Furthermore, these verses are almost the most admired in Statius, and yet uniformity is marred in the phrase, "now shield by shields," for as the lines go on they speak of bosses in the same number, and then swords and feet and spearpoints. Not so, though, with shields, since one word is

singularis numeri, reliqua pluralis. Dixisset ergo melius, ut videtur, "iam clipei clipeis." Sed adhuc laederetur iterum uniformitas ex eo quod de aliis fit mentio in singulari numero, de clipeis in plurali. Dixisset ergo adhuc melius sic, "iam clipeo clipeus," nisi quia auctor vitavit ibi nostram licentiam quam nos appellamus penthemimerim. Item laeditur uniformitas ubi dicit, "ense minax ensis." Male enim habet haec dictio "ensis" adiectivum cum aliae non habeant.

2 Item in fabula de Pyramo et Thisbe, in hiis versibus,

> Dum pietas pueros castigat sedula, mulcet
> nunc amor illecebris, nunc tonat ira minis.

contra hanc dictionem "amor" ponit diversitas hanc dictionem "ira." Ex uniformitate est quod similiter contra hanc dictionem "illecebris" ponitur haec dictio "minis," et contra hoc verbum "tonat" hoc verbum "mulcet." Similiter in commendatione Pyrami, si sic diceretur,

> Militat in membris Hector, callescit Ulixis
> ingenio, puro ridet in ore Paris,

laederetur uniformitas ex eo quod haec dictio "in" ponitur cum primo ablativo et ultimo, et non cum medio. Unde utilius dicitur, "callescit Ulixis in sensu." Item in hiis versibus,

> Quid quod tam sapiens sine sensu, quod sine lingua
> rhetor, discretus quod rationis inops?

hic laeditur uniformitas ex eo quod haec dictio "quod" bis ponitur ante primam dictionem suae rationis, tertio post.

singular, the other plural. He'd have done better, it seems, to write, "now shields by shields." But uniformity is marred again anyway by the fact that the others are mentioned in the singular, shields in the plural. So he'd have done even better to write, "now shield by shield," unless he was avoiding here the license that we call penthemimer. Uniformity is marred again when he writes, "threatening sword by sword," because it is wrong for "sword" to have an adjective when the other nouns do not.

Likewise in the story of Pyramus and Thisbe, in the lines, 2

> While the pious busybodies chide the young people,
> one minute love soothes them with its charms, the
> next anger bombards them with threats.

it is diversity that opposes the word "anger" to the word "love," and uniformity that similarly opposes "charms" to "threats," and "soothes" to "bombards." Again, in the praise of Pyramus, if it said,

> Hector soldiers in his limbs, Ulysses schemes with his
> intelligence, Paris smiles in his fine face,

uniformity would be marred because "in" accompanies the first and last ablatives, but not the middle one. So it is more effective to say, "Ulysses schemes in his sense." Again, in these lines,

> What of the fact that so wise a man is without sense,
> that a rhetorician is without a tongue, that a man of
> discretion is devoid of reason?

uniformity is marred here because the word *quod* is twice put before the first word of its argument, the third time after it.

3   Item Ovidius:

> Tres sumus imbelles numero: sine viribus uxor
>   Laertesque senex, Telemachusque puer.

Quidam, quibus gravis est concussio inter hanc dictionem "uxor" et hanc vocem "sine viribus," dicunt sic punctum debere fieri: "Tres sumus imbelles numero sine viribus," non advertentes quod, dum conantur Ovidium a Scylla eicere, proiecerunt in Charybdim. Haec vox enim "uxor" sic esset sine determinatione, cum haec vox "Laertes" suam habeat determinationem, et "Telemachus" suam, et sic uniformitas graviter laederetur. Est ergo haec vox "sine viribus" determinatio huius vocis "uxor." Latius solvat qui velit. Nec tamen est penitus uniformitas illaesa, cum haec vox "sine viribus" non sit simplex dictio appositiva, sicut haec vox "puer" et haec vox "senex." Cum uniformitate maiori posset dixisse, "Tres sumus imbelles numero tibi: debilis uxor, Laertesque, etc." Nec tamen adhuc esset penitus uniformitas depurata, cum haec dictio "debilis" sit adiectiva, haec dictio "puer" et haec dictio "senex" substantivae.

4   Item qui de Davo dixit,

> Fomentum sceleris, mundi sentina, ruina
>   iustitiae, legum laesio, fraude potens,

per hunc finem "fraude potens" vehementer laesit uniformitatem. Item in metaphora similiter laeditur uniformitas, ut hic:

PART 5

Again, Ovid:

> Though three in number, we are unfit to fight: a wife without strength, Laertes an old man, and Telemachus a boy.

Some people, to whom the clash between "wife" and "without strength" is a serious fault, say it ought to be punctuated like this: "Though three in number, we are unfit to fight and without strength," not noticing that as they try to thrust Ovid away from Scylla they have plunged him into Charybdis. For then "wife" would have no modifier, while "Laertes" has its modifier and "Telemachus" has its, and thus uniformity would be seriously flawed. Therefore the phrase "without strength" modifies "wife." Let whoever wants to explain this more extensively go ahead. However, the uniformity is not utterly flawless, since the phrase "without strength" is not a simple appositive word, like "boy" and "old man." It could have been expressed with greater uniformity, "Though three in number, we are unfit to fight for you: a weak wife, and Laertes, etc." And yet the uniformity would still not be completely perfect, since "weak" is an adjective and "boy" and "old man" are nouns.

Again, the poet who wrote of Davus:

> Encourager of crime, dregs of the world, ruin of justice, violator of laws, able in fraud,

by the ending "able in fraud" gravely damaged uniformity. Uniformity is likewise damaged by a metaphor, as in this case:

> Pronus ad insidias, ad commoda lippus, ad iram
> velox, ni noceat se sibi deesse timet.

Auctoris pace, dixerim haec dictio "lippus" inutiliter ibi ponitur transumptive, cum haec dictio "pronus" et haec dictio "velox" non transumantur. Item in synonymis laedi potest, ut hic:

> Vivendi modus est una gaudere, dolere
> coniunctim, pariter ire, sedere simul.

Hic uniformis est diversitas synonymorum — si vero bis poneretur haec dictio "pariter," sic,

> Vivendi modus est pariter gaudere, dolere
> coniunctim, pariter ire, sedere simul,

sic laederetur uniformitas. Per haec exempla possunt infinita alia dinosci subtiliter intuenti.

5 Munditia consideratur in debita et ornata positione dictionum de quarum quibusdam agere libet, scilicet de hiis: "adhuc," "porro," "ecce," "quippe," "et," "-que," "quoque," "etiam," "[nec]," "sed," "tamen," "vel," "atque." Haec vox "adhuc" quadrupliciter ponitur. Pro praesenti, ut hic: "Non adhuc recedis ab Oxonia." Pro futuro, ut hic: "Adhuc veniam Oxoniam." Pro praeterito, ut hic: "Dum licuit adhuc tecum vixi." Pro praesenti confuso, ut in Bernardo dicente, "Cui sol dulcis adhuc primo blanditur in ortu," id est, quando sol oritur.

PART 5

> Prone to treachery, blind to what is good, quick to anger; unless he does harm, he fears he is untrue to himself.

My apologies to the author, but I would say that "blind" is ineptly used here metaphorically, since "prone" and "quick" are not metaphors. Uniformity can be flawed by synonyms too, as in this case:

> Their way of life is to share joys, to be sad in unison, to walk together, to sit at the same time.

The uniformity here is the diversity of the synonyms—but if you said "together" twice, thus,

> Their way of life is to share joys together, to be sad in unison, to walk together, to sit at the same time,

the uniformity would be flawed. These examples will enable anyone who studies them carefully to recognize any number of others.

Purity of style is seen in the proper and ornamental use of words some of which I intend to treat, such as: *adhuc* (still), *porro* (further), *ecce* (behold), *quippe* (indeed), *et* (and), *-que* (and), *quoque* (too), *etiam* (also), *nec* (nor), *sed* (but), *tamen* (yet), *vel* (or), *atque* (and). The word *adhuc* (still) is used in four different ways. With reference to the present, as here: "You are still not leaving Oxford." With reference to the future, as here: "I shall still come to Oxford." With reference to the past, as here: "I still lived with you while it was permitted." In a gnomic present, as in Bernard, when he writes, "Which the sweet sun still soothes at its first coming up," that is, at sunrise.

"Porro" adversative habet poni. Unde illud: "Porro unum est necessarium." "Ecce" semper novitatem aliquam introducit, ut in fabula de Pyramo:

> Ecce rudis teneros infantia vagit amores,
> cum non possit adhuc lingua tenella loqui.

Lucanus:

> Ecce nefas belli! reseratis agmina portis
> captivum traxere ducem.

Haec fuit mira novitas.

6 "Quippe" secundum Devoniensem idem est quod "certe." In quibusdam quidem locis difficile est aliter exponere. Secundum quosdam interrogative habet poni, et exponitur fidelius, "quippe," id est, "quid mirum?" Huic positioni consentio vehementer. Unde de rubore sito super collem faciei dictum est,

> Hic velut in solio regnat rosa: quippe pudorem
> regem virgineae simplicitatis habet.

Exponitur: "quippe," id est, "quid mirum si regnat, regem habet in maritum." Bernardus: "Homines, quia locum incolunt inquietum, tumultus instar veteris, motus permutationum necesse est experiri. Quippe quae de caelo sideribusque discesserat potentius expurgata, in inferioribus remansit ad plurimum silvae necessitas influentis." Idem alibi: "Mercurio virga levis in manibus, pes alatus, expeditus accinctus. Quippe qui deorum interpretis legatique muneribus fungebatur." Exponitur: "quippe," id est, "quid mirum"; "qui,"

PART 5

Porro (further) can be used adversatively. Thus: "Further, one thing is necessary." *Ecce* (behold!) always introduces some novelty, as in the story of Pyramus:

> Behold! Unformed infancy bewails its tender desires,
> since the baby tongue cannot yet speak.

Lucan:

> Behold the criminality of war! The gates were opened,
> and the troops dragged out their captive general.

That was a strange and amazing event.

According to Roger of Devon, *quippe* (indeed) is the same as "certainly." And indeed in some places it is hard to explain it any other way. According to some, it can be used questioningly, and then *quippe* is explained more accurately, as "why wonder?" With this position I strongly agree. Thus of the blush on the hillside of a face it has been said, 6

> Here the rose reigns as on a throne: no wonder
> (*quippe*) — it possesses modesty, the king of maidenly
> simplicity.

To explain, *quippe,* that is, "no wonder if it reigns, it possesses the king for its husband." Bernard: "Because men live in a restless place, the image of ancient chaos, they necessarily experience the disturbances of its changes. And why wonder, for the necessity of matter, ever in flux, which had been vigorously expelled and had departed from heaven and the stars, remained for the most part in the lower regions." And the same writer in another passage: "Mercury had a light wand in his hands, wings on his feet, equipped lightly. No wonder, since his job was to function as interpreter and messenger of the gods." To explain: *quippe,* that is, "no

id est, "quia ille fungebatur, etc." Sive igitur exponatur, "quippe," id est "quid mirum," sive "quippe," id est "certe," officium eius purissimum censeo, ut introducat rationem aliquam proximo supradicti.

7   De positione huius coniunctionis "et," notandum quod in coadunatione dictionum vel orationum multiplici, si assit tamen unica coniunctio copulativa vel disiunctiva, oportet ut vel cum ultima oratione vel cum finali veniat dictione. Cum ultima oratione, quantum ad adiunctum, ut hic,

> In stellis Codri paupertas, copia Croesi,
>   incestus Paridis, Hippolytique pudor.

Statius: "Iam clipeus clipeis, umbone repellitur umbo, etc." Cum finali dictione, quantum ad polysyndeton, ut hic:

> Pectora, mamma, latus, venter, femur, ilia, lumbi,
>   brachia, spina, genu, crura pedesque latent.

Si alibi ponatur, vel erit vitium vel figura, antiquis forte excusabilis, modernis inexcusabilis. Si plures fuerint coniunctiones quam una, necesse est ut vel ubique ponatur excepto principio, et copulative teneatur, vel ubique sine exceptione, et distributio resultabit. Copulative, ut hic:

> In stellis pugil est Pollux, et navita Tiphys,
>   et Cicero rethor, et geometra Thales.

Distributive, ut hic:

> Dum rex, dum proceres, dum starent pergama, Troia
>   et decus et species et caput orbis erat.

wonder," "who," that is, "because he functioned, etc." Really, whether we explain it as "no wonder" or as "certainly," I think its basic purpose is to introduce some rationale for what was spoken most recently.

As to the positioning of the conjunction "and," it should be noted that in a multiple accumulation of words and phrases, if there is only one copulative or disjunctive conjunction, it ought to come with the last phrase or the final word. With the last phrase as a connective, as here,

> In the stars are the poverty of Codrus, the wealth of Croesus, the unchastity of Paris, and the modesty of Hippolytus.

Statius: "Now shield is repelled by shields, boss by boss, etc." With the final word as a polysyndeton, as in this case:

> Breasts, pap, side, belly, thigh, abdomen, loins, arms, spine, knee, shins, and feet—all are hidden.

If it is put anywhere else, it will be either a fault or a figure, maybe excusable for the ancients but not for moderns. If there are more "ands" than the one, either it has to be put everywhere except the beginning, and is taken copulatively, or everywhere without exception, and then it will be distributive. Copulatively, as in this case:

> In the stars are the boxer Pollux, and the sailor Tiphys, and Cicero the orator, and the geometer Thales.

Distributively, as in this case:

> While the king, while the chief men, while the citadel remained standing, Troy was both the glory and the splendor and the head of the world.

Sine prima coniunctione posset stare sententia, sed tunc non esset ibi distributio, sed tantum copulatio. Secundum hanc regulam hii versus Bernardi vitiosi sunt:

> Astrorum motus et quae sit cuique potestas,
> ortus et occasus, puncta, gradus, numeri.

Melius dixisset pluraliter, "ortus, occasus" sine coniunctione—et forte vitio scriptoris apposita est copula. Ponuntur etiam venustissime istae duae dictiones "et," "-que," pro "etiam," scilicet adjective. Ovidius: "Iam seges est ubi Troia fuit resecandaque falce"; "-que" pro "etiam," quasi diceret, "Non solum est, sed etiam apta resecationi."

8 Haec dictio "quoque" duplicem habet positionem commendabilem. Praeter enim officium copulative (si quod habet), notat tum concomitantiam, tum difficultatem. Pure copulative ponendam non censeo diligenti. Nec enim tales commendo, "Socrates, Plato quoque, legunt, Cicero currit, Virgilius quoque legit." Invenitur tamen quandoque poni pro "et," scilicet pure copulative, ut in Bernardo:

> Militat in thalamis, tenero quoque servit amori
> Tactus, et argute saepe probare solet.

Et stultum est niti contradicere—quin multotiens sic ponatur. Sed ibi reputo summam diligentiam defuisse: et consultum est a tali positione plenius abstinuisse.

Without the first conjunction the sentence could stand, but then it would not be distribution but only copulation. According to this rule, these verses of Bernard's are faulty:

> The movements of the stars, and what power belongs to each, their rising and setting, points, degrees, numbers.

He would have better written *ortús,* plural (risings, settings), without a conjunction—though perhaps the conjunction was introduced by a scribal error. Also, the two words *et* (and) and *-que* (and) are used very elegantly instead of *etiam* (also), that is, with an additional sense. Ovid: "Where Troy stood is now a wheat field, and ready to be cut down by the sickle." Instead of *etiam, -que* is used, as if he were saying, "It not only is there, but is even ready for harvesting."

The word *quoque* (too) has two approved uses. Besides its copulative use (if it has any), it denotes concomitance and difficulty. I don't think a careful writer should use it simply copulatively. Nor do I recommend such things as, "Socrates also Plato are reading, Cicero is running, also Virgil is reading." It is sometimes found substituted for "and," that is, in a purely copulative sense, as in Bernard:

> Touch is a good soldier in the bedroom, and *(quoque)* does service to tender love, accustomed often to cunningly assess the situation.

And there is no sense expending effort in arguing against that usage—for indeed it is frequently used that way. But in such cases I think that the greatest care has been lacking: my recommendation is to abstain completely from this usage.

Haec dictio "quoque," prout concomitantiam notat, exponi solet per "similiter," ut hic, "Patres nostri mortui sunt, nos quoque moriemur," id est, "similiter," "sicut patres nostri." Prout difficultatem notat, per "etiam" solet exponi, ut hic: "Venus, subiugato humano genere, Samsonam quoque devicit," quasi diceret, "Etiam Samsonam, qui tam fortis fuit." Sic ergo haec dictio "quoque," utroque modo posita, respectiva est alicuius positi vel intellecti extra dictionem vel orationem quam introducit. Utraque tamen venustior erit si id quod respicitur non apponatur, sed tantum subintelligatur. Bernardus:

> Influit Eridanus caelum quoque, tramite nostro
> notus, et ad superos non leve nomen habet.

Expone: "caelum quoque," id est, "similiter"; subintelligitur, "sicut et terram." Boethius: "Verum omnis mutatio subita rerum non sine quodam quasi fluctu contingit animorum; sic factum est ut tu quoque paulisper a tua tranquilitate discederes." "Tu quoque," hoc est, "Etiam tu qui tantus eras quod quondam caelo liber aperto suetus in aetherios ire meatus." Lucanus de Catone ait, "Iusto quoque robur amori / restitit." "Quoque," hoc est, "etiam iusto," quasi diceret, "non solum iniusto"—et tamen de iniusto nulla praecessit mentio. Eadem "etiam" subintelligentia pulchra est, cum haec vox "et" pro "etiam" ponitur. Ut ibi, "Numquid et vos vultis abire?" Maluit subintelligere quam dicere, "sicut et alii abierunt."

Quandoque determinatur respectus huius dictionis "quoque" positae in uno libro per aliquod dictum authenticum positum in alio libro, ut si dicam, "Traditionem suam luit

PART 5

When *quoque* denotes concomitance, it is usually interpreted as "similarly," as here: "Our fathers died, we too *(quoque)* shall die," that is, "similarly," "like our fathers." When it denotes difficulty, it is usually interpreted as "even," as here: "Venus, once she had the human race under her thumb, overcame even Samson," as if it said, "Even Samson, who was so strong." So then, *quoque,* used in either of these ways, has reference to something present or understood beyond the word or phrase it introduces. But both will be more appealing if the reference isn't added but only understood. Bernard:

> Eridanus, well known in our journeying, flowed into heaven too, and has no slight name among the gods.

Explain: "heaven too," that is, "similarly"; "as on earth" is understood. Boethius: "But every sudden change in circumstances brings with it some fluctuation in spirits, and so it has happened that even you *(tu quoque)* are departing a little from your peace of mind." "Even you," that is, "Even you who were so great that once you were accustomed, free in the open sky, to travel the paths of the heavens." Lucan says of Cato, "His strength resisted even sanctioned lovemaking." "Even *(quoque),*" that is, "even *(etiam)* sanctioned," as if it said, "not only illicit"—and yet there has been no mention of illicit love. The same word *etiam* (also) is attractively unstated but understood when the word *et* is used instead of it, as here: "Will you also go away?" He preferred to leave unstated but understood, "as the others went away."

Sometimes the reference of *quoque* in one book is determined by some authoritative text from another book, as if I should say, "Ganelon too expiated his betrayal by hanging

suspendio Gueno quoque," subintelligitur ex authenticis voluminibus evangelistarum, "sicut et Iudas." Virgilius in tertio dicit, "Vivite felices, quibus est fortuna peracta iam sua." Propter illud authenticum ait Statius in decimo de Hopleo et Dymante,

> Vos quoque sacrati, quamvis mea carmina surgant
> inferiore lyra.

"Inferiore," intellige, "quam Virgilii." Ubi dicit, "vos quoque," expone, id est, "similiter sicut Helenus et Andromache," de quibus agit Virgilius.

"Etiam" eodem modo quandoque concomitantiam, quandoque difficultatem notat, licet in sola difficultate soleat usualiter "quoque" pro "etiam" exponi.

9 Haec coniunctio "nec," praeter generalem sui positionem, quandoque significat idem quod haec vox "etiam non," ita quod intellectus huius coniunctionis "etiam" respiciendo quiddam subintellectum includit negationem, ut hic, "Crudelis est qui nec patrem diligit." Innuitur latenter eum non alios diligere.

"Sed" coniunctio venustissime tenetur quando ponitur inter adiectivum et suum substantivum, et notat quandam adversationem inter adiectivum et substantivum occultam, ut hic: "pulchra sed pudica." Lucanus de Afranio: "Gerit omnia victi—sed ducis." Item, si ponatur inter verbum transitivum et suam determinationem, ut hic: "Nero diligit sed iniquos." Item per syllabicam adiectionem huius vocis "et," additive habet teneri, ut ibi, "Sed et si per errorem calculi quantitatem indebitam promisisti, condictio liberationis tibi competit."

himself," there is implied, from the authoritative books of the gospels, "as Judas also did." Virgil in book three says, "Live and be happy, those whose fate has now run its course." And because of this authoritative passage Statius can say, in his tenth book, of Hopleus and Dymas,

> You too are made sacred, even though my songs rise from a lesser lyre.

"Lesser," understand, "than Virgil's." Where he says, "you too," explain, that is, "Like Helenus and Andromache," about whom Virgil is talking.

Etiam, like *quoque,* sometimes denotes concomitance, sometimes difficulty, although normally it is only in the case of difficulty that *quoque* is explained as *etiam.*

The conjunction *nec* (nor), besides its general use, sometimes means the same thing as *etiam non* (not even), so that our understanding of the conjunction *etiam* with respect to something unspoken includes negation, as in this case, "Cruel is he who does not even love his father." The hidden implication is that he does not love others.

The conjunction *sed* (but) is used most elegantly when it is placed between an adjective and its noun and denotes a certain hidden opposition between the adjective and the noun, as in this case: "a beautiful but modest woman." Lucan on Afranius: "He showed all the bearing of a beaten man— but a beaten general." Also, if it is put between a transitive verb and its object, as in this case: "Nero feels affection, but for the wicked." If you just add the single syllable *et,* it has to be taken additively, as in this case, "And also *(sed et),* if by an error in calculation you have promised more than you owed, you can file a claim to have it canceled."

10   "Tamen" venustissime notabit adversationem inter adiectivum et suum substantivum, ut hic: "Pulchra, pudica tamen." Item inter verbum et suam determinationem, ut hic, "Iste paret libenter—tamen suis." Cum dictum esset "libenter," videretur quod omnibus, et ideo sequitur "tamen suis," quasi diceret, "non alienis." Lucanus: "Invita peragam, tamen omnia dextra." Sensus est, "Peragam, invita quidem existente dextra, et licet invita, tamen peragam." Item venustissime ponitur, si inter unum adiectivum et suum substantivum introducat per parenthesim quiddam eis adversans. Statius de Iove ait,

> Mediis sese arduus infert
> ipse deis, placido quatiens tamen omnia vultu.

11   "Vel" praeter discretionis officium dupliciter tenetur, quandoque pro "saltem," quandoque pro "etiam." Pro "saltem": Solinus introducit Atym, filium Croesi, dicentem, "Parce patri meo, Cyre, et hominem te esse vel casibus disce nostris," quasi diceret, "Si per alios non vis, saltem per patrem meum disce." Pro etiam, ut hic: "Caesareos titulos vel pauper Amyclas ampliat," id est, "Non solum divites sed etiam pauper Amyclas."

De hac coniunctione "atque" breviter notandum quod ea expedit.

PART 5

Tamen (yet) will denote an opposition between an adjective and its noun very elegantly, as here: "A beautiful, yet modest girl." Also between a verb and its object, as in this case, "this man submits freely—yet to his own." After the word "freely," it would seem to mean "to everybody," and therefore there follows "yet to his own," as if to say, "not to strangers." Lucan: "I will do everything, yet with an unwilling hand." The sense is, "I will do it, though my hand indeed is unwilling, but though it is unwilling I will still do it." It is also used elegantly if it inserts parenthetically between an adjective and its noun something at odds with them. Statius says of Jove,

> He bears himself high amid the gods, making everything shake, yet with a calm face.

Vel (or), besides its regular disjunctive use, has two further uses, sometimes for *saltem* (at least), sometimes for *etiam* (even). For *saltem:* Solinus brings in Atys, the son of Croesus, saying, "Spare my father, Cyrus, and learn that you are a man, at least from our misfortunes," as if he said, "If you don't want to learn that through others, at least learn it through my father." For *etiam,* as here: "Even poor Amyclas swells Caesar's titles," that is, "not only the rich but even poor Amyclas."

As for the conjunction *atque* (and), let me just say that it is useful.

6

Consequenter utile est nosse rationem coniecturalis probationis rethoricae, quae consistit in locis vel argumentis. Haec utilis est ad alliciendum animos auditorum, ad favorem adipiscendum, ad quidlibet persuadendum. Nota igitur ratione inveniendi adiectiva, determinationes etiam huiusmodi alias praeostensas, non sunt omnia indistincte ponenda: sed ea quae maxime faciunt ad propositum. Verbi gratia, Lucanus in fine ait de Caesare,

>   Respexit in agmine denso
> Scaevam perpetuae meritum iam nomina famae
> ad campos, Epidamne, tuos. . . .

Facta igitur mentione de perpetua fama, quam Scaeva meruerat, ad probandum illud meritum subdit,

>   ubi solus apertis
> obsedit muris calcantem moenia Magnum.

Ubi dicit "solus," optimum est argumentum a difficultate faciendi. Commendabilius enim fuit quod solus fecit quam si cum sociis fecisset. Minus ergo utiliter, quamvis adeo vere, ibidem posuisset hanc dictionem "fortis." Item in hac dictione "apertis" latet argumentum meriti. Difficilius enim fuit hoc, quam si clausi essent muri. Ubi dicit "obsedit,"

PART SIX

As a next step, it is useful to know the theory of inferential proof in rhetoric, which consists in the topics and arguments. It is valuable in engaging the minds of one's audience, in securing their favor, and in persuading them to something. So while the theory of finding adjectives has been established, and also of finding other modifiers of this kind as have already been set forth, they must not all be used indiscriminately, but rather use the ones that best serve your purpose. For example, Lucan at the end says of Caesar,

> He fixed his gaze in the crowded troop on Scaeva, who had earned eternal fame on your fields, Epidamnus. . . .

Having mentioned the eternal fame that Scaeva had earned, he adds, to prove he'd earned it,

> where all by himself, after the walls were breached, he laid siege to the Great Man as he trod the ramparts underfoot.

Where he says, "all by himself," he makes the best argument, from the difficulty of acting. For it was more commendable that he did it by himself than had he done it with others. It would have been less effective, though perfectly true, if he had used the word "brave" in that passage. There is also a concealed argument for his merit in the word "breached," since his exploit was harder than if the walls were intact.

minus utiliter dixisset "defendit" vel huiusmodi. Hoc enim minus esset laudis. Ad defensionem enim castri coguntur inclusi quodammodo necessario. Sed iste, cum discessisse posset si vellet, obsedit exercitum ne transiret. Argumentatur etiam efficaciter ubi dicit "calcantem moenia," quasi diceret, "Non obsedit segnem vel otiosum, sed calcantem moenia." In proprio etiam nomine non deficit argumentum, ubi dicit "Magnum." Ibi enim est illud exilissimum argumentum a nomine. Melius tamen dixit "Magnum" quam si dixisset "Pompeium," quasi diceret, "Non parvum aliquem obsedit, sed magnum."

2 Ideo sciendum est quid persona, quid negotium, quod etiam quaedam attributa sunt personae, alia negotio. Attributa sunt personae xi: nomen, natura, convictus, fortuna, habitus, studium, affectio, consilium, casus, facta, orationes. Attributa negotio sunt ix: summa facti; causa facti; triplex administratio ante rem, cum re, post rem; facultas faciendi; qualitas facti; tempus; locus. Attributorum negotio, quaedam sunt continentia cum negotio, quaedam in gestione negotii. Item quaedam sunt adiuncta negotio, quaedam consequentia negotium.

Haec contingit abundanter in omni commendabili reperiri scriptura. Per huiusmodi locos commendavit Bernardus caelum quadrupliciter, dicens,

PART 6

When he says, "laid siege," he'd have spoken less effectively had he said "defended," or the like. This would be less praiseworthy, since those inside a camp to a certain degree necessarily defend it. But Scaeva, though he could have run away if he wanted to, besieged Pompey's army to keep it from coming through the breach. There is further effective argument where he says "trod the ramparts underfoot," as if he were saying that "Scaeva didn't besiege a lazy or inactive man, but one treading the ramparts underfoot." In the proper noun too the argument loses nothing by calling him "the Great Man." In that passage the argument from his name is very weak. He did better to say, "the Great Man" than had he said, "Pompey," as if to say, "He besieged not some little person but a big one."

It is important to know, then, what is a person and what are actions, and that some things are attributes of persons, others attributes of actions. There are eleven attributes of persons: name, nature, manner of life, fortune, demeanor, interests, attachments, judgment, fortunes, actions, speeches. There are nine attributes of an action: a summary of what happened; the cause of an action; its threefold performance (before the action, at the time of the action, after the action); the capacity for acting; the quality of the action; time; and place. Of the attributes of actions, some are connected to the action, some are part of its actual performance. Likewise some are adjuncts to it, some follow upon it.

This can be found fully treated in any reputable text. It is with topics of this kind that Bernard praises heaven in four ways, saying,

> Caeli forma teres, essentia purior ignis,
> motus circuitus, numina, turba deum.

Sic commendat aulam caelestem: a forma, a materia, a statu, ab inhabitantibus. Psalmista quoque multipliciter et egregie creatorem suum commendavit, dicens, "Deus autem rex noster; ante saecula operatus est salutem in medio terrae." A benignitate, ubi dixit "Deus": haec dictio enim "Deus" semper in benignitatem seu clementiam sonat. A potentia, ubi dixit, "rex." Ab humanitate, ubi dixit, "noster." Ab aeternitate, ubi dixit, "ante saecula." Ab humilitate, ubi dixit "operatus est." A commoditate, ubi dixit, "salutem." A communitate, ubi dixit, "in medio terrae." Et alibi: "Ploremus coram Domino, qui fecit nos, quia ipse est Dominus Deus noster." "Dominus," ergo potest misereri. "Deus," ergo vult. "Noster," ergo debet.

De huiusmodi igitur locis, quoniam valde necessarii sunt, rhetoricas consulamus et in istis contenti simus Cicerone.

3 De artificiali ordine vel naturali narrandi historias, de modo philosophico procedendi, de triplici stilo—grandiloquo scilicet, humili, et mediocri—agere, meum stilum excedit. Ad regulas stilum verto tantum versibus speciales.

PART 6

> The rounded form of the sky, its essence a purer fire, its motion a circle, the divine beings, the throng of gods.

Thus he praises the palace of heaven: in its form, matter, order, and inhabitants. The psalmist also has praised his creator exceptionally well many times, saying, "But God, our king, before the ages hath wrought salvation in the midst of the earth." For kindliness, when he said, "God": since the word "God" always has overtones of kindliness and clemency. For power, when he said, "king." For humanity, when he said, "our." For eternity, when he said, "before the ages." For humility, when he said, "hath wrought." For beneficence, when he said, "salvation." For commonality, when he said, "in the midst of the earth." And in another psalm: "Let us weep before the Lord that made us, for he is the Lord our God." "Lord," and so he can be merciful. "God," and so he wants to be merciful. "Our," and so he should be merciful.

About topics of this kind, therefore, because they are exceedingly necessary, let us consult works of rhetoric, and among them be content with Cicero.

It is beyond the scope of my pen to treat the artificial or natural order for constructing narratives, the philosophical mode of proceeding, and the three styles—that is, high, low, and middle. I turn that pen to rules that pertain just to verse.

7

In versibus igitur monosyllabarum dictionum nimietas praecavenda, ne vel totus versus vel eius maior pars ex monosyllabis constiterit dictionibus. Quales sunt illi versus iocosi de lenone et meretrice:

> Res fit ab hiis sed ob aes; dat hic aes, fit ab hoc et ab
>   hac res.
>   Quod fit ab hoc et ab hac, non fit in hoc sed in hac.

Huiusmodi non sunt inter authenticos interserendi. Item in fine versus monosyllabam non ponamus nisi sit enclitica coniunctio, ut hic, "Ad sensum perfecta Cherub propiusque magisque, etc." Hic autem vitiosus: "Mancipiis locuples eget aeris Cappadocum rex." Et, quod mirum est, cum vitium sit ibi monosyllabam ponere, pulchrius est duas ponere quam unicam tantum, unde hic versus minus reprobabilis:

> Diversis paries tectis interiacet, in quo
>   rimula colloquiis obsequiosa latet.

Contingit etiam in fine vitioso tres monosyllabas invenire, ut hic:

> Immutat mores aetas mutata—nec est in
>   fructu maturo qui fuit ante sapor.

PART SEVEN

In poetry excessive use of monosyllables should be avoided, lest a whole verse, or the greater part of it, consist of monosyllables. Of this kind are the comic lines about a lecher and a whore:

> The thing is done by them, but for cash; he gives the cash, and the thing is done by him and by her. What is done by him and by her is done not in him but in her.

Things of this kind don't belong in serious poetry. Also, we should not put a monosyllable at the end of a line, except an enclitic conjunction, as in this case: "Perfect in understanding, the cherub (discerns) closely and more fully, etc." But this is faulty: "The king of the Cappadocians is rich in slaves but not cash." And, what is remarkable, though it is a fault to use a one-syllable word in that place, it is more attractive to use two than to use only one, and so this verse is less blameworthy:

> A wall lies between two houses, in which there is a hidden chink that makes conversation easy.

Sometimes you also find three one-syllable words in a faulty line ending, as in this case:

> With a change in years one's ways change too—and ripe fruit doesn't have the taste it had before.

Sed duarum positio magnum vitium est, unius maius, trium vel plurium maximum.

2   Item versus hexametri prima syllaba quinti pedis et secunda in diversas dictiones cedere non presumant, nisi eiusdem pedis secunda syllaba dictio enclitica fuerit. Unde hic versus non est vitiosus: "Legerat huius Amor titulum nomenque libelli." Hic autem vitiosus:

> Rex sedet in cena turba cinctus duodena.
> Se tenet in manibus, se cibat ipse cibus.

Sed talium alius magis vitiosus, alius minus. Magis ubi prima syllaba quinti pedis non est integralis dictio, sed pars maioris dictionis ibidem terminatae, quale praedictum exemplum. Minus vitiosus ubi prima syllaba quinti pedis monosyllaba est dictio, ut in epitaphio abbatis Gauteri, qui tumulatus est in die Ascensionis Domini et Inventionis sanctae crucis,

> Tempore quo rapitur Christus, quo crux reperitur,
> vir crucis et Christi tumulo fuit insitus isti.

Manifestum est igitur in *Apollonio* auctorem hoc vitium ignorasse.

3   Versus pentameter in monosyllabam vel monosyllabas indecentius terminatur, unde peccasset Martialis, nisi stilus specialis et suus reprehensionis modus eum excusasset, cum dixit,

PART 7

To use two is a great fault, one a greater fault, and three or more the greatest fault.

The first and second syllables of the fifth foot of a hexameter should not take it upon themselves to fall in different words, unless that second syllable is an enclitic. Thus this line is not faulty: "Love had read the name and title of this book." But this is faulty:

> The king sits at dinner surrounded by a band of twelve. He holds himself in his hands, the food feeds itself.

However, some lines like these are more faulty others less. The more faulty ones are where the first syllable of the fifth foot is not a whole word but the end of a longer word, as in the example just given. The less faulty are where the first syllable of the fifth foot is a monosyllable, as in the epitaph for Abbot Walter, who was buried on the feast of the Ascension of the Lord and the Invention of the Holy Cross.

> On the day when Christ is taken up, and the cross is found, a man of the cross and of Christ was laid in this tomb.

It is clear in his *Apollonius* that the author did not know that this is a fault.

It is improper for a pentameter to end in one or more monosyllables, and so, if his distinctive style and satiric mode hadn't excused him, Martial would have been at fault when he wrote,

Pro togula debes: hoc ad te pertinet, Ole.
Quadrantem nemo iam tibi credit: et hoc.

Ultima igitur dictio versus pentametri semper sit disyllaba, quamvis contingat in auctoribus trisyllabas vel tetrasyllabas—quae secundum quosdam commendantur—plenius invenire. Caveamus ad plenum illas auctorum licentias, synaloepham scilicet et ellipsim, ut, "ille, ego qui quondam," "magnanimum Aeaciden." "Caveamus," inquam, non propter turpitudinem sed propter usum, quia nescio qua iniuria eis aures modernorum laeduntur. Sciatis quod istas licentias apud meam conscientiam non condemno.

4   Antipenthemimerim vero, hepthemimerim, posthepthemimerim omittamus. Sola nobis penthemimeris est relicta. De hoc autem vehementer admiror quod adeo audaces sumus in penthemimerim incidisse, quam auctores adeo vitaverunt. Inspicite Ovidium *Heroidum:* fere semel tantum est ibi hanc licentiam invenire, ubi dicit, "mittit Hypermnestra, etc." In magno rarissime. (Nec enim illos computaverim quos summo vitio deturpavit, qualis est hic: "et fauni et satiri et monticolae silvani.") Secundum Priscianum tamen, alia potest esse solutio super huiusmodi, "mittit Hypermnestra": Graecorum enim nominativi terminati in *-a* apud auctores nostros saepe producuntur, quia apud Graecos semper. Consilium igitur est ut raritas pariter licentiam hanc excuset et sententiosa necessitas, ut contingit in illis versibus de Pyramo et Thisbe:

PART 7

> You owe for your toga: that is your business, Olus. Nobody will lend you a penny anymore: this is your business too.

In short, the last word of your pentameter should always be a word of two syllables, even though in the authors you often find three-syllable or four-syllable words—and some people even admire them. And let's be extremely cautious about the license the authors allow themselves of synaloepha and ellipsis, as in "I am he who once," "greathearted Aeacides." I don't say, "Let's be cautious" because they disfigure, but only for practical reasons, because they cause some injury to the ears of people today. Be assured that in my personal feelings I do not condemn these licenses.

Let's leave out the antipenthemimer, hephthemimer, and posthephthemimer, so we just have the penthemimer left. As for it, I am amazed at how bold we are in having broached the subject of the penthemimer, since the authors have avoided it so. Look at Ovid's *Heroides:* about the only place you find this license there is when he says, "Hypermnestra sends, etc." In his big poem you find it extremely rarely. (I'm not counting the lines that he disfigured with some huge fault, lines such as this: "fauns and satyrs and wood gods in the mountains.") Priscian, though, gives another solution for lines such as "Hypermnestra sends": Greek nominatives that end in *-a* are often lengthened in our authors, because the Greeks do it all the time. The recommendation, then, is that infrequent use and sentence requirements excuse this license, as in these lines on Pyramus and Thisbe:

4

Iunge relativa quos nodat gratia, foedus
copulat alternum, mutuus unit amor.

Generalem tamen et usitatissimam concedimus esse hanc licentiam, sicut et leonitatis in singulis versibus vel in distichis, ubi non est multorum versuum collectio, utputa in epitaphiis et proverbiis et sigillis. In productis autem materiis, caesura haec licenter fit et frequenter, nec tamen temperantiam excedamus si syllabae terminentur in consonantes, quae per hanc licentiam producuntur, ut ibi: "Omnia vincit amor; et nos cedamus amori."

5   Caveantur inter caetera multisyllabae dictiones, quales sunt "Oedipodionides"—nisi tales in quibus iocunda sonoritas invenitur, quales sunt dictiones pentasyllabae pedem dactilum continentes in sui principio. Circa has dictiones regulariter admonendum ut, quotiens poterimus, penultima dictio versus pentametri sit pentasyllaba, nec distinguendum an terminetur in *-osus* an in *-asus,* vel quomodo terminetur. Bernardus: "Ardua iam poterant exhilarasse deas." Alibi: "Leges humane conditionis habent. . . ." Haec regula, cum illa de quinto pede superius tradita, a memoria non recedat. Illa enim semper, ista multotiens observanda.

Per talem dictionem pentasyllabam versus hexameter venustius inchoatur. Architrenius: "Velificatur Athos." Quidam admirantes huiusmodi magnas dictiones, inutiliter et turpissime versum clauserunt sub duabus dictionibus vel tribus. Unde quidam ait, "Versificabantur Constantinopolitani"; alius, "Plenus honorificabilitudinitatibus esto."

PART 7

> Join those whom fondness for each other ties together, whom a reciprocal compact couples, whom mutual love makes one.

Still, we grant that this license is general and commonplace, just as is the practice of leonines, whether in single lines or couplets, where there is not a sequence of many verses, for example in epitaphs and proverbs, and on seals. In longer material, however, this caesura is frequent and permissible, and yet we should not go beyond moderation if syllables lengthened by this license end in consonants, as here: "Love conquers all; let's yield to love too."

Among other things, care should be taken with polysyllabic words, words such as *Oedipodionides* (the son of Oedipus)—except for those that display a happy euphony, such as five-syllable words that start with a dactyl. On these it should be laid down as a rule that whenever we can, the next-to-last word of a pentameter should be of five syllables It makes no difference whether it ends in *-osus* or *-asus,* or indeed how it ends. Bernard: "The hardships (overcome) already could have cheered the goddesses." And in another place: "The laws of the human condition ensure...." This rule, and the one I just gave about the fifth foot too, should be retained in your memory. The one should always be observed, the other frequently.

A five-syllable word makes an attractive beginning for a hexameter. Architrenius: "Athos is sailed over." Some people who admire long words of this kind have ineffectively and very clumsily filled up a line with just two or three words. Thus one says, "The Constantinopolitans were versified"; and another, "Be full of honorificabilitudes." Claudian,

Claudianus tamen versum hexametrum pulcherrime sub tribus clausit dictionibus, dicens, "Bellerophonteas indignaretur habenas." Excusat enim eum raritas talium et iocunda sonoritas dictionum. Ovidius similiter pentametrum pulcherrime dicit: "Incustoditae diripiuntur opes."

6 Omnis praeterea versus, si duo primi pedes dactili fuerint, venustior resultabit, ut hic: "Arma virumque cano." Quod si fieri non possit, quotiens poterimus saltem primum pedem dactilum faciamus, ut hic: "pagina maeroris." Venustissimus erit modus si quilibet pes praeter ultimum dactiletur, ut hic: "Nil prius in Venere neque post nisi cauda Chimaerae." Quamvis autem non ubique dactilos habere possimus, ad dactilos tamen summa diligentia desudandum. Haec est observantia propter quam etiam a non intelligentibus hunc modum plenius commendatur *Architrenius* propter sonos dulcissimos dactilorum.

7 Duorum etiam versuum copula venustior erit si in tres clausulas distinguatur, ut hic:

> Militat in membris Hector, callescit Ulixes
> in sensu, puro ridet in ore Paris.

Sed adhuc erit venustior si per contrarietatem fiant. Verbi gratia,

> Audaces fortuna iuvat timidosque nociva
> praegravat; inde deae stat favor, inde furor.

Ecce prima pars de audacibus est, secunda de timidis, tertia de utrisque. Hic est modus venustissimus tractandi proverbia. Aliud simile:

though, wrote a complete hexameter beautifully in three words, saying, "He (Pegasus) would disdain Bellerophon's reins." What saves him from blame is the rarity of such lines and the pleasing euphony of the words. Ovid similarly writes a very attractive pentameter: "Their unguarded possessions are plundered."

Any line, furthermore, will be made more attractive if the first two feet are dactyls, as here: "I sing of arms and a man." But if that should not be possible, we should at least make the first foot a dactyl as often as we can, as here: "a page of grief." This mode will be most pleasing if every foot except the last is a dactyl, as here: "There is no before or after in sex but the tail of the Chimera." But even though we can't have dactyls in every position, we should labor as hard as we can to procure them. It is because of this practice—that is, because of the very sweet sounds of dactyls—that *Architrenius* is praised so highly even by those who don't understand the rule.

A couplet will be more elegant if it is divided into three clauses, as in this case:

> Hector soldiers in his limbs, Ulysses schemes in his brain, Paris smiles in his unblemished face.

But it will be more elegant still if the division is made by opposites. For example,

> Fortune favors the brave, and ill fortune daunts the timid. On one side stands the favor of the goddess, on the other her anger.

As you see, the first part is about the brave, the second about the timid, the third about both. This is the most elegant way to handle proverbs. Another, similar example:

THE ART OF MAKING VERSES

> Qui cito dat bis dat: meritum dilata minorant
> munera; plus laudis hinc fluit inde minus.

Venustissima est etiam repausatio in septima syllaba, ut hic: "Audaces fortuna iuvat."

8 Notandum etiam quod pulchriores sunt versus hexameter et suus pentameter si in terminis suis consonantia inveniatur, saltem vocalium ultimarum, ut hic:

> Troia iacet certe, Danais invisa puellis;
> vix Priamus tanti totaque Troia fuit.

Per hunc modum versus authentici decorantur.

9 Sunt etiam versus retrogradi, quidam littera ad litteram, quidam verbo ad verbum, quidam etiam verborum et sensuum, ut hic:

> Canonicum fore me vellem, nec gaudia mundi
> diligo; quod, regum rex, tibi confiteor.

10 Sed non possumus de omnibus agere quae necessaria sunt versificatoribus. Debent enim omnia genera literaturae partialiter cognoscere, et idem de versificatoribus censeo quod Vitruvius de architectis, qui ait, "Non potest, nec debet, esse architectus grammaticus, quemadmodum fuerat Aristarchus, sed non agrammatos; nec musicus, ut Aristoxenus, sed non amusos; nec pictor, ut Apelles, sed graphidis non imperitus; nec plastes, quemadmodum Myron seu Polyclitus, sed rationis plasticae non ignarus; nec denuo medicus, ut Hippocrates, sed non aniatrologetos." Quibus etiam natura tantum tribuit sollertiae, acuminis, et memoriae ut

PART 7

He who gives quickly gives twice: delayed gifts diminish the credit; more praise flows from the one, less from the other.

Also particularly elegant is a caesura at the seventh syllable, as in this case: "Fortune favors the brave."

It should be noted further that a hexameter line and its pentameter are more attractive if there is assonance in the two endings, at least of the last vowels, as in this case:

Troy is fallen, sure, hated by Greek girls; scarcely was Priam, scarcely Troy, worth so much.

The verses of the canonical authors are beautified in this manner.

There are also retrograde verses. Some go letter by letter, some word by word, and some reverse the sense as well as the words, as here:

I would like to be a canon; I don't love worldly pleasures; this I confess to you, king of kings.

But we can't treat every last thing necessary for poets. For they ought to be partially familiar with every kind of literature, and I think the same about poets as Vitruvius did about architects. He said, "An architect cannot and should not be a critic, as Aristarchus had been, but should not be without critical ability; nor a musician like Aristoxenus, but should not be unmusical; nor a painter like Apelles, but not unskilled with his pencil; nor a sculptor, as Myron was or Polyclitus, but not ignorant of plastic art; nor finally a physician like Hippocrates, but not ignorant of medicine." And those whom nature endowed with so much skill, acuity, and

geometriam, astrologiam, musicam, arithmeticam, triviales etiam et ethicas at physicas et theologicas disciplinas penitus habere possint notas praetereunt officia versificatorum, ipsorum tamen commendantur opera in quibus de huiusmodi fit mentio temperata.

Perfecto versificatori non hiemet, non aestivet, non noctescat, non diescat sine astronomia. Iuvenalis loco istorum verborum "mane" vel "paulo ante mane" ait,

> Sideribus dubiis aut illo tempore quo se
> frigida circumagunt pigri sarraca Bootae.

Per motus enim astronomicos probatur sarraca circumacta esse modico ante diem. Item nec varietur ei tempus, nec pelagus transeatur, nec de rebus philosophicis fiat mentio sine philosophia. Lucanus in primo, ubi mentionem facit de fluxu et de refluxu oceani, movet quaestionem philosophicam, dicens, "Ventus ab extremo pelagus sic axe volutet, etc." Et item in obsidione Ilerdae philosophicam facit inundationem aquarum. Similiter Caesar, transire volens ab Epiro in Ausoniam, non sine philosophia navigavit.

Sic igitur perfecto versificatori de qualibet re secundum naturam suae materiae loquendum est.

Erant adhuc et multa alia a versibus eliminanda, ut huiusmodi dictiones: "cursitat" (nec enim verbum maturi animi videtur); item, "praeambulant" et "praeire" et huiusmodi composita ex duobus integris habentibus vocalem ante vo-

memory that they are able to master geometry, astrology, music, mathematics—not to mention the subjects of the trivium and even the disciplines of ethics, physics, and theology—go beyond the functions of poets, and yet their poems are honored in which there is judicious mention of these subjects.

For a perfect poet, it should not be winter or summer or night or day without astronomy. Juvenal, instead of saying "in the morning," or "a little before morning," says,

> When the stars are fading, or at the time when the cold wain of sluggish Bootes is wheeling itself around.

For according to the movements of the celestial bodies, it is shown that the wain has wheeled around just before daybreak. Likewise, for a poet the season should not change, nor the sea be crossed, nor any mention be made of philosophical matters without philosophy. Lucan in his first book, where he brings up the back-and-forth flow of the ocean, asks a philosophical question, saying, "Does a wind from the faraway pole roil the sea so?" and so on. And again in the siege of Ilerda, he makes the flood philosophical. In the same way, too, when Caesar wanted to cross from Epirus to Italy, he made the voyage not unaccompanied by philosophy.

Therefore, a perfect poet must write on any subject in accordance with the nature of his material.

There were still many other things to be eliminated from verse: words such as *cursitat* (which does not seem to be a verb that a grown-up would use); likewise *praeambulat* and *praeire* and compounds like them, made from two words with a succession of two vowels if those vowels in a line of

calem, si illae vocales in versu sint diversarum syllabarum. Lucanus enim ait, "Non deest prolato ieiunus venditor auro." Sed huiusmodi rara sunt.

12   De legendis, de audiendis versibus essent regulae praenotandae. Quidam enim sunt qui sic legunt fere ut scandunt, nec legendo sciunt distinguere ubi versus, ubi clausula finiatur. Quidam audiendo turpiter admirantur, vel pede pulsant, vel sibilant, vel cachinnant. Huiusmodi inhonesta sunt clericis. Sed sub tractandi compendio non clauduntur.

verse belong to separate syllables. Lucan says, "When money is on offer, there is no dearth of sellers, however hungry." But instances are rare.

Rules for reading verse aloud, and for listening to it, would need to be laid down in advance. Some people read almost as they scan, and they don't know how to distinguish in reading where a line or a clause ends. Some listeners show their enthusiasm in uncouth ways. They either stamp their feet or hiss or guffaw. Conduct like that is improper for clerics. But this treatise is too short to include it.

8

Dictamen est congrua et apposita literalis compositio de aliquo quod vel mente retinetur, vel litteris seu voce significatur, secundum Bernardi sententiam. Huius quidem tria sunt genera: metricum, rhythmicum, et prosaicum. De versibus dictum est; de aliis metris et rhythmo omittimus. Prosaicum dictamen est oratio a lege metrorum differens, congrua et longa continuatione procedens. Lex enim metrorum considerat utrum syllaba brevis vel longa. Quod siquidem in prosis faciendis penitus amovetur, grammaticae quidem artis ratio conservatur; et ipsa nimirum adeo prosa in longum debet extendi quod ex verbis eius vel sententia ad minus pentameter versus constituatur. Quod profecto ab eiusdem nominis proprietate satis convenienter posse sumi videtur; nam "prosa" a *proson* Graeco dicitur, quod "longum" Latini dicere volunt. Beda in libro de arte metrica: "Prosa est longa oratio a lege metri soluta, quae infra heroici non debet quantitatem mutilari. Ultra vero, quantum provido dictatori placuerit, valet prolixior sine reprehensione constitui."

Huius duae sunt species: alia enim per simplicem fit constructionem, id est, per rudem identitatem; alia fit per appositionem, id est, per politam identitatem vel contrarietatem vel similitudinem.

> Per simplicem constructionem cum scribimus idiotis et minus peritis.

PART EIGHT

A literary work, according to Bernard's definition, is a correct and appropriate literary composition about something which is either stored in the mind, or communicated by voice or writing. Its three kinds are metrical, rhythmic, and prose. The subject of verse has been treated; I pass over other meters and rhythm. Prose composition is discourse that shuns the laws of meter, advancing in a lengthy and well-ordered progression. The laws of meter consider whether a syllable is short or long. If those laws are wholly laid aside in writing prose, the rules of grammar at any rate are observed; and prose itself certainly ought to reach such a length that from its words or sentiments at least a pentameter verse may be constituted. This can certainly be very simply deduced from the proper meaning of its name, for "prose" comes from *proson* in Greek, which is "long" in Latin. Bede in his book on the art of meter: "Prose is long discourse freed from the laws of meter, which should not be any shorter than the length of a hexameter. But it is possible to compose at greater length, as far as the prudent writer likes, without incurring blame."

There are two kinds of composition: one made by simple construction, that is, by straightforward identity, the other by apposition, that is, by polished identity or by opposition or likeness.

> By simple construction, when we write to the ignorant and those less learned.

Appositio est dictionum ordinatio a constructionis serie remota. Appositio tunc recte formabitur si in singulis dictionibus partes congrue locabuntur. Unde nobis notandum quod Victorinus ipse fatetur "in omni genere dictaminum tres esse distinctiones, quas et ratio probat et bene legentis iudicium. Quarum prima est suspensiva, secunda constans, tertia finitiva." Suspensiva dicitur illa qua audita animus auditoris quasi suspenditur, et adhuc aliud audire praestolatur; et est ipsa acuto accentu pronuntianda. Constans dicitur illa qua audita animus auditoris nihil audire intendit, intentio tamen dictatoris est inexpleta. Finitiva est qua finitur oratio et ipsa dicentis intentio. Hiis et nos subicimus quod, sicut in versibus et metris modicas, sic in dictamine decet prosaico longas admodum et sonantiores erigere dictiones—tamen modestia conservetur.

3   Cum autem a lege decantationis metricae soluta sint dictamina, necesse est ut in illis accentus fidelius observetur lectori specialiter deputatus. Decens est igitur omni clausulae ut in quadratam cubitam terminetur. Terminetur igitur omnis clausula tetrasyllaba dictione cuius penultima producatur, vel praecedente monosyllaba trisyllaba sit finalis, cuius etiam penultima sit producta. Quaeratur autem productio non tempore, sed accentu, ne vel phrenesim eligas in fine, vel effugias symphoniam. Cavendum autem semper in fine ne vel dissyllaba simus contenti vel tetrasyllabas excedamus. Semper vero trissyllabe vel deinceps sint penultimae dictiones, quarum penultimae brevientur, secundum quod

PART 8

Apposition is an arrangement of words that departs from the sequence of the construction. Apposition will be formed correctly if in individual expressions the components are fittingly placed. And here let me remind you that Victorinus said that "in every kind of writing there are three categories, which both reason and the judgment of the good reader approve: the suspensive, the constant, and the conclusive." The suspensive is when a listener's mind is as it were suspended at what he hears and waits to hear something further; it is to be pronounced with an acute accent. The constant is when the listener's mind looks to hear nothing more than what he has heard, and yet the intention of the writer is incomplete. The conclusive is what the sentence ends with, the very intention of the writer. To these terms I too subscribe because, just as it is fitting in verse and meter to bring in a limited number of words, so in literary prose it is fitting to construct quite long and resonant sequences of words — though moderation must be preserved.

However, though prose compositions are freed from the laws of metrical chant, in them accent has to be observed unusually faithfully, as the special province of the reader. It is fitting, then, that every clause end in a squared-off elbow. Thus, every clausula should end in a four-syllable word whose penult is long or, if a monosyllable precedes it, in a trisyllable whose penult also should be long. But the length should be sought not in time but in accent, lest you choose to end in disarray or abandon harmony. You always have to be alert never to be content at the end with two disyllables, or to exceed the length of four syllables. But penultimate words should always have three syllables or more with a short penultimate syllable, according to what I said above

supra diximus in accentu. Hic igitur non devites "Paraclitum, sed sophiam." Visa igitur tam penultimae regula quam finalis, satis competenter hinc eligetur "Paraclitus," hinc "Maria." Istae regulae semper et ubique nullatenus omittendae.

4   Sunt et aliae quas observant quidam gloriosius procedentes. Distinguitur enim sic: omnis dictio cuius penultima producitur in accentu dicatur spondeus pes; similiter omnes dissyllabae et monosyllabae. Omnis vero dictio trium vel plurium syllabarum quae corripitur in penultima dactylus appellatur. Dicunt ergo in omni clausula spondeos coniunges quot volueris, numquam duo dactyli coniungantur; nec licet, nisi raro, vocalem ante vocalem diversis in dictionibus, et hoc si summa necessitas exigat invenire. Praedictum autem finiendi modum licet in metro prosae, licet et in puncto cum libeat observare, id est, et in fine constantis et in termino suspensivae. In harum autem terminis commodius est ut dactylus eligatur, praescito quod in fine cuiuslibet partis dissyllaba sit vitanda.

Notandum etiam quod partem ultimae dictionis (quantum ad hoc artificium tradendum) censeo monosyllabam si praecedat, ita tamen si monosyllaba cum sequenti dictione tetrasyllabam non excedat. Penultima vero, quam dactylum pedem futuram praediximus, quandoque assumit sibi monosyllabam terminalem. Bernardus: "Ad cuius rei spectaculum mora consumpta est aliquanta." Et alibi: "Cuius partes duodecim laboriosior visa est peragrare." Et in hoc articulo valet plenius vocalis ante vocalem.

about accent. On these grounds, then, you will not avoid *Paraclitum, sed sophiam*. So, now that you have seen both the rule for the penult and the rule for the last word, it will be fine to choose *Paraclitus* in one place and *Maria* in the other. These rules are never, anywhere, in any way to be ignored.

There are other rules that some people observe who are striving to write more ambitiously. Distinction is won in the following ways: every word whose penult is long and accented should be called a spondaic foot, and likewise all disyllables and monosyllables. But every word of three or more syllables whose penult is short should be called a dactyl. And so they say that in any clause you will join as many spondees as you like, but two dactyls may never be joined; and it is not permitted, or only rarely permitted if dire necessity forces it on you, to place a word that ends in a vowel before a word that starts in a vowel. But it is permitted to keep that kind of ending in the versicle of a sequence and, when it pleases, at a punctuation point, that is, at the ending of a constant or termination of the suspensive. In endings like these, though, it is more fitting to use a dactyl, as long as you know that at the end of any part dissyllables are to be avoided.

It should be noted that I think that a monosyllable is part of the last word (at least for the purpose of communicating this device) if it comes first, just as long as the monosyllable with the following word does not exceed four syllables. But the penult, which I have already said will be a dactylic foot, sometimes takes a monosyllable at the end. Bernard: "But some time was taken to observe that spectacle." And elsewhere: "Whose twelve parts she (Nature) seemed to travel through with more difficulty." And in this phrase a vowel followed by a vowel is more fully acceptable.

5 Adiecit etiam magister Johannes de Hauvilla decorum existere consonantiam invenire, scilicet ut aliqua dictio quae fini vicina ponitur finali dictioni consimiliter terminetur, dum tamen penitus color exulet leoninus. Clausulas enim huiusmodi condempnavit: "Qui non diligit amicum, diligat inimicum." Et hanc: "Ignis subtilis est, terra reflexioris et corpulentiae grossioris."

6 Per praedicta patet quod aliqua oratio sub uno ordine versus turpissimus est et sub eodem prosa pulcherrima, ut haec: "Terra es, et in terram ibis, et in cinerem redigeris." In omni igitur prosa, versus et metra, quicquid alii iudicent, censeo fugienda, quae cum suis stringantur legibus legem prosaicam faciunt claudicare.

7 Est et alius modus clausulas finiendi, scilicet ut ultima dictio trissillaba sit tantum media producta, penultima dictio trissillaba vel deinceps, cuius similiter penultima producta. Bernardus: "Confortatis caespitibus vis occulta surrepsit." Et alibi: "Vultu quodam festivitatis occurrit." Sed hic modus magnae prosae raro, modice nullatenus imponatur. Hic modus in antiquis decretalibus epistulis observatur.

8 Notandum quod magister Johannes bene admisit vocalem post aliam, sed circa hoc nos perfectius instruit Isidorus, dicens, "Purum et honestum eloquium carere debet omnibus vitiis, tam in litteris quam in verbis quam etiam in sententiis, ut iunctura apta et conveniens sit. Observandum igitur ne praecedentis verbi extrema vocalis in eandem

PART 8

Also, Master John of Hauville has added that beauty is 5
created by finding coincidence of sound: namely, that a word
set next to the end should end in the same way as the last
word, as long as the leonine color is scrupulously avoided.
For he has condemned clauses such as this: "Let him who
does not love my friend love my enemy." And this: "Fire is
subtle, earth is more bendable and of more solid corporeality."

It is clear from what I have said that a sentence in a certain 6
order is very bad verse but in the same order very good
prose. This, for instance: "You are earth and will return to
earth and be reduced to ash." Therefore, whatever others
may say, I think that in all prose, verses and meters must be
shunned because when they are constrained by their own
rules they cause the rule of prose to limp.

There is another way to end clauses, namely for the last 7
word to be only a trisyllable with only the middle syllable
long, and the next-to-last word a trisyllable or longer, also
with a long penult. Bernard: "As the sod took on strength,
a hidden power sprang up." And elsewhere: "(Everything)
came to meet (Nature) with a certain air of joyfulness." But
this mode is introduced rarely in high-style prose, and not at
all in the middle style. It is a mode practiced in ancient decretal letters.

It should be noted that although Master John found quite 8
acceptable two vowels in a row, Isidore has instructed us in
this matter more perfectly, saying, "Good, pure speech
should be devoid of every fault in letters, words, and sentences so that juxtapositions are appropriate and well
matched. Care should be taken, then, not to let a final vowel
in one word clash with the same vowel at the start of the

vocalem primam incidat verbi sequentis, ut 'feminae Aegyptiae,' quia structura melior fit, si consonantes vocalibus applicantur. Trium quoque consonantium quae in se incidentes stridere et quasi rixari videntur vitanda iunctura—id est, *r, s, x*—ut 'ars studiorum,' 'rex Xerxes,' 'error Romuli.' Fugienda et consonans *m* illisa vocalibus, ut 'verum enim.'" Hoc tamen ultimum non observavit Bernardus in prosa.

next word, as *feminae Aegyptiae* (Egyptian women), because the construction is better if consonants follow vowels. Also juxtaposition of three consonants—that is, of *r, s,* and *x*—which when they clash with each other seem to hiss and, as it were, fight, should be avoided, as *ars studiorum* (the art of studies), *rex Xerxes* (King Xerxes), *error Romuli* (the error of Romulus). A clash between the consonant *m* and vowels should also be avoided, as *verum enim* (but in fact)." But this last injunction Bernard did not follow in his prose.

Abbreviations

Architrenius = Johannes de Hauvilla, *Architrenius,* ed. and trans. Winthrop Wetherbee, Dumbarton Oaks Medieval Library 55 (Cambridge, MA, 2019)

CCCM = Corpus Christianorum continuatio medievalis

Colores = Geoffrey of Vinsauf, *Summa de coloribus rhetoricis,* in Faral, *Les arts poétiques,* 321–27, and Wollin, "Die erste Poetik," 403–35

Cosmographia = Bernard Silvestris, *Cosmographia,* ed. and trans. Winthrop Wetherbee, in *Poetic Works,* by Bernard Silvestris, Dumbarton Oaks Medieval Library 38 (Cambridge, MA, 2015)

Documentum = Geoffrey of Vinsauf, *Documentum de modo et arte dictandi et versificandi,* in Faral, *Les arts poétiques,* 263–320

Faral, "Le manuscrit 511" = Edmond Faral, "Le manuscrit 511 du 'Hunterian Museum' de Glasgow," *Studi medievali* 9 (1936): 18–119

Faral, *Les arts poétiques* = Edmond Faral, *Les arts poétiques du XIIe et du XIIIe siècle: Recherches et documents sur la technique littéraire du moyen âge,* Bibliothèque de l'École des hautes études, Sciences historiques et philologiques 238 (Paris, 1924; reprint, Paris, 1962)

Gräbener, *Ars poetica* = Hans-Jürgen Gräbener, ed., *Ars Poetica,* by Gervaise of Melkley, Forschungen zur romanischen Philologie 17 (Münster, 1965)

Harbert, *A Thirteenth-Century Anthology* = Bruce Harbert, ed., *A Thirteenth-Century Anthology of Rhetorical Poems: Glasgow MS V.8.14* (Toronto, 1975)

ABBREVIATIONS

HB = Louis Holtz, *Donat et la tradition de l'enseignement grammatical: Étude sur l'*Ars Donati *et sa diffusion (IV–IX*ᵉ *siècle) et édition critique* (Paris, 1981), 653–74; an edition of Donatus's *Barbarismus,* which is part 3 of his *Ars maior;* cited by page and line number

John Gray = *Magnus Alexander,* a Latin poem celebrating the installation of John Gray as bishop of Norwich, probably by Gervase, in Harbert, *A Thirteenth-Century Anthology,* 47–52, and Faral, "Le manuscrit 511," 109–12

KB = Heinrich Keil, ed., *Grammatici Latini* (Leipzig, 1855–1888; repr., Hildesheim, 1961), vol. 4, pp. 392–402; an edition of Donatus's *Barbarismus;* cited by page and line number

LLT = Library of Latin Texts, updated December 29, 2023, https://clt.brepolis.net

Mathematicus = Bernard Silvestris, *Mathematicus,* ed. and trans. Winthrop Wetherbee, in *Poetic Works,* by Bernard Silvestris, Dumbarton Oaks Medieval Library 38 (Cambridge, MA, 2015)

PL = J. P. Migne, ed., *Patrologiae cursus completus, series Latina,* 221 vols. (Paris, 1844–1868)

Poetria nova = Geoffrey of Vinsauf, *Poetria nova,* in Faral, *Les arts poétiques,* 197–262

PT = *Pyramus and Thisbe,* a poem perhaps by Gervase, in Faral, *Les arts poétiques,* 331–35, and Harbert, *A Thirteenth-Century Anthology,* 54–60

RAH = *Rhetorica ad Herennium,* ed. Harry Caplan, Loeb Classical Library 403 (Cambridge, MA, 1954)

Rosiene, "The *Ars versificaria*" = Alan M. Rosiene, "The *Ars versificaria* of Gervase of Melkley: Structure, Hierarchy, Borrowings," in *Le poetriae del medioevo latino: Modelli, fortuna, commenti,* ed. Gian Carlo Alessio and Domenico Losappio, Filologie medievali e moderne 15 (Venice, 2018), 205–24

TLL = *Thesaurus linguae Latinae*

ABBREVIATIONS

Tria sunt = *Tria sunt: An Art of Poetry and Prose,* ed. and trans. Martin Camargo, Dumbarton Oaks Medieval Library 53 (Cambridge, MA, 2019)

Wollin, "Die erste Poetik" = Carsten Wollin, "Die erste Poetik Galfrids von Vinsauf: Eine verläufige Edition der *Summa de coloribus rhetoricis,*" *Mittellateinisches Jahrbuch* 49 (2014): 393–442

Note on the Text

The Manuscripts

This edition is based on a collation of the following four manuscripts, which to my knowledge are the only extant copies of the work.

A = Oxford, Balliol College 276, fols. 127r–53v, mid-fifteenth century. Has Geoffrey of Vinsauf's *Poetria nova* and Matthew of Vendôme's *Ars versificatoria*, as well as Alan of Lille's *Anticlaudianus* and Terence's comedies.

B = Oxford, Balliol College 263, fols. 153v–76r, early fifteenth century. Martin Camargo, *Medieval Rhetorics of Prose Composition: Five English Artes dictandi and Their Tradition,* Medieval and Renaissance Texts and Studies 115 (Binghamton, NY, 1995), 109, has called Balliol 263 "a rich compendium of materials for studying the verbal arts." Like H and A, it contains Matthew of Vendôme and Geoffrey of Vinsauf as well as Gervase, and several treatises on *dictamen* also.

D = Douai, Bibliothèque municipale 764, fols. 119r–85r, ca. 1400. Made in Oxford, and also a rich compendium: the contents include *Tria sunt,* Geoffrey of Vinsauf's *Poetria nova,* Alan of Lille's *De planctu Naturae,* and several treatises on *dictamen.*

H = Glasgow, Hunterian Museum, V.8.14, formerly MS 511, and so named in the published catalogue, John Young and P. Henderson Aitken, *A Catalogue of the Manuscripts of the Library of the Hunterian Museum in the University of Glasgow* (Glasgow, 1908), 417–19, and by most scholars who have written about it. It is dated to the first quarter of

NOTE ON THE TEXT

the thirteenth century and was probably made while Gervase was still alive, perhaps with his assistance. It is a handbook of the rhetorical art, containing several other treatises and a number of poems, some perhaps by students, some almost certainly by Gervase, that illustrate the rhetorical art of poetry in practice. The other texts are these: Matthew of Vendôme's *Ars versificatoria,* which opens the volume (fols. 1r–33r), and Geoffrey of Vinsauf's *Summa de coloribus rhetoricis* (fols. 36r–45v), *Documentum de modo et arte dictandi et versificandi* (fols. 46r–67r), and *Poetria nova* (fols. 72r–97v). Alan Rosiene has suggested that they are probably arranged in chronological order.[1] Edmond Faral printed all four of these in *Les arts poétiques du XII* et du XIII* siècle* (Paris, 1924; repr., Paris, 1962), the first three from H, and the *Poetria nova* from H and several other manuscripts. Gervase's *The Art of Making Verses (Ars versificatoria)* comes after them all, on fols. 103v–33v, being the last in order. The rhetorical poems are interspersed among the treatises; the texts of many are in Edmond Faral, "Le manuscrit 511 du 'Hunterian Museum' de Glasgow: Notes sur le mouvement poétique et l'histoire des etudes littéraires en France et en Angleterre entre les années 1150 et 1225," *Studi medievali* 9 (1936): 18–119, and of all in Bruce Harbert, *A Thirteenth-Century Anthology of Rhetorical Poems: Glasgow MS V.8.14* (Toronto, 1975). Rosiene thought that Gervase took part in the composition of the manuscript.

Previous Editions

Faral did not include Gervase's text in *Les arts poétiques,* but contented himself with a two-page summary. In "Le manuscrit 511," he focuses on "some notable traits" ("quelques traits notables," p. 63) of the last pages of the work, printing excerpts, commencing at 6.10 (p. 64), where Gervase cites Vitruvius on the wide knowledge required of architects and says the same of poets. He then gives the entirety of 7.10, and the instructions for reading aloud, 7.12, summarizes the teachings on *dictamen* in part 8, and prints part 8 in full

(pp. 67–69). Later he returns to Gervase on similitude, and prints 2.2–17 (p. 97–103).

In 1965 Hans-Jürgen Gräbener published a critical edition, under the title *Ars poetica*. It had been his doctoral dissertation at Münster, supervised by Hennig Brinkmann and Heinrich Lausberg, to whom the book is dedicated. His text, like mine, is based on Hunterian V.8.14, but he collated the two Balliol manuscripts as well, and used readings from them in his text when he judged them superior to H's, as have I (adding Douai, which Gräbener did not know). Useful as this edition has been to scholars over the years, it is not in the end reliable, as the reviews by Rino Avesani, in *Studi medievali* 7, no. 2 (1966): 749–60, and Franz Josef Worstbrock, in *Zeitschrift für deutsches Altertum und deutsche Literatur* 96 (1967): 99–107, made clear right away. The present edition has more than four hundred divergences from Gräbener's text, all recorded in the Notes to the Text.

Other Gervase Material in Manuscript H

In manuscript H, *The Art of Making Verses* is preceded and followed by materials apparently related to Gervase. In front of it, starting on the first line of fol. 102v, which starts a new quire, is a short treatise on *dictamen,* beginning *In componendis epistulis,* and ending on fol. 103r, *delectari nolumus sed prodesse.* This is followed by a sentence that says, *Quoniam nulla doctrina fidelior exemplari, quaedam opera nostra iam dictis regulis supponemus, a beata Virgine exordium sumentes, ut qui voluerint post regularem doctrinam concipiant exemplarem* (Since no teaching is more trustworthy than an example, we are appending to the rules we have stated some pieces of our own,

NOTE ON THE TEXT

starting with the blessed Virgin, so that those who want an example after the teaching of the rules may have it). The first example is a rhymed poem starting *In honorem matris Dei* (In honor of the mother of God), and the second a begging letter from a student in Paris named R. de Bruelas to his "second father," A. de Pleissetz. The Mary poem is cited twice in *The Art of Making Verses,* at 3.7 and 3.12. All three items, the short treatise on *dictamen* and the two examples with their sentence of introduction, are printed by Faral, "Le manuscrit 511," 58–61, and by Gräbener, *Ars poetica,* as an appendix on pp. 234–42. The poem and letter are only in H; the short treatise on *dictamen* is in the late manuscripts, appearing as an integral part of *The Art of Making Verses,* at its very end. If one supposes that the speaker of *opera nostra* (some pieces of our own) is Gervase, as seems probable, then all three are his.

Six poems follow the treatise, on folios 133v to 138v, Harbert's numbers 39 to 44, on pages 45 to 61 of *A Thirteenth-Century Anthology.* Of these, *John Gray* (no. 40) and *Pyramus and Thisbe* (no. 43) are quoted often in the treatise; *Gloria felicis* (no. 41) and *Contra cognatum* (no. 42) are quoted once each, at 3.7 and 1.80; and *Parmenides rupis* (no. 39) and *Fama loquax* (no. 44) appear on stylistic grounds to be by Gervase. (For *Parmenides rupis,* see the Introduction; in *Fama loquax,* see the comparisons of Cecilia to Penelope, Helen, and Marcia alongside the teaching in *The Art of Making Verses* 2.21, and see the later punning on *ave* and *Averenchis.*) All six, then, have a relation to Gervase; Alan Rosiene in his New Orleans paper plausibly called the entire run of pages, from 102v to 138v, "the Gervase section of the manuscript."

NOTE ON THE TEXT

Though I think that all of these—the short treatise on *dictamen,* the sample poem and letter, and the six poems that come after the treatise—are by Gervase, since they are not actually parts of *The Art of Making Verses* I do not include them.

The Present Text and Translation

The superior value of H is evident: it is contemporary with Gervase, surrounds the treatise with materials he probably wrote and certainly used, might well have been supervised by him, and is carefully made throughout. The other three manuscripts were made two hundred years later and clearly derive from a common ancestor already compromised by numerous errors. Nevertheless, I have collated them carefully and on occasion have preferred their shared reading to that of H. Still, I regard what I have produced as essentially an edition of H with normalized spelling and occasional corrections, some from the other manuscripts and some conjectural. Capitalization and punctuation are mine. The Notes to the Text record all departures from H, and also from Gräbener's edition. The translation, as is standard in the Dumbarton Oaks Medieval Library, is literal enough to enable a reader to use it to see how the Latin works. Occasionally I have strayed from literalness to reproduce a rhetorical effect.

In the Notes to the Text which follow, Glasgow Hunterian V.8.14, formerly 511 (H) is the base text. The notes record all places where I have varied from it, and mention as well all places where I have varied from Gräbener (G). Any manuscript not mentioned has the reading of the lemma.

NOTE ON THE TEXT

My conjectures are marked with an asterisk. If Gräbener has the same conjecture as my own (sometimes it seems to be just a misreading of H), the letter G does not appear among the variants listed. Glosses and corrections in H are not recorded. Manuscript A is Balliol 276, B is Balliol 263, and D is Douai 764.

Notes

1 My citation of Rosiene here is to a paper offered to the International Society for the History of Rhetoric at its meeting in New Orleans in July 2019, to which he referred in several emails to me later that summer. Sadly, Alan Rosiene died of COVID-19 in January 2020. His widow, Sandra Bruner, has sent me what she could find on his computer relating to the ISHR meeting, including what looks like the actual paper, although since much of it was on slides, I have only a few pages of prose and then the titles of the slides, on which Alan seems to have spoken extempore. His paper is clearly an important contribution to our understanding of the text of H. I have learned from it, and I am pleased to be able to honor his memory by citing it.

Notes to the Text

Preface

1   versificatoriae: versificarie *HG*; versifica^rie *B*; versificatorie *D*; *A omits the entire prologue*
2   *psittacus: spitacus *H*; psitacus *BDG*; *A missing*
     *praesumpsisse: presuisse *H*; presumere *BDG*; *A missing*
4   intellecto: intellectio *G*
5   Nasonis: *G marks the start of fol. 105r in manuscript H, erroneously for 104r; this error continues throughout his text (all G's indications of new pages in H are one number too high)*
6   etiam: *omitted H*
7   Hauvilla: Hanvilla *G (throughout)*
     de Darete: darete de, *corrected H*
     Darete Phrygio: Frigio Darete *AG*
9   communia: communes *G*

Part One

1   positae: minute *ABDG*
     ubertatem: venustatem *HG*
2   simplici praedicato: praedicato *HG*
3   vitio quod: vitiis que *HG*
     *Devoniensis: Dovenensis *HG*; Devonensis *ABD*
4   figurae: figura *H*
     ut olli: et olli *G*
     mutatio: notatio *G*
     alio sanguineis: *omitted H*
     concentu: contemptu *AG*

NOTES TO THE TEXT

      melancholicis: melancolicicis *G*
      vitium: vitum *G*
      relinquimus: reliquimus *G*
5   similitudinarie: similitudine *HG*
      contrarie: contrario *HG*
      contrariis et: contrario sed *ABDG*
      puta: picta *HG*
7   habet[1]: *omitted G*
8   euphonomaton: eufonomyaton *H*
      *Tautoparonomion: tautoparartomyon *H*; tautocimonum *A*; tautoparamiom *B*; tantoparimon *D*
      tangunt: tangit *G, which treats this phrase as text, not as an example*
      dictionum: dictionem *G*
9   et in medio: et medio *H*
      sic: ut hic *ABDG*
10   schemata: scemata idest due figure *HG*
      Paromoeon: paranomeon *H*
      repetitio: repititio *G*
      episcopum: episcopatum *G*
      ergo: igitur *AG*
      in oscula: oscula *HG*
      Ad: Adeo *G*
11   unde: ut *HBG*
      carcer *(twice)*: carere *G*
      g et c: *omitted H*
      i: r *ABD*
      versibus hiis: hiis versibus *G*
12   retentio: annominatio *HG*
      polyptoton: polipteton *H*
      honesto: egregio *H*
      Quicquid: quisque *HG*
      sit haec syllaba phy: hec sillaba fi sit *HG*
13   etiam et: etiam *HG*
      terminatur ut hic: terminatur ut huiusmodi *H*
      illis: hiis *H*
14   dupliciter: duplciter *G*

PART I

        in eis ait: meis ait *HBDG*
        *ut hinc inde: hinc inde ut *H*; hinc autem *ABD*, ut *G*
15   facit: faciunt *G*
        ponantur: ponatur *H*
        *Vanoque: varioque *HG*; maneque *ABD*
        citra: circa *BG*: cura *AD*
        Callistus: Calixtoe *HG*; calixtoneo *A*; calixtones *D*
        Hic sapit . . . salus: *mislineated G*
        est: *omitted H*
        paronomasia: paranomasia *H*; paranomasiam *B*
16   parit *(first three)*: facit *H*
        repetitionem[2]: repetitionum *G*
        antonomastice: antonomasice *HADG*
        vox[2]: *omitted HG*
        mala: male *HGBD*
        Non amor . . . amans: *mislineated G*
18   pervigiles: pervigigiles *H*; perviliges *G*
19   decorari: decorare *G*
        monoculi: monocili *G*
        exemplum: exemplam *G*
        exponendo: exprimendo *HG*
        praenotetur: pernotetur *G*
        Angliae: *omitted HG*
20   *peperit pignus: pignus peperit *HABDG*
        Lucanus . . . ait: Vicimus Aufranio *H*
21   sed suis: sed quod suis *HG*
        Norvicensi: Norvici *G*
        viscera: viscere *G*
22   extollimus: exclamamus *ABDG*
23   cum petit: competit *G*
        parta: perta *G*
        minuatur: miniatur *G*
24   *agis: ages *HABD*
        ita: ista *G*
25   interpolatam: interpositam *HG*
        quadam: sub quadam *ABDG*

NOTES TO THE TEXT

	*in hoc exemplo: hoc exemplo *HABD*
26	Iohannes: Iohannis *G*
	Byblidem: bimblidem *H*
	praescindit: precidit *G*
	subaudis: subauditur *ABD*; subausculta *G*
	Benedictus[1]: bene *H*
	Praescindimus: precidimus *HG*
	rei: connomini rei *A*; cognomini rei *BDG*
27	et subtracti: vel subtracti *HG*
	potest hic modus fieri: hic modus potest fieri *HG*
	possessionem: possessionem suam *HG*
28	Tydei: Thedidis *G*
	*equidem: quidem *HABD*
	modicum: modicim *G*
	quiddam: quoddam *HG*
29	alia est occupatio *HG*
30	inchoandis: in inchoandis *ABDG*
	*Schesis onomaton: scesomaton *H*; scesonomaton *ABD*
31	hic est utilis: hoc est utilis *G*
	hic similiter est utilis: hoc similiter est utile *G*
	quandoque etiam: quandoque *HG*
32	Adiunctum est: ergo adiunctum est *HG*
	Extra vagantia: *omitted ABD*; Extravaganter *G*
	secundum quamlibet sui speciem: secundum qualibet sui speciem *A*; vel quelibet sua species *G*
33	vobis: nobis *G*
	verbis: mente *H*
	quem praedicat: qui predicat *HG*
	vindicta: vindicata *G*
	occurritur morbis: occuritur morbus *G*
	sententiae: eiusdem sententie *HG*
	Polinici tydea: polita fidea *G*
35	cum fit: cum hoc fit *H*; cum hic fit *G*
	ita frequenter: *omitted* ita *HG*
	alternum: alterutrum *HG*
36	Venustissimum est: venustissimum est igitur *HG*

PART I

37 quamvis etiam: quandoque etiam si *HG*
praecedat: precedit *H*
et tunc: sed tunc *HG*
fortis: fātis *H (reported as* fatuitatis *by G)*
38 rhetoricos²: dialecticos *G*
39 terminus non casualis: non terminus casualis *H*
caloris: coloris *G*
40 smaragdus¹: sgmaragdus *H*
41 albus: abbus *H*
Epitheton aliud: Epythetum aliud *ABDG*
lentus: lentus vel segnis *HG*; segnis *ABD*; *see Rino Avesani, review of Ars poetica, by Gervase of Melkeley, ed. Hans-Jürgen Gräbener, Studi medievali 7 (1966): 756*
Ulixes: Ulixis *G*
42 ut si dicam: ut si dico *H*
discernit: decernit *H*
sensus: Urbs *G*
43 Cum fit mentio: Ut (?) cum fit mentio *H*
opera divina: omnia divina *HG*
dictu: dictum *HG*; dicto *A*
suo: sui *H*
44 appositum: appositam *G*
Parvipontani ... dicamus: *G prints as verse*
Quae appositio: Appositio *G*
45 communitatis: converitatis *G*
Socrates qui: Socrates qui qui *(at page break) H*
apponi: appono *G*
47 e converso: converso *A*; eius modo *G*
48 posset: possit *HG*
quod senectute: quod vel senectute *H*
49 vicit: vincit *H*
50 Quaelibet: quelibet igitur *HG*
multipliciter: multiplciter *G*
resolvitur: resolvetur *G*
51 Prisciano: Prisciane *G*
*Socrates: se *HG*; *omitted ABD*

NOTES TO THE TEXT

52   Bononia: Bolonia *HG*
Non est sensus[1]: non est is sensus *HG*
ex parte appositi: ex parte apposita *G*
Regitur: retinetur *HG*
Hectorem: hectora *H*

53   partiunculas: clausulas perversas *G*
dictionem: dictiones *ABDG*

54   quam et genitivus: quam genitivus *G*
hic tempestates: Hii tempestates *HG*
Obliquus: obscurius *HG*

55   quandoque[1]: q$\overline{m}$ *H*
*voce ipsa: voce ipsa vel vocis significato *HAB*; voce ipsa vel vocis significatio *G*
appellato: appellatio *G*

56   macilento: macilente *G*
Pellis: pelex *G*

59   sed: sed sed *H*
istas inferiores: inferiores *HG*

60   Fit . . . vocis: *ends previous paragraph in* G
quando: est quando *HG*
Nisi: Niso *G*

62   sub aequalitate: Erit sub equalitate *HG*
In hac: *pronoun refers to* locutione
elucescat: elucescar *G*
pro hac: *pronoun refers to* locutione
cupido: Cupido *G*
convertitur: pure convertitur *HG*
Item: Iterum *G*
rudis est: rudis *HG*
est aequalitas: *omitted* est *HG*
locutio: *omitted HG*
arbori sic: arbori sit *H*
haec mutatio: hec commutatio *H*; bene commutatio *G*

64   eisdem: eiusdem *H*

66   in hiis: *omitted* in *H*

PART I

    synonymis: sininimis *G*
    collectio: collocatio *G*
    synonymorum: sinomimorum *G*
    huiusmodi exemplum: hoc exemplum *HG*
    iuncta: iucta *(nasal bar omitted) H*
67 per hoc innuat: hoc innuat *H*
68 periphrasis Plutonis: periphrasis est Plutonis *ABDG*
    ponuntur quando: ponuntur quandoque *G*
    protractio[2]: portractio *G*
69 id est dignissima: *omitted* id est *H*
70 se: *omitted HG*
    imitationem: mutationem *ABD*; immitationem *G*
    peremit: premit *G*
    signans, signato, signatur: significans, etc. *G*
    consequente: consequenti *H*
    Horatius: Ovidius *G*
    decembres: decembros *HG*
    intelligatur: intelligatur ut comprehendatur *ABDG*
    illic ingens: ingens illic *HG*
    semperque: superque *G*
    laborant: laborat *HG*
    repetant: repetunt *HG*
    Laborare animalium est: *G prints as part of the Lucan passage*
71 graece permutatio latine: grece pronuntiationem sonat *ABD*;
      igitur permutatione latior *G*
    est quotiens: est ergo quotiens *HG*
    quia: quod *HG*
    ea: eo *G*
72 potes: *omitted ABD*; potest *G*
    segeti[3]: segetis, *corrected* segeti *H*; segetis *G*
    mutari: et mutari *HG*
    incandentis: incandescentis *G*
    tantum ... tantum: tum ... tum *G*
73 unica: una *G*
    consonat: sonat *H*

NOTES TO THE TEXT

74 dubitari: dubitare *G*
generaliter: *omitted H*
75 et mentem: *omitted* et *HG*
monachalem: monochalem *H*
omnia fraterna: onmia fraterna *G*
76 *turrit: currit *HABDG*
77 Quandoque[1]: quando *H*
augmentantem: augmentative *ABDG*
*videbatur: *add* nunc pro aliquando *HABDG*
horrere: horrore *G*
sui: sua *G*
commissuras: commisuras *G*
78 transvertitur: transumitur *HG*
utantur: utuntur *ABDG*
79 *Hic dividitur: hec dividitur *HABD*
*synchysis: sinthesis *HABDG*
Inque: in quod *G*
peroptime: per optime *G*
dicendum: demonstrandum *G*
dolor: *omitted G*
80 ubi: nisi *G*
pulchrior: pulcerior *B*; pulcherrimus *HG*
actis: aetas *G*
81 *Synchysis *(twice)*: Sinthesis *HABDG*
nuncupamus: *add* idest color sic vocatus *HG*
*synchysim: sinthesim *HABDG*
vix: fix *G*
haec vox caeca: *omitted* haec *H*
pluraliter: plurale *G*
diversitate: deversitate *G*
Excepta: Extra *G*
*synchysi: sinthesi *H*; sineresi *ABD*; sinthesim *G*
82 superlatio: superlocutio *G*
color: colorum *G*
83 modum *(twice)*: modis
84 praenotandus: pernotandus *G*

PART 2

quidem: quedam *G*
Melius: melius est *ABDG*
quattuor: auditori *G*

Part Two

2	Rectus enim: Rectus enim nominis barbari *ABDG*
3	tum: tamen *G*
	semiporcus: semicorpus *H*
4	nota: vota *G*
6	imitantur: mutantur in *ABDG*
8	callide: callident *H*; callidet *G*
9	Contulerat: conculcat *G*
	*comantibus: *omitted HG*; domantibus *ABD*
	*novamentis: ornamentis *HG*; nova indictis *ABD*
10	eliminantur: elimantur *G*
11	quae tamen: que tantum *G*
	grossitiem: grossitudinem *G*
	praesentius: expressius *HG*
12	Bernardus ... substiterunt: *omitted H*
	*singulo: singulum *ABDG*; *H missing*
	etiam et: *omitted* et *HG*
	audienti: gradienti *HG*
13	Telamonis: Thelamonius *G*
	prosiliit: prosiluit *G*
	est: *omitted H*
	vocatos: vocatus *G*
	proprium: prorrium *G*
	dicunt: dicant *G*
	inveniri: invenire *G*
	*illa: illi *H*; ista *ABD*; illa *G*
	dicentes licuit: dicentes lucuit *H*
	intellige: intelligere *H*
	praesente nota: signatum praesente nota *G*
	enucleat: enucliat *G*
	fere comparativis: comparativis fere *HG*

NOTES TO THE TEXT

14	uter: *omitted ABD*; utique *G*
	germine: gramine *HG*
	Videtur: Videretur *G*
	*Devoniensem: Dovenensem *HG*; Devonensem *ABD*
	illi: illii *H*; alii *G*
	videtur: vero *HG*
	*synanchen: squinatem morbum *H*; squinantem *ABD*; synanchem morbum *G*
	*synanchen: squinantem *HABD*
	*argyranchen: arginantem *HABD*; argynanchen *G*
	Acceperat: deceperat *HG*
16	repraesentantur: representatur *HAG*
	vox v[1]: vox quinte *H*
	enim: etiam *HG*
17	distinctione: distincte *ABDG*
	intolerabiliorem: tolerabiliorem *HG*
18	per[2]: *omitted HG*
19	Phyllida nosti: Phillidam nostri *G*
	salutem *(twice)*: salutat *G*
	Spiritus: specie *H*; Spem *G*
20	terminorum illius: *omitted* terminorum *HG*
	fuit Tantalus: *omitted* Tantalus *HG*
	egenus: egens *G*
	Si respicitur: Si respiciatur *ABDG*
21	Censu: Sensu *G*
22	accidens filius: accidens filium *G*
	a Virgilio: Virgilius *HG*
23	*propriorum: priorum *HABD*
24	disgregativus: degeneratus *G*
	disgregativus visus vel Lilia sunt color: *omitted HG*
	transumptio: determinatio *H*
25	alienam: *omitted ABDG*
26	nomini: nomine *G*
27	apertum: opertum *G*
	vellus: velus *G*
28	ut ... procedatur: *construed with previous sentence G*
	approbat: apropriat *H*

PART 2

   et est simplex ... plura: *omitted H by eyeskip, added in margin in a different hand*
   secundum quod: per quod *H*
29 luce clarius elucescat: *construed as an example by G*
   legens: leges *H*
   virebat: virebant *HG*
   loquitur, fatetur: loquor, fateor *G*
   curam: curiam *HG*
   diescat: diescit *HG*
31 calidus idest: *omitted* idest *HG*
32 Utinam: Aut *G*
   per fidem: perfecte *H*; perfectus *G*
   nosse: scire *ADG*; scire, *corrected* nosse *B*
33 amantum: amantem *G*
   relativis: relatoris *G*
34 Item cura: Item pro hac cura *ABDG*
35 Janus: inanis *AB*; maius *D*; sanus *G*
   dempta: depta *D*; derepta *G*
   et e converso: *construed with* Cassiodorus *G*
36 dederat: desiderat *ABDG*; *see 2.35 above*
   Quod sequitur: quia sequitur *HD*
   licet: *construed with* nivea pro alba *G*
37 aliqua: alia *ABDG*
   efferebat: offerebat *ABDG*
38 animo: animi *G*
39 tantum: *omitted HG*
   intermixtio: intermixto *G*
   incepta: incepto *H*
   praemonstravi: permonstravi *G*
   *cui: qui *HAB*; quia *D*
   lenioris: levioris *G*
   Eum: Cum *G*
40 autem adhuc: autem *HG*; adhuc *A*
41 utimur: utimus *G*
42 nevit *(twice)*: venit *ABDG*
   filum: fili *ABD*; filium *G*
43 quod quodlibet: *omitted* quod *H*

NOTES TO THE TEXT

        lacte: lactis *ABDG*
        id est de: *omitted* id est *H*
        nive: nivis *ABDG*
44   *Asteismon(s) *(four times)*: antismon(s) *HABDG*; astismos *Donatus, KB 401.30*
        *satis: magis *HABDG*; satis *Donatus, KB 401.30*
        *expolitum: expositum *HABDG*; expolitum *Donatus, KB 401.30*
45   solem: sol solet *G*
        Cynthum: Cinthium *G*; Sinthium *ABD*
46   seram: levem *ABDG*
        Inde: Inter *G*
47   praedicationum: predictionum *H*
        praedicatio: predictio *H*
        est durae: *omitted* est *H*
        asinus: *omitted ABD*; alius *G*
        *Bis: qui bis *HABDG*
        Ideo: Iohanne *G*
        Hectorem *(twice)*: Hectora *H*
        litoten: liptote liptoten *G*
49   Haec enim: Hec autem *HG*; Hec tamen *A*
50   gaure cum: gaure tamen *G*
51   accidunt: accident *G*
        similis: similes *H*
        Hortetur: Hortatur *ABDG*
        movens: monens *G*
        studendi: studenti *G*
        oneri: honori *G*
52   etiam: etiam et *AG*; etiam in *BD*
53   nuncupatur: nuncupantur *H*
        Haec icon est; *D omits from here to* ut hic Iste *in 3.3*

Part Three

1   *Maeciliane: ciciliane *HG*; ceciliane *AB*; *D missing*
        *fututorum: futurorum *HABG*; *D missing*
        dictu: dicta *G*

PART 3

    quaeris Line Nomentanus: *all three marked for transposition in H, though what new order is desired is not clear*
    *Nomentanus: momentanus *HABG*; *D missing*
2   Marci: marcii *H*
    per: propter *ABG*; *D missing*
    *dicis: *omitted HAB*; *D missing*
3   prius: *omitted* HG
    vorator: venetor *AB*; venator *D*; narrator *G*
    proprio filio: propria filia *G*
    *generas ut futues: futuas generas ut, *with* ut *marked for transposition* H; generas ut firmas *ABD*; generatas futuas tu *G*
    Alam *(twice)*: Alimenta *G*
    quaesumus: quesimus *G*
4   tantum: tamen *G*
    apposuisse: aposuisse *G*
    non malis: malis *HG*
    prioris: prio/oris *H*
    commodum: incommodum *G*
    vincas: unitas *G*
6   videtur: videretur *HG*
7   Heri: Hesterni *G*
    Fiet: Fit *G*
8   Sensus: sensus est *ABDG*
    inexpressum ... expressum: expressum ... inexpressum *HG*
    de la Yde: de Lahyde *A*; de la hyde *BD*; de Layde *G*
    *Lycoris: luscus *H*; liquoris *ABD*
    scelus ignorare ... nefas: etc. *HG*
    *timentque: timent quia *ABD*; *HG missing; see Pref. 8 above*
    aliquo: alio *G*
    ex more: et ex more *H*
    unde: inde *G*
    dampnas: dampnans *H*
9   illud: aliud *ABDG*
    Deo *(four times)*: Domino *G*
    contermino: contrario *G*
    non aurum: non est aurum *ABDG*

NOTES TO THE TEXT

    demum: deinde *HG*
    qualis: quales *G*
    hunc: hunc esse *ABDG*
    Ieronimi: Ieronimus *G*
10   sola falsitate: scola falsitatis *HG*
    instabilitate: infidelitate *H*
    Amicitia . . . hic: *omitted G*
    sententias: materias *G*
    Fortunae: fortunae ait *ABDG*
    conquestione: questione *HG*
    efficit: effecit *G*
11   tum praetendit: tamen pretendit *G*
    habente: *omitted G*
    positio: predicatio *HG*
    deificari: divinificari *G*
    *censerentur: censeretur *H*; censetur *ABD*; censentur *G*
    demonstrato: demonstratio *G*
    *Hercule: eche *(h crossed) H*; ethere *ABD*; Ethiocle *G*
12   vera: vera sunt: *G*
13   Ovidii: Ovidius *G*
    cuilibet: quelibet *G*
    Lundoniensis: Lundunensis *G*
    *Avite: Avita *HG*; a vita *ABD*
    vere: veritate *G*
    positive: positione *G*
    dominus . . . meus: *G prints as if an example*
    adverbium: verbum *G*
    quid *(twice)*: quidque *G*
    *Fannius: Faustinus *HABDG*
    ipse: *omitted G*
    attollit: attolit *G*
    cohaereat: coherceat *H*

Part Four

1   *tautoparonomion: tantoparoymion *H*; tantoparoyminon *ABD*
2   vulneris: vulueris *G*

PART 5

    partus: pertus *G*
    translaticia: translatia *H*
3   translaticias: translatias *H*
    vocabat: vocavit *H*; vocant *G*

Part Five

1   est conservanda: *omitted* est *HG*
    postea¹ . . . ensibus: umbonibus *and* ensibus *reversed H*
    iterum uniformitas: uniformitas iterum *G*
    singulari: sigulari *G*
2   sensu quod: sensu tantum quod *H*
    tertio post: *omitted H*
3   concussio: contractio *H*; concutio *G*; *the readings* concutio *A and*
      concucio *B are alternate spellings of* concussio, *pronounced like it*
    telemachus suam: thelemachusque suam *HG*
4   *ni: ne *HABDG*
    sic laederetur: *omitted* sic *G*
5   *nec: *omitted HABD*
    recedis: recedes *ABDG*
    necessarium: necessum *G*
    Haec . . . novitas: *G prints it as part of Lucan's line*
6   *Devoniensem: dovenensem *HG*; devonensem *ABD*
    In inferioribus: *omitted* in *HG*
7   orationum: orationis *H*
    oportet ut: *omitted* ut *HG*
    oratione: *omitted G*
    et copulative: vel copulative *G*; copulative *ABD*
    resecandaque: reserandaque *HG*
8   tenero: teneri *G*
    multotiens: multotiens in auctoribus *ABDG*
    positi vel intellecti: *omitted* vel *H*
    aetherios: etheros *G*
    restitit: restituit *G*
9   *Afranio: Africano *HG*; Affricano *ABD*
10 venustissime: similiter venustissime *ABDG*
    Mediis: medius *H*

NOTES TO THE TEXT

	quatiens: quotiens *H*
11	*esse: *omitted HABDG*

Part Six

1	nosse: noscere *AG*
	ad quidlibet: et ad quodlibet *AG*; et ad quidlibet *BD*
	*Epidamne: epidaure *HABDG*
2	reperiri: reperire *ABDG*
	teres: ceres *G*
	quoniam: quin *G*
3	De artificiali ordine: *ABD start the next part here, with a decorated capital; they may be right*

Part Seven

1	perfecta: perfectam *G*
	propiusque: propriusque *ABDG*
	Mancipiis . . . mirum est: *printed by G as if from one poem, not recognized as Horace, and mislineated*
	plurium: plurimum *G*
2	terminatae: termanantis *G*
3	modus: motus *G*
	togula: tegula *H*
	*Aeaciden: eacidam *H*; eandem *ABD*; ea sidam *G*
4	silvani: silvam *G*
5	Oedipodionides: dedipodionides *H*; epidipodionides *AG*
	in quibus: *omitted* in *HG*
	poterant: poterat *H*
	dicit: dicens *HG*
6	Pagina: Pergama *HG*
7	hinc: hic *H*
8	etiam: igitur *G*
	Priamus: Piramus *G*
10	*Vitruvius: Victrinius *HABD*
	*Polyclitus: Poliditus *HABDG*
	*aniatrologetos: aniatrolicus *H*; aniatrologus *ABD*

PART 8

Perfecto: Perfectio *ABDG*
sarraca *(twice)*: sarrata *G*
*Bootae: boete *HABDG*

Part Eight

1 siquidem: quidem *H*
  mutilari: minuere *G*
3 decantationis: determinationis *H*
  cubitam: cubicam *G*
  paraclitum: parasitum *H*
  paraclitus: parasitus *H*
4 finiendi: inveniendi *H*
  Penultima: penultimam *H*
5 consimiliter: similiter *ABDG*
  color: odor *G*
  reflexioris: refixior *G, following Bernard; see Notes to the Translation*
7 finiendi: sonendi *H*
  surrepsit: subresit *H*
8 aliam: m *H*
  consonantium: *omitted H*
  studiorum: studior *ABDG*
  Romuli: romulo *H*

Notes to the Translation

Preface

1 *John White*: Probably John Blund (that is, "blond," or *albus*), an Oxford grammar master, for whom see Josiah Cox Russell, *Dictionary of Writers of Thirteenth-Century England* (London, 1936), 56–58. Apparently Gervase had studied under him and was now his colleague at Oxford.

2 *Matthew of Vendôme . . . Geoffrey of Vinsauf . . . Bernard Silvester*: For the first two, see Edmond Faral, *Les arts poétiques du XIIe et du XIIIe siècle* (Paris, 1924; repr., Paris, 1962). Bernard's *Poetria* is lost. See Hans-Jürgen Gräbener, ed., *Ars poetica,* Forschungen zur romanischen Philologie 17 (Münster, 1965), nos. 31–32, pp. xv–xxvii; Monika Klaes, "Die '*Summa*' des Magister Bernardus: Zu Überlieferung und Textgeschichte einer zentralen *Ars dictandi* des 12. Jahrhunderts," *Frühmittelalterlichen Studien* 24 (1990): 198–234, esp. 199–202, 232–33; Martin Camargo, "A Twelfth-Century Treatise on *Dictamen* and Metaphor," *Traditio* 47 (1992): 161–213, on pp. 165–69. Or it may never have existed. Douglas Kelly, *The Arts of Poetry and Prose,* Typologie des sources du Moyen Âge occidental, fasc. 59 (Turnhout, 1991), 58–59, argues that Gervase was simply recommending Bernard's *Cosmographia* as containing the whole art of both poetry and prose; Alan M. Rosiene, "The *Ars versificaria* of Gervase of Melkley: Structure, Hierarchy, Borrowings," in *Le poetriae del medioevo latino: Modelli, fortuna, commenti,* ed. Gian Carlo Alessio and Domenico Losappio (Venice, 2018), 217n60, agrees with him.

NOTES TO THE TRANSLATION

a parrot in prose: This remark has been taken to be a slap at Bernard, but in fact Gervase is praising him for his flow of words; see 2.38 below.

3 *abbreviated ... redundant*: Gervase wittily claims to commit two of the faults listed by Donatus in the *Barbarismus*, which he is about to mention: *eclipsis*, being too brief, leaving things out, and *perissologia*, saying too much; see KB 395.5, 395.11, and HB 659.1, 659.6. Manuscript H glosses *ecliptica* (abbreviated) with *defectiva* (defective).

beginners: Boys still in the grammar course and starting to create Latin verses. Gervase mentions student versifiers or beginners again at 1.47, 1.48, 1.61, and 1.72.

Barbarismus: The third part of Donatus's *Ars maior*, treating schemes and tropes as well as vices. See KB 392–402, HB 653–74. Gervase cites it often, and sometimes copies it without citing it.

Donatus: Faults: KB 392–95, HB 653–60; figures: KB 397–99, HB 3–66.

5 *Seneca's Controversies*: In 2.2.12 of that work.

Both ... bull: See Ovid, *Ars amatoria* 2.24.

6 *The easiest mistake ... to avoid*: Apparently because it is made inadvertently but is obvious to a proofreader—a wrong case ending, for instance.

7 *John of Hauville*: John lived from about 1160 to around 1210. See Winthrop Wetherbee, ed. and trans., *Architrenius*, Dumbarton Oaks Medieval Library 55 (Cambridge, MA), p. vii. Since he taught in the cathedral school at Rouen, Gervase must have studied there. Of the writers mentioned in this paragraph, John, Bernard, Statius, Lucan, and Ovid are all cited often; Virgil, Dares Phrygius, and Alan of Lille, the author of *Anticlaudianus*, almost never.

A careful reading ... mind: Quoted by the author of *Tria sunt*, 10.3.

8 *before he knew ... rhetoric*: This anecdote backs up Gervase's assertion that his teaching is for beginners. For attributes of persons and things, see 1.62 and 6.1 below, with their notes.

insinuatio: Insinuatio is a way of beginning subtly; see *RAH* 1.4.6,

PART I

1.6.9–7.11; and Cicero, *De inventione* 1.17.23–25, which it is drawn from.

9   *common . . . special*: The special rules come briefly at the end: verse in part 7, prose in part 8. The great bulk of the book applies both to verse and prose, though Gervase's bias toward verse is obvious. The book is aimed at boys learning to write hexameters and pentameters.

Part One

1   *sameness, likeness, and opposition*: For this apparently original way of thinking about figurative language, and organizing a book about it, see the Introduction.

2   *Donatus*: KB 397–99, HB 663–66.

barbarism or solecism: According to Donatus (KB 393.9, HB 655.7), barbarism is a fault in a single word, such as a misspelling, while solecism is a fault in the relating of words to each other, such as putting a plural verb with a singular subject.

3   *Ennius's book is condemned*: See Alan of Lille, *De planctu Naturae* 18.9, and *Anticlaudianus* 1.165–66, ed. and trans. Winthrop Wetherbee, *Literary Works*, Dumbarton Oaks Medieval Library 22 (Cambridge, 2013), pp. 208 and 238. See also Ovid, *Tristia* 2.424, and *Amores* 1.15.19. Horace famously slights Ennius at *Ars poetica* 258–62, but treats him better at *Epistle* 2.1.50.

of barbarisms and solecisms as well as of figures: In the *Barbarismus*, Virgil is cited twenty times in the three sections on vices (KB 392–95, HB 653–60), and thirteen in the section on figures (KB 397–99, HB 663–66).

Roger of Devon: Not otherwise known. He is mentioned again at 2.14 and 3.13.

4   *figures . . . colors*: Gervase consistently uses "colors" for what other writers call "figures of words," and "figures" for their "figures of thought." See *RAH* 4.18.13, *verborum et sententiarum exornationes*. Sometimes he uses *schema* as a synonym for *figura*; I have translated both words as "figure." In general, figures come from the grammatical tradition and have Greek names,

NOTES TO THE TRANSLATION

while colors come from the rhetorical tradition and have Latin names. See *Tria sunt* 8.5, where the author attempts to distinguish between figures and colors, quoting this passage from Gervase at length, but does not make the matter very clear.

exceed and are exceeded equally: Metaphor, say, exceeds literal statement but can itself be excessive.

if you change . . . illi: *Per immutationem litterae sicut olli pro illi,* KB 392.16, HB 654.1.

Antithesis . . . illi: KB 397.1, HB 663.1.

mutation: See 1.76 below.

praecones for praedones: Since *praeco* means "herald" and *praedo* "robber," it's hard to imagine a context for this mutation.

hard metaphors: Starting with the first line, which Gervase quotes at 1.31 below.

5   *the topic "from likeness" . . . "from contraries"*: See Boethius, *De differentiis topicis*, PL 64:1197.

verbal or factual: An example of what Gervase means can be seen at 1.32 below. Repeating a word several times makes a verbal figure, repetition, but synonymy, "repetition in reality," is more beautiful.

rhyme: *Leonitas,* the quality of leonine verse, apparently a coinage of Gervases's.

6   *Cicero . . . clarify*: I cannot find that Cicero says that, or the author of *RAH*. Again and again in discussing the tropes, however, whose nature is to "depart from the ordinary meaning of . . . words" (4.31.42), the *RAH* author (who does not use the word "trope") speaks of not calling things by their normal name. Catachresis, for example, is "the inexact use of a like and kindred word in place of the precise and proper one" (4.33.45). Likewise Cicero, at *De oratore* 3.161, in a discussion of metaphor, says that "there is nothing in nature whose name we can't use for other things" *(nihil enim est in rerum natura cuius nos non in aliis rebus possimus uti vocabulo et nomine).* Nowhere, however, is any of this said to be done to teach and clarify. But in *De oratore* 24.82, speaking of metaphors, Cicero does say, "if a thing

does not have its own name, the metaphor seems to be made not playfully but in order to teach" *(si res suum nullum habet nomen, docendi causa sumptum non ludendi videtur)*, and in 24.92, again speaking of metaphor, he actually uses the word *mutare* (change). See also the color hypallage, which Gervase calls a *genus transmutationis* (kind of transmutation), in 1.79 below; Cicero mentions it in *De oratore* 27.93; in it "words are, as it were, exchanged for words" *(quasi summutantur verba pro verbis)*.

8 *tautoparonomion*: From Greek *tauto* (the same) and Late Latin *paroemia* (proverb). Defined again as "a proverb of sameness," that is, a nonmetaphorical proverb, at 4.1 below.

euphonomaton: Greek *euphonia onamoton* (euphony of names).

Things foreseen hurt more lightly: See pseudo-Cato, *Disticha* 2.24. Bartlett J. Whiting, *Proverbs, Sentences, and Proverbial Phrases; from the English Writings Mainly before 1500* (Cambridge, 1968), p. 455, no. P146 (before 1450), "lichtlear hurtis that is fore-sen."

General troubles touch us more lightly: Claudian, *De raptu Proserpinae* 3.197, the nurse Electra to Ceres, wishing that "a general trouble" such as an attack by Titans had happened to Proserpina, instead of the rape she is about to describe.

One word beforehand is better than two afterward: A pentameter verse.

later: "Later" refers to 1.26 and 4.1; see the note at 1.26 below.

9 *The violence . . . running*: Geoffrey of Vinsauf, *Colores,* ed. Faral, *Les arts poétiques,* p. 323, and Carsten Wollin, "Die erste Poetik, Galfrids von Vinsauf: Eine verläufige Edition der *Summa de coloribus rhetoricis,*" *Mittellateinisches Jahrbuch* 49 (2014): 412.

Trivalli: Trivalli was Trifels in Bavaria, where Richard I was imprisoned in 1192. The phrase may be a fragment from something about Richard.

Ulysses . . . supercheekiness: Gräbener, *Ars poetica,* p. 11, cites Ovid, *Ars amatoria* 2.123: *Non formosus erat, sed erat facundus Ulixes* (Ulysses was not handsome, but he was eloquent). Perhaps Gervase set that line as a prompt, and one of his students came up with this. The line has three spondees, suggesting student

NOTES TO THE TRANSLATION

writing. See Gervase's praise of dactyls in 7.6 below, and my discussion of the matter in Traugott Lawler, "Langland *Versificator*," *The Yearbook of Langland Studies* 25 (2011): 70–71.

The plane tree ... valleys: Bernard, *Cosmographia* 1.3.267.

10 *Isidore*: See *Etymologies* 1.36.14, where Isidore quotes *O Tite*, but says that Virgil moderates that well by confining alliteration either to the beginning or the end of a verse, and the two examples he gives from the *Aeneid*, 1.295 and 3.183, alliterate on three words each. He does not, however, declare a three-word limit. Gervase apparently copied the declaration from Matthew of Vendôme, *Ars versificatoria* 3.16, ed. Faral, *Les arts poétiques*, 171, where it appears in just these words, and is ascribed to Isidore.

O Titus Tatius: Ennius, *Annales*, supposedly 1.108. It is Isidore's example, also in *RAH* 4.12.18, and Donatus, KB 398.21 and HB 665.13; Matthew of Vendôme used it as well (see note above).

The plane tree ... shore: Bernard, *Cosmographia* 1.3.267–68.

Bernard: Gräbener, *Ars poetica*, no. 58, p. xlvii, says *ipse*, which I have here translated as "Bernard," means Isidore; maybe so.

He is ... such a man: John Gray 117–19. This poem may well be by Gervase, he quotes it so often. If so, he seems to say here that Bernard Silvester would have given it his blessing—and to give himself a further pat on the back in what he says after the quotation.

11 *There hangs ... plotting against them*: *PT* 95–96. If, as I (and many others) think, Gervase wrote this poem too, he here gives himself a slap in the face to offset the pat on the back. Robert Glendinning has argued persuasively not just that Gervase wrote the poem but that he wrote it when he himself was in school. See his "Pyramus and Thisbe in the Medieval Classroom," *Speculum* 61, no. 1 (1986): 51–78. See also the note to 1.80 below.

While ... sits by: Probably another student performance. The excessive punning sounds are *fu-fu-fe-fa, prop-prop,* and *nutri-nutri*.

12 *strict structure*: See 1.21 below.

Abundant wit ... drinking: John of Hauville, *Architrenius* 2.285.

PART I

Now shield . . . lance: Statius, *Thebaid* 8.398–99. John of Garland, *Parisiana poetria* 1.18, ed. Traugott Lawler, Dumbarton Oaks Medieval Library 65 (Cambridge, 2020), 38, cites these lines to exemplify *traductio,* the Latin equivalent of polyptoton. Gervase brings this couplet up again in 1.66, 5.1, and 5.7.

hare: That is, a hermaphrodite. On the hare's reputation for ambiguous sexuality, see Beryl Rowland, "Animal Imagery and the Pardoner's Abnormality," *Neophilologus* 48 (1964): 56–60; her *Animals with Human Faces* (Knoxville, 1973), 91; and Bruce Harbert, *A Thirteenth-Century Anthology of Rhetorical Poems: Glasgow MS V.8.14* (Toronto, 1975), 53n3. Harbert is annotating no. 39 in the anthology, a poem Gervase quotes at 1.41 below, and probably wrote. There is a wealth of information about hares; see the index under "hare" in John Boswell, *Christianity, Social Tolerance, and Homosexuality: Gay People in Western Europe from the Beginning of the Christian Era to the Fourteenth Century* (Chicago, 1980).

13 *Cicero*: The reference is probably to *De oratore* 44.149–50, which says explicitly that a final syllable should not grate with the following initial syllable. See also *De oratore* 25.84 and *RAH* 4.12.18, which have Ennius's "O Titus" line, and *RAH* 4.22.32–4.23.32.

The short roach . . . plaice: Bernard, *Cosmographia* 1.3.438.

A dead goose . . . urn: That is, a meal of goose goes better with wine. The aphorism shows up in Thomas Levacher de la Feutrie, *L'École de Salerne, ou, l'art de conserver la santé* (Paris: 1779), 136: *Auca petit Bacchum mortua, viva lacum* (A dead goose asks for Bacchus, a live one for a pond). And in French, "L'oison a toujours soif, mort aussi bien qu'en vie, / mais c'est de vin à table, et d'eau dans la prairie" (A goose is always thirsty, whether dead or alive, but for wine at the table and for water in the field).

Ida . . . Paris's rape: Bernard, *Cosmographia* 1.3.340.

14 *venit, ait*: Ovid, *Metamorphoses* 6.43.

Donatus: KB 398.22, HB 665.14.

15 *did not want to compose . . . in rhyme*: Gervase's point is that in the

NOTES TO THE TRANSLATION

four places where Ovid might have rhymed, he has *-on, -em, -am,* and *-um.*

The one ... descended: John of Hauville, *Architrenius* 8.38–39, 8.36–37. The "other color" is presumably the play on *Lucifer* (Lightbringer) and *Letifer* (Deathbringer). *Quo Numa devenit* (where Numa descended) echoes Horace, *Epistles* 1.6.27.

Oh, how terrible ... judge: John of Hauville, *Architrenius* 7.246. The line is completed by another *heu quam*; thus the second member of the rhyming pair, *immobilis,* is indeed near the end of the line.

She is better ... beauty: Gervase seems to ascribe this elegiac couplet to "Architrenius," the name he frequently uses for John of Hauville. Wetherbee says John might have written a poem on Callisto, "though the lines quoted by Gervase could have been coined for teaching purposes" (*Architrenius,* p. xxiii n2).

Donatus: KB 398.24, HB 666.1.

one on the pope and a king: By Matthew of Vendôme, *Ars versificatoria,* ed. Faral, *Les arts poétiques,* 169. Matthew says it is a comparison of either a pope and a king or of a monk and a robber.

usually called paronomasia: Gervase oddly insists that paronomasia applies only to punning on the ends of words, and is a figure, not a color; see the second sentence of 1.10 above.

16 *repetition ... conversion ... complexion*: As Gräbener, *Ars poetica,* p. l, points out, these are the first three colors that appear in Geoffrey of Vinsauf's poem illustrating the colors in *Poetria nova* (lines 1098–1100), and also the first three colors defined in his *Colores* (ed. Faral, *Les arts poétiques,* 321, and Wollin, "Die erste Poetik," 409); Gräbener presumes that Geoffrey is Gervase's source here.

Both please me: All the unidentified examples in this paragraph are probably by Gervase or his students.

Oh, hateful one ... bloodshed: PT 135–36. Whereas the previous example makes quasi-leonines by putting all the instances of *vires* in the rhyme position, this passage avoids that by placing the three instances of *caedi*s in other positions.

17 *Donatus*: KB 400.4–6, HB 668.11–13. On metalepsis, see John

338

PART I

Hollander's appendix, "The Trope of Transumption," in *The Figure of Echo* (Berkeley, 1981), 133–49.

Wrath . . . help: Matthew of Vendôme, *Ars versificatoria* 3.42, ed. Faral, *Les arts poétiques,* 177; also in Geoffrey's *Colores,* ed. Faral, *Les arts poétiques,* 323, and Wollin, "Die erste Poetik," 411, along with the next example but one ("He came . . .").

Thus love consoles . . . sustains: *PT* 147–48.

He came . . . madness: From a poem entitled "Causa magistri Gaufredi" in Hunterian manuscript V.8.14, formerly 511, fol. 101r–v, printed in Faral, "Le Manuscrit 511," 56–57, and discussed by him in *Les arts poétiques,* 16–18. It is an appeal to the archbishop of Canterbury to restore Geoffrey's teaching job, taken from him forcibly by his former friend Robert. Geoffrey is apparently Geoffrey of Vinsauf, who used this couplet from the poem to exemplify *gradatio* (climax) in *Colores,* ed. Faral, *Les arts poétiques,* 323, and Wollin, "Die erste Poetik," 411. The poem is also in Harbert, *A Thirteenth-Century Anthology,* 42–44.

I wouldn't dare condemn it: A second welcoming of a fourth member when the limit is three, as Gräbener, *Ars poetica,* p. lii, notes; see the end of 1.10 above, on paronomasia: "these lines are thought by some to be very beautiful."

18 *I hammer away at my last*: One meaning of *galla* is a shoemaker's last. A lawyer whose disreputable wife's name was Galla asked a shoemaker in court what he did; this was his witty reply: "I hammer away at Galla" (Macrobius, *Saturnalia* 2.2.6).

I broke a leg: A thief who broke images of gods in order to steal the gold once broke his own leg in the process; when asked by a lawyer what he did, he said, "I broke a leg," thus admitting his crime but seeming not to. See Virginia Cox and John Ward, eds., *The Rhetoric of Cicero in Its Medieval and Early Renaissance Commentary Tradition* (Leiden, 2006), 440, where they print from the *RAH* commentary they call *Ut ait Quintilianus* remarks on *RAH* 1.6.10, *ambiguo,* giving both this story and the previous one about the shoemaker. In a note they cite another commentary, perhaps by William of Champeaux, that has the "I broke a leg" story and identifies the lawyer questioning the

NOTES TO THE TRANSLATION

man as Cicero, and they mention the commentary by one Master Alanus, which also has both stories. Gervase clearly knew one or more of these commentaries, probably used them in his teaching, and expected his readers to know them.

Once Croesus has crossed the Halys... kingdoms: The original of this famous story is in Herodotus, *Histories* 1.53. Gervase probably drew this hexameter exemplifying ambiguity from Matthew of Vendôme, *Ars versificatoria* 4.12, ed. Faral, *Les arts poétiques*, 183, who treats ambiguity as a vice; it appears also in Thomas Aquinas's (later) commentary on Boethius's *Consolation of Philosophy*, book 2, prose 2.34, and as line 2.451 of John of Garland's *De triumphis ecclesiae*.

Nothing escapes... complaints: Statius, *Thebaid* 2.335–36. The ambiguity is in which of the two nouns, *suspiria* (sighs) and *questus* (complaints), is the subject and which is the object.

Who denies... mother: Suetonius, *Nero* 39.

19   *These men... money bag*: These verses, in rhyming pentameters, and playing in the fourth line on *locus/locum* (topos/place), are not otherwise known, and probably by Gervase.

Isidore: *De differentiis verborum*, 312, ed. *PL* 83:43, with *ultro* (spontaneously) for *inopinate* (unexpectedly), though not in reference to Ovid's verse, *Metamorphoses* 1.654–55, *tu non inventa reperta / luctus eras levior:* Io's father Inachus is addressing her; after a long search he has found her changed to a cow by Jove. Losing her was a grief; finding her a cow is a greater grief.

What will you do?... future: Geoffrey of Vinsauf, *Poetria nova* 348–52. Alan Rosiene has shown that Gervase never names the *Poetria nova* and takes no doctrine from it, quoting from it only Geoffrey's illustrative poems on King Richard, which probably circulated independently, and so there is no proof that he knew it ("The *Ars versificaria*," 214–16).

20   *In him... enemy*: Line 13 of a poem on the fall of Troy *(De excidio Troiae)*, by Simon Chèvre d'Or, printed by J. P. Migne with Hildebert's works *(PL* 171:1447), but with *ignes* (fires) for *hostem* (enemy), as Gervase has it in the next paragraph; see the note there. See Faral, "Le Manuscrit 511," 44; André Boutemy, "La version

parisienne du poème de Simon Chèvre d'Or sur la guerre de Troie (Ms. Lat. 8430)," *Scriptorium* 1 (1946–47): 267–88.
He showed... general: Lucan, *Pharsalia* 4.342–43.
In a short time... one: *PT* 89–90.
Beautiful yet chaste: John of Hauville, *Architrenius* 9.295.
Though... all: Lucan, *Pharsalia* 1.378.

21 *the house... small*: Geoffrey of Vinsauf, *Colores*, ed. Faral, *Les arts poétiques*, 323, and Wollin, "Die erste Poetik," 411. Geoffrey also adds that correction is better when joined with annomination.
In him... family: Simon Chèvre d'Or, *De excidio Troiae* 13–14, ed. *PL* 171:1447 again. Line 14 of *De excidio Troiae* has the words in a different order: *sed sibi, sed Priamo, sed mala cuncta suis*. Both versions scan, but Gervase's, with *mala cuncta* (every evil) close to *tela* (weapons) and *ignem* (fire), seems right to me. Gräbener, *Ars poetica*, p. liv, says that by using the same example for both adversative and additive correction Gervase shows his uncertainty about whether correction belongs under vehemence, but here by adding the second line he gives a good example of climax, and the total of five instances of *sed* (but) is certainly additive. The example appears for a third time in 1.30, exemplifying polysyndeton.
Religion... itself: John Gray 90–93.
Oh... God: John of Hauville, *Architrenius* 5.331–33.

22 *O sorrow... death*: Geoffrey of Vinsauf, *Poetria nova* 386–87.
above: In 1.19.
You impose... call you?: Marbod of Rennes, *De ornamentis verborum; Liber decem capitulorum: Retorica, mitologia e moralità di un vescovo poeta (secc. 11–12)*, ed. Rosario Leotta, Per verba 10 (Florence, 1998), 126, and *PL* 171:1692, where, with three more lines, it is Marbod's example of *dubitatio* (indecision). Geoffrey used it both in *Documentum* 277 and in *Colores*, ed. Faral, *Les arts poétiques*, 324, and Wollin, "Die erste Poetik," 413, and Evrard de Bethune in *Graecismus* 3.85–88; thus Gervase's *nota*. It also appears in *Tria sunt* 3.18.

23 *Anna, sister... life*: Not otherwise known, but the death of Dido must have been common material for school exercises.

NOTES TO THE TRANSLATION

What are you carrying? ... No: Likewise unknown.

You can find ... Seneca the tragedian: An unusually early reference to Seneca's tragedies. See R. J. Tarrant, "Tragedies," in "The Younger Seneca," in *Texts and Transmission: A Survey of the Latin Classics*, ed. L. D. Reynolds, rev. ed. (Oxford, 1986), 378–81.

A miser ... smaller: Marbod of Rennes, *De ornamentis verborum*, ed. Leotta, p. 44, and *PL* 171:1692, exemplifying *ratiocinatio* (reasoning by question and answer). Marbod has *dives avarus egit* (a rich miser is needy); the change to *semper* (always) alludes to Horace, *Epistles* 1.2.56, *semper avarus eget*. See also Geoffrey of Vinsauf, *Colores,* ed. Faral, *Les arts poétiques,* 322, and Wollin, "Die erste Poetik," 410; and Eberhard, *Graecismus* 3.23–24.

24 *O father ... children*: Lawrence of Durham, *Hypognosticon* 93–100. I read *agis* (you do) in the first line with Susanne Daub, ed., *Gottes Heilsplan — verdichtet: Edition des Hypognosticon des Laurentius Dunelmensis* (Erlangen, 2002). The same example is also used in Geoffrey of Vinsauf, *Documentum* 2.2.28, and *Tria sunt* 3.17.

25 *Mutation*: The subject for the remainder of the first part, divided into subtraction (26–28), addition (29–60), and diversion (61–83).

Are you crying ... Call him: In Geoffrey of Vinsauf, *Documentum* 2.3.168, and *Tria sunt* 7.63.

The senate ... companion: Lucan, *Pharsalia* 7.84.

26 *Who hurt you ... what you want*: John of Hauville's poem on Byblis and Caunus is lost. Gervase quotes it again in 1.81 and 7.6 below. The present passage is given as an example of aposiopesis in *Tria sunt* 7.63. For the story of Byblis's unlawful passion for her brother Caunus, see Ovid, *Metamorphoses* 9.453–665.

I forgive ... tongue: Bernard Silvester, *Mathematicus (The Astrologer)* 593–94. *Parricidalis,* the title Gervase gives, of course means "The Parricidal One," but I have used the standard title.

Great the works of the lord: Psalms 110:2.

Faithful all his commandments: Psalms 110:8.

One word beforehand better than two afterward: Perhaps the pentameter of an elegiac couplet; treated above at 1.8, and again near the end of the treatise, 4.1. Not otherwise recorded as a

PART I

Latin proverb, but see Whiting, *Proverbs,* p. 665, no. W576, "Better ys a word by-fore thanne afterward three," from the poem *Firumbras,* cited also by Sibylle Hallik, *Sententia und Proverbium* (Köln, 2007), 344n. "Forewarned is forearmed" is the same idea, and the whole tradition of the value of counsel, such a central issue in Chaucer, is implicit.

There was a man . . . name: Gregory, *Dialogues* 2.1.

One man plucks flowers, one books: The ancient comparison of reading to picking flowers, as in "anthology" and *florilegium.*

Aeneas . . . mother: See 1.18 above.

Each James shines because of his laurel: From the sequence *Alleluia nunc decantet,* celebrating the apostles; Franz Mone, *Lateinische Hymnen des Mittlealters: Heiligenlieder* (Freiburg, 1855), 64. The laurel is the crown of martyrdom. James the son of Zebedee was put to death by Herod, Acts 12:1–2; James the son of Alphaeus is traditionally thought to have been crucified in Egypt.

28   *This . . . ancestors*: Statius, *Thebaid* 2.462–64.

29   *Why . . . belly*: Geoffrey of Vinsauf, *Documentum* 2.3.167.

I omit . . . beauty: John Gray 69–71.

30   *adjunction*: See *RAH* 4.27.38.

Acamas . . . Neoptolemus: See *Aeneid* 2.263; used to illustrate polysyndeton by Donatus, KB 399.5–6 and HB 666.12–13; Matthew of Vendôme, *Ars versificatoria* 3.14, ed. Faral, *Les arts poétiques,* 171; and Eberhard, *Graecismus* 1.50.

She . . . herself: See above, 1.20–21.

Rich in arms . . . glory: Marbod of Rennes, *De ornamentis verborum,* ed. Leotta, 58–60, and *PL* 171:1689, illustrating *articulus;* also used by Geoffrey of Vinsauf, *Colores,* ed. Faral, *Les arts poétiques,* 322, and Wollin, "Die erste Poetik," 410; and Eberhard, *Graecismus* 3.35–36.

In riches . . . well favored: This couplet, like all the Io lines, seems clearly by Gervase, but the first line here imitates the opening line of Simon Chèvre d'Or, *De excidio Troiae,* ed. *PL* 171:1447 (see the note to 1.20 above), a poem that uses polysyndeton over and over.

schesis onomaton: See Donatus, KB 398.17–19 and HB 665.9–11.

31 *Leaves ... flowers*: Geoffrey of Vinsauf, *Colores,* ed. Faral, *Les arts poétiques,* 324, and Wollin, "Die erste Poetik," 412.
Mount Athos ... hills, etc.: John of Hauville, *Architrenius* 1.1–2.
a Marcia in judgment: Marcia, the wife of Cato. See Lucan, *Pharsalia* 2.326–71.
The poor lovers ... ill-omened love: *PT* 141–42.

32 *The elephant ... forehead*: Bernard, *Cosmographia* 1.3.205–6.
Donatus: KB 399.4, HB 666.10, though Donatus says nothing of the sort.
Waters ... ground: Bernard, *Cosmographia* 1.3.167–68.
There was ... ancestors: Bernard, *Mathematicus* 3–4.
Appetite ... fish: Bernard, *Cosmographia* 2.14.93–94.
Their way ... time: *PT* 79–80.

33 *His severity ... mind*: A schoolroom moment, apparently: a teacher talking to the boys about another teacher.
For I ... handmaid: Psalms 115:16.
You ... two: Juvenal, *Satires* 6.641–42.
He is your son ... zones: Bernard, *Mathematicus* 381–82, 385–86, 383–84.
Crimes ... crimes: This is in Geoffrey of Vinsauf's *Colores,* ed. Faral, *Les arts poétiques,* 325, and Wollin, "Die erste Poetik," 414, but is also the first two lines of a forty-six-line poem on Deucalion and Pyrrha in Harbert, *A Thirteenth-Century Anthology.* Harbert had also printed it in his essay, "The Achievement of Matthew of Vendôme," *Medium Aevum* 43 (1975): 225–37, on 235–36, arguing convincingly that Matthew is the author.
contrary to what Cicero teaches: See *RAH* 4.13.19–4.14.21, treating four figures of repetition, the first four figures of diction. At the end the author says, "there inheres in the repetition an elegance which the ear can distinguish more easily than words can explain" (4.14.21). And yet a little later synonymy is described and praised (4.28.38).
Whatever ... health: Bernard, *Cosmographia* 2.9.3.
May this love ... bind us now: Verses celebrating an alliance between King Stephen and Henry, Duke of Normandy, in 1153. See Matthew Paris, *Historia Anglorum,* ed. Frederic Madden,

PART I

Matthaei Parisiensis, monachi Sancti Albani: Historia Anglorum, sive, ut vulgo dicitur, Historia minor (London, 1866–1869), vol. 1, p. 297.

34 *I beg... pact*: This seems to spell out in prose the gist of the previous verse, but without mentioning Tydeus and Polynices. And love pacts are still the subject in the Pyramus quote below.

35 *Join us... unites*: PT 137–38.

36 *Modification*: This subject occupies 1.36–62.

add... fall short: I'm not sure what Gervase means here, though it's obvious enough how an adjective adds to our understanding of its noun; perhaps it takes away by being partitive: a handsome man, say, reduces the larger category "man."

We are three... a boy: Ovid, *Heroides* 1.97–98. Gervase's point is that in Ovid's version, *sine viribus* (without strength) is not parallel to *senex* (old man) and *puer* (boy). He suggests substituting the adjective *debilis* (feeble) for *sine viribus*. See 5.3 below, where this couplet of Ovid's comes in for further treatment.

37 *A white man is running*: The first of a series of sample sentences between here and 1.75 that come from Aristotle's logical works, particularly the *Categories* and *De interpretatione*, as translated and commented on by Boethius, and that either use his stock terms (Socrates, Plato, man, animal, urine, run, walk, live, white, black) or repeat entire sentences. Those, such as "Socrates is curly haired," that aren't used by Boethius himself can be found in other, later logical works, particularly the anonymous *Glossae "Doctrinae sermonum"* (on *De interpretatione*), Abelard on *De interpretatione*, and Alan of Lille's *Summa "Quoniam hominis,"* all three roughly contemporary with Gervase. William of Ockham and Aquinas, later than Gervase, have most of them, illustrating their continued currency. I have not identified each, but they can be found easily in LLT.

38 *Hell, I will be thy bite*: Hosea 13:14.

There are two Ajaxes... Telamon: See Boethius on Aristotle's *De interpretatione* 2.1, ed. PL 64:486.

39 *creature of salt*: That is, "the creature salt," or "salt, a created thing." When salt was exorcised and blessed for sacramental

345

NOTES TO THE TRANSLATION

use, it was addressed, in a hendiadys, as *creatura salis*. It is a grammatical sophism; see Irène Rosier, "Les sophismes grammaticaux au XIIIe siècle," *Medioevo* 17 (1991): 220.

In that thence of place ... generation: Bernard, *Cosmographia* 1.3.145–46.

It was ... Most High: Bernard, *Cosmographia* 1.2.13 (prose).

40 *I am not ... fingers*: John of Hauville, *Architrenius* 1.87–88, 1.90–91.

The plain possesses the sleepy poppy: Bernard, *Cosmographia* 1.3.364.

Sad wormwood ... fields: Ovid, *Epistulae ex Ponto* 3.1.23–26. *Tristis* here actually means "bitter," rather than "sad," but that is not how Gervase understands it.

41 *a white swan*: Ovid, *Heroides* 7.2. "White" is excessive simply because all swans are white.

dread Celaeno: Virgil, *Aeneid* 3.311, cited by Donatus, KB 400.21 and HB 669.8, as an example of epithet; Celaeno was a harpy—and all harpies are dire.

Byrrhia: Perhaps an error for Pyrrhia; see Horace, *Epistles* 1.13.14.

Ulysses the eloquent: Ovid, *Heroides* 3.129.

Alexander the great: The opening words of the poem on John Gray, quoted at 2.51 below. The phrase also occurs, about a different Alexander, in poem no. 39 in Glasgow, Hunterian V.8.14, formerly 511 (Harbert, *A Thirteenth-Century Anthology*, 46), thought to be by Gervase.

42 *Donatus*: KB 400.23–24, HB 669.10.

Adrastus: Polynices married Adrastus's daughter Argia; see Statius, *Thebaid* 2.266, 4.74; and Tydeus married her sister Deipyle—but Gervase has invented this scene.

43 *Athos ... terebinth*: Bernard, *Cosmographia* 1.3.183, 1.3.186. *Cithaera* for *Cithaeron* is Bernard's form. See Wetherbee's notes on these lines, in Bernardus Silvestris, *Poetic Works*, Dumbarton Oaks Medieval Library 38 (Cambridge, MA, 2015).

By the shallows ... swan: Ovid, *Heroides* 7.2. For Ovid on faults that beautify, see Pref.5 above.

44 *An adjective ... Christ*: This entire section was printed by R. W. Hunt in his essay, "Studies on Priscian II: The School of Ralph

PART I

of Beauvais," in *The History of Grammar in the Middle Ages: Collected Papers,* ed. G. L. Bursill-Hall (Amsterdam, 1980), 39–94, on pp. 93–94.

Parvipontani: The "Little Bridge" school of logicians in twelfth-century Paris, led by Adam of Balsham. I have not found this statement in his or others' writings.

is understood from the same perspective as the principal noun: That is, is synonymous with it.

45 *Both appositions and relative modifications*: Either *quaedam* here takes a partitive construction, oddly, or it modifies an omitted noun that would govern the two genitives.

specify a commonality: That is, "mount" and "man" are common nouns; the apposition "Ossa" and the relative clause "who is white" specify them.

this is incorrect: Apparently because only part of Socrates is curly; the man in the previous example is all white.

uniform but indirect partition: These terms have been introduced in 1.39 above, though there "direct" and "indirect" have been applied only to nonuniform partition. Apparently, *Mons Ossa* (Mount Ossa) and *homo albus* (man who is white) are direct because the genus appears before the species; in these new examples, *homo* comes after *Leo* and *belua* comes after *canis,* and so they are indirect (though uniform because both words are in the same case).

The dog ... fierce: That is, a seal or seadog. Another example from logic, appearing often, for instance, in Abelard's *Dialectica.*

46 *I believe ... a lot of*: Ovid, *Heroides* 2.49.

May death ... finally stop these tears: The phrase *mors ultima linea rerum* (death, the end of evils) is Horace, *Epistles* 1.16.79, but the rest of the verse is Gervase's. Similarly, in the next example, beginning *mors meritum vitae,* the first line is Gervase's but the second line is John of Hauville, *Architrenius* 7.75, quoted below at 1.68.

In death ... merits: See Romans 2:6, "he will render to each according to his works."

47 *made it last for two lines*: This, along with the next section, is the

347

NOTES TO THE TRANSLATION

clearest indication that the typical classroom exercise in versification was composing couplets—or perhaps, when a student had made a verse, the teacher would say, "Good. Now turn it into a couplet."

49 *active, modest, bashful*: One of Gervase's examples of *articulus;* see 1.30 above.

Io was ... character: Gervase's example of conjunction; see 1.31 above.

Empty ones ... asyndeton: A baffling pair of statements, since either type seems capable of being used with or without conjunctions, and with one verb or several. For the terms used in this sentence, see 1.30 above. Gervase never defines asyndeton; probably he thought it evident enough that it is the opposite of polysyndeton.

50 *with something in between, some verb*: Apparently the elegance would be to say, "Plato will speak eloquently," or maybe, "That man is so white he must sunburn easily," or "That mountain towering above us is Ossa." Or it may only be to say, instead of "Mount Ossa," "That mountain is Ossa," and so on, which does not seem particularly elegant. The rest of the paragraph seems merely to say that the form of a verb indicates tense and mood as "cosignifiers" as well as the base meaning.

rough sameness: Simple predication; see 1.2 above.

51 *Priscian*: See Priscian, *Institutiones grammaticae* 17.82, ed. Heinrich Keil, *Grammatici Latini* (Leipzig, 1855–1888; repr., Hildesheim, 1961), vol. 3, p. 154.

52 *third predicate element*: *Tertium adiacens* is Boethius's translation of Aristotle's *triton proskategorethe* (a third thing predicated besides); *Categories* 10, ed. *PL* 64:343. It is simply the copulative "is," added to "Socrates white" as a third element of the predication. See Gabriel Nuchelmans, *Secundum/tertium adiacens: Vicissitudes of a Logical Distinction* (Amsterdam, 1992). Scholars usually leave the Latin phrase untranslated.

Juvenal: Juvenal, *Satires* 11.61–62.

the apposed verb: That is, the verb ("will come" in the first example) that leads to the apposition, here of "Hercules" and "Ae-

neas," the "subsequent nouns," with "you." That unusual meaning for *appositi* (literally, "the apposed thing") in this sentence is made clear by the full phrase *ex verbo apposito* (by the apposed verb) in the next sentence.

Achilles ... Hector: Unfound; probably a line of student verse.

53 *Break down ... texts*: Not found, but the basis is Lamentations 4:4, *Parvuli petierunt panem et non erat qui frangeret eis* (The little ones have asked for bread, and there was none to break it unto them), and Matthew 14:19 (Mark 12:10, Luke 20:17), where Jesus takes the five loaves, breaks them, and distributes them to five thousand. Both passages were interpreted by exegetes as referring to the need for teachers to break down the hard passages of scripture.

54 This paragraph is about using nouns (*termini,* or "terms," but Gervase clearly means nouns) absolutely (that is, without a verb), but declining them as if a verb were there—and then subsequently clarifying their use. Thus in Bernard's sentence, *Auster* (the West Wind, apparently, though usually the south wind) and *Eurus* (the East Wind) are in the nominative but have no verb to govern, and then they are replaced in the next line by the pronouns "this one" *(Eurus)* and "that one" *(Auster)*, and finally get their verbs. In the next example *lapidem* (stone) is accusative, though no verb governs it, and it is replaced in the next line by *hic.*

The North Wind ... weather: Bernard, *Cosmographia* 1.3.157–58.

oblique: That is, the accusative *lapidem* (stone); see the note just above.

The stone ... become: Psalms 117:22, quoted by Jesus at Matthew 21:42 (Mark 12:10, Luke 20:17), and again by Saint Peter in Acts 4:11.

The cold North wind ... clothe it: Bernard, *Cosmographia* 2.8.19–20.

55 *simplicity ... simply*: Gervase is being very coy here through 1.60, using "simple" where we surely would use "double" and "simplicity" for what looks more like duplicity. His excuse would seem to be that to refer to only one meaning of a double-meaning term is to "simplify" it.

NOTES TO THE TRANSLATION

a double meaning, as was said above: See 1.26.

the adjectives: "Common" and "proper," which are used "materially," referring to the word "Idonea." This paragraph is murky to me.

56   The illustration seems off because *intumescere* (swell) is a verb and the subject is adjectives. But it shows up in the illustration as the participle *intumescens* (swelling), a verbal adjective. Gervase of course draws on yet a third meaning of the word that we are left to guess.

57   *as I said above*: See 1.43, where the line about raven and swan has first appeared.

The tall . . . Phyllis: Bernard, *Cosmographia* 1.3.295–96.

58   *He is oppressed . . . Judas's*: From a short poem probably about Henry II, who had Thomas Becket's blood on his hands. The poem, whose first two lines are quoted below at 3.7, uses the "hare-hermaphrodite" idea that appears above at 1.12 and is probably by Gervase. It is in the Hunterian manuscript, near Gervase's treatise with several other poems probably by him, printed in Harbert, *A Thirteenth-Century Anthology*, 53. Gervase's point here is that the neuter relative pronoun *quod* refers not to the feminine *seditione* (treachery) but to *nomen* (name), that is, *ipsam vocem* (the word itself). Taking *Iudaica* as "Judas's" is a suggestion of Harbert.

59   *Inachus is swollen by Jupiter, his son-in-law*: Statius, *Thebaid* 4.121.

The sacred . . . usefulness: Bernard, *Cosmographia* 1.3.25–26.

60   *He urges . . . swords*: Statius, *Thebaid* 2.485–87 (compressed).

Nisus's . . . groin: Ovid, *Ars amatoria* 1.331–32.

The cautious . . . daughter: Ovid, *Remedia amoris*, 737. Ovid here confuses Nisus's daughter Scylla, who was changed into a bird, with Scylla the daughter of Phorcys, the famed monster at the straits of Messina, transformed by Circe (see Ovid, *Metamorphoses* 14.52), and Gervase corrects him.

Metamorphoses 11: The manuscript readings *undecimo* ("eleven," in manuscript H) and IX° (the numeral nine, in manuscripts ABD) perhaps go back to an original XIV° erroneously transmitted as XI°.

PART I

That is how we are coming to war: Statius, *Thebaid* 2.703. Tydeus, the ambassador of the previous quotation from Statius, has left Thebes after failing to convince Eteocles to cede the throne to Polynices, his year being over. Eteocles has sent fifty men to ambush him—the ambush mentioned just above—but he has killed them all but one, Maeon, and is sending him back to Eteocles to tell him to prepare for war, saying, "Look around at this field, smoking *(fumantem)* from my sword: that is how we are coming to war." The word *fumantem* refers to the field; Tydeus apposes *tales* to it, applying it to himself and his comrades in arms.

61 *Caesar, raging for arms*: Lucan, *Pharsalia* 2.439.

From confusion ... emerges: Bernard, *Cosmographia* 1.2.8.

the section on dictamen: Part 8 below.

62 *the Rhetorics*: Cicero, *De inventione* ("First Rhetoric") and *RAH* ("Second Rhetoric"), regarded as Cicero's.

Cicero ... attributes of persons ... of actions: Cicero, *De inventione* 1.24–25 (persons), 26–28 (actions). For persons, see also *RAH* 4.63.50–65.51.

Is it to be supposed ... desire: Ovid, *Heroides* 5.129.

loaded: "Weighed down" *(onerata)* by more words.

63 *What was being pounded ... confusion*: Bernard, *Cosmographia* 1.2.4.

64 *the copula*: The "third predicate element" *(tertium adiacens);* see above, 1.52 and note.

And since ... work: Bernard, *Cosmographia* 1.2.2.

66 *There is ... beast*: Ovid, *Fasti* 4.495–96.

a certain mode mentioned above: 1.12; the mode is "cognate annomination."

Now ... spear: Statius, *Thebaid* 8.398.

words utterly different: Gervase, following his master John Blund (see note to 1.1 above), champions what H. W. Fowler in his *Dictionary of Modern English Usage* (Oxford, 1926) contemptuously labeled "elegant variation." See also 1.33 above, praising synonymy.

Thus ... pious man: Bernard, *Mathematicus* 21–22, cited also, as an example of an adjective *(iuncta)* followed by several datives, by

NOTES TO THE TRANSLATION

Geoffrey of Vinsauf, *Documentum* 2.3.73, and ascribed to Hildebert.

His Procne ... man: Unidentified, perhaps student work. The pentameter line does not seem to scan.

67 *Donatus*: The reference is apparently to Donatus's definition of a trope, KB 399.13–14, HB 66.2: *Tropus est dictio translata a propria significatione ad non propriam similitudinem* (A trope is a word brought over from its own meaning to one not its own but like it).

Terrible ... kingdoms: Statius, *Thebaid* 1.240–42. The old man is Oedipus.

We will speak of comparison elsewhere: In part 2, on likeness.

Babylon ... apex of the world: PT 3–4.

digression in the consecration of the slain Archemorus: The Nemean games, celebrating Archemorus's memory, in which various of the seven Argive kings perform gloriously, take up the whole of book 6 of the *Thebaid*; at the beginning of book 7, Jupiter has to send Mercury to get the army to resume its campaign.

Lucan describes the place: Lucan, *Pharsalia* 4.581–661: Hercules and Antaeus at 581–655, Scipio at 656–61, and then comes the sentence about Curio.

Curio ... battle: Lucan, *Pharsalia* 4.661–62.

68 *At last ... to him*: Statius, *Thebaid* 1.615–16.

the hour ... blessed: John of Hauville, *Architrenius* 7.75, quoted above at 1.46 as part of an example by Gervase.

70 *Metonymy*: Why metonymy and synecdoche, and later hyperbole, all of which other writers treat as tropes, turning away from the literal, belong under sameness is a puzzle. The best answer I can give is that Gervase is committed to his three categories, and these tropes don't fit under similitude or contrariety either—so he persuaded himself that "inclusiveness"—the ring includes the gold it's made of, and so on—makes them literal. See 1.67 above, "This proximity I don't call similitude, as Donatus does."

Donatus lists three kinds ... examples: KB 400.7–14 and HB 668.14–

PART I

669.2, though Donatus does not mention possession for possessor, and the example of the chattering field is not his.

In my bowl . . . Bacchus: The first line of a witty epigram by Hugh Primas condemning mixing wine with water. See C. J. McDonough, ed., *The Oxford Poems of Hugh Primas and the Arundel Lyrics* (Toronto, 1984), 48, and A. G. Rigg, *A History of Anglo-Latin Literature, 1000–1422* (Cambridge, 1992), 143–44 and 358n253. It also appears as an example of *significatio* in Geoffrey of Vinsauf, *Colores*, ed. Faral, *Les arts poétiques,* 326, and Wollin, "Die erste Poetik," 429.

Aulus Gellius's Attic Nights: 1.8.

Let him know . . . Decembers: Horace, *Epistles* 1.20.27.

exigitive and constitutive: "Exigitive" means "requiring," "demanding." A body is required to have a surface, and a line is required to be divisible into points. Aquinas, *Summa theologiae,* book 2, part 2, quaest. 49, art. 5: *Et quia ea quae exiguntur ad perfectionem prudentiae dicuntur exigitivae vel quasi integrales partes prudentiae, inde est quod ratio inter partes prudentiae connumerari debet* (And since all the things that are required for the perfection of prudence are called exigitive or, as it were, integral parts of prudence, reason has to be counted among the parts of prudence).

wherever this mode appears there is emphasis: "This mode" is property for subject, not all metonymy. Emphasis is defined just below as attributing to the accident what belongs to the subject, and a property is an accident.

Mighty . . . contact: Lucan, *Pharsalia* 3.62–63.

71 *Emphasis*: The English word "emphasis," as used here and in section 72 following, is misleading. The Greek word means a reflection in a mirror or a pool, that is, something at one remove. The Latin term in *RAH, significatio* (the sign maker), is good: the reflection in a mirror is a sign only of the person looking at it. Thus it is understatement, or, as *RAH* has it, it "leaves more to be suspected than has actually been asserted" (4.53.67–54.67). So Gervase is basically right: to speak of an attribute or property instead of the subject is to speak of a reflection, to

understate—and yet he seems to me not really to grasp the full import of the figure. *RAH* 4.3 and *Tria sunt* 7.93 make it much clearer. Gervase is right to sniff at expressions like "Davus is crime itself": they do say the subject is the attribute but are hardly understatements—but his own examples about weather and wheat and the sun shining on the wall seem merely wordy rather than understated or sly. In the next section he says it's the same as circumlocution, and indeed it seems to be nothing more. Why it should be the perfect thing to teach boys is anybody's guess—because boys like puzzles?

as in the previous example: Well, sort of. The sea doesn't labor, humans do, but the sea is not really an "accident."

Many Latin speakers: One of them is John of Garland, who defines emphasis as "the strong expression of praise or blame," and gives as an example, "The virgin of virgins is chastity itself" (*Parisiana poetria* 4.17).

72   *The weather is bad for wheat*: See 1.36 above.

changed, as was described above: See 1.61–66.

He who gives quickly gives twice: Publilius Syrus: *Inopi beneficium bis dat qui dat celeriter* (He gives a gift to a needy person twice, who gives it quickly). The briefer *bis dat qui cito dat* was proverbial. See Whiting, *Proverbs,* p. 226, no. G76; Hans Walther, *Proverbia sententiaeque Latinitatis Medii Aevi: Lateinische Sprichwörter und Sentenzen des Mittlalters in alphabetischer Anordnung,* Carmina Medii Aevi posterioris Latina 2, 9 vols. (Göttingen, 1963–1986), nos. 2032–34. Gräbener, *Ars poetica,* p. 72, cites Bernard, *Mathematicus* 673–74, which looks like the source of Gervase's couplet.

73   *circumlocution in colors is the same as emphasis in figures*: See Geoffrey of Vinsauf, *Documentum* 2.3.30, and also *Colores,* ed. Faral, *Les arts poétiques,* 325, and Wollin, "Die erste Poetik," 414–15. Geoffrey makes a little more sense of this device by treating it as designed to create difficulty.

Stay brothers . . . born to: Pseudo-Hegesippus, *De excidio urbis Hierosolymitanae* 1.39, ed. Vincenzo Ussani, *Hegesippi qui dicitur historiae libri V* (Vienna, 1932). Fraternal love, which can be

PART I

thrown away, is an accident of blood brotherhood, which cannot; in actually saying, of the accident, "Don't throw away fraternal love," Herod seems to be saying, understatedly of the subject, "Don't throw away your kinship." In the second example, the "subject" is the women's actual bodies, and the "accident" is some false appearance of high station dependent on cosmetics or dress.

74 *Caesar is curly*: Probably not a reference to Crispus son of Constantine, declared a Caesar by his father, but rather just a variation of *Socrates est crispus* (Socrates is curly), earlier in 1.45.

now the year most beautiful: See Virgil, *Eclogues* 3.57.

substitution . . . attribution: Gervase is focusing on his verbs. In metonymy, we were told, one thing "is put for" another; in synecdoche, part or whole "is attributed to" the other. Attribution is bolder, or more definitive. But it certainly seems true to say that synecdoche is simply one kind of metonymy.

we have not received . . . Donatus: See 1.70 above, where Gervase has taken Donatus's "examples for those who like examples" as warrant for broadening the list of kinds of metonymy.

75 *Donatus*: KB 400.28–29, HB 669.13–14.

He praised . . . halfway: Ovid, *Metamorphoses* 1.501.

property: See section 70 above, where "property for the subject" appears under metonymy, not synecdoche, and DMLBS, under *proprietas* 4, "characteristic feature" (such as Socrates's white foot)—but Gervase's point is not very clear.

Benedict . . . cowl: See 1.26 above.

But though . . . precedence: Statius, *Thebaid* 10.654.

76 *Transversion*: Another mode of diversion; see 1.61 above.

periti . . . perditi: An extremely common pun; those that follow are much less common. Geoffrey of Vinsauf uses it and *archidiabolus/archidiaconus* in the same example at *Documentum* 2.3.167.

displicina . . . disciplina: Donatus, KB 392.20, HB 654.4–5.

metaplasms: Both examples are from Donatus on metaplasm, KB 397.1–3, HB 663.1–3. Anathesis and metathesis are an alteration of vowels and a transposition of letters, respectively. *Evandre* is an alternative form of the vocative, used at Virgil, *Aeneid* 11.55.

NOTES TO THE TRANSLATION

77 *Why, perfidious soldier ... army*: Geoffrey of Vinsauf, *Poetria nova* 382–84.

It is good ... etc.: Psalms 117:9.

A more abundant ... settled: See Bernard, *Cosmographia* 1.2.2.

For now ... head: Boethius, *Consolation of Philosophy,* book 1, prose 1.9–11.

You see ... forests: Bernard, *Cosmographia* 2.1.5.

the language ... displaying: Donatus KB 400.4, HB 668.11.

Then ... heart: Statius, *Thebaid* 2.544. Statius's verbs are infinitives.

And if ... came from: Bernard, *Cosmographia* 2.5.15.

78 *tragoedía, comoedía ... tragédia, comédia*: Manuscript H actually has the accent marks, on the *i* for Greek and on the *e* for Latin.

Yxewirde ... Yxewirdia: The English name is stressed on the first syllable, the Latin on *wird,* the antepenult. This is probably Ixworth in Suffolk, home of a Blund family and perhaps John Blund's birthplace.

Melkley: Now Mentley, in Hertfordshire, just north of London. Writing it *Saltus lacteus* is the same device as writing John Blund *Iohannes Albus* at the start of the Preface.

they keep Latin accent: That is, they stress the penult since, being a diphthong, it is long.

79 *hypallage*: The Greek word means "interchange," and in rhetoric usually refers to making an adjective modify the wrong noun, such as saying "the honey of the sweet bee" for "the sweet honey of the bee." Ovid, *Metamorphoses* 1.1, means "bodies changed into new forms," not "forms changed into new bodies"; Lucan, *Pharsalia* 5.15, means "as soon as the crowd kept silence."

arms and a man: Gervase (like Eberhard, *Graecismus* 1.56–67) takes Virgil's opening phrase as really meaning either "the arms of the man" or "the man-at-arms," but one needn't.

Donatus: KB 401.4–23, HB 670.6–671.11. Donatus gives five kinds of hyperbaton; Gervase rejects three but keeps two, parenthesis (which he calls *interpositio*) and synchysis (spelled *sinthesis* in the manuscripts).

PART I

tmesis: Tmesis is cutting. In the first example, taken from Horace, *Epistles* 1.1.14, *quocumque* (wherever) is cut into by *me* (me). In the second example, the idea is that *invicem* (in turn) is cut in half by the enclitic *-que* (and), for example, at Ovid, *Metamorphoses* 6.631.

A cold snake ... grass: Virgil, *Eclogues* 3.93.

His father ... to it: Bernard, *Mathematicus* 57–58.

They affirmed ... death: Bernard, *Mathematicus* 371–72.

80 *Against my kinsman ... I stood*: Harbert, *A Thirteenth-century Anthology,* 54, a poem probably by Gervase, who refers to himself coyly here as *alius* (another poet). See the same usage at 2.28, 2.39, and 2.41, the last introducing a couplet from *PT*: this is tantamount to an admission by Gervase that he wrote it.

You have been endowed ... pile up high: Statius, *Thebaid* 2.430–32.

But see ... builder: *PT* 115–16.

81 *Synchysis*: The Greek word means "flowing together." The definition is word-for-word from Donatus, KB 401.18–19, HB 671.7.

But their teenage plan ... time: *PT* 89–90. Also used above, in 1.20.

the example Donatus gives: Virgil, *Aeneid* 1.108–9, used at KB 401.20–23 and HB 671.8–11. It is a figure not a color, because it only rearranges the words from their normal order; it does not, in Gervase's view, adorn.

Christ ... without-end God: Matthew of Vendôme, *Ars versificatoria* 4.51.1, ed. Faral, *Les arts poétiques,* 192.

Juno ... love: Apparently by Gervase. Reading across, each line is a hexameter; reading down, each column of words is a complete sentence, containing one verb and five nouns, each in a different case; I have rendered these sentences in my translation.

The forehead ... likeness: Alan of Lille, *Anticlaudianus* 1.277–78.

doesn't exculpate: That is, leaves it clear that both are killers.

This page ... hand: From John of Hauville's now-lost poem on Byblis and Caunus; see the note to 1.26 above. The first two words are quoted again at 7.6 below.

NOTES TO THE TRANSLATION

Love . . . Greeks: John of Hauville, *Architrenius* 7.116–17. The ambiguity comes perhaps in the periphrasis "Phrygian shepherd" for Paris.

There exults . . . tree: PT 169–70.

there is nothing to object to in the construction: Gervase accepts the zeugma: *comburo* (burn) means something slightly different in each case. The implicit construction is *pastorem combussit amor, Pergama combussit ignis, Graecos combussit ira* (love consumed the shepherd, fire consumed Troy, wrath consumed the Greeks).

82   *No small . . . life*: Bernard, *Cosmographia* 1.1.37–38.

Hyperbole . . . turtle: KB 401.24–25, HB 671.12–13.

Before the face . . . fades: PT 41–42.

83   *diversion*: Gervase's subject since 1.61.

This . . . country: Lucan, *Pharsalia* 2.380–82.

84   *It is better . . . deceived*: See Geoffrey Chaucer's "He hasteth wel that wisely kan abyde," in *Melibee* B2239 and *Troilus* 1.956. This proverb appears again at 4.1 below. A current of advice to be patient runs all through Gervase's book, as through so much other medieval writing.

Part Two

3   *John of Hauville said "vernifluous"*: Not in *Architrenius*.

4   *new verbs happen to be invented*: Cited by *Tria sunt* 5.10, though as *novas dictiones,* new words, rather than new verbs; all the examples offered, however, including *tantalizat,* are verbs.

It was allowed . . . mintmark: Horace, *Ars poetica* 58–59.

5   *Accordingly someone said*: John of Hauville, according to manuscripts AB; see 2.3 above.

8   *And so the Usiarch . . . all things*: Bernard, *Cosmographia* 2.3.10.

9   *Theodulus*: *Eclogue* 83–84. Genesis 11:8: *virentibus foliis* (with green leaves).

The earth . . . forests: Bernard, *Cosmographia* 2.1.5.

The first quarter . . . spring: Bernard, *Cosmographia* 2.5.11.

10   *He is rockier . . . Hydra*: John of Hauville's line has too many feet. Perhaps he wrote a pentameter (*Petrior est petra / tigre tigrior*

PART 2

Hydra), with *hydrior* as the first foot in another line. The revised version is not verse. *Visa ... abradi* suggests that Gervase is remembering a classroom moment, John having his pupils write the verse on their tablets and then delete it.

appellatives and substantives: The substantive (noun) is divided into proper substantives and appellatives *(vir, femina),* but proper nouns can become appellatives, such as "Caesars."

11 *It was possible ... mirror*: Bernard, *Cosmographia* 1.2.13.

And when ... way: Bernard, *Cosmographia* 1.2.7.

12 *When ... middlemost*: Bernard, *Cosmographia* 1.2.8.

13 *simply ... equivocally*: The distinction here is unclear to me, but perhaps it means there can be only a limited number of Ajaxes, whereas there is no end to the pluralizing of a common object such as a stone.

The Seine ... Charleses: Bernard, *Cosmographia* 1.3.261–62.

Martial the Cook: The first-century-poet Martial acquired this nickname in the Middle Ages.

Mantua ... Lucan: Martial, *Epigrams* 1.61. Maro is Virgil, born in Mantua; the Paeligni are a people of central Italy. Ovid (Naso) was born in the Paelignian city of Sulmo. Cordoba, in Spain, was the birthplace of both Senecas and Lucan.

Crazy ... Virgils: Martial, *Epigrams* 3.38.

And he marries elms to vines: Compare Columella, *De re rustica* 11.2.79: *ulmi vitibus maritantur.*

matrimony: The standard definition is *viri mulierisque conjunctio, individuam vitae consuetudinem continens* (the joining of a man and a woman, maintaining an indivisible habit of life; *PL* 161:1409).

White ... fruit: Clearly about Thisbe's dropped veil after the lion has bloodied it, though the version of Gervase's *PT* that we have stops before reaching this incident. This seems to be from it, though, suggesting that the poem was longer but its ending lost. See Glendinning, "Pyramus and Thisbe," however, who argues that the poem was never finished, and this distich not from it.

Many things ... reborn: Horace, *Ars poetica* 70.

New . . . adapted: Horace, *Ars poetica* 52–53.
You . . . new: Horace, *Ars poetica* 47–48.

14 *There the mildness . . . fruits*: Bernard, *Cosmographia* 1.3.321–22.
From heaven . . . creation: Bernard, *Cosmographia* 1.3.3–4.
Roger of Devon: Unknown; mentioned above, in 1.3.
Horace's line: Horace, *Ars poetica* 59. The full statement is quoted at 2.4 above, along with John of Hauville's interpretation, which Gervase obviously prefers to Roger's. What is allowed is coining new words. Perhaps Roger applied it to memory because memory systems advocated creating memorable images.
Your friend . . . farting: Martial, *Epigrams* 4.87.
Servius: The story comes not from Servius but from Aulus Gellius, *Attic Nights* 11.9. Plutarch is the ultimate source.

15 *Tartarus . . . obba*: Obba seems clear enough: when you say it your lips form a bowl; as for Tartarus, if you trill the r's it sounds like hell.

16 *Sometimes it happens that what is short . . . dishonor*: For the example Gervase offers, "There is long love . . . ," see Mario Esposito, "On Some Unpublished Poems Attributed to Alexander Neckham," *English Historical Review* 30 (1915): 453n; the previous line in that poem has *decus* (honor) and *dedecus* (dishonor) also. See also Josiah Cox Russell, "Alexander Neckham in England," *English Historical Review* 47 (1932): 260–68. Also Phillip Damon, "A Note on the Neckham Canon," *Speculum* 32 (1957): 99–102. Both lines are pentameters. In the first, the *a* in *amor* is lengthened the first time. In the second, the *e* in *decus* is lengthened, implying spurning perseverance in honor.
Master John . . . the same way: The whole point of this anecdote is that the cup is v-shaped: its shape says, "I am five." But the explanation is decidedly murky; something may be lost. Possibly, *incausti* (ink) should be *crateris* (bowl) or *cuppae* (cup), though that would be an odd error.
I'm so wealthy . . . marks: The line is a hexameter, with a spondee in the fifth foot.
the shape of the ink: That is, the shape of the written letter.

PART 2

17 *Cicero*: *Tusculan Disputations* 4.31.66. He distinguishes between pleasure *(laetari)* and (undue) joy *(gaudere)*.

Hegesippus: Pseudo-Hegesippus, *De excidio urbis Hierosolymitanae* 2.1.

18 *Metaphor*: The second of the three large categories of likeness; see 2.1. It is the largest, treated from here through 2.50.

The beach is being plowed: To plow the beach *(litus arare)* is to do something worthless, to labor in vain, as Gervase explains at 2.47 below. Thus the whole sentence is a metaphor, whereas in "The meadow is laughing," only the verb is a metaphor. As Alan Rosiene, "The *Ars versificaria*," 215n50, points out, these examples also appear together in two contemporary logic texts. Both are commonplaces and both are used by Geoffrey of Vinsauf, as Gräbener, *Ars poetica*, p. 108 observes; Gräbener also quotes Ernst Robert Curtius, who calls "the meadows smile" "an old school-example."

Donatus: KB 399.17–30, HB 667.6–668.7. The four kinds are animate to animate, inanimate to inanimate, animate to inanimate, and vice versa. Gervase replaces this classification with his own of absolute and respective—the same way he divided *ostentio* (demonstration) at 1.42—holding off the latter until 2.32.

19 *Pamphilus*: From Terence's *Andria*, as are Byrrhia and Davus, mentioned just below, in 2.21.

A friend greets . . . His Theseus greets: Salutations in letters.

Simon is dead: Simon de Montfort the elder, fifth Earl of Leicester (ca. 1175–1218); Matthew Paris, *Historia Anglorum* 240. Matthew explains the names as Gervase does, and names the poet, Rogerus de Insula. This reference puts Gervase's treatise after June 25, 1218, the date of Simon's death.

20 *The knot . . . Pyramus*: PT 83–84.

21 *amass*: See Geoffrey of Vinsauf, *Poetria nova* 1767–80.

A Marcia . . . Io: Already used in 1.31 above, to exemplify conjunction.

22 *the accident*: A son literally "falls to" his father.

NOTES TO THE TRANSLATION

If only ... palace: See Virgil, *Aeneid* 4.328.
But if ... palace: Juvenal, *Satires* 5.137–39.
Now ... Ucalegon is burning: Virgil, *Aeneid* 2.311.
Ucalegon ... odds and ends: Juvenal, *Satires* 5.198–99.
He will put ... house: Juvenal, *Satires* 12.117–19.
Three in number ... war: Ovid, *Heroides* 1.97; see 1.36 above.

23 *A new page ... verse*: John of Hauville, *Architrenius* 2.2.
A parrot ... poetry: Gervase's quip about Bernard Silvester; see Pref.2 and note above, and 2.38 below.
just as with proper nouns: See 2.21 above.
He was a dwarf ... mind: A pentameter, unidentified.
An ass ... follow: From the *Prophecies of Merlin,* in Geoffrey of Monmouth, *History of the Kings of Britain,* ed. Michael Reeve, trans. Neil Wright, Arthurian Studies 69 (Woodbridge, 2007), 150.

24 *These tears ... has*: Bernard, *Cosmographia* 1.1.41.
There ... ages: Bernard, *Cosmographia* 1.2.13; my translation is Wetherbee's (*Poetic Works*, 11), modified.
content that I spoke of earlier: 1.32 above.
Whiteness ... vision: *Color disgregativus visus* is Boethius's translation of Aristotle's definition of whiteness as *chroma diakritikon opseos* in *Topica* 3.5.31 (*Topicorum Aristotelis ... Boetii interprete* 3.4, ed. *PL* 64:939). It became a commonplace phrase.
Lilies mixed with roses ... face: Probably from a lost poem on Pyramus and Thisbe, perhaps by Gervase, as Glendinning has posited in "Pyramus and Thisbe," 56–60.
Harmonious ... tooth: *PT* 39–40.

25 *call moonlight "day"*: Well, moonlight does follow daylight, but all the same this is an odd example of antecedent for consequent. For *lux aliena* meaning moonlight, see a poem attributed to Isidore of Seville, ed. *PL* 83:1113.
Content with the day ... went: *PT* 185–86.
mutation, which we have treated above: In 1.25–84, a giant category, comprising subtraction (25–28), addition (29–60), and diversion (61–84).

PART 2

what a word is transferred to: Which would normally be the same part of speech.

26 *exigitive*: That is, compelling, demanding: they force themselves on you.

27 *a windowed net*: Windowed, because nets have little windows.

Earth ... species: Bernard, *Cosmographia* 1.3.355.

From the clarity ... purity: Bernard, *Cosmographia* 2.7.9.

A lamblike master ... goatlike: A leonine hexameter, probably by Gervase.

28 *Donatus's order*: That is, the order in which Donatus treats the parts of speech: first nouns (including adjectives), then pronouns.

convertibility of terms: That is, of the pronoun and the noun it stands for.

an emotion of yours imposes a noun on your work: That is, choice of language can be dictated by our emotional involvement in the subject.

simple relation: See 1.58 above.

May the gods grant that my I not die without me: Apparently a prayer by Pyramus after he thinks Thisbe is dead, from a Pyramus and Thisbe poem by John of Hauville. See Glendinning, "Pyramus and Thisbe," 62, where this is the first example he gives of shared ideas in poems 1–3: Pyramus and Thisbe are the same person (*PT* 83–84; see 2.20 above). The line is quoted in Anne Grondeux, ed., *Glosa super "Graecismum" Eberhardi Bethuniensis, Capitula I–III: De figuris coloribusque,* CCCM 225 (Turnhout, 2010), 167, as an example of an additional mode of *alleotheta,* the use of one grammatical case for another: the mode is using one grammatical person for another, here the first person for the third, since *ne moriatur "ego"* (literally, "that my 'I' not die") means "that my girlfriend, whom I love as myself, not die." Also quoted by Aquinas, attributed to *poeta* (a poet), in his *Commentary on the Sentences,* book 1, distinctio 4, quaestio 2, articulus 2. Robert of England, *La "Sophistria" de Robertus Anglicus,* ed. Anne Grondeux and Irène Rosier-Catach (Paris, 2006),

NOTES TO THE TRANSLATION

159, 166, and elsewhere, used it as an example of a "sophism," defined in the *Dictionary of Medieval Latin from British Sources* as an "ambiguous or puzzling sentence" (see "Sophisma," Logeion, accessed January 11, 2022, https://logeion.uchicago.edu/sophisma). The whole elegiac couplet is: *Non ego solus ego sed ego sumus unus et alter. / Dii faciant sine me ne moriatur ego.* (I am not only I, but we—the one and the other—are I. May the gods grant that this I not die without me.) Grondeux and Rosier-Catach, *La "Sophistria,"* 92–93, discuss the distich, arguing that it is a student "pochade" (a rough sketch, or hurried piece of writing) based on a collage of New Testament phrases, especially from the gospel of John. Robert (Grondeux and Rosier-Catach, *La "Sophistria,"* 170) says that the speaker wants to signify the unity of him and his girlfriend, that they are one in love. The couplet is also in Robert Kilwardby, *Sophismata grammaticalia,* and *Sicut dicit Remigius;* see Rosier, "Les sophismes grammaticaux," 221.

While we drank . . . you: Unfound.

The girl herself . . . of herself: Ovid, *Remedia amoris* 344.

29 *A vine loves elms*: See 2.13 and note above.

The Lord . . . silent: See Matthew 8:26.

A baby: Literally, Hebe, goddess of youth.

A new page . . . verse: John of Hauville, *Architrenius* 1.42, quoted at 2.23 above.

The speech . . . hearing: Bernard, *Cosmographia* 1.2.3.

But he flourished with female progeny: Statius, *Thebaid* 1.393–94.

Let the work . . . wrote it: Alan of Lille, *Anticlaudianus* 6.364.

I will make . . . flesh: Deuteronomy 32:42.

His face . . . hair: John of Hauville, *Architrenius* 1.216.

With my . . . day: John of Hauville, *Architrenius* 9.479, the last sentence of the poem.

30 *Abundant malignity . . . up*: See Bernard, *Cosmographia* 1.2.2.

we don't spend time . . . and the reverse: Gervase shows his disdain for the modern fashion of applying logic and dialectic to grammar, replacing Donatus with Priscian, the practical with the speculative; see also 1.44 above. Peter Helias's widely used

PART 2

twelfth-century *Summa super Priscianum* is an example; he has the common sample sentence *Socrates videt Platonem* ("Socrates sees Plato"; Peter Helias, *Summa super Priscianum*, ed. Leo Reilly [Toronto, 1993], vol. 2, p. 898). The sentence about touching the ceiling is probably not a quotation but Gervase making fun of questions such as *quantus est Socrates* (Peter Abelard, *Glossae super Praedicamenta Aristotelis*, ed. B. Geyer, Beiträge zur Geschichte der Philosophie des Mittelalters 21.3 [Münster, 1921], 185), though Abelard raises it not because he cares how tall Socrates was but as a way of discussing the Aristotelian category quantity.

32 *Various examples of this idea*: That is, of an inconstant man.

I wish ... vomit you out: See Revelation 3:15–16.

as ... yours: This example is opaque. Something has dropped out, I think.

It (matter) ... appearances: Bernard, *Cosmographia* 1.2.4.

Aeschines: A disciple of Socrates and the author of several Socratic dialogues. Called "Aeschines Socraticus" to distinguish him from the orator Aeschines.

33 *A verb that evokes ... refers*: This sentence is difficult to understand, especially since the example that follows has no noun in the accusative case.

35 *untransferred likeness*: That is, apparently, a likeness that exists but is not yet expressed in a metaphor. The phrase occurs again in section 2.38 below.

if it is intransitive: That is, apparently, if one simply said, "The snow melts by emaciation." Compare 2.40 below.

They bowed down ... redeemer: See Gregory, *Dialogues* 2.8: *Sub leni redemptoris iugo cervicem cordis edomarent.* (They subdued the neck of their heart beneath the easy yoke of the redeemer.) Gervase's *suave jugum* (gentle yoke) is Matthew 11:30.

It is not fitting ... world: Gervase seems to be thinking of Bede's commentary on Luke 1:15, in which the angel says to Zachary, "He shall drink no wine nor strong drink, and he shall be filled with the Holy Ghost": *Decet enim vas coelesti gratiae mancipatum a saeculi illecebris castigari, nec vino, in quo est luxuria, inebriari eum*

NOTES TO THE TRANSLATION

qui musto Spiritus sancti desiderat impleri. (For it is fitting that a vessel that has been handed over to heavenly grace be held back from the snares of the world, nor for him who desires to be filled with the new wine of the Holy Spirit to be drunk on the wine in which lust resides.) Gervase adjusts the statement to his needs, particularly by replacing *inebriari* (to be drunk on) with *haurire* (to drink in).

we read in Gregory's Dialogues: 3.7.

we should admire: Since old people use canes, "staff" and "old age" make for *advocatio* (evocation).

You have taken the staff of our old age: Tobit 5:23. The Vulgate has the singular *tulisti* for "you have taken": Anna is rebuking Tobias, after the angel has left with their son. The plural used here would simply mean, "You and the angel have taken."

36 *He was ... minds*: Geoffrey of Vinsauf, *Poetria nova* 390–91.

37 *Let us bow ... redeemer*: See above, 2.34 and note.

a philosopher ... sample: See Alan of Lille, *De planctu Naturae* 2.

38 *untransferred likeness*: Defined at 2.18 above.

From a person, doubly: That is, either transferring to a person the nature of a nonperson (such as, in the examples below, saying a person is an ox), or transferring to a nonperson the nature of a person (such as saying someone with an emaciated face is a philosopher).

parrot ... nightingale: See Pref.2 above, where Gervase uses these phrases to praise Bernard Silvester.

39 *Red hair ... faithfulness*: See 2.35 above.

teaching assistant: Since later in the section this person turns out to be a teacher, not a pupil, I have taken *discipulus* to mean a young scholar working closely under a master.

white ink ... pen: A series of somewhat strained double entendres comparing sexual intercourse to writing. I take *tripus* (apparently neuter here) to be a three-legged stool on which a scholar sits at his desk in the daytime. The point is clear enough, though some bafflement on the part of scribes may account for the variant *tempus* (time) in manuscripts ABD.

PART 2

Claudian: Gervase is surely thinking of Claudian's invectives. In *Against Eutropius,* for example, the eunuch Eutropius is called a slave, then a pimp, then a maidservant, then an old dog, and each new role is developed in extensive detail, just as with Gervase's teacher-farmer.

consistency of proceeding: That is, the alternation of "evocations" of the metaphor and the literal term, described earlier in the section.

In his customary . . . reason: Alan of Lille, *Anticlaudianus* 1.136, 1.135 (Gervase has reversed the lines).

40 *My hair . . . old age*: John of Hauville, *Architrenius* 1.86–87.

41 *Springs . . . valley*: Bernard, *Cosmographia* 1.3.367–68.

Roses . . . cheeks: *PT* 33–34.

42 *Hercules . . . Venus's*: John of Hauville, *Architrenius* 7.118.

Hercules . . . woman: John of Hauville, *Architrenius* 7.124–25.

This town . . . hatreds: Pseudo-Hegesippus, *De excidio urbis Hierosolymitanae* 3.4.1.

43 *The white masks . . . truth*: *PT* 173.

The white beguilements . . . limbs: Joseph of Exeter, *De bello Troiano* 4.176. Gervase is insisting that the standard reading *lactea* (milky) is wrong, and *candida* (white) is right.

44 *washing a brick*: A common Latin idiom. See Shakespeare, *The Two Noble Kinsmen* 3.5.41–42, "We have, as learned authors utter, wash'd a tile, / we have been fatuous, and labored vainly."

asteismos: Generally defined as urbanity; see *TLL*.

If he doesn't . . . billy goats: Virgil, *Eclogues* 3.90–91. Both Isidore, *Etymologies* 1.37.30, and Donatus, KB 401.30, use this same example to illustrate *asteismos*.

Caesar . . . son-in-law: See Lucan, *Pharsalia* 2.652.

45 *As Cynthia comes . . . Thetis*: An unidentified line of rhythmical verse in the Goliardic stanza, like the Archpoet's *Aestuans intrinsecus ira vehementi* (*Carmina Burana* 191).

46 *expressions . . . imagined*: Thus, in Bernard's line below, the goddess Lachesis, who doesn't really exist, is used to designate death, the literal idea.

NOTES TO THE TRANSLATION

with what desire: To write verse as good as Bernard's, apparently. A remarkably personal moment.

The penis . . . Fates: Bernard, *Cosmographia* 2.14.165–66.

these verses belong under sameness: Apparently because Lachesis is unreal, and so there is no real comparison.

And the swan . . . death: Bernard, *Cosmographia* 1.3.449–50. There is no main verb here because the swan is one in a list of aquatic birds.

Juno's . . . sport: Bernard, *Cosmographia* 1.3.459.

In this way . . . life: Martial, *Epigrams* 10.23.7–8, with *ampliat* (increases) for Gervase's *duplicat* (doubles). Gervase seems to misunderstand Martial, who is not speaking of posthumous fame but of looking back over one's own life.

one of the moderns: Probably Gervase himself.

William of Nunchamp: This is William de Longchamps, bishop of Ely and chancellor and justiciar of England (d. 1197). He died in Poitiers and was buried in the abbey of Notre Dame du Pin; I have not found any other report of his epitaph.

47 *an ass to the lyre*: Boethius, *Consolation of Philosophy,* book 1, prose 4.1.

He will trample . . . feet: Geoffrey of Monmouth, *History of the Kings of Britain*, 7.112.

He will yet draw beans from a pot: Not a common saying, but since it is apparently a way of asserting that someone is dishonorable, it may mean something like, "He'll surely end up in prison" (standing in line for his meals).

48 *emerging from its cradle*: See 2.33 above for a literal use of the phrase *cunis egrediens*.

Now I am preparing . . . theme: Statius, *Thebaid* 1.33.

49 *as it were syllabic*: That is, divisible into more than one meaning, as a word is divisible into syllables. In the example, "wash" is divided into its literal meaning and a metaphorical meaning.

Demophoon . . . winds: Ovid, *Heroides* 2.25, Phyllis to Demophoon.

You spoke dishonestly: When he promised to return to Phyllis within a month.

50 *And now . . . horses*: Virgil, *Georgics* 2.542, cited and explained (*Hoc*

est, carmen finire, "This is, to end the poem") by Donatus, KB 401.26–27, HB 671.14–15.

something else is meant than is said: Donatus, KB 401.26, HB 671.14, reads: *Allegoria est tropus quo aliud significatur quam dicitur.*

If allegory ... too little: Gervase has just declared that what Donatus calls allegory is what he, Gervase, calls sentence metaphor, which he has not quite defined as meaning something other than what is said, but only "something removed" *(alienam)* but like. He seems to take Donatus's *aliud* (something else) here as meaning "the opposite of what is said," as if Donatus were claiming that allegory somehow combines likeness and oppositeness.

gaure: Possibly English *gaure* (stare), which Chaucer uses in the fourteenth century, but which is not attested this early. More likely it is the name from Martial, in the vocative, that appears in *Epigrams* 8.27, cited below in 3.8. Conveniently, it starts with G and rhymes with *aure* to create a leonine hexameter, as in the previous line, where the odd passive *haberi* (literally, "to be had") rhymes with *operi* (work), at least by sight. The solution is "Gervasius." The next couplet, where the two lines rhyme with each other, clearly presents *LVX* (light).

My mother ... from me: Donatus, KB 402.7, HB 672.11. A common example of enigma among the ancient grammarians, not just Donatus; see Manuela Bergamin, *Aenigmata Symposii: La fondazione dell'enigmistica come genere poetico,* Per verba 22 (Firenze, 2005), 93. Two indispensable modern treatments are Eleanor Cook, "The Figure of Enigma: Rhetoric, History, Poetry," *Rhetorica* 19, no. 4 (2001): 349–78, and Curtis A. Gruenler, *"Piers Plowman" and the Poetics of Enigma: Riddles, Rhetoric, and Theology* (Notre Dame, 2017).

indicating ... known: Donatus, KB 402.21–22, HB 673.12–13.

according to Donatus: See KB 402.22–24, HB 673.14–15. The example is his, from Virgil, *Aeneid* 1.589, of Aeneas.

Paradigm: See Donatus, KB 401.28, HB 674.5.

hanged himself with a halter: Matthew 27:5.

Peter wept: Luke 22:62.

NOTES TO THE TRANSLATION

Great Alexander ... burden, etc.: The opening lines of the poem on John Gray likely written by Gervase.

Socrates ... thumb: Diogenes Laertius says that Socrates learned to play the lyre when he was old, and Quintilian mentions the fact, *Institutio oratoria* 1.10.13.

with this device: Architrenius opens with a "coadunation of paradigms," a series of examples to show that *ingenii furor instat,* a frenzy of ingenuity is upon us (1.4).

52   *this answer of Aristotle's*: I have not found this story. Aristotle is citing the fable "The Wolves and the Sheep," in both Babrius and Aesop. See Ben Edwin Perry, "An Analytical Survey of Greek and Latin Fables in the Aesopic Tradition," in *Babrius and Phaedrus: Fables,* Loeb Classical Library 436 (Cambridge, MA, 1965), no. 153, p. 450.

A certain man ... Jericho: Luke 10:30, the parable of the Good Samaritan.

I will ... parables: See John 16:25, where *in parabolis* (in parables) is a common variant for the received text's *in proverbiis* (in proverbs). It is the reading of the Clementine Vulgate.

53   *Donatus*: KB 402.24–25, HB 674.1.

For the fame ... abundance of comparisons: Quoted in *Tria sunt* 3.23. The *Thebaid* has twice as many similes as the *Aeneid*. On this interesting issue, see William J. Dominik, "Similes and Their Programmatic Role in the *Thebaid*," in *Brill's Companion to Statius,* ed. William J. Dominik, Carole E. Newlands, and Kyle Gervais (Leiden, 2015), 266–90.

like Tiphys ... mouth: *John Gray* 40–41. Tiphys was the helmsman of the Argonauts.

like a ship ... drawn: Claudian, *Panegyric on the Fourth Consulship of the Emperor Honorius* 223–24.

For everything ... point: *John Gray* 141–43. The location of "hard Gargara" is disputed: either the peak of Mount Ida in Phrygia or a town at its foot. See Virgil, *Georgics* 1.100 and 3.269. Servius Auctus, *In Georgica* 1.102, explains it as one famous mountain for all famous mountain peaks. Macrobius, *Saturnalia* 5.20, contains a whole *quaestio* on the place-name.

Part Three

1   *Five kinds ... pertain to opposition*: Donatus, KB 401.29–30, HB 672.1–2, lists seven "preeminent" species of allegory; from these Gervase excludes aenigma and *astismos*. All his definitions of the types are taken from Donatus, KB 401–2, HB 672–73.
There wasn't ... guy: Martial, *Epigrams* 1.73.
What a great ... horses: Alluding apparently to Phaeton, of whom Ovid, *Metamorphoses* 2.192, says, *Nec retinere valet nec nomina novit equorum* (He cannot hold the reins and he does not know the horses' names).
Euphemism: *Charientismos*, Greek for "gracefulness," part of a large word family that includes such English words as "charity," "caress," and "charisma." As a trope it really means "graceful irony."
Put me ... covenant: Statius, *Thebaid* 7.540–41, Tydeus speaking sarcastically of King Eteocles's hostile treatment of him in book 2; see the passage quoted from book 2 in 1.28 above.
You ask me ... seeing you: Martial, *Epigrams* 2.38.

2   *Cicero's Topics*: 13.55–14.56.

3   *How will a person ... when he had a partner*: Marbod of Rennes, *De coloribus verborum*, ed. Leotta, 52–55, and *PL* 171:1689, also defining *contrarium* (reasoning by contraries). Also in Geoffrey of Vinsauf, *Colores*, ed. Faral, *Les arts poétiques*, 322, and Wollin, "Die erste Poetik," 410. The last two examples are in Eberhard, *Graecismus* 3.32–33.
You won't die ... yours: Seneca, *Controversiae* 3.9.
I will feed ... eating: Seneca, *Controversiae* 3.1.

4   *They would rather ... win*: Lucan, *Pharsalia* 7.109.
as long as you wouldn't rather: I think *non malis* ("you wouldn't rather," manuscripts ABD) is right, not *malis* ("you would rather," manuscript H). The pimp's point seems to be that the request is not to help him have her but to help him deceive her, and his job is to promote having.
Your priestess ... man: Seneca, *Controversiae* 1.2.1.
Be angry ... victim: Seneca, *Controversiae* 8.4.1.

NOTES TO THE TRANSLATION

I am moved . . . murderer: Seneca, *Controversiae* 1.2.9.

made one a little bit chaste: That is, he speaks as if the opposites, whoredom and chastity, are interchangeable.

Forgive . . . winner: Lucan, *Pharsalia* 4.355–56.

5 *a certain man . . . grandson*: See Seneca, *Controversiae* 2.4.1.

He adopted . . . out: Seneca, *Controversiae* 2.4.6.

6 *Man is an idle thing . . . he will not be*: These verses, not by Gervase, appear in Geoffrey of Vinsauf's *Colores,* ed. Faral, *Les arts poétiques,* 322, and Wollin, "Die erste Poetik," 410, likewise exemplifying contention. They are also quoted by the anonymous author of *Distinctionum monasticorum et moralium libri v,* probably a contemporary of Gervase's, in his entry *De homine,* as quoted by J. Pitra in his edition of the *Clavis Melitonis,* Spicilegium Solesmense 2 (Paris, 1855), 191.

You are turned on . . . Bassa: Martial, *Epigrams* 3.76.

7 *You will live . . . yesterday*: Martial, *Epigrams* 5.58.7–8. The "local modifier" has occurred in line 5: "Is tomorrow hiding in Parthia or Armenia?" Gervase apparently regards the whole poem as familiar to his readers.

If you obey . . . accomplice: Publilius Syrus, *Sententiae,* ed. Eduard von Wölfflin, *De nugis philosophorum quae supersunt: E codicibus et auctoribus vetustis eruit* (Basil, 1855), 109.

Admonish . . . openly: Publilius Syrus, *Sententiae,* ed. Wölfflin, *De nugis,* 103.

Fear this; don't fear the other: See 3.2 above.

Let the general . . . older: Lucan, *Pharsalia* 2.561. The gloss on *miles* (soldier), apparently Gervase's, refers back to line 480.

Laetinus . . . swan: Martial, *Epigrams* 3.43.1–2.

This we ask . . . with you: Lucan, *Pharsalia* 4.362, from the same speech of Afranius quoted at 1.20 and 3.4 above; see note at 3.4.

A little mound . . . enough: See 3.9 below.

Hail . . . is born: From the poem on Mary by Gervase in Hunterian V.8.14, formerly 511, ed. Gräbener, *Ars poetica,* 230, and Faral, "Le Manuscrit 511," p. 60, lines 10–21.

prophecy of Isaiah: Gervase is perhaps thinking of Matthew 1:23, where Matthew asserts that Jesus fulfills the prophecy of a virgin bearing a son in Isaiah 7:14.

372

PART 3

David's giant: Jesus was called a giant based on Psalms 18:6: *Exultavit ut gigas ad currendam viam* (He as a giant rejoiced to run the way). See *Piers Plowman* C.20.261, "Iesus as a geaunt with a gin cometh 3ende [yonder]."

If you obey . . . free: Gervase alters the proverb cited just above, which he attributes to "Seneca," in order to make a sharper contrast with *servus* (slave).

Though no day . . . no fool: Martial, *Epigrams* 8.20.

I who once . . . refrains: Boethius, *Consolation of Philosophy*, book 1, meter 1.1–2.

The glory . . . old man: The opening lines of a twelve-line poem in Hunterian V.8.14, formerly 511, ed. Harbert, *A Thirteenth-Century Anthology*, no. 41, and Faral, *Les arts poétiques*, no. 42, perhaps about Henry II (as Harbert suggests) or King John (as Faral does); perhaps by Gervase.

8 *Too much humility is pride*: Simon of Tournai, *Die "Institutiones in sacram paginam" des Simon von Tournai: Einleitung und Quästionenverzeichnis*, ed. Richard Heinzmann (Munich, 1967), 87. A popular thought in Gervase's world, appearing also in Peter Chanter, John of Salisbury, and the English *Vices and Virtues;* see Stephen Pelle, "The Date and Intellectual Milieu of the Early Middle English *Vices and Virtues*," *Neophilologus* 99 (2015): 151–66, on 161–63. It and the next example are cited by the author of *Tria sunt* as examples of contention; he then says that Gervase shows the varieties of contention *plenissime* (most fully).

the abbot of Hyde . . . monks: A blunt report of this lurid event, which Gervase brings up again at 3.13, appears in the annals of Winchester Abbey, which include entries about Hyde Abbey, for July 27, 1201: "At almost midnight on the night of the feast of the Seven Holy Sleepers, a calamity took place, a monstrous one that caused much weeping, an attack by two false brethren of Hyde on the testicles of the abbot of Hyde, and because of it a lot of people endured a lot of punishment they did not deserve, and serious loss" (*Media fere hora noctis sanctorum septem Dormientium, enormis quaedam et nimis luctuosa evenit dissonantia inter duos pseudofratres de Hida et geminos eiusdem loci abbatis, unde perplures plurimam quam non meruerunt poenam perpessi sunt et*

NOTES TO THE TRANSLATION

grave dispendium). See Henry R. Luard, ed., *Annales monasterii de Wintone, AD 519–1277*, Rolls Series 36, vol. 4 (1869), 77. The abbot was John Suthill, who had been abbot since 1181 and kept his job despite this mishap until his death in 1222—that is, he was still alive when Gervase was writing about him. With *pseudofratres* (false brethren), see 2 Corinthians 11:26: *periculis in falsis fratribus* (in perils from false brethren).

The son ... father: Gervase may be the author. The "unexpressed antitheton" seems to be between *caro* (flesh) and *pater* (father). The couplet at 3.13 clarifies this one: the event will make the abbot a better spiritual father.

Faustinus ... sees: Martial, *Epigrams* 3.39. The page from Troy is Ganymede.

it has been said: By one of Gervase's young students in the couplet quoted below; see Pref.8 above (with *nil scire* for *ignorare*).

The only hope ... safety: Virgil, *Aeneid* 2.354.

Gaurus ... Die: Martial, *Epigrams* 8.27.

the previously mentioned opinion of Ovid: "A face is more beautiful if it has a blemish in it." See Pref.5 above.

If you accuse ... condemn her: Cicero, *Topics* 13.55; see 3.2 above.

9 *unmodified*: Robert Glendinning, "Eros, Agape, and Rhetoric around 1200: Gervase of Melkley's *Ars poetica* and Gottfried von Strassburg's *Tristan*," *Speculum* 67 (1992): 892–925, on 905–9, has an interesting discussion of the section on antitheton, but I think he goes wrong here to translate *indeterminatum* as "unsolved" (907) rather than "unmodified." It makes what Gervase is teaching here seem deeper than it really is.

To serve God is to reign: A common aphorism among late medieval writers, as searching for the phrase in the LLT reveals.

the word you'd naturally supply: That is, "real" or "really."

A false penny isn't a penny: A common point of comparison, both in logic and in general discourse. For examples, search *falsus denarius* in LLT.

When a woman ... good: Publilius Syrus, *Sententiae* 1.20.

It is suspicious ... smell good: Martial, *Epigrams* 2.12.3–4.

He who denies ... arms: Lucan, *Pharsalia*, 1.348–49: Caesar, rousing his men to fight the usurper Pompey, and suggesting that

PART 3

armed revolt is the way to right injustice. A line often cited, it is fully discussed by Edward Paleit, "The 'Caesarist' Reader and Lucan's *Bellum Civile,* ca. 1590–1610," *Review of English Studies* 62 (2011): 212–40. The dative phrase *arma tenenti* (to one bearing arms) explains the opposition of *negat* (denies) and *dat* (grants).

A little mound . . . little: Gervase's attribution of this distich to Geoffrey of Vinsauf is the only evidence we have that he wrote it; Ralph of Diceto, *Radulfi de Diceto decani Lundoniensis opera historica: The Historical Works of Master Ralph Diceto, Dean of London,* ed. William Stubbs (London, 1876), vol. 2, p. 65, quotes it as Henry II's epitaph, but does not name an author. See Martin Camargo, "From *Liber versuum* to *Poetria nova:* The Evolution of Geoffrey of Vinsauf's Masterpiece," *Journal of Medieval Latin* 21 (2011): 1–16, on 4–5. It later appeared in the *Latin Anthology* as if the epitaph of Alexander the Great, perhaps because of Juvenal's line about Alexander (*Satire* 10.168), to which the Henry epitaph alludes: *Unus Pellaeo iuveni non sufficit orbis* (One world is not enough for the Pellan youth).

To love . . . hate them: Repeated from 3.8 above; see the explanation there, reinforced by an epigram from Martial.

When the sense . . . doing: Jerome, *Against Jovinian* 2.8, frequently quoted, as by Abelard in his first letter to Heloise. The antitheton comes at the end: "to do what it doesn't do."

10   *Byrrhia*: From Terence's *Andria.* See note to 2.19 above.

supplementary verb: *Verbum adjectivum,* a phrase invented by late medieval grammarians and logicians, modeled apparently on *nomen adjectivum,* an added noun or adjective; it seems just to mean any verb added to a subject other than the verb "to be," which is a *verbum substantivum*.

Here is Fortune's mansion . . . tumbling: Alan of Lille, *Anticlaudianus* 8.13–14.

She fixes . . . stability: Bernard, *Cosmographia* 1.3.59–60.

We poor . . . cruel love: *PT* 141–42.

Pleasing Scylla . . . sweet love: *PT* 143–44.

False . . . pain: *PT* 145–46.

11   *Whatever . . . give away*: Martial, *Epigrams* 5.42.7–8.

NOTES TO THE TRANSLATION

This visible girl ... reveals: That is, the wax seal with its imprinted image of a girl keeps the letter private.

And she ordered ... heaven: *Satires* 6.622–23.

You will fall this way, Antaeus: That is, you will fall onto me, not the earth; Lucan, *Pharsalia* 4.649. Hercules, having realized that Antaeus draws strength from the earth, has lifted him into the air.

Here is how ... nourishes: PT 147–48.

12 *A virgin ... immortal*: Lines 10–12 of Gervase's poem on Mary, ed. Gräbener, *Ars poetica*, 230, and Faral, "Le Manuscrit 511," 60.

The eternal one ... local: From a hymn printed in *Nachrichten von der Königlichen Gesellschaft der Wissenschaften zu Göttingen: Philologisch-historische Klasse* 6 (1908): 476.

Our mortality ... weakness: Not an exact quotation from the *Dialogues,* but Gervase seems to be thinking of 2.23, near the end, where, speaking of the power of binding and loosing given to Saint Peter, Gregory, *Dialogues,* trans. Odo John Zimmerman, Fathers of the Church 39 (New York, 1959), 93, says, "The Creator's very purpose in coming down from heaven to earth was to impart to earthly man this heavenly power ... What raised our weakness to these heights was the descent of an almighty God to the depths of our own helplessness."

13 *And although unfound ... discovered*: See note to 1.19 on Isidore above.

William of London: Unidentified. See Russell, *Dictionary,* 194, and Richard Sharpe, *A Handlist of the Latin Writers of Great Britain and Ireland before 1540* (Turnhout, 1997), 783.

You ask ... poet: Martial, *Epigrams* 10.102.

Who gives me ... nothing: See 3.8 above, where it is one of the general examples of antitheton.

The woman ... everything: See 3.2 and 3.8 above.

Even if ... nothing: Ovid, *Ars amatoria* 1.151. "There" is in the lap of one's date at a stadium.

a certain master and friend of mine: Probably John White, described in this way in the opening sentence of the treatise.

PART 4

the monk of Hyde: See 3.8 above. Apparently *abscidit* (cut off) and *abstulit* (removed) are "verbs of abnegation."

another wise man: Socrates: see Lactantius, *De ira Dei* 1, and Plato's *Apology* 5–10. The first wise man is probably Plato, since Lactantius points out that Socrates taught this and Plato handed it down. The negation here is simply the litotes "it is no small" in place of "it is great" or "the only thing I know" in the original sayings.

Galla . . . means: Martial, *Epigrams* 3.90. *Credere* (believe) is *dicere* (say) in standard texts of Martial, which makes better sense: I can't say what she means.

A mother . . . sister: Martial, *Epigrams* 2.4.7–8.

While fleeing . . . die: Martial, *Epigrams* 2.80.

Both the man . . . die: Pseudo-Hegesippus, *De excidio urbis Hierosolymitanae*, 3.17.

In his books . . . attempt: Jerome, *Against Jovinian* 1.1.

Every time . . . none: Jerome, *Against Jovinian* 1.3.

Part Four

1 *One word . . . after*: Treated above at 1.8 (where it is given as an example of *tautoparonomion*) and 1.26; see the note there. All the proverbs in this paragraph are proverbs of sameness because they are not metaphorical.

It is better . . . deceived: This proverb also appears at 1.84 above.

Harping on it . . . evil: *PT* 99–100. The first statement here is the *materia* (subject matter); the second, "Harmful anxiety leads to deadly evil," is the epiphoneme.

Hidden snares do more damage: The obverse of the two proverbs quoted under *tautoparonomion* at 1.8 above, *Praevisa levius laedunt* (Things foreseen hurt more lightly) and *Levius communia tangunt* (Shared troubles touch us more lightly), both deriving from pseudo-Cato, *Disticha* 2.24.

2 *Besides . . . harvesting*: Ovid, *Ars amatoria* 3.81–82.

3 *The one . . . caused it*: Publilius Syrus, *Sententiae* 31.

I think ... unhappy: Seneca, *De providentia* 4.3.
My friend ... stock: Seneca, *Controversiae* 1.23.

Part Five

1 *we mentioned uniformity above*: See 1.30*, 1.33*, 1.36, 1.39, 1.45, 1.61*, 1.66*, 2.39, 2.53. The asterisked sections also mention diversity. Section 1.66 cites Statius's *clipeus* line under the rubric "uniform variation."
Now shield ... boss: Statius, *Thebaid* 8.398.
penthemimer: The first two-and-a-half feet of a hexameter. In the full hexameter, *clipeus* would require stressing a short syllable, whereas Statius's *clipeis* ends properly in a long syllable. Gervase's obsession with uniformity seems to trip him up here.

2 *While the pious busybodies ... threats*: PT 97–98.
Hector ... face: PT 63–64, except that Gervase has replaced *in sensu* (in his sense) with *ingenio* (with his intelligence), for the moment, to make his point.

3 *Though three ... boy*: Ovid, *Heroides* 1.97–98; see 1.36 above.

4 *Encourager ... fraud*: Matthew of Vendôme, *Ars versificatoria* 1.53.3–4, ed. Faral, *Les arts poétiques*, 125, and *PL* 205:983.
Prone ... himself: Matthew of Vendôme, *Ars versificatoria* 1.53.15–16, ed. Faral, *Les arts poétiques*, 125. The couplet is omitted in the version printed in *PL* 205.
Their way ... time: PT 79–80.

5 *gnomic present*: *Praesens confusum*, a grammatical term met with occasionally, in the classical period as well as in the Middle Ages, opposed to *praesens determinatum*. It means the present of a continuously existing state, as opposed to an action now. See C. H. Kneepkens, "From Eternal to Perpetual Truths: A Note on the Mediaeval History of Aristotle, *De Interpretatione*, Ch 1, 16a18," *Vivarium* 32 (1994): 161–85, on 179–80.
Which the sweet sun ... coming up: Bernard, *Cosmographia* 1.3.319.
Further, one thing is necessary: Luke 10:42.
Behold ... speak: PT 75–76.
Behold ... general: Lucan, *Pharsalia* 2.507–8.

PART 5

6   *Here the rose . . . simplicity*: *PT* 37–38. Thisbe's blushing cheeks have just been compared to roses on a hillside in lines 33–34, quoted above at 2.41.

Because men . . . lower regions: Bernard, *Cosmographia* 2.5.19.

Mercury . . . gods: Bernard, *Cosmographia* 2.5.16.

7   *In the stars . . . Hippolytus*: Bernard, *Cosmographia* 1.3.41–42.

Now shield . . . boss, etc.: Statius, *Thebaid* 8.398. For the full couplet, with *et* (and) before the last of five phrases, see 1.12 above. Gervase expects us to remember the whole couplet, which he has discussed so often.

Breasts . . . hidden: *PT* 51–52.

In the stars . . . Thales: Bernard, *Cosmographia* 1.3.45–46.

While the king . . . world: Simon Chèvre d'Or, *De excidio Troiae* 3–4, ed. *PL* 171:1447 (see the note above on 1.20).

The movements . . . numbers: Bernard, *Cosmographia* 2.8.7–8.

Where Troy stood . . . sickle: Ovid, *Heroides* 1.53.

8   *Touch . . . often*: Bernard, *Cosmographia* 2.14.105–6.

Eridanus . . . gods: Bernard, *Cosmographia* 1.3.113–14. *Tramite nostro* (in our journeying) is an error for *climate nostro* (in our clime). Apparently Gervase, quoting from memory, wrote *tramite;* the ABD group of manuscripts have a lame attempt at correction, adding *climate nostro* after *influit,* and retaining *tramite nostro.*

But every . . . peace of mind: Boethius, *Consolation of Philosophy,* book 2, prose 1.

once you were accustomed . . . heavens: Gervase quotes Lady Philosophy's words in Boethius, *Consolation of Philosophy,* book 1, meter 2.6–7.

His strength . . . lovemaking: Lucan, *Pharsalia* 2.379–80.

Will you also go away: John 6:68. "He" in the next sentence is John.

Ganelon . . . hanging himself: *Gueno* is Ganelon, who betrayed Charlemagne and Roland. See the poem *De tradicione Guenonis,* ed. and trans. William Paden and Patricia Harris Stäblein, *Traditio* (1988): 201–51. Ganelon does not commit suicide; Gervase is saying, "Suppose I wrote *(ut si dicam)* that Ganelon hanged himself: I could say 'too,' meaning 'just like Judas.'"

NOTES TO THE TRANSLATION

Live and be happy ... course: Virgil, *Aeneid* 3.493–94.
You too ... lyre: Statius, *Thebaid* 10.445–46.
Helenus and Andromache: It is indeed this pair who are addressed in *Aeneid* 3.493–94, but Gervase has cited the wrong Virgilian place. Statius compares them in his next sentence to Nisus and Euryalus, so Gervase should have cited *Aeneid* 9.446–49.

9 *He showed ... general*: Lucan, *Pharsalia* 4.342–43; see 1.20 above.

10 *A beautiful ... girl*: John of Hauville, *Architrenius* 9.295; see 1.20 above.
I will do ... hand: John of Hauville, *Architrenius* 1.378.
He bears ... face: Statius, *Thebaid* 1.201–2.

11 *Spare my father ... misfortunes*: Solinus, *Collectanea* 2.112.
Even ... titles: John Gray 15–16.

Part Six

1 *It is valuable ... something*: Gervase's version of the classical formula *reddere audientes attentos, benevolos, dociles* (to make listeners attentive, well-disposed, and apt for instruction); see, for example, *RAH* 1.4.6.
He fixed ... Epidamnus: Lucan, *Pharsalia* 10.543–45. Here, where Lucan's poem breaks off, Caesar, under siege in Egypt, recalls Scaeva's earlier one-man stand against Pompey and his army after they had breached the walls of Caesar's camp, narrated by Lucan at 6.140–262.

2 *eleven attributes of persons*: Cicero, *De inventione* 1.34; Matthew of Vendôme, *Ars versificatoria* 1.77, ed. Faral, *Les arts poétiques*, 136.
nine attributes of actions: Cicero, *De inventione* 1.37; Matthew of Vendôme, *Ars versificatoria* 1.93, ed. Faral, *Les arts poétiques*, 143.
The rounded ... gods: Bernard, *Cosmographia* 1.3.5–6.
But God ... earth: Psalms 73:12.
Let us weep ... God: Psalms 94:6–7.

Part Seven

1 *The thing ... in her*: Barthélemy Haureau, *Notices et extraits de quelques manuscrits latins de la Bibliothèque nationale* (Paris, 1890),

315, prints this couplet, from manuscript Bibliothèque nationale lat. 6765. It is a riddle, as Haureau says, and an obvious one—though as he also says, he didn't get it. Born yesterday, apparently.

Perfect ... fully, etc.: Bernard, *Cosmographia* 1.3.13.

The king ... cash: Horace, *Epistles* 1.6.39.

A wall lies ... easy: Apparently from a poem, perhaps by a student, on Pyramus and Thisbe.

With a change ... before: Perhaps another piece of student work, graded B by Gervase.

2 *Love ... book*: Ovid, *Remedia amoris* 1.

The king ... itself: A couplet on the Last Supper, perhaps one more piece of imperfect student work.

Abbot Walter: Ascension Thursday fell on May 3, the feast of the Finding of the Cross, in 1190, 1201, and 1212. Walter of Ghent, abbot of the Augustinian abbey at Waltham, Essex, died May 2, 1201, and so is clearly the Walter at issue here. I have not found the epitaph elsewhere.

Apollonius: The reference is to Godfrey of Viterbo's *Pantheon*, a twelfth-century telling of the story of Apollonius of Tyre in three-line stanzas, each consisting of two hexameters and a pentameter. The hexameters violate Gervase's rule about the fifth foot often, especially in the "faultier" way.

3 *You owe for your toga ... too*: Martial, *Epigrams* 7.10.11–12.

I am he who once: The first words of the spurious four-line introduction to the *Aeneid*. One must elide the final *e* of *ille*.

greathearted Aeacides: The first two words of Statius's *Achilleid;* one must elide the final *um* in *magnanimum*.

4 *antipenthemimer, hephthemimer, posthephthemimer*: These words refer to the lengthening of a naturally short vowel at various places in the hexameter line. The main one, the penthemimer ("five halves," or two and a half), has the lengthening in the beginning of the third foot, ordinarily making a caesura, as in *mittit Hypermnestra* (Hypermnestra sends). In the antipenthemimer, the lengthening comes at the beginning of the second foot; in the hephthemimer ("seven halves"), at the beginning of

NOTES TO THE TRANSLATION

the fourth foot; and in the posthephthemimer, at the beginning of the fifth foot.

Hypermnestra sends: Ovid, *Heroides* 14.1.

fauns . . . mountains: Ovid, *Metamorphoses* 1.193. Ovid actually wrote *Faunique satyrique et monticolae silvani*. The fault, according to what Gervase has just taught, is that the fifth foot consists of parts of two words.

Priscian: Priscian, *Institutiones grammaticae* 6.10, ed. Keil, *Grammatici Latini*, vol. 2, pp. 202–3.

Join . . . makes one: PT 137–38. The scansion requires lengthening the final *a* in *relativa*.

epitaphs . . . seals: See 1.15 above. For a leonine epitaph, see 7.12; for a leonine on a seal, see 2.11.

Love conquers all . . . love: Virgil, *Eclogues* 10.69.

5   *the son of Oedipus*: Polynices; see Statius, *Thebaid* 1.313. Unless *quales sunt* is attracted into the plural by *dictiones*, Gervase must have given at least one other example of a polysyllabic word here, which might have dropped out because of its strangeness.

The hardships . . . goddesses: Bernard, *Cosmographia* 2.6.2.

The laws . . . ensure: Bernard, *Mathematicus* 2.

Athos is sailed over: John of Hauville, *Architrenius* 1.1.

The Constantinopolitans were versified: Unfound.

Be full of honorificabilitude: The word *honorificabilitudinitatibus*, made famous by being used in *Love's Labor's Lost* for its substantial length. It is the subject of a learned and entertaining article in Wikipedia ("Honorificabilitudinitatibus," Wikipedia, accessed January 11, 2022, https://en.wikipedia.org/wiki/Honorificabilitudinitatibus). The line Gervase cites is also cited by John of Bath in his notes to the *Derivationes* of Osbern of Gloucester; see R. W. Hunt, "The Lost Preface to the *Derivationes* of Osbern of Gloucester," in Bursill-Hall, *History of Grammar*, 279.

He . . . reins: Claudian, *Panegyric on the Fourth Consulate of the Emperor Honorius* 560.

PART 7

Their unguarded . . . plundered: Ovid, *Tristia* 3.10.58.

6 *I sing of arms and a man*: Virgil, *Aeneid* 1.1.

a page of grief: From John of Hauville's lost poem on Byblis and Caunus; see the note on 1.26 above. Also see 1.81, where the couplet begun by these words is quoted in full.

There is no before . . . Chimera: Unfound; probably a versifying by Gervase or one of his students of Walter Map's *Dissuasio Valerii* 28. See also Boethius, *Consolation of Philosophy,* book 3, prose 7. Part of the wit of the hexameter is that *Venere* (sex) and *Chimere* (in its Medieval Latin form) make a sight rhyme.

7 *Hector . . . face*: PT 63–64; see above, 5.2.

Fortune . . . anger: The couplet is unfound, though the first three words are common; see Virgil, *Aeneid* 10.284: *Audentes fortuna iuvat* (Fortune favors the daring).

He who gives . . . other: See above, 1.72.

the caesura at the seventh syllable: In both lines of the couplet, though the added example is odd, since a caesura between *fortuna* and *juvat* seems unlikely.

8 *Troy . . . much*: Ovid, *Heroides* 1.3–4, spoken by Penelope. The assonance is the repetition in *fuit* of *u* and *i* from *puellis*.

9 *I would like . . . kings*: Perhaps by Gervase. The meaning is indeed reversed, since read backward the lines mean, "I confess to you, king of kings, that I love worldly pleasures, and I would not like to be a canon" *(Confiteor tibi, rex regum, quod diligo mundi / gaudia nec vellem me fore canonicum)*. The key to the meter is to put *mundi* (worldly) in the other line. *Mundi* serves as the sixth foot of the hexameter in both distichs.

10 *An architect . . . medicine*: Vitruvius, *De architectura* 1.1.13.

When the stars . . . around: Juvenal, *Satires* 5.22–23.

Does a wind . . . so: Lucan, *Pharsalia* 1.412.

the flood: Lucan, *Pharsalia* 4.45–120.

he made the voyage . . . philosophy: Lucan, *Pharsalia* 5.597–677.

11 *When money . . . however hungry*: Lucan, *Pharsalia* 4.97. It is hard to see how the meter works in this line if *deest* is two syllables; modern editors print *dest*.

NOTES TO THE TRANSLATION

Part Eight

1 *a correct and appropriate . . . writing:* See Bernard, *Ars dictaminis,* ed. Mirella Brini Savorelli, "Il 'Dictamen' di Bernardo Silvestre," *Rivista critica di storia della filosofia* 20, no. 2 (1965): 202.

Prose is a long discourse . . . blame: This definition is not in Bede, but is taken (loosely) from Bernard, *Ars dictaminis,* ed. Savorelli, "Il 'Dictamen,'" 202–3.

2 *Victorinus:* Franz Josef Worstbrock, review of Gräbener, *Zeitschrift für deutsches Altertum und deutsche Literatur* 96 (1967): 105, and R. Avesani, review of Gräbener, *Ars poetica, Studi medievali* 7, no. 2 (1966): 759, cite Victorinus Maximus, *Ars grammatica,* ed. Keil, *Grammatici Latini,* vol. 6, p. 192. Here, under the heading *De distinctione,* Victorinus says that you put a punctuation mark in three places in a sentence: at the end, when the sense is complete *(nota finalis);* in the middle, to give the reader a pause for breath *(mese);* at the beginning, to induce suspense *(subdistinctio).* The terms "suspensive," "constant," and "conclusive" emerged later and became standard, used by John of Garland, Alberic, and Alexander of Ville-Dieu among others; see Charles Sears Baldwin, *Medieval Rhetoric and Poetic (to 1400) Interpreted from Representive Works* (Gloucester, MA, 1928; repr., 1959), 218–19.

To these terms I too subscribe: That is, even I who write for beginners; see the Preface.

3 *as the special province of the reader:* Here Gervase clearly has letters in mind.

in a squared-off elbow: A puzzle. In the first place, the word should be *cubitum* (neuter, "elbow" or "cubit"). If you put your elbow at a right angle, your hand and forearm may seem to be roughly three times as long as your upper arm from the crook to the armpit, which may be like a long penult followed by a short fourth syllable. A desperate guess!

you will not avoid Paraclitum, sed sophiam: Apparently *sed* is thought of as part of the last word, as Gervase says just below. *Paracli-*

PART 8

    tum is the penultimate word, with a short penultimate syllable, and *sed sophiam* the last word, with a long penultimate syllable.

4   *monosyllables*: That is, pairs of monosyllables.

    But some time . . . spectacle: Bernard, *Cosmographia* 2.3.7.

    Whose . . . difficulty: Bernard, *Cosmographia* 2.3.8.

5   *the leonine color*: That is, rhyme. In the examples in the next sentence, *inimicum* (enemy) rhymes with *amicum* (friend), and *grossioris* (more solid) with *reflexioris* (more bendable).

    more bendable: As Worstbrock, review of Gräbener, *Ars poetica*, 105, points out, Gervase has taken a phrase from Bernard's *Cosmographia* 1.2.8 (*refixior et corpulentiae grossioris*, "more fixed and of more solid corporeality"), and altered it, inventing a word *reflexus*, in order to create a rhyme with *grossioris* to illustrate the point.

6   *You are earth . . . ash*: See Genesis 3:19 (Vetus Latina).

7   *As the sod . . . sprang up*: Bernard, *Cosmographia* 2.9.4.

    Everything . . . joyfulness: Bernard, *Cosmographia* 2.9.4.

8   *Good, pure speech . . . in fact*: Isidore, *Etymologies* 2.19.

    Bernard did not follow in his prose: For example, just in the first three sentences of *Megacosmus* 2 in Bernard, *Cosmographia* 2.1: *cum ad loquentem oculos* and *quam utique*.

Bibliography

Editions and Translations

Giles, Catherine Yodice. "Gervais of Melkley's Treatise on the Art of Versifying and the Method of Composing in Prose: Translation and Commentary." PhD Dissertation, Rutgers University, 1973.

Gräbener, Hans-Jürgen, ed. *Ars poetica*. Forschungen zur romanischen Philologie 17. Münster, 1965.

Further Reading

Bernardus Silvestris. *Poetic Works*. Edited and translated by Winthrop Wetherbee. Dumbarton Oaks Medieval Library 38. Cambridge, MA, 2015.

Camargo, Martin. *Essays on Medieval Rhetoric*. Farnham and Burlington, 2012.

——, ed. and trans. *Tria sunt: An Art of Poetry and Prose*. Dumbarton Oaks Medieval Library 53. Cambridge, MA, 2019.

Caplan, Harry, trans. *Rhetorica ad Herennium*. Loeb Classical Library 403. Cambridge, MA, 1954.

Copeland, Rita. *Rhetoric, Hermeneutics, and Translation in the Middle Ages: Academic Traditions and Vernacular Texts*. Cambridge, 1991.

Faral, Edmond. "Le manuscrit 511 du 'Hunterian Museum' de Glasgow: Notes sur le mouvement poétique et l'histoire des etudes littéraires en France et en Angleterre entre les années 1150 et 1225." *Studi medievali* 9 (1936): 18–119.

——. *Les arts poétiques du XIIe et du XIIIe siècle*. Paris, 1924. Reprint, Paris, 1962.

Friis-Jensen, Karsten. "Horace and the Early Writers of Arts of Poetry."

In *Sprachtheorien in Spätantike und Mittelalter,* edited by Sten Ebbesen, 360–401. Tübingen, 1995.

Glendinning, Robert. "Eros, Agape, and Rhetoric around 1200: Gervase of Melkley's *Ars poetica* and Gottfried von Strassburg's *Tristan.*" *Speculum* 67 (1992): 892–925.

———. "Pyramus and Thisbe in the Medieval Classroom." *Speculum* 61 (1986): 51–78.

Harbert, Bruce, ed. *A Thirteenth-Century Anthology of Rhetorical Poems: Glasgow MS V.8.14.* Toronto, 1975.

Holtz, Louis. *Donat et la tradition de l'enseignement grammatical: Étude sur l'Ars Donati et sa diffusion (IV–IXe siècle) et édition critique.* Paris, 1981. See especially *Donati ars maior* 3, pp. 653–74.

Hunt, R. W. "English Learning in the Late Twelfth Century." *Transactions of the Royal Historical Society* 19 (1936): 19–42.

Hunt, Tony. *Teaching and Learning Latin in Thirteenth-Century England.* 3 vols. Cambridge, 1991.

Johannes de Hauvilla. *Architrenius.* Translated by Winthrop Wetherbee. Dumbarton Oaks Medieval Library 55. Cambridge, MA, 2019.

Keil, Heinrich, ed. *Grammatici Latini.* 7 vols. Leipzig, 1855–1880. Reprint, Hildesheim, 1961.

Kelly, Douglas. *The Arts of Poetry and Prose.* Turnhout, 1991.

Klopsch, Paul. *Einführung in die Dichtungslehren des lateinischen Mittelalters.* Darmstadt, 1980.

Purcell, William M. *Ars Poetriae: Rhetorical and Grammatical Invention at the Margin of Literacy.* Columbia, SC, 1996.

Rosiene, Alan M. "The *Ars versificaria* of Gervase of Melkley: Structure, Hierarchy, Borrowings." In *Le poetriae del medioevo latino: Modelli, fortuna, commenti,* edited by Gian Carlo Alessio and Domenico Losappio, 205–24. Venice, 2018.

Russell, Josiah Cox. *Dictionary of Writers of Thirteenth-Century England.* London, 1936.

Index of Names

Abraham, 2.2
Achilles, 2.1, 2.10, 2.13, 2.16, 2.19
Adam, 2.2
Aeneas, 2.22
Agenor, 2.21
Ajax, 2.13
Alan of Lille: *Anticlaudianus,* Pref.7, 1.81, 2.29, 2.39, 3.10; *De planctu Naturae,* 2.37
Amyclas, 5.11
Archelaus, 2.17
Aristotle, 2.52
Ascolon, 2.42
Athos, 2.3
Atys, 5.11
Aulis, 2.22
Aulus Gellius, *Attic Nights,* 1.70

Bede, 8.1
Bernard Silvester, Pref.2, Pref.7, 8.8; *Ars dictaminis,* 8.1; *The Astrologer,* 1.26, 1.32–33, 1.66, 1.79, 7.5; *Cosmographia,* 1.9, 1.10, 1.13, 1.32–33, 1.39–40, 1.43, 1.54, 1.57, 1.59, 1.61, 1.63–64, 1.77, 1.82, 2.8, 2.9, 2.11– 14, 2.24, 2.27, 2.29–30, 2.32, 2.41, 2.46, 3.10, 5.5, 5.6–8, 6.2, 7.1, 7.5, 8.4, 8.7
Boethius, *The Consolation of Philosophy,* 1.77, 3.7, 5.8
Byrrhia, 1.41, 2.21, 3.5, 3.10

Cassiodorus, 2.35
Cato (pseudo-Cato), *Distichs,* 1.8, 2.19, 4.1
Chèvre d'Or. *See* Simon Chèvre d'Or
Cicero, 5.8, 6.2; *Rhetorics,* Pref.3, Pref.5, 1.6, 1.13, 1.33, 1.62, 2.17; *Topics to Trebatius,* 3.2, 3.8
Claudian, Pref.7, 2.39; *Panegyric on the Fourth Consulship of the Emperor Honorius,* 2.53, 7.5; *The Rape of Proserpina,* 1.8
Cynthia, 2.45
Cynthus, Mount, 2.45

Dares Phrygius, Pref.7
Demosthenes, 1.70, 2.14
Deuteronomy, 2.29

INDEX OF NAMES

Devon. *See* Roger of Devon
Dido, 2.22
Donatus, *Barbarismus,* Pref.3–5, 1.2–4, 1.14–15, 1.17, 1.32, 1.42, 1.67, 1.70, 1.74–75, 1.79, 1.81–82, 2.18, 2.28, 2.44, 2.50–53

English, 1.78
Ennius, 1.3, 2.10
Eteocles, 2.32

Ganelon, 5.8
Ganymede, 2.10
Geoffrey of Vinsauf, Pref.2, 1.2, 1.16, 1.17, 2.18, 3.9; *Poetria nova,* 1.19, 1.22, 1.77, 2.21, 2.36
Gervase of Melkley, Pref.1, 3.7, 3.12. *See also* Melkley
Godfrey of Viterbo, *Pantheon,* 7.2
Greek, 1.78, 2.8
Gregory, *Dialogues,* 1.26, 2.35, 3.12
Grey, John (bishop of Norwich), 1.21, 2.51, 2.53, 5.11

Hauville. *See* John of Hauville
Hebe, 2.33
Hector, 2.10, 2.19, 2.47, 5.1, 7.7
Hegesippus (pseudo-Hegesippus), *De excidio urbis Hierosolymitanae,* 1.73, 2.17, 2.42, 3.13
Helen, 2.21
Hercules, 2.13, 2.42
Herod, 2.10, 2.17, 2.19, 2.21
Homer, 3.2
Horace: *Art of Poetry,* Pref.3, 2.4, 2.13, 2.14; *Epistles,* 7.1

Hyde, abbot of, 3.8, 3.13
Hydra, 2.10

Innocent III (pope), 3.3
Iphigenia, 2.22
Isidore: *De differentiis verborum,* 1.19; *Etymologies,* 1.10, 8.8

Jerome, *Against Jovinian,* 3.9, 3.13
Jerusalem, 2.42
John (evangelist), 2.52
John Grey. *See* Grey, John
John of Hauville, 2.10, 2.12–13, 2.28, 7.6, 8.5, 8.8; *Architrenius,* Pref.7, 1.4, 1.12, 1.15, 1.21, 1.26, 1.31, 1.40, 1.66, 1.68, 1.81, 2.3, 2.4, 2.5, 2.8, 2.29, 2.40, 2.42, 2.51, 5.10, 7.5, 7.6
John White. *See* White, John
Joseph of Exeter, *De bello Troiano,* 2.43
Judas, 1.58, 2.51, 5.8
Juvenal, *Satires,* 1.33, 1.52, 2.3, 2.8, 2.22, 3.11, 7.10

Laertes, 2.22
London. *See* William of London
Longchamps. *See* William of Nunchamp
Lucan, *Pharsalia,* Pref.7, 1.20, 1.25, 1.67, 1.70, 1.79, 1.83, 2.42, 3.4, 3.7, 3.9, 3.11, 5.5, 5.8–10, 6.1, 7.10–11
Lucretia, 2.21
Luke (evangelist), 2.51, 2.52

Marcia, 2.21
Mars, 2.19

INDEX OF NAMES

Martial the Cook, *Epigrams,* 2.13–14, 1.46, 3.1, 3.6–9, 3.11, 3.13, 7.3
Matthew (evangelist), 2.51
Matthew of Vendôme, Pref.2, 1.81, 5.4
Melkley, 1.78. *See also* Gervase of Melkley
Mercury, 2.46
Merlin, 2.47

Nero, 5.9
Nunchamp. *See* William of Nunchamp

Ovid, Pref.6, Pref.7, 1.3; *Ars amatoria,* Pref.5, 1.60, 3.8; *Epistolae ex Ponto,* 1.40; *Fasti,* 1.66; *Heroides,* 1.15, 1.36, 1.43, 1.46, 1.62, 2.22, 2.49, 5.3, 5.7, 7.4, 7.8; *Metamorphoses,* 1.19, 1.75, 3.13; *Remedia amoris,* 2.28, 7.2; *Tristia,* 7.5

Paris (mythical hero), 2.19, 2.21, 5.1, 7.7
Parvipontani, 1.44
Paul, Saint, 1.69
Penelope, 2.21
Plato, 2.4, 2.30, 3.13, 5.8
Polynices, 2.32
Pompey, 6.1
Priscian, Pref.5, 1.51, 7.4
Psalms, 1.33, 1.77, 6.2
Publilius Syrus. *See* Seneca
Pyramus and Thisbe, 1.11, 1.16, 1.20, 1.32, 1.35, 1.47, 1.67, 1.80–81, 2.13, 2.20, 2.24–25, 2.41, 2.43, 3.10–11, 4.1, 5.1, 5.4–7, 7.4, 7.7

Revelation, book of, 2.32
Roger of Devon, 1.3, 2.14, 3.13, 5.6

Samson, 5.8
Scaeva, 6.1
Seneca (Publilius Syrus), 3.7, 3.9
Seneca (rhetorician), 2.39; *Controversies,* Pref.5, 3.3–5; *De providentia,* 4.3
Seneca (tragedian), 1.23, 1.28
Servius, 2.14
Simon Chèvre d'Or, *De excidio Troiae,* 5.7
Socrates, 2.30, 2.51, 3.13, 5.8
Solinus, 5.11
Statius, Pref.7; *Achilleid,* 7.3; *Thebaid,* 1.12, 1.18, 1.28, 1.59–60, 1.66–68, 1.75, 1.77, 1.80, 2.29, 2.48, 2.53, 3.1, 5.1, 5.7–8, 5.10, 7.5

Tantalus, 2.20
Telemachus, 2.22
Thais, 2.8
Thebes, 2.32
Theodulus, 2.9
Theseus, 2.20
Thule, 2.6
Tityrus, 2.12
Tobias (book of Tobit), 2.35
Troy, 2.22

Ucalegon, 2.22
Ulysses, 5.1, 7.7

INDEX OF NAMES

Venus, 5.8
Victorinus Maximus, *Ars grammatica*, 8.2
Virgil, Pref.7, 1.3, 1.69, 5.8; *Aeneid*, 1.47, 1.79, 2.22, 7.6; *Eclogues*, 1.74, 2.42, 7.4
Vitruvius, *De architectura*, 7.10

Walter, Abbot, 7.2
White, John, Pref.1
William of London, 3.13
William of Nunchamp (Longchamps), epitaph for, 2.46

Index of Literary and Rhetorical Terms

accent, 8.3
accumulation, 1.31, 1.32
adjectives, 1.37–38, 1.40–41, 1.44, 1.49, 1.55–57, 1.72, 1.84, 2.8, 2.11, 2.21, 2.23, 2.27, 2.43, 3.10, 6.1
adjunction, 1.49
adverbs. *See* conjunctions and conjunctive adverbs
adversity, 3.3
advocation, 2.33–36
allegory, 2.50, 3.1
alliteration, 1.10
ambiguity, 1.17
anastrophe, 1.79
annomination, 1.9–13, 1.16–17, 1.21
anomaly, 3.12
antiphrasis, 3.1
antithesis, 3.3
antitheton, 3.8–13
antonomasia, 1.16, 1.69
aposiopesis, 1.25–27
apposition, 1.44–49, 1.59–60, 8.2
appropriation, 2.16
argument, 6.1
articulus, 1.30

assonance (in verse), 7.10
assumption. *See* coinage
asteismos, 2.44
astronomy (in verse), 7.9
asyndeton, 1.49
attributes (of both actions and persons), 1.8, 1.62, 6.2

catachresis, 2.17
circumlocution, 1.68
clause endings (in prose), 8.4
climax, 1.16–17, 1.34, 1.82
coadunation, 2.53, 3.7, 3.11
coalescence, 1.29–31
coinage (assumption), 2.1–17
colors, 3.7
comma, 1.30
comparatives, 2.10, 2.12
comparison, 2.51, 2.53
complement. *See* suspensive, constant, and complement
complexion, 1.16
compound words, 2.3
conclusion by contraries, 3.2
conjunction, 1.31–32

393

INDEX OF LITERARY AND RHETORICAL TERMS

conjunctions and conjunctive adverbs, 5.5–11
consonance, 1.14–15
constant. *See* suspensive, constant, and complement
contention, 3.3, 3.6–7
contraries, 3.3, 7.7
conversion, 1.16, 3.2
correction, 1.20–21

dactyls (vs. spondees), 7.6
dialogue, 1.22
dialyton, 1.32
digression, 1.61, 1.67
disjunction, 1.31, 1.82
diversion, 1.25, 1.83
diversity. *See* uniformity and diversity
duplication, 1.33

each to each, 1.81, 3.7
ellipsis, 7.3
emphasis, 1.71–72
enigma, 2.50
enthymeme, 2.2–3, 4.1, 4.3
epiphoneme, 4.1–2
epitaphs, 7.4
epithet, 1.41
equivocation, 2.42
euphemism, 3.1
euphonomaton, 1.8
exclamation, 1.20, 1.22
exsuperation, 1.82

hendiadys, 1.79
homoeoptoton, 1.14

homoeosis, 2.51, 2.53
homoeoteleuton, 1.15
hypallage, 1.79
hyperbaton, 1.79, 1.81
hyperbole, 1.79, 1.82
hypophora, 1.23–24
hypozeuxis, 1.31
hysteron proteron, 1.79

icon, 2.51, 1.53
identity, rough. *See* rough identity
indecision, 1.20, 1.22
inferential proof, 6.1
insinuation, Pref.8
interposition, 1.7
invention, Pref.8
invention of verbs. *See under* verbs
irony, 3.1, 3.4

leonine rhyme, 1.14–16, 7.4
letters, 8.2
likeness, 1.1, 1.31, 2 *throughout*
line endings in verse, 7.1
litotes, 1.79, 1.82

metalepsis, 1.17
metaphor, 2.18–50, 3.5
metaphorical proverb *(translaticia)*, 4.1–2
metathesis, 3.3, 3.5
metonymy, 1.69–70, 1.74
mintmarks, 2.4–6, 2.13
modification, 1.29, 1.36, 1.43, 1.45, 1.50, 1.55–56, 2.38, 3.6–10, 6.1
mutation, 1.25, 2.25

INDEX OF LITERARY AND RHETORICAL TERMS

nouns, 1.13, 1.19, 1.21, 1.23–24, 1.26, 1.28, 1.32, 2.10, 3.10

one-syllable words, 7.1. *See also* polysyllables in verse
onomatopoiea, 2.15
opposition, 1.1, 1.5, 1.31, 3 *throughout*

parable, 2.53
paradigm, 2.51–52
paralipsis, 1.29
paranomasia, 1.10, 1.15
parenthesis, 1.79
paroemia, 3.1, 4 *throughout*
participles, 2.8–9, 2.11, 2.29
partition, 1.38–39
pentameter, 7.3
penthimimer, 5.1, 7.4
perissologia, 1.5
polysyllables in verse, 7.5. *See also* one-syllable words
polysyndeton, 1.30, 1.32
predicate element, third. *See* third predicate element
progression, 1.21
prolepsis, 1.25, 1.28
pronouns, 2.28, 2.32
prose, 8 *throughout*. *See also* verse, rules for
prosopopoeia, 1.25
proverb, 4 *throughout,* 7.4, 7.7
punctus, 8.4

reading verse aloud, 7.12
reiteration, 1.33

removal, 3.13
retrograde verses, 7.9
rhyme. *See* leonine rhyme
rough identity, 1.62, 8.2

sameness, 1.1 *and throughout*
sarcasm, 3.1
schesis onomaton, 1.30
sentence-metaphor, 2.44, 2.49–50
similiter cadens, 1.15
similiter desinens, 1.15
spondees. *See* dactyls
superlatives, 2.12
suspensive, constant, and complement, 8.2, 8.4
synaloepha, 7.3
synchysis, 1.79, 1.81
synecdoche, 1.74, 1.75
synonymy, 1.33, 1.35, 1.61–66

tautoparonomion, 1.8, 4.1
third predicate element, 1.52–53
tmesis, 1.79
topics, 6.1–2
transcendence, 1.79
translaticia. See metaphorical proverb
transmutation, 1.76–77, 1.79
transplacement, 1.16
transumption. *See* metaphor
transversion, 1.76
trope, 3.1

uniformity and diversity, 1.30, 1.33, 1.61, 1.66, 5.1–4

INDEX OF LITERARY AND RHETORICAL TERMS

vehemence, 1.20

verbs: in antitheton, 3.11; invention of, 2.4–5, 2.8–9, 2.13–14; metaphors in, 2.29, 2.32

verse, reading. *See* reading verse aloud

verse, rules for, 7 *throughout*. *See also* prose

zeugma, 1.31